About the Authors ...

Michael J. Corey is Chief Operating Officer for
New England's oldest relational database
consulting firm, Database Technologies, Inc.
Michael is also very proud to announce his
company a recent winner of the New England
Fast 50 award, for being the 11th fastest growing
hi-tech firm in all of New England. They're also a
winner of the National 500 award. For many
years, Michael has been a driving force in the
Oracle Users community through the numerous
User group organizations in which he

participates. For over four years, Michael was the president of the
International Oracle Users Group–Americas, and is currently an active
board member. Currently, he is the director of conference for the IOUGA–
Live Conference held every spring. He is a founding member of the
Worldwide Affinity program, founding member of the ECO conference,
founding member of the President's Council and a past president of the
Northeast Oracle Users Group. In addition to being one of the most visible
forces in the User community, Michael is also a highly recognized expert
and speaker at various technical conferences on Oracle and its related
technologies around the world. Michael has been using Oracle, since early
Version 4 of the product, on a variety of platforms from PCs to mainframes.
He is co-author of *Tuning Oracle, Oracle: A Beginner's Guide, Oracle8
Tuning*, and *Oracle8: A Beginner's Guide* (the first Oracle8 book on
the market).

Michael Abbey lives in the Ottawa, Canada area,
supplying Oracle7/8 technical services to a
hungry national capital region. As the successful
co-author of six works in the Oracle Press Series,
Michael communicates with Oracle users around
the globe. He has a passion for pre-CBS Fenders
as well as just about anything having to do with
Oracle and good LOUD music. He can be
reached at masint@istar.ca on e-mail.

Ian Abramson currently lives and works in Toronto, Ontario, Canada. He has over 12 years of Oracle experience building an Oracle consulting practice for his own company, Ian Abramson Systems Inc. Ian has experience in designing and developing all types of Oracle systems, from operational systems to data warehouses. He is a regular presenter at Oracle conferences and is an active member of the conference committee. Most recently he worked  with Hexagon Computer Systems, where he helped to start their Data Warehousing practice in the Toronto office. Ian can be contacted by e-mail at: ias@magi.com.

Ben Taub is a Project Manager / Senior Warehouse Architect with Dataspace Incorporated, a data warehouse consultancy with offices in Ann Arbor, Chicago, and Kansas City, as well as founder of the firm. He is also the data warehousing focus area manager for the International Oracle User Group–Americas (IOUG–A) conference committee. During his career Ben has held information technology positions with both Andersen Consulting and MicroStrategy, Incorporated. Ben, a certified public accountant, holds a Bachelor of Science degree from Lehigh University and a Master of Business Administration degree from the University of Michigan. His e-mail address is btaub@dspace.com.

Oracle Press™

Oracle8 Data Warehousing

Michael J. Corey
Michael Abbey
Ian Abramson
Ben Taub

Osborne/**McGraw-Hill**

Berkeley New York St. Louis San Francisco
Auckland Bogotá Hamburg London Madrid
Mexico City Milan Montreal New Delhi Panama City
Paris Sáo Paulo Singapore Sydney
Tokyo Toronto

Osborne/**McGraw-Hill**
2600 Tenth Street
Berkeley, California 94710
U.S.A.

For information on translations or book distributors outside the U.S.A., or to arrange bulk purchase discounts for sales promotions, premiums, or fund-raisers, please contact Osborne/**McGraw-Hill** at the above address.

Oracle8 Data Warehousing

1234567890 AGM AGM 901987654321098

ISBN 0-07-882511-3

Publisher Brandon A. Nordin	**Technical Editors** Andrew Flower Kevin Downey	**Indexer** Richard Shrout
Editor-in-Chief Scott Rogers	**Editorial Assistant** Ann Sellers	**Computer Designer** Jean Butterfield Roberta Steele Michelle Galicia
Acquisitions Editor Scott Rogers	**Copy Editor** Dennis Weaver	**Illustrator** Brian Wells
Project Editor Mark Karmendy	**Proofreader** Stefany Otis	**Series Design** Patricia J. Beckwith

To my wife Juliann and my three children,
John, Annmarie, and Michael.
Michael J. Corey

This book is dedicated to my parents, Rhoda and Sydney
Abbey, who always fascinate me with their energy and
enthusiasm, not to mention my Dad's unique sense of humor.
Michael Abbey

I would like to dedicate my involvement in this book to my
wife Susan and my children Baila and Jillian. Although I may
not say it enough, you all help to make me complete.
Ian Abramson

I would like to dedicate my effort to my children Jimmy and
Katie and my wife Jane, who bear far more of the burden of
my career than I care to admit.
Ben Taub

Contents At A Glance

Contents

Foreword

hen the phone call from Mike Corey came with a request to write a foreword to another book co-authored by Michael Abbey, I was not surprised. Indeed, their text on Data Warehousing is immensely popular as a primer to Oracle developers everywhere. Practical guides are well suited for senior managers and technical personnel alike. I knew immediately that the follow-on text would become an instant success. So, I quickly agreed to write the foreword for this book.

I last wrote about the use and development of data warehouses at the cable TV company where I headed Information Technology. This company is well on its way to redefine itself as a "broadband" company. A so-called "broadband" company is one that delivers beyond traditional cable television boundaries. Such a company will offer other services through its pipe, or fiber optic networks, data, voice, video, and other new interactive services. Intimate knowledge of customers, trends, competitive data, and of countless other information elements is a critical factor in achieving the new identity the company seeks. At the heart of this strategy remains the investment in data warehousing.

Recently I joined The Weather Channel. Again, as if struck twice by lightning, I was seduced by the incredible opportunities that surround the use of data warehousing. To be sure, The Weather Channel acquires enormous amounts of data on a daily basis. This data is useful in Real time and offers great potential as a historical repository. Target audiences such as pilots and large-scale farmers, for example, could benefit a great deal from properly mined data. Numerous weather-related products can spawn from such a mining process. Presently, the company's senior managers are becoming aware of the potential for such a warehouse; initiation of a full-scale project is now underway.

In both positions, (as an information distributor for cable TV and a content creator for The Weather Channel), I rank the importance and impact of data warehousing projects in the top three inside the IT portfolio. Harvard Business School's case library is full of studies where companies flourish as a result of warehouse initiatives. Lexus, for example, can analyze all customer movement in the luxury market, and avoid the pitfall of studying its own performance in isolation. WAL-MART also uses sophisticated database techniques to ensure that inventory and store management reflect customer demands without guesswork.

Data Warehousing systems, however, do not come cheap. Each Lexus dealer has invested in its own IBM AS400 and a satellite dish to transmit sales and service information to the company's U.S. headquarters in Torrance, California. In addition to the equipment cost, budgets for several servers, databases, and developers needed to be allocated. Getting a handle on the costs of data warehouse projects (hardware, software, and development) is a difficult task. Working through the business case and achieving the significant breakthroughs in detailed customer knowledge are paramount to initiate such projects. Of course, access to books that provide a practical guide to these juggernauts can only help educate project constituents.

This is a book about "how to." It is written by "doers." I hope that it will be read as a call to action. It will first challenge the reader to ask, "What in my organization could a data warehouse provide that would truly make a difference? How will it work? What data should we collect and what should we mine?" And I am sure that it will then motivate each reader to DO it.

Robert Strickland
Senior Vice President, Chief Technical and Information Officer
The Weather Channel, Inc.

Mr. Strickland lives near Boston, Massachusetts and is senior vice president, chief technical and information officer for The Weather Channel. The Weather Channel is headquartered in Atlanta, Georgia and is owned by Landmark Communications, Inc. Previously, Mr. Strickland was senior vice president for information systems at MediaOne, Inc.

Acknowledgments

I would like to thank my wife Juliann, and my children John, Annmarie, and Michael. Having lived through five books already, I want to thank them for their love, understanding, and continued support. To my friend and co-author Michael Abbey, HEY THANKS. To the new members of the team, Ian and Ben, welcome aboard. To my business partner and friend David Teplow, this book and Database Technologies (The Finest Consulting House on the East Coast) would not be possible without your help, HEY THANKS. Special HEY THANKS goes to Rob Strickland for writing another great foreword. It's a pleasure to work with you again. Thanks to the Staff at Database Technologies for all their help. Thanks to Jack Nevison (Mr. Project Manager). To the Osborne/McGraw-Hill team, HEY THANKS A BUNCH. To Scott Rogers at McGraw-Hill, thank you again for another opportunity to work with you. To the avid readers of our first five books, thank you for having confidence in us and buying the book. Thank you very much for all the wonderful e-mails I have received.

Michael J. Corey

Many thanks to my fellow authors, Mike, Ian, and Ben, without whom this would not have come together. Thanks as well to Kevin Downey and Andrew Flower as a co-tech editors. The gang at Osborne (as usual) was awesome. I would like to thank Mike Mallia for a large part written in Chapter 17, Andrew Flower for the engine-based tools piece in Chapter 8, and Kevin Downey for the Prism piece.

Gracias (big time) to Mike Ault and the gang in Waltham, MA, USA for the help with the Express chapter. I would also like to mention many of the people I rub shoulders with all the time, including Mark Farnham, Mike Teske, John Richer, David Teplow, and Mark Kerzner, who continually prop me up when I need help.

Michael Abbey

I would like to thank my co-authors, Michael Abbey, Michael Corey, and Ben Taub. When you get a chance to work with the best, it makes you better. Thanks to you all! I will not soon forget the lesson that my friends Michael and Michael have taught me: "This is not rocket science."

Thanks to all my relatives who are too numerous to mention. From the oldest to the youngest, you are all part of the total package. Special thanks to my father, without whom I would not be who I am. Thanks to my friends who have been around this year. It was a big transition for me.

A special thanks to Jeremy Fitzgerald, Director of Business Intelligence of Hexagon Computer Systems, who helped me with the query and OLAP chapters as they relate to the Cognos' toolset. Thanks to everyone at Oracle who helped me discover the Discoverer product. Thanks to Ed Meyers who helped provide the inspiration to many of our cable company examples.

There are not many opportunities in which one can apply all his experience towards a project that helps get people excited about a technology. This subject excites me, and this book has allowed me to express that to you.

Ian Abramson

I would like to thank my co-authors, Michael Abbey, Michael Corey, and Ian Abramson for giving me the opportunity to participate in this effort. I would also like to acknowledge the input and efforts of my co-workers at Dataspace Incorporated, the most talented group of data warehousing professionals with whom I have had the opportunity to work.

Ben Taub

Introduction

Data Warehousing—two words that conjure up visions of massive amounts of data accessed by a hungry user community. Where do all these users come from? What do they want? Why are they here? What can systems professionals do to make them happy? Many of us remember the Kevin Costner film, *Field of Dreams*, about an American family that built a fantasy baseball diamond in their front yard, hoping the greats would magically appear; they did! The theme of that movie was "If we build it, they will come." Guess what? A data warehouse is the exact opposite; thus, we would like to call it a *Dream of Fields*, categorized by a twist on the movie theme: "If they come, we will build it." The most important player in the data warehouse stadium is the user; we build what they want, when they want it. We have the technology, what's the holdup?

We see a data warehouse as a new way to do an old thing. In the 1980s many of us cut our technological teeth with spreadsheet software, gazing for days at figures representing business sales, receipts, debits, credits, receivables, payables, and then some. We delighted at the thought of proceeding to cell AB67 and changing the number 12,390 to 24,780 and watching the change ripple through the screen. This was the first venture into "what-if" analysis. There have been many generations of decision support solutions since those days—all the way from the most rudimentary to the most sophisticated products of the modern day.

Warehousing turns data into information. Systematic collection of business-related data from a wide range of sources is part of the exercise. Presentation of that data is another. Proliferation of access to that data is yet another. Simply stated, we use data warehouses to get information to a wide range of users—those in the trenches to those who enjoy privileges in the corporate board room.

Oracle8 Data Warehousing marries the experience of four industry resources, familiar with the design, building, and rollout of a data warehouse as well as the implementation specifics with Oracle8. We cover many "whats" and "whys" related to warehousing, discuss issues that will help ensure that the warehouse becomes a reality, and delve into one of the most awkward areas of any project—office politics. All too may projects flounder, cough, and die before their time because the participants simply can't get along!

The *design* of the data warehouse is a multi-discipline design task. "Design" does not just mean designing a database; it also means that you need to design your data extractions, data loading, and end-user access to the warehouse. Many of today's data warehousing books explain the basics of designing the warehouse—normalization, denormalization, and star schemas. This book does all that, but it also provides you with a proven approach to designing the data warehouse. We explain how to approach the design of the warehouse, the questions that you need to ask, and all the aspects of the warehouse that together will help you design and develop your database. Our approach guides you through collecting requirements that will form the basis of your data warehouse's database. *Oracle8 Data Warehousing* is also unique in that:

- ■ Our approach embraces the user—many data warehouses today are built in isolation of user requirements.

- ■ Our approach shows you how the user will be involved in the design—the user must be highly involved in the design of the warehouse to ensure its success in your organization.

- ■ Our approach will guide you through this design transition and help you to build successful warehouses—the design method used in the warehouse is a paradigm shift from the ways we design operational systems today.

We touch on many aspects of bringing the datamart/warehouse from the drawing board to a hungry community. Previous offerings of the Oracle Server product delivered significant enhancements to bring Oracle Corporation closer to the forefront when companies were looking for the database to solve their storage and quick retrieval requirements. In *Oracle8 Data Warehousing* we cover Oracle8 specifics and concentrate on getting the most from the software. We look at generic issues in the expanding suite of data warehouse solutions. The politics of bringing the project in on time and on budget are discussed alongside the Oracle8 technical issues that we believe wise to attend to early in the game and on an ongoing basis. This data warehousing assignment, should you decide to accept it, will change your life. Read on.

CHAPTER

1

Warehouse: What Is It, Who Needs It, and Why?

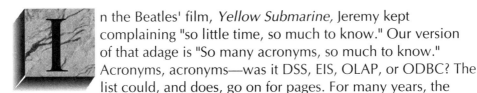n the Beatles' film, *Yellow Submarine,* Jeremy kept complaining "so little time, so much to know." Our version of that adage is "So many acronyms, so much to know." Acronyms, acronyms—was it DSS, EIS, OLAP, or ODBC? The list could, and does, go on for pages. For many years, the computer industry has been enamored with acronyms and new terminology. In fact, the term *data warehouse* is just another iteration of a concept that has been around for years. Remember using Lotus 1-2-3? This was your first taste of "what if?" processing on the desktop. This is what a data warehouse is all about—using information your business has gathered to help it react better, smarter, quicker, and more efficiently.

Contrary to popular belief, most companies are not building data warehouses simply to test the patience of their technical staff. Data warehouses are, instead, a key component of well-reasoned decision support architectures. This chapter will help you understand what users require from a decision support system and why a data warehouse is often necessary to satisfy these demands. We'll answer the following questions:

- What is decision support?

- What are the business and technical goals of decision support?

- What is data warehousing?

- What are the business drivers of data warehousing?

- What are the technical drivers of data warehousing?

A Particularly Bad Awful Day

Well, you've finally made it—chief information officer (CIO). Who would have thought when you started 18 years ago as an accountant turned COBOL programmer that you would be sitting in such a key spot? Who would have thought that your organization would someday put you in a strategic role? Who would have thought that all your jokes about CIOs spending their days at expensive vendor junkets or on the golf course were close to the mark? Who knew?

So, flush with the knowledge that you shot a 76 yesterday (and will likely shoot a 74 today), you check the value of your new stock options on the Internet. Suddenly, pandemonium breaks loose. You hear the angry voices outside your office. "Hey," you think, "that sounds like John Valjon, our vice president of sales and Norman Richelieu, our chief financial officer." You listen closely to the near screaming. "I don't care if he's busy, I'm seeing him NOW! Henchard just chewed us out and I want some answers!"

You think, "Now Richelieu is a bit uppity, but, I've never heard Valjon so agitated. I wonder what's up?" In storm the two gentlemen, flushed with anger, beads of sweat gathering on their foreheads.

Richelieu starts, "We spent $27 million on computers last year alone. Why is it that when John and I go into a meeting with the big man, our reports don't even match? How can it be that John thinks he sold 45,000 units in October while my reports show 42,500? How could your people possibly get such a simple thing wrong?"

John continues, "and that's just a touch of the problems I'm having with you folks. Last week I had a meeting with Ed Kramden, the purchasing chief at FutureChef Industries. I'm sure I don't have to remind you that on our list of top ten target accounts, FutureChef ranks third. I know they're having a problem with late deliveries from their current vendor. It would have been great to show up at the meeting with a report showing our delivery record to each of the cities where they have facilities. You know our logistics department is among the best and this report could be critical to winning the account.

"Anyway, the appointment was scheduled for 3:00 P.M. I called your guys at 8:00 A.M. and requested the report. Do you know what they told me? Since my request was obviously important, they would push it to the 'top of their stack.' It would only take four days to write the programs and deliver the report. Four days! What good is that? I can't imagine how long it takes a non-VP to get a critical report.

"Beyond that, we have two sales systems—one for wholesale sales and the other for retail sales. Sometimes I am interested in looking at just wholesale accounts or retail accounts. But, believe it or not, there are times when I need information about sales of particular products, regardless of where they occurred. It wastes my time and the company's money for me to have to go to two different systems, find the related figures, and plug them into a spreadsheet to figure out what the sales of product X were."

Then, it was Richelieu's turn again. "And another thing. How the heck (Richelieu has always been fond of saying, 'How the heck') can I possibly forecast our cash needs when our general ledger system keeps only six months of history online? With the seasonality in our industry, even two years wouldn't be enough.

"And hey, I'm a finance guy. I live in spreadsheets. If I can't sort it, summarize it, or chart it, I'm cranky. So, why is it that you can only give me data in paper reports? My salary costs the company over 300K per year. I'm spending half my time typing numbers from your paper reports into my spreadsheet. Does this make sense? Frankly, I'm getting a bit tired of this."

You start thinking, "300K, my deal is good but it's not that strong. Mental note: renegotiate employment contract."

"Well guys," you say, "let me chew on this for a while. I'll get back to you in a few days after I've figured it all out." The truth is, you're scared. After all, how secure is a CIO's job? You're the fourth that your company has had in the past six years. You never really asked why the others were 'shown the door.' Could it have been related to these same problems? Have there always been reporting problems here? How wise was it to take out a $450,000 mortgage last week?

Problems with the Current Reporting Architecture

After thinking about the heated conversation, you start analyzing the issues. What were your users really saying? Their concerns seem to break into a few categories. Users are concerned about the following:

- **Accessibility**   Can I get to my information when I need it?

- **Timeliness**   How long after transactions occur do I get my information?

- **Format**   Can I get my data in spreadsheets or graphs or maps or using other analytic tools, or can I only get it in paper reports?

- **Integrity**   Can I believe the data I get?

It's not hard to see that such concerns bring into question the competence of the IS (information systems) department. Even more importantly, answering such concerns can have a huge impact on the profitability of the company. How much, for instance, would it be worth to the company to have been able to provide Valjon with the report that could have won the FutureChef account? Do you think that was the only opportunity to leverage reporting to grow the company? In all probability, similar concerns arise all the time. Support this type of request and you build a new future for your company.

The Goal: Decision Support

As we noted earlier, the data warehouse is simply one component of modern reporting architectures. The real goal of reporting systems is decision support, in other words, to help people make better decisions. While you might not realize it, virtually all computer systems have some decision support component. That component is the reports produced by these systems. People take these reports and make decisions based on the information that they contain.

Since the introduction of computer systems, decision support has evolved greatly. Originally, computer systems produced paper reports. Users generally received information on a periodic basis via daily, weekly, monthly, annual, etc. reports. To receive custom reports, users would contact the IS department and have a programmer assigned to write a program to create the report. This task would take anywhere from a few hours to, in extreme cases, months. We have heard stories about companies that had an 18-month turnaround time on report requests. Eighteen months!

Of course, paper reports provided very little formatting and analytic flexibility. For example, did you ever try to sort a paper report? It really works only if you have scissors, tape, and a lot of time. And don't try to graph the data on a paper report unless you have a box of crayons!

Around 1980, a new technology entered the scene. What was that technology? That's right, the personal computer. When we got a personal computer, we generally bought two programs to go along with it—a word processor and a spreadsheet. We used the word processor to work on our resume. We used the spreadsheet to work with data. Did the spreadsheet give us access to any more data? Absolutely not—it gave us the ability to have our high-paid executives waste hours copying their data from our paper reports into their spreadsheets. But, our users could now analyze and format data. The inefficiencies and possibilities for errors are obvious.

In the early 1990s, spreadsheet companies recognized these problems and started building database connectivity into their products. The only thing missing was ease of use. This brings us to modern decision support. A decision support system is, therefore, a system that gives users access to their data and allows them to analyze and format the data as needed. Figure 1-1 shows the high-level evolution that has come to be called *decision support* in the 1990s.

Believe it or not, the fascination with end-user access to data is not quite new. Perhaps you remember a relic called COBOL—the COmmon Business Oriented Language. When COBOL was first developed, virtually all programming was done in assembler language. COBOL was an attempt to make computers accessible to users. The first business applications were accounting systems and therefore most users were accountants. The stories of accountants who became IS folk are legion. You've got to find it just a bit interesting that our first attempt to give end users reporting capabilities succeeded primarily in turning them into us. There have been successive attempts—each with similar, or even less auspicious, outcomes. Perhaps it's time to surrender, to realize that we really do want to turn our users into programmers, just not full-time programmers.

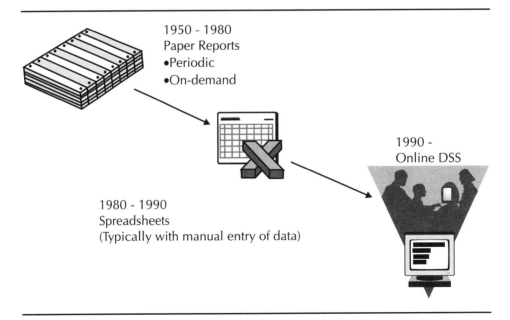

1950 - 1980
Paper Reports
•Periodic
•On-demand

1980 - 1990
Spreadsheets
(Typically with manual entry of data)

1990 -
Online DSS

FIGURE 1-1. *The road to modern decision support systems*

An Automatic Teller Machine (ATM)—For Data

Another way to view a modern reporting system is as an ATM for data. The parallels are interesting (OK, maybe not thrilling, but at least interesting) and hold a great number of lessons for the design of your reporting system.

When banks first introduced ATMs, what did they really do? In essence, they turned you into a teller, a virtual bank employee (how can anyone write a computer book nowadays without including the word "virtual?"). Now, if you consider a teller's job, you realize that it entails interacting with a complex computer system in order to execute transactions. You became a teller, but did you go through your bank's ATM training? We have yet to meet a person who answers "yes" to that question.

But, why would you be willing to become a bank employee? Because there are benefits for you. In fact, the benefits are so great that many banks now charge $1.50 per transaction for the right to become their teller. What are these benefits? Well, you now have access to your money wherever and whenever you need it—evenings, weekends, holidays—New York, Chicago, Copenhagen, Ann Arbor—your money is accessible. Can you do every conceivable banking transaction through an ATM? Well, no, there are still some complex transactions, like applying for an ill-advised $450,000 mortgage, that require help from real bank employees.

In a modern reporting environment, we are trying to do the same thing—but with data. Don't tell your users that we are really trying to shift programming work to them (i.e., to make them into programmers). They'll use point and click tools that generate queries in languages like SQL. If we do our jobs well, these tools will be so easy to use that we won't have to expend excessive effort in training our users how to use them. Why will computer-phobic users be willing to become "virtual" programmers? Because of the benefits to them. They will suddenly be able to get the information they need when they need it. IS will no longer be a bottleneck, requiring long lead times for responding to simple requests.

If you think about it, we're really trying to shift work from IS to our users. In the past, IS was an information conduit. All requests for data flowed through the IS department. We wrote programs and the results passed back through our department to the requestors. In the future, we want to be conduit builders. We want to put the tools and structures in place that allow users to access their own data. Our jobs don't go away, they're just transformed. Instead of writing report programs, we now build data warehouses and configure query tools to give simple access to our users. Figure 1-2 shows how IS has gone from being the conduit to being the builder of the conduit—a facilitator as opposed to a provider.

So, What's a Data Warehouse?

A modern reporting environment will give users access to their data. But, it doesn't solve all the problems our users have. Just because users have access to data doesn't guarantee the integrity of that data. It doesn't guarantee that system response times will be adequate. It doesn't guarantee that your systems won't purge old data before its useful life is passed. In fact, giving users access to data says little about that data.

To address many of these data problems, Bill Inmon speaks of the data warehouse. In fact, Inmon is frequently referred to as the "father of the data warehouse;" still, we recommend against calling him "dad." In his book,

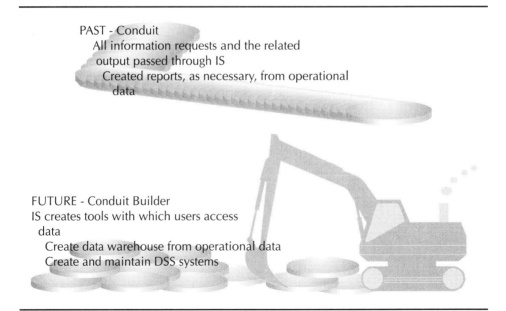

PAST - Conduit
    All information requests and the related
    output passed through IS
        Created reports, as necessary, from operational
            data

FUTURE - Conduit Builder
IS creates tools with which users access
    data
        Create data warehouse from operational data
        Create and maintain DSS systems

FIGURE 1-2.   *The effect of data warehousing on the IS department*

Building the Data Warehouse (John Wiley & Sons Inc., 1996), Inmon describes the warehouse as a "subject oriented, integrated, nonvolatile, time variant collection of data in support of management decisions."

Data warehouses are databases used solely for reporting. This is opposed to traditional data capture or online transaction processing (*OLTP*) systems. Classic examples of operational systems include the following:

- General ledger
- Accounts payable
- Financial management
- Order processing
- Order entry
- Inventory

Data warehouses are populated with data from two sources. Most frequently, they are populated with periodic migrations of data from OLTP systems. The second source is made up of external, frequently purchased, databases such as lists of income and demographic information that can be linked to internal data. The group of users supported by data warehouses grows all the time. Now these databases support more than just managers, but the basic concepts still apply. So, let's pull apart the definition in the next section.

Subject Oriented

OLTP databases are usually intended to hold information about a small subset of the organization. For example, a retailer might have separate order entry systems and databases for retail, catalog, and outlet sales. Each system will support queries about the information it captures. But, suppose a user wants to run a query on all sales, not simply the sales captured by a particular system. In your case, Valjon wants a report that describes the sales of a particular product, regardless of the channel responsible for that sale. Your data warehouse database will be subject oriented, organized into subject areas, like sales, rather than around OLTP data sources. Figure 1-3 shows how the three sales data sources come together in the sales subject area of the warehouse.

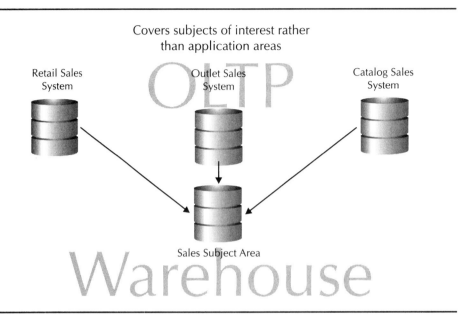

FIGURE 1-3. *Evolution into subject—oriented sales information*

When one of us worked for a major computer vendor early in his career, the employees could not answer a simple question like, "Who are our top ten customers?" They could tell you who the top ten mainframe customers were. They could tell you who the top ten mini customers were. They could tell you who the top ten PC customers were. But these answers in themselves were not entirely accurate; when they took the time (and were given the ability) to analyze total volume of sales of all customers across all product lines, two or three customers emerged as the best. The fact that these two or three were some of the company's best customers was lost when sales were isolated by computer size.

Imagine how much time was wasted every time senior management came back with a new question. Because no central repository existed to go to, each request was a painful process. Because it was a manual process, it also had the possibility of being fraught with manual error. Yet this was the best information available, and many decisions were made based on what data he and the other employees could supply to senior management.

Integrated

Consider the situation where you're bringing together data from three order entry systems into one warehouse. It is possible, in fact likely, that each of these systems codes their data differently. Perhaps the retail system has a product code consisting of seven numeric digits (e.g., 8909321—all numbers), the outlet system consisting of nine alphanumerics (e.g., TH67AF678—letters and numbers in no special order), and the catalog system consisting of four alphanumerics and a four character numeric (e.g. HHYU7815—letters and numbers where the last two digits are the sum of the previous two digits). To create a useful subject area, the source data must be integrated. In other words, the data must be modified to comply with common coding rules. This doesn't necessarily mean that the coding in the source systems must change but, instead, some process must be able to modify the data coming into the warehouse to assign a common coding scheme. Figure 1-4 illustrates this difficulty—the marriage of different coding schemes into one for the warehouse data.

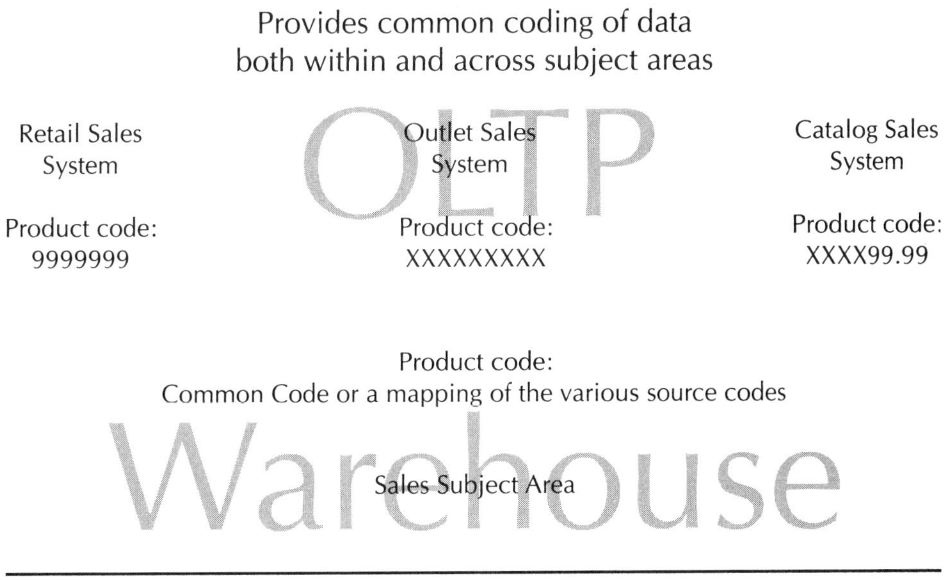

Provides common coding of data
both within and across subject areas

OLTP

Retail Sales System	Outlet Sales System	Catalog Sales System
Product code: 9999999	Product code: XXXXXXXXX	Product code: XXXX99.99

Product code:
Common Code or a mapping of the various source codes

Warehouse

Sales Subject Area

FIGURE 1-4. *Integration of coding schemes*

Nonvolatile

Nonvolatile is a 50-cent word (U.S., or 65 cents CAD) meaning that the warehouse is read-only; users can't write back. As opposed to OLTP databases, warehouses primarily support reporting, not data capture. As we will see, the warehouse is a historical record. Allowing users to write back to the warehouse would be akin to George Orwell's concept of rewriting history. Figure 1-5 illustrates this fundamental difference between OLTP and the data warehouse.

Time Variant

Much business analysis requires the analysis of trends. Trend analysis requires access to historical data. Generally, more than one year of history is required, particularly when the business is seasonal. Most OLTP systems, on the other hand, do not store large amounts of history. This is because large quantities of data are the enemy of fast response times. Since OLTP systems are designed for immediate response, they often purge data within a few months of its capture. Warehouses, on the other hand, hold large amounts

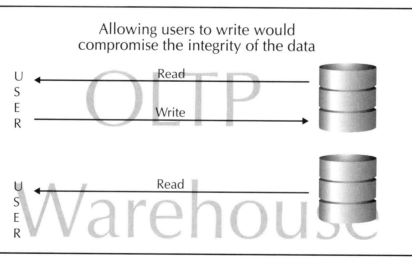

FIGURE 1-5. *OLTP read/write vs. data warehouse read-only*

The time dimension is key to most
management decisions

FIGURE 1-6.   *Time variant in the warehouse vs. OLTP*

of history. This is one of the main reasons why warehouses are often huge
databases. Figure 1-6 reiterates this time component.

Keep in mind, though, that not all history must be kept at the same level
of detail. For example, one past client operated in the wholesale food
business. This customer's warehouse kept track of the detail of each sales
transaction for a month. When the data was a month old, it was summarized
into weekly summary values. After two years, the data was kept only as
monthly summaries. Not only does this help data warehouse query
performance, but it also makes business sense. The details of any individual
transaction generally become less important as we get farther in time away
from that transaction. Three years from now, how important will it be to
know that customer Y bought a sack of freeze-dried okra on January 26?
On the other hand, if we are trying to estimate the winter demand for
freeze-dried okra, it might be important to know how much freeze-dried
okra was sold in total during the month of January.

Decision Support Differs from Transaction Processing

So, we're saying that you can't do hard core reporting and OLTP work in the same database. Why not? Well, first of all, while your users will demand a reporting system that adheres to Bill Inmon's four criteria of a data warehouse, most OLTP environments do not support these. In addition, think about the differences between decision support computing and OLTP computing:

- OLTP systems are designed to work with small pieces of information. For example, when taking an order, an OLTP user typically works with one customer, one order, one shipment, etc. at a time. Data stored in an OLTP database is designed to support this form of use. As a result, OLTP schema are highly normalized. Decision support queries, on the other hand, frequently work with huge blocks of information. For example, imagine what happens when the president of McDonald's wants to see a report of total sales for 1997, broken down by geographic region. Running this query of the OLTP database would entail reading billions of transaction records and summarizing the results to put on the report.

- OLTP data must frequently be updated in real time. For example, consider a bank whose systems did not provide real-time updates. A customer could go from branch to branch, withdrawing the full balance from her checking account, over and over again. In the decision support arena, on the other hand, data almost never needs to be updated in real time. This is because DSS users work with high-level, summary data. There is a real cost associated with obtaining data in real time. Before paying that cost you must ask, "Is there anything that could have happened in the past five minutes that could, or even should, have an effect on a decision that a manager will make?"

- OLTP schema are designed for rapid data input. Companies can't afford to make customers wait for order takers to finish transactions on slow order entry systems. In a data warehouse, on the other hand, no data is entered by users—remember, nonvolatile. Instead, the goal is to get data out as quickly as possible.

- OLTP users need immediate response. When the "Accept order" key is hit, the screen had better be available for the next order in under a second. DSS users, while they should not have to wait months for answers, generally don't need such blazing response times. When they get a response from the system, they consider it for a while and then take the next step.

- OLTP usage patterns are relatively predictable. System designers can tell how much work it will take to process a transaction and when most transactions will occur. In a decision support environment, on the other hand, usage patterns are not quite so stable. Who knows when a question might arise that requires complex analysis. Thus, the system might be heavily used for about four hours on Monday and then not touched again until Friday.

- OLTP schema are very complex. It is difficult to build an easy to use "ATM for data" on top of a complex schema.

Data Warehousing: A Dirty Little Secret

If you've picked up any IS-related publication over the past few years, it's apparent that warehouses are widely accepted, widely implemented tools. Database, tool, and consulting vendors love them. But amidst all the hype is buried a dirty little secret. Philosophically, in the opinion of many, data warehousing is a silly idea; even though many may feel that way, it's the best answer for the foreseeable future. Corporate data is already stored in computers that are accessible throughout the organization. Who in their right mind would get involved in moving data to new computers, cleaning it, and suffering through the headaches of making sure that this movement happens correctly, completely, and automatically? Who, in their right mind, would pick up a book the size of this one to learn how to move that data?

The original dream of relational databases was that we would store all of our organization's data in one central, integrated place. All transactions would be performed against that central database. All reporting would be out of that database. With the exception of the transaction processing, doesn't this sound a bit like a data warehouse?

Come to think of it, rather than copying data from your various OLTP systems into a data warehouse, why not get back to the original dream? Why not spend all that data warehousing money integrating your various OLTP systems? Couldn't we just place views over the new database to make it user friendly and then let users report directly from it? Wouldn't this save us from the philosophically ugly alternative of building a separate database just for reporting?

Well, an oddly related question is "How many MIPS do you have?" *MIPS* stands for millions of instructions per second, and has become one of the measurements of the processing power of a computer—more MIPS translates to faster processing. Imagine that you had infinite MIPS. Then, indeed, you could do all the processing for your company on one computer. Therefore, because you had infinite computing power, the response to any query would be instantaneous (and, incidentally, you could probably play some pretty cool computer games). Sadly, hardware vendors have let us down on this account. They have yet to deliver a computer with infinite computing power.

Instead, we live in a world where machines, including computers, can only do a fixed amount of work in a given period of time. Even large computers can only do so much work. Try, given this limitation, to run your OLTP and reporting systems on a single machine. Reporting and decision support queries frequently require a large amount of computing power as they summarize and report on millions of records. Now, imagine these queries sharing computer time with OLTP transactions and complex OLTP schema that are highly normalized. Your response time will likely be agonizingly slow. Also, these compute-intensive queries will slow down the performance of your OLTP systems. Do you want to be the one responsible for the line, "I'm sorry Mr. Kramden (of FutureChef), but we can't process your $10 million order right now because our president, Mr. Henchard, is running his monthly sales report and it's slowing down all of our systems. Could you please call back in about four hours?"

But, there is an important point here, a point that most companies don't consider. A data warehouse is not always required. For example, imagine a near-infinite MIPS situation. Suppose you run your entire company's finances on the personal finance software package called Quicken. Also, suppose this package is running on a Cray supercomputer. In this situation, you'll likely have enough MIPS to run both your OLTP and reporting systems on that one computer. While this is an extreme example, it does show that there is a range of options.

A data warehouse is frequently, but not always, the most cost-effective or even the best solution. In fact, we sometimes recommend that companies ease into data warehousing. It is often advisable to start by building summarized reporting structures in the OLTP database. These structures can eventually be ported to a warehouse as your reporting needs mature.

Return on Investment

To gain approval to pursue a systems development effort, one thing that most companies require is a financial analysis. This analysis is intended to determine whether the proposed investment will be a wise, profitable effort. Of course, no one will be sure until the effort is actually complete whether this prediction was correct or not. Even after completion, it is frequently difficult to tell whether or not a system is 'paying for itself.'

A number of formulae are used to determine whether or not a particular investment is wise. You've undoubtedly heard of these formulae. They have names like return on investment (*ROI*), internal rate of return (*IRR*), and payback period. Bean counters spend endless hours debating which of these is most appropriate and which is so ill-advised that the simple mention of its name will lead your project, and likely your entire organization, to certain bankruptcy.

Regardless of the formula you use, it will likely involve estimating the cost to construct your system and comparing it to the expected benefits that the system will provide. Costs include items like hardware, software, and developer and consulting fees. Benefits include items like estimated reductions in costs and increases in revenues.

In some systems efforts, the costs and benefits are relatively easy to estimate. For example, if you expect a new OLTP system to allow order entry operators to enter orders twice as fast, you can expect to need only half as many, reducing your personnel costs. In a data warehouse effort, the costs are as easy to estimate as in an OLTP environment. The benefits, on the other hand, are far less tangible.

A new sales warehouse will allow us to better market our customers, but, how much better? What is the value of:

- More rapid access to data

- More reliable reporting

- More flexible data presentation

Thus, many companies that require cost justification for every five-dollar systems purchase will forgo such analysis for the construction of a warehouse. Perhaps the exact benefits can't be quantified, but hopefully they are there.

One reason why warehouse benefits are so hard to quantify is that the exact target audience of these systems is rarely completely known when the effort is started. For example, most companies start their data warehousing efforts in the sales and marketing area. Why? Because the sales figure is usually the largest number on the company's income statement. A small percentage of improvement in this number can lead to a large dollar increase in the company's profitability. But, in our experience, while these systems are targeted at the company's sales and marketing force, an unexpected audience frequently follows close on their heels. Who? The controller's group. They're after the warehouse as an accurate place to verify exactly how the company is doing, without succumbing to the dirty data issues that are often rampant in OLTP environments.

A recent study by a company called IDC, which used information gathered from more than 60 organizations that had implemented data warehousing, found that data warehousing generated an average ROI of 401 percent over three years. Even if you're not a bean counter, 401 percent of anything is pretty good, right?

With an average ROI like that, it's no wonder we see such growth in corporations developing data warehouses and data warehouse strategies. In fact, economics is the major motivation for many of the trends we have lived through already. Downsizing became a reality when the corporate world realized it was now cheaper to reengineer or downsize applications than it was to keep them intact. With these kinds of ROIs, it's no surprise the majority of the corporate world is building or planning to build a warehouse.

One more point about estimating benefits. While most decision support efforts start in the sales and marketing subject area, they rarely end there. Decision support tools, such as data warehouses, are about optimizing operations—not just maximizing sales. Thus, while the sales department is generally interested in maximizing sales, other groups might be interested in helping by minimizing some factor. For example, perhaps the human resources (*HR*) department is trying to minimize headcount. In both the sales and HR examples, the groups are trying to optimize the company's performance.

In general, your warehousing go—no go decision should be based on questions like:

- Does it give us a competitive advantage?

- Does it improve the bottom line?

- Will it deliver on all its promises?

- Will it be delivered on time?

- What is the risk if we don't do it?

- What is the risk if we do it?

- Will it be delivered on budget?

While it is important to discuss the benefits of a planned warehouse, it is usually impossible to quantify these benefits in dollar terms. Sadly, the decision to construct the warehouse must frequently be a leap of faith. This fact does, though, bring us back to our earlier infinite MIPS discussion. Sometimes it's advisable to ease into warehousing by adding reporting structures to your existing OLTP database. This can be a lower risk path that allows you to "test the waters" before diving in completely.

This Book

The remainder of this book will discuss building your own data warehouse—the repository of information your business needs to thrive in the information age. We will help you understand what a data warehouse is and what it is not. You will learn what human resources are required, as well as the roles and responsibilities of each player. You will be given an overview of good project management techniques to help ensure the data warehouse initiative does not fail due to poor project management. You will learn how to physically implement a data warehouse with some new tools that help with the migration and transformation of legacy data into the warehouse. Once you understand how the warehouse is loaded, you will learn about query analysis and reporting software. This software is the technologist's power tool, helping you capitalize on your new information asset to mine those nuggets of value hidden in the vast expanses of data you've stored in the warehouse.

Oracle produces some of the world's best and most tested tools for warehousing and analysis. Throughout this book, Oracle8 specifics will be discussed, allowing you to leverage this powerful family of technologies to your competitive advantage.

A Career-Saving Happy Ending

Now it's Friday, and you have big plans for the weekend. You don't want to spend the evenings lying awake, worrying about reporting problems. You've got to go shopping for your new Mercedes. You send out an email to Valjon, Richelieu, and Henchard (as though those guys ever actually check their email). It reads as follows:

```
Folks:

It has recently come to my attention that there may be a bit of
dissatisfaction with our current reporting systems. We've been
following this situation closely over the past few months. I think
I've hit on a novel solution. Please expect to see a new budget
request for constructing a data warehouse. I won't get into exactly
what a warehouse is because you probably wouldn't understand
anyway. Suffice it to say that I think this warehouse will help to
solve many of our reporting problems.
```

Fasten your seatbelts and, if any children under the age of 13 are in the front seat, they should be in the back if your car has airbags. Time and time again, so many find the data warehouse project a new way of thinking. New ways of thinking, new ways of doing things, new stuff to consider and, in some cases, unlearning of the way we have done things in the past. This is what the next chapter of *Oracle8 Data Warehousing* is about. Et tu Bruté, then read Caeser…

CHAPTER
2

Things to Consider

iving a know-it-all author a chapter title like "Things to Consider" is a bit like giving an axe murderer a chainsaw. What to do, what to do? There are a ton of things to consider. For example, consider the fact that humans have inhabited the earth for over 200,000 years but writing was invented only about 5,000 years ago (about the same time as the wheel). What does that say about the pace of technology? Well, 5,001 years ago we couldn't even write, and now we write so much that we need data warehouses to store it all!

In Chapter 1, we provided some idea of what a data warehouse is and what it isn't. In this chapter, we will address a number of "guiding principles" of data warehousing. These are insights that we've gained through years of experience and struggle. Consider them as you read the rest of this book and as you build your warehouses and marts. Let's start with a big one, one that essentially says, "Sometimes it may be a good idea to ignore what you read in this book."

Don't Listen to What We Say... Be Pragmatic

So, what are you building? Is it a data mart or a data warehouse? Can you tell the difference? Does it matter?

The data warehouse industry generates a lot of great terminology and rules. The problem with it is that people new to the field feel that they must adhere to these rules. We've been on projects where team members have told us things like, "You can't do X or Y, this is a warehouse."

At times like these, we have to ask, "Are we trying to build a warehouse or solve a set of business problems?" Our point here is that you have to stay pragmatic. Build the system that solves the user's problem, not the one that looks like a pure data warehouse.

Articles and Books Contain Opinions, Not Facts

Over the past few years there have been a lot of very intelligent individuals (and a few not-so-intelligent ones) writing and speaking on the topic of data warehousing. Magazine articles are very alluring. If it appears in print, it must be true.

Keep in mind, though, that not all words in print are gospel. *CompInfoTimes* is not the Bible. Opinions, even those of respected professionals, are just that, opinions—not facts. This, of course, puts more pressure on you. Now, the only one you can blame for mistakes is yourself. Protect yourself. Thoroughly think through your design decisions before you commit.

Start with Business Requirements—Not Technology

What made you interested in building systems? For many of us, it was a love of technology. We love being able to write snappy systems that put pretty pictures on some undeserving user's screen. The answer to virtually every problem is to "build a new system."

Well, sadly, data warehousing is not about technology. Data warehousing is about solving business problems. In fact, some of the best data warehousing specialists we know have degrees in business, not in computers. One key to successful data warehousing is to start by focusing on what information the organization needs to flourish, NOT on how to deliver that information.

Query technologies are "cool," and developers tend to want to play with them. In fact, we have seen a project where the team spent the first six months picking the query tool and then learning how to use it. Data structures were given a back seat. Managers aren't dumb people. They can tell when real progress is being made…and when it isn't. In the end, this company's managers got so frustrated that they canceled the project. It restarted, but with a new project manager who was instructed to deemphasize tools.

It's important to remember that most properly designed warehouses will be accessed by a variety of technologies. Once the warehouse is built, it may support the following:

- Programs that export data to data marts
- Report writers

- OLAP and analysis tools

- Data mining tools

- Custom-coded executive information system (EIS) tools

- Geographic information system (GIS) tools

- Any number of other query technologies

Thus, focusing on any one query technology can distract the team from building the necessary flexibility.

Keep in mind that query technologies come and go. The flavor of the day may be Cognos, but tomorrow it may be Business Objects. Regardless of what a query tool vendor may say, the real strategic piece of the warehouse is the data. It is vital that the data structures accurately reflect the demands of the business and that they contain correct, reliable data.

There is one caveat. Certain query tools require specific types of data structures in order to work. These can be powerful tools. We generally recommend that such tools be viewed as limited-function data mart technologies rather than enterprise-wide data warehouse tools.

What Goes into the Warehouse?

Many new warehouse designers view the warehouse as the final repository for all the company's data. They will make naïve statements like, "All corporate reporting will be done from the warehouse." This is generally not a viable approach. As we noted in the first chapter, the warehouse is only one component of an enterprise reporting strategy, albeit a big component.

This distinction is important for a number of reasons. For one, the vast majority of warehouses are updated in batch rather than in real time. Thus, transactions are not immediately loaded into the warehouse but, instead, wait until the end of the day or the end of the week. Certain reporting requests, on the other hand, require a real-time, current view of the company's data. For example, a clerk answering telephone calls from customers may need to be able to tell whether or not a particular payment has been received. Supplying that clerk only with data from a warehouse that is loaded once a week is a sure formula for customer irritation.

Another reason why it is important to "position" the warehouse in the corporate reporting architecture is to protect the project from overbuilding. In systems development, increases in size increase risk. Each new table, each new column, each new constraint increases the amount of development work that must be estimated, scheduled, and performed. They also increase the possibility that an object in the architecture will fail. Thus, positioning the warehouse effectively is a tool for managing its scope, and also a tool for helping ensure success.

Given this, we recommend that in designing your warehouse you explicitly state where the warehouse will fit into the corporate reporting process. This statement should detail the rules that will be used to determine what data goes into the warehouse and what data is excluded. An example of such a statement might be, "The warehouse will focus on delivering data that has value in an aggregated format or in grouping large segments of the population. Data unique to relatively small numbers of the population, such as the second alternate address, will not be included." Statements like this (perhaps with a little more detail) give warehouse developers a basis for deciding what is included in, and what is excluded from, the warehouse. This warehouse position should be developed while you are gathering business and user requirements.

The user community should signify their understanding and agreement with the warehouse position statement. Not only does this help them understand the role of the warehouse, but it also gives them another way to plan for how to use it.

Data Mart or Data Warehouse?

One of the first questions that always springs up tries to address this nagging issue—what are data warehouses and data marts, and which do we build first? In this book you'll read a lot about data warehouses and data marts. One of the big topics in reporting systems nowadays is the dreaded data warehouse versus data mart altercation (aren't automated thesauri wonderful?). Companies are trying to figure out the following:

- Do we need a data warehouse?

- Do we need data marts?

- Come to think of it, what is a data warehouse?

- For that matter, what is a data mart?

- If we need both, which do we build first?

Time for some brief descriptions. As we noted in the first chapter, per Bill Inmon, a data warehouse is a "subject oriented, integrated, nonvolatile, time variant collection of data in support of management decisions." To us, a data warehouse is "broad" data store. It contains a number of subject areas. A data mart, on the other hand, typically focuses on a more narrow part of the business. It usually covers a single subject area and/or type of analysis. For example, your corporate data warehouse might include information about sales, finance, and human resources. Your company may also maintain a number of data marts. Perhaps there is a data mart targeted at analyzing product movement through the retail channel. Another, located in a regional headquarters, might be used for analyzing sales in that region. Perhaps the company has yet another targeted at employee turnover.

There are two basic ways that companies create data marts. The first is to capture data directly from OLTP systems into the marts that need it. The second is to capture data from OLTP systems into a central data warehouse and then to feed the data marts with data from the warehouse. There is a great deal of disagreement on which is the best approach. The first approach quickly gets you a data mart. But at what cost?

When you build an enterprise data warehouse, you typically start by defining an enterprise data model. This entity-relationship model shows the key entities in your warehouse and the relationships between these key entities. When you start to build your population routines, you will likely not populate all these entities at once. Still, you have defined how they relate to each other. Once the model is fully populated, users will be able to extract data that crosses functional lines (for example, the trend in sales per person employed). This query crosses the boundary between the sales and human resources subject areas. It provides a new level of information, a level not attainable in the traditional, stovepipe, transaction-oriented systems of the past.

Now, assume that you build a few data marts by extracting data directly from OLTP sources. In most cases, you get the mart up quickly, but you ignore cross-subject area relationships. Thus, the sales-per-headcount query we just mentioned remains as difficult as ever.

So, what to do? As in all our advice, the answer will vary according to a number of factors but, in general, we recommend that you adopt an enterprise-wide approach from the start. But, do this in a way that delivers results before the warehouse is complete. How do you do this? Start by quickly defining a logical, enterprise data warehouse, showing only the organization's key entities and relationships. Then attack one subject area, and develop an architecture to populate that area. Determine whether queries can occur directly from the warehouse or if the relevant data must be moved into a mart. If a mart is necessary, building it will be far less complex than building it directly from OLTP systems, and it should therefore be completed fairly quickly.

One point to note: In this warehouse-feeding-mart architecture, your warehouse becomes a source system to your marts. In designing that warehouse, you can take steps to ease construction of these downstream marts. One thing, in particular, that you can do is create structures, such as last update time stamp columns, to track changes in warehouse data. While these structures will slightly increase the size and complexity of your warehouse, they will greatly ease the amount of work necessary to build downstream data marts.

Data marts can also contain data that is important for the purpose of the mart but is unimportant to the rest of the company. For example, perhaps the telecommunications department needs to analyze long-distance usage on a monthly basis. It will build its mart using two data sources:

1. It will gather data from the corporate data warehouse about every employee, their phone number, and their department.

2. It will gather data from its long-distance provider about the long-distance usage from each phone.

Notice that while the usage data is very important to this particular department, it is relatively unimportant to the rest of the company. Thus, it is unlikely that the usage data would be captured in the enterprise warehouse. Basic employee information, on the other hand, is quite important and would be captured in the enterprise warehouse.

Here's one more interesting concept about data marts: you can consider each report that your company produces to be a little data mart. This is especially true if the data is delivered in an electronic format that can later be manipulated and analyzed. Once the data is moved into Excel or Access, for example, the user can further analyze and manipulate that data. How is this different from a data mart that is explicitly called a data mart? This point is important for a few reasons:

1. It forces us to think about what it really takes to build a data mart.

2. It highlights some of the security concerns that accompany the greater access to data we are striving for when we build our warehouses and marts.

3. It also highlights the fact that a mart can be a one-time, single-use structure. Perhaps we need to do headcount reporting by race and gender to support a government audit of hiring practices. Once the audit is over, we no longer need the data. It is not necessary to build a complex architecture for every data mart needed. It is quite acceptable to use warehouse queries to build single-purpose marts to support these one-time requests.

Big Bang Vs. Small Iterations— Development Phases

Everyone knows that data warehouses are built iteratively, not in one large step, right? There is an endless stream of consultants and vendors screaming about rapid delivery and iterative development. Still, what do these terms really mean (we suspect that even these vendors and consultants don't always think this through)? Does this mean that a warehouse has no thought given to architecture? To user requirements? Do we just keep iterating until we get it right?

You can probably guess that the answer to those questions is "no." If you're building a system that management is going to rely upon, building one that is slapped together—missing things like basic controls and checks—is counterproductive, at least as a driver of your career success. So what, then, does this iterative development look like?

Well, the warehouse is certainly built in small pieces, or iterations. But, not all of these iterations are the same size. In terms of the amount of data delivered, the first iteration is pretty small. In terms of the amount of work required, the first iteration is frequently the largest.

Why is this? Well, a good deal of the effort of your first release will focus on building a robust warehousing infrastructure. Think about it—to complete this first release, you need to do a lot of things that you'll never have to do again, at least not for a long time. These include things like:

- Developing the high-level enterprise warehouse model
- Training the warehouse team on technologies and strategies
- Selecting data movement and query technologies
- Creating the network and server environments and support mechanisms

Later releases will capitalize on this infrastructure, allowing you to deliver more data with far less work.

Long Live RI

Data warehouse developers have a secret weapon to help them fight their way through the administrivia that most companies force traditional applications through—administrivia like data model reviews and director sign-off. This secret weapon? The phrase, "Well this is a warehouse, and in a warehouse we do things differently." What a great cop-out! If only such excuses worked elsewhere (for example, "Well, officer, this is a Japanese car and, therefore, doesn't have to adhere to U.S. speed limits").

While we hate to give away such a powerful tool, we're afraid that the "but we're developing a warehouse" excuse (hereafter we call this the BWDAW excuse) gets used far too often. Yes, you are developing a warehouse. No, you are not developing an altogether new form of reality. Warehousing is not computing anarchy. In general, unless you can come up with a really good justification for breaking the rules we all know and live by, don't break them.

The most frequent area where the BWDAW excuse is used is referential integrity (RI). To refresh your memory, Oracle allows a developer not only to define tables of information but also the relationships between those tables. The act of ensuring that these references are enforced is called enforcing referential integrity. You can tell Oracle, for example, "Reject any sales transaction for which a related customer record does not exist in the CUSTOMER table." Should you try to insert data about a sale to John Smith and Mr. Smith doesn't have a record in the customer table, the database will vomit back your data. Thus, though enforcing RI requires computer time when loading data into the warehouse, it does not affect query response times.

Even though tones have been written about the need for data quality in the warehouse, developers seem dying to turn off one of their key tools for ensuring quality—RI. Why? The most frequent justification goes something like this, "We don't want to pay the performance penalty that enforcing RI entails and, besides, we're programmatically checking RI, we don't need the database to do this for us."

Well, let's think about the "programmatically checking" argument for a moment. Who in their right mind ever wrote a serious business application that intentionally violated referential integrity? We dare say, desperately few developers who lived to tell about it. We enforce referential integrity to protect us from ourselves—to help ensure that we don't accidentally commit programming errors that violate the basic tenets of our business.

As for the performance penalty, most of the people who use this excuse have never tested the database with RI turned on. Try your system with RI turned on. In terms of performance, one of two things will happen:

1. Performance will be adequate and you'll be a referentially correct hero

2. Performance will be inadequate and you'll have to find a way to improve it. In this case, you'll have a few options:

   ■ Analyze your load jobs to see if they can be tuned.

   ■ Analyze your schema to see if it can be tuned.

   ■ Reevaluate your hardware selection.

   ■ Disable referential integrity (if you're willing to take the risk).

The point here is that you don't start your project by turning off one of your best data quality tools. Turn it off only if there is no other way to get the load performance you need.

One last note about RI. Frequently, you will validate the data from your source against a list of valid values before you put it into the warehouse (i.e., programmatically check referential integrity). What do you do with "bad values?" Do you reject them? Well, one technique we've used is to alter the bad records. The technique goes as follows:

1. Into each of your lookup tables (i.e., lists of allowable values), insert an additional record with a description like "Unrecognized data received."

2. When a record that violates integrity is received, make a copy of it into some log for later checking.

3. Take the original record and change the offending value to point to the "Unrecognized data" record in the related lookup table.

4. Insert this modified record into your warehouse.

This approach has a lot of value. For one, it allows you to completely populate your warehouse. Second, it adheres to referential integrity rules while still keeping a record of data that must be investigated. Third, and most important, it allows you, or a user, to run queries showing the impact of "bad data." Suppose you run a sales query and get a result indicating that 20 percent of all sales were to customers that the system could not identify. You can now start to look at your OLTP systems with an eye toward forcing those systems to capture this essential data.

Query Tools—You Will Have More than One

As we noted earlier, you may very well build a data mart specifically to support a particular query tool—especially if that tool requires its own proprietary data structures. On the other hand, other marts and most data warehouses should be tool independent. To get the warehouse's full value, it will likely be queried by a variety of tools. These might include things like:

■ Report writers

■ Online analytical processing (OLAP) databases and tools

■ Statistical analysis and data mining packages

- Client/server programming languages

- Geographic information system (GIS) mapping tools

- Executive information systems (EIS)

Thus, developing the warehouse should not be viewed as an exercise in query tool selection. Instead, it should be geared toward developing and populating powerful, tool-independent data structures. Data structures and data are a strategic investment. Well done, these will last for years. Query tools, on the other hand, are nonstrategic. The "flavor of the day" will change from year to year. Design specifically for today's flavor and you'll be in bad shape tomorrow.

Data Warehouse Differences— A Developer's Perspective

Skills and habits formed while building an assortment of operational system work has prepared many DSS analysts and developers for data warehouse project work. All that operational system "big bang" work is not out the door. In many ways, data warehouses are not that different from those systems that you've always built. Think of a data warehouse as consisting of two separate yet intertwined architectures—the data loading architecture and the end-user data access architecture. To a great extent, the loading architecture is really just a well-designed batch system in a client/server environment. The data access architecture may be a bit different, but it really just builds on tools that you've already acquired—tools like SQL and client/server and/or Internet concepts. Chapter 19 speaks at length about the Internet.

In other ways, data warehouses—systems for delivering rather than capturing data—are vastly different than anything you've ever built before. In Chapter 1, you learned that data warehouse projects are different by nature. Now you will see how participants in data warehousing projects need to learn how to deliver a system that is radically different from any other they have delivered before.

This reorientation is good for IT professionals who are fortunate enough to participate in warehousing projects. Not only does it allow them to hone their client/server skills, it also gives them an opportunity to work on projects that are typically very visible to management and the company at large. This visibility, though, does have its downside. Because they gather data from other systems using other technologies (that were possibly built at times when the business looked very different than it currently does), data warehouse projects can be quite demanding and, at times, tense. Participants on data warehouse projects should be prepared to accept the visibility that comes along with such a project, and at the same time be prepared to deliver under some very demanding conditions.

Developers new to the data warehouse world must be ready for a significant mindshift, a shift away from a data-capture mindset and to one of data distribution. Warehouse developers must develop a mindset that focuses on rapidly delivering large quantities of data. The question is no longer, "How quickly can I insert this row in the database?" The question now becomes "How can I deliver results to a query that summarizes 10 million rows in a reasonable amount of time? Beyond that, how can I ensure adequate performance to a variety of similar queries that I can't even foresee today?"

The thinking is very different. For example, in a data-capture world, you index your data very lightly. In a reporting world, you put a lot of indexes on your data, paying a price when loading in batch that pays off in faster response time when users run a variety of unforeseen queries.

Another example, one that data modelers in particular have difficulty grasping, is the concept of normalization. In the OLTP world, schema are highly normalized. A transaction may need to join a few tables together, but this generally accesses only a few records in each of these tables. If you were to join the same tables in a reporting environment and try to bring back millions of records, your query would die—and you'd get an angry phone call from some disgruntled user (and his boss). Thus, you denormalize tables together in the data warehouse.

Think a minute about denormalization. What are you really doing when you denormalize? In a way, aren't you doing the following:

1. Predicting the work that a user will request

2. "Predoing" it in a batch job so that the system doesn't have to do it when the user submits his or her query?

A good way to approach many of the performance issues you'll encounter in the data warehousing world is to ask yourself, "Is there anything else I can predo when I load the data to save the user from having to do it at run time?" Hey, what about creating summary tables to support certain summary queries that I know the user will run? Etc., etc., etc.

The point? Developers moving from an OLTP environment to a data warehousing environment must get used to the fact that they are going to break traditional rules in an effort to satisfy their users' lust for data (did you ever think you'd see the words "lust" and "data" in the same sentence?).

Data Warehouse Differences— The User's Perspective

Here's a sobering thought: In many cases, use of the data warehouse is optional. If a user doesn't want to use the warehouse, she won't. If using the warehouse is more trouble than it's worth, the user will circumvent it. "Circumvent it how," you ask? Well, remember that the warehouse contains data gathered from other systems. Perhaps our user will get reports directly from those systems. Perhaps she'll set up her own mini IS department to write programs and circumvent the overbearing, central IS department that tried to force her to use that damned warehouse. Perhaps she'll do her best to go without reports altogether.

Clearly, a warehouse holds a ton of promise. What would make a user avoid it? Well, how about the following:

- **Unreliable data?** How many times does our user have to make bad decisions or look bad in front of her boss, because your warehouse delivered bad data, before she loses interest?

- **Poor response time?** Perhaps immediate response time isn't necessary, but how user friendly is it to lock up the user's PC for four hours waiting for a report to run?

- **Complex user interfaces?** Have you ever tried to teach an executive how an outer join differs from an inner join? Do it once and you'll never try again (assuming, of course, that you remain employed). How willing will your user be to use your warehouse if you give her a tool that requires her to define her own joins?

Of course, this is different than the OLTP world. In OLTP, for the most part, users have to use the system that they're given. If your job is to enter sales transactions into a database, the only way you'll be able to do this is to use the system that the IS department gave you.

The point here is that the data warehouse is one of the few places where the user really can vote on whether or not she likes the system. If she likes it, she'll use it to no end. If she dislikes it, she'll avoid it like the plague. How would the face of business change if users had such voting power over all the systems we gave them?

Empowering Users

How many times in the past few years have you heard that company X or Y is restructuring? Everyone's doing it. If you read deep enough into the details of restructuring announcements you usually find somewhere that management in the new organization will empower its (remaining) employees. What do they mean by "empower?" Well, they mean that now employees will be allowed to make many of the decisions that used to be directed up the management chain. Think about it, though. How effective will employees be at making decisions if they don't have data with which to make those decisions?

Implementing a data warehouse is one way to deliver this data. Not only is it tied to freeing users from running to management, but, surprisingly, it also frees users from having to run to IS.

Empowerment allows users control of their own destiny—no running to the programmers asking for reports programmed to satisfy burning needs. How many times in operational environments are new reports identified, scoped, and programmed, after which you discover that, by the time they are ready, the user has found other sources for the desired output? An inevitable time delay exists between the identification of new requirements and their delivery. This is no one's fault; it is simply reality.

Using reporting tools against a data warehouse empowers users to get and analyze data and make informed decisions by themselves. For example, OLAP tools allow users to do forecasting, drill-down, and digging for trends in all aspects of their business. The data warehouse user can slice and dice data in ways never dreamed of before. New information is uncovered and a new way of thinking is born. Armed with the freedom to report on what they want, when they want, the operational application development personnel are free to build new applications. These applications may be tailored to implement business decisions made by executives and management, based on information gleaned from the data warehouse. They may even be applications to correct some of the dirty data issues that the warehouse uncovers. If this sounds like the best of both worlds, it is.

Why Oracle for Data Warehousing?

Oracle the company and Oracle the product have been supplying relational IT solutions to the marketplace for almost two decades. In a previous life, the company was called Relational Software, with its roots in the late 1970s. Since its inception, Oracle has established itself as a significant provider of software, services, and support. Businesses moving into the relational technology environment have always had a wide range of choices to make. What they continue to look for is a one-stop shopping supplier; they want to leverage existing investments when they move toward setting up DSS systems in the 1990s.

Total Solutions

Oracle has established a network of partnerships with hardware vendors and other software vendors. By leveraging the products of these vendors, Oracle allows organizations to take advantage of their own data warehouse features as well as those of their business partners. Oracle is so pervasive today that vendors cannot afford to avoid it. Oracle is the first database engine supported by most tools created nowadays. Choose Oracle and all doors are open to you. Not all database technologies can boast of such wide support.

OLAP and Universal Server

Oracle has deliberately based their data warehouse and OLAP solutions on their cooperative server technology. Many organizations looking at the data warehouse solution already use Oracle. Their development personnel are used to programming against the Oracle database, and their learning curve is flattened when the Oracle warehouse solution is selected.

With release of the Oracle8 Server, significant enhancements have been made to speed up data retrieval, query processing, and optimization.

Optimization is a process whereby Oracle selects a plan to follow when executing queries such that the time spent until the query results are presented to the user is minimized.

The transformation and migration of data to the data warehouse centers around the Oracle8 Server technology coupled with its Parallel Query Option (PQO). The PQO allows computers with more than one processor to partition query processing among the processors. It is designed to provide for faster throughput of queries. The PQO has been available since release 7.1 of the database (circa January 1995), and it is a player in the information warehouse environment. Transforming and migrating data into the warehouse are, by nature, operations that can take advantage of multiple processors. Oracle installations not exploiting PQO can still take advantage of parallel data loading, starting with release 7.3, which has been available in many platforms since March 1996. Parallelization increases performance by partitioning work among a handful of processes that work alongside one another. By definition, parallel processing is faster than *linear* (one process) processing.

Using Oracle Open Gateway technology, data architects, DSS analysts, and programmers can access non-Oracle data sources such as DB2, CA/IDMS, Informix, and CA/Ingres. The Gateway technology handles and deals with inconsistencies in data types between Oracle and the other product being accessed.

Part of the data loading process in some warehouses involves moving data from a wide range of operational systems; Oracle can handle getting that data for the warehouse by issuing SQL statements against these data stores. Structured Query Language (SQL) has become the industry standard for access to relational databases. SQL standards define syntax for statements and govern what can be accomplished and how to use industry-accepted "rules and regulations."

Oracle also provides data acquisition and transformation tools. These are tools specifically designed for moving and transforming data from source systems and moving it to the data warehouse or data mart. Later in the book, we will talk about the Oracle Data Mart Suite and the Sagent suite of tools.

Later chapters discuss tools from Oracle to access the data in your warehouse. As we'll learn, there are two basic approaches to storing data for OLAP: multidimensional and relational. Oracle covers both bases. Discoverer 3 is a critically acclaimed tool for accessing data in a relational database. Oracle's Express is a leading suite of tools that address the multidimensional approach; Chapter 17 is dedicated to Oracle Express.

Oracle multidimensional OLAP technology can access operational systems as well as legacy systems using a non-Oracle database. The product line is made up of a few of the following:

- **Oracle Express Server**   This is the heart of the Oracle Express solution that facilitates OLAP tool features permitting presentation of warehouse data in an assortment of easy-to-understand formatted outputs with graphic capabilities.

- **Oracle Express Objects**   This is a developer tool that enables programmers to build applications that permit decision making and forecasting efforts based on the data residing in the data warehouse. Oracle Express Objects is fully Windows-compliant, and its rapid application development capabilities allow quick delivery of modules to the customer (end user).

- **Oracle Express Analyzer**   This is an end-user OLAP tool that permits subject-oriented analysis by a wide range of users of the data warehouse. The product allows the end user to become self-sufficient for reporting and analysis needs.

One Repository/Many Solutions

For many years, companies have invested significant dollars in writing, and then rewriting, operational systems that allow them to go about their daily business. Many have moved on to later releases of Oracle, and they are in the midst of spending time and effort moving to client/server-based systems. The bottom line? By using the existing technology, companies can protect current investments and at the same time make use of state-of-the-art data warehouse solutions.

Data warehouse management, just like OLTP system management, requires a database administrator (DBA). The work involved is similar—except the extraction, scrubbing, and loading processes may be new to some DBAs. Many of the tasks performed and tools used by the database administrator are the same, regardless of whether or not they support the operational system or the data warehouse.

Existing Relationships

Most in-house personnel responsible for technical support of the Oracle product suite know their way around the Oracle sales and support organizations. In some cases, relationships have been ongoing for over a decade. Sometimes we find ourselves getting that personal touch when we speak with Oracle Worldwide Customer Support. Does this mean existing customers get better support than new ones? Definitely not! Oracle provides the same level of service and attention to detail to all customer contacts regardless of whether they are new or existing customers. By leveraging existing professional relationships with support analysts, the support process is smoother, it can be more satisfying, and it can end up producing more useful results.

Return on Investment

Organizations that adopted Oracle technology many years ago have spent time and money training their developers and database administrators. The Oracle product suite has undergone radical changes over the past few years; however, the skills acquired by developers, especially in using SQL to manipulate data, are protected when Oracle is used for DSS initiatives. No additional learning curve exists. Because Oracle standardized on its procedural SQL programming language PL/SQL, work developers have done is not lost. As Oracle brings new products to market, they are committed to using PL/SQL as one of the new product's programming languages.

Chapter 3 discusses details about building the data warehouse team. Building a data warehouse is a complex undertaking that requires personnel with a wide range of skillsets. We will model an existing data warehouse team and discuss the various roles of each participant, along with the skills that each needs to bring to the table. This is the first step to help you build your own team from the pool of resources and individual sets of skills you have available.

CHAPTER
3

Building the Team

hen we began writing this chapter, the intent was to supply you with a successful organizational chart, which could be used as the basis to build a data warehouse team. But, the more we thought about it, the more we realized that would be the equivalent of implying only one correct way exists for you to organize a data warehouse team. In truth, correct ways to solve any problem or meet any challenge depend upon many factors, all of which are specific to available resources and your particular time constraints.

With this in mind, it became clear this chapter would be of more value if it discussed various roles that should be part of a successful data warehouse initiative. After looking at the individuals—their unique abilities and time constraints—you have available, you can use this chapter as a sounding board when you build your team. In addition, it will act as a reference tool to see if you have covered all necessary bases.

The Data Warehouse Team Checklist

No matter which task you choose to analyze, as you break it into its various components, you quickly realize that no matter how simple the task seems, it is not as easy as it looks. To illustrate this point, look at how complicated it is simply to take a container of milk from a refrigerator and pour that milk into a glass. As you look at this problem in more detail, you might derive the following task list:

1. Locate the refrigerator.

2. Open the refrigerator door.

3. Scan the current contents of the refrigerator to locate a container of milk.

4. Determine how to move any items in the refrigerator that stand in your way so you can obtain the milk.

5. Remove the milk container from the refrigerator and place it on the kitchen counter.

6. Remove the milk cap.

7. Place the milk cap on the kitchen counter.

8. Determine where the clean glasses are located.

9. Open the kitchen cabinet door that contains the clean glasses.

10. Determine which hand to use and how to hold and retrieve the clean glass.

11. Inspect the glass for chips because it is breakable.

12. Bring the glass to the bottle of milk.

13. Pour the milk into the glass.

This list represents the task list of pouring a glass of milk in its simplest form, but what if a problem occurred. What if the bottle of milk was almost empty? What if the bottle of milk was a paper carton? What if the milk was in a plastic container? What if the glass you were about to use was chipped? What if the glass you picked up was not properly cleaned? What if you wanted the milk warmed?

As you can see from this simple example, many tasks must be performed and many different scenarios must be considered. Each one of these situations will affect how long it takes to get a glass of milk. The old native saying, "Don't judge people until you have walked in their moccasins," applies here. The significant attribute of a professional athlete is the ability to make a sport look so easy you want to try it yourself. When we watched Larry Bird of the Boston Celtics play basketball or Bobby Orr of the Boston Bruins play hockey, they made it look so easy. (It's not hard to see a few of us are very big Boston sports fans. On a side note, we do not want to hear how good the Chicago Bulls are until they win 16 world championships. They are still a very far cry from the legacy of the Boston Celtics—sorry, Boston pride overwhelmed us there for a minute.) Yet when we pick up a hockey stick or a basketball, we are very quickly brought to the realization that it's not so easy.

When you look at the listing of data warehouse roles, do not underestimate the complexity of the undertaking on which you are about to embark. Be it a data mart or a full-blown, enterprise-wide data warehouse, it is a lot of work to take your organization's data, scrub it, clean it, and repackage it so that you have easy access to slice and dice it any way you want. No matter how easy your team makes it look, under the surface, a lot of effort was expelled to get you there. In much the same way the professional athlete makes a particular sport look so easy, a successful data warehouse implementation team will make what they do look easy at first glance. Yet, when you take the time to look under the covers, a lot of tasks were completed and a lot of very hard effort made it all possible.

Let's take a high-level look at a data warehouse roles checklist; these are some of the areas of responsibility you need to cover in your effort to build a warehouse. Since there is a great deal of overlap, we will only go into detail on the major items. The next listing shows a data warehouse roles checklist—use this as your guideline when building the team.

```
Data warehouse project manager
Data warehouse architect
Database administrator
System administrator
Data migration specialist
Legacy system specialist
Data transformation/grooming specialist
Data provision specialist
Data mart development leader
Operations/data center
Configuration management
Organization consultant
Change management consultant
Quality assurance/testing specialist
Infrastructure specialist
Production control analyst
Power user
Trainer
Technical writer
Public relations person
Metadata steward
Corporate sponsors
Help desk functionality
End-user business executive
Tools specialist
Vendor relations person
Web master
Metadata repository manager
New technologies analyst
New technologies manager
End users
Consultants
```

TIP
Your particular situation will determine how these roles are allocated. On a very large data warehouse effort, these roles would be spread among 7 to 30 individuals; on a smaller warehouse effort, a single person might accomplish two, three, or even all these roles.

As you can see from reviewing the data warehouse roles checklist, you must think through and account for many different roles. Your level of success will depend on how you manage the resources you have available to accomplish the tasks associated with these roles. On a very large data warehouse effort, these roles might represent a particular individual; on a smaller effort, a single person might accomplish two or more of these roles.

Roles Needed for Your Data Warehouse Team

As you read the detail of these roles, remember your particular situation and the personalities involved. Review your situation from two different perspectives:

- The job function—the nature of the job that has to be performed
- The person or individual—the nature of the person performing a task

For example, you must decide which person or what team will be responsible for the functions of a system administrator, who should be responsible for determining whether or not the backups are working, and if the correct system patches are installed. As we stated before, you must determine if the person you choose has the right technical breadth of experience coupled with an appropriate personality. If not, perhaps a team should fulfill this function. Let's proceed by having a look at the major players on the data warehouse team, their abilities, and their responsibilities.

Data Warehouse Project Director

The person you consider for project director should have a quick wit and a solid understanding of the business and its technology vision. More importantly, this person must understand why the business needs a data warehouse and how to sell this concept to senior management to obtain the needed funding. The project director must have the ability to talk about the data warehouse initiative from the 10,000-foot view. Project directors should spend much of their time working with senior management to keep them up to date on the status of the project and to ensure that the direction of the warehouse project will meet the business directives. A project director typically holds the purse strings for the project; he or she is the type of person who can take the vision of the corporation and make certain everyone in the team understands it. The project director must have strong leadership qualities. The project director must "sell" the warehouse to both senior management and potential users; yes, many users are part of the design team. This selling job is to users that may end up coming on board after seeing the results on corporate desktops around the organization.

Abilities/Responsibilities

- The perspective of this person is that of a bird flying over a maze. This image represents the project director's need to take a global view of the project to see where it is headed. Like the bird, a project director sees the paths of the maze and where they all head, yet he or she may not see every pitfall hidden within the maze.

- Must have strong leadership skills. The project director should constantly communicate the vision of the project. This ability to motivate and inspire will, in effect, energize all team members and enable them to overcome any barriers to change. These barriers will come in many forms, from political obstacles to resource problems.

- Must know how to establish a vision for the future and how to relate this vision to the needs of the business. They must develop strategies to produce all necessary changes to accomplish the vision.

- Must have strong political skills. The project director must know how to package and sell the efforts of the team to senior management. He or she must understand the importance of each business unit within the company and ensure that the priorities of the warehouse project are in synch with the priorities of the business.

- Must have strong communication skills, including written ability, oral ability, and the ability to listen effectively.

- Must have strong financial skills. The project director will have ownership of the warehouse budget as well as ownership of the preparation of the budget. He or she will also have to ensure this budget adheres to the standard corporate practices.

- Must have power over the technology. The project director must be able to talk the talk but not necessarily walk the walk.

- Must be responsible to senior management for the status of the project. The buck stops with the project director. If anything goes wrong, the problem rests on his or her shoulders.

- Must be responsible for monitoring the major milestones of the project and for making certain the milestones are in tune with corporate needs.

- Must be able to educate top management on the various applications and the impact data warehousing will have on those efforts.

- Must be adept at obtaining the necessary economic support within the business units.

- Must be able to educate users on the data warehouse and its capabilities.

- Should be participating in user group meetings and industry associations.

- Must be able to define budgets and schedules.

- Must be able to identify applications and prioritize between applications.

Data Warehouse Project Manager

Unlike the data warehouse director, the data warehouse project manager does not need a quick wit. He or she needs sound organizational skills and sound management capabilities. The data warehouse project manager should spend time managing the initiative and directives of the project. He or she must understand the data warehouse initiative from a rat's view of the maze; however, having the ability to see over the maze is also very important.

The project manager must understand and oversee all the details of the project. He or she owns the project plan and oversees it daily. This person must understand how to be a great negotiator because he or she will constantly be dealing with conflict resolution and task prioritization. The project manager must understand what a critical path is and how to manage a project against it. He or she should constantly be working with the team leaders to appraise the technical soundness of each task.

When you visualize a project manager, you may have a mental image of a burly sort of person who has an ability to hold people's feet to the fire physically. The project manager's role is not that of a visionary, but he or she must know how to follow the vision. This is not the job of a corporate politician, but he or she must understand the politics of the team members. The project manager needs to be a great negotiator; success on the job hinges on the ability to navigate through the stakeholders' convergent needs. He or she understands that a successful project plan contains tangible results. The project manager must understand that a task is either 100 percent complete or it is not done at all. He or she understands that no task should take more than three weeks. The best analogy to this position is that of the majority whip in the U.S. Senate. The whip makes certain the right players are present; he or she pushes what must be pushed through and delegates what must be delegated. The whip is skilled at sidestepping the nonissues and overcoming the hurdles. He or she is the person who drives the car.

TIP
The most important attribute of a great project manager is the ability to keep an eye on milestones constantly and never lose sight of the project commitments.

Abilities/Responsibilities

- This person is not a corporate politician but, instead, a person with strong team-building skills. The project manager understands how to make a group of people work together as one toward a common goal.

- Must have strong organizational skills and pay very close attention to detail.

- Must have strong planning skills.

- Must have strong management skills, but also must understand technology. On the job, the project manager will constantly be dealing with team members who have varied skillsets. He or she must understand technical mumbo-jumbo. Put another way, they should have a good idea how long a particular task should take. When a task falls behind schedule, they should be able to look under the covers to ensure the process and procedure the technical staff member is using is appropriate.

- Must be able to plan effectively and allocate available resources. A staff member with too little to do is as dangerous for a project as a team member with too much work to do. Both these situations will lead to team member fatigue.

- Must be able to deal with resource shortages effectively. People leave projects and move on. This is a fact of life. A project manager who does not deal with this easily is sure to fail. A project manager who panics every time a resource leaves is not in control and is not doing his or her job.

- The project manager must be a diplomat. The project manager will constantly deal with stakeholders who feel their needs are the most critical. Stakeholders typically only see their needs. A good project manager must assess each stakeholder's need and see where those needs fit into the overall vision of the project.

■ Must know how to deliver bad news and how to circulate good news. They realize one of the keys to success is a well-informed team member.

■ Must be able to set up and *control* a meeting. They must be able to provide team members with the needed nudge when they don't appear for meetings.

■ Must be in control of the project scope. The project manager must be able to control scope creep. *Scope creep* happens when requests come in that will affect the delivery date of a project. The project manager must know how to take this problem to the appropriate ears, and then he or she must obtain the necessary documentation to support the approval of the scope creep.

■ Must be able to do appropriate risk management. For example, when the project manager is working with new technology, he or she must understand how this new technology may affect the project plans. In a data warehouse environment, this is critical because you are constantly dealing with bleeding-edge technology. *Bleeding-edge technology* is state of the art and introduces new ways to do something with new functionality. If you don't want your project to die from this, you must understand risk assessment.

■ Must listen well. The project manager must pay attention; he or she must know when to interrupt and when to listen.

■ Must have the ability to harmonize the team. The project manager must be able to reconcile disagreements.

■ Must be able to play the role of gatekeeper. The project manager helps facilitate participation by the team members. He or she must constantly monitor to see if everyone is satisfied with the approaches. The project manager should make certain the team understands the priorities.

TIP
Project managers must take the time to understand the contribution of every one on the team. Team members that are treated like mushrooms do not thrive. Only mushrooms thrive in the dark.

- Must be an excellent negotiator—able to admit an error and to look for the compromise that will get the project back on track.

- Must be able to determine the performance of the project. They realize tasks are not 50 percent complete—it's all or nothing. A task is not done till it's 100 percent. Trying to manage a project by partial completion does not work.

- Must realize that sick projects will not get better on their own. The project manager knows sick projects require corrective action immediately.

- Must realize he or she cannot be a developer at the same time. The position of a data warehouse project manager is a full-time, dedicated position.

- Must be able to select team members and then motivate them.

- Must be able to evaluate team members and perform performance appraisals.

- Must be able to run a project to a budget.

- Must be able to educate users on the data warehouse and how it will impact the particular business unit.

- Must be able to monitor industry trends and identify emerging technologies that should be considered for adoption.

- Like the director of data warehousing, he or she should be able to identify and solidify economic support for the project.

Data Provision Specialist, Business Analysts

Data provision specialists are the people who go out and meet with various department heads and key end users to define the business needs of the organization; then they communicate those needs to the rest of the team. To be successful, data provision specialists must have strong people skills. They must be able to extract information from nontechnical people and to convey pertinent information to the technical teams. This information takes many forms—from current business practices to the current invoice forms used. They must have enough political savvy to identify the key decision makers and power users. In a nutshell, data provision specialists must be able to determine what information must be available if the warehouse is to meet various business unit needs.

Abilities/Responsibilities

- Must know how to phrase questions to determine the end users' needs.

- Must have excellent writing skills and the ability to convey the end users' needs to the technical teams.

- Must be able to develop the database schema and be familiar with data concepts like the star schema.

- Must take responsibility for defining the scope statements. Must work with the technical teams and the user community to obtain the necessary consensus so the project moves forward.

- Must have excellent people skills. Data provision specialists not only must be diplomats, they must also be eloquent communicators. Much of the success of the data warehouse project hinges upon the ability of the data provision specialist to work well with the user community.

- Must have enough political savvy to identify key decision makers. They must then know how to make the best use of the key decision makers' time when they have it.

- Must be able to assist the end users in how to find the information they need from the warehouse.

- Must be able to help train the end users.

- Must be able to develop EIS and decision support systems.

- Must be able to develop and implement test plans for new applications. This includes monitoring data quality. Dirty data will destroy a data warehouse project very quickly.

- Must be able to gain consensus among different users' departments for the good of the warehouse. This means helping to develop and implement common data definitions and key performance indicators.

- Must be able to identify and document the inflows and outflows of data to the warehouse. This includes identifying possible incompatibility of data in the warehouse to other systems. For example, he or she must ensure that the financial data in the warehouse reconciles to the source financial systems.

- Must be able to evaluate new software from middleware, reporting tools, and front-end software to data mining "OLAP" software.

Data Warehouse Architect

The data warehouse architect is a technical Jack or Jill of all trades. To achieve success in this career, the architect must understand both the technical side (i.e., familiarity with the software and hardware involved) and the business needs. He or she will take the findings of the data provision team and interpret those findings into a road map of the data warehouse. This road map is typically the *entity relationship diagram* that maps out the tables and the relationships between the assortment of tables in the data warehouse.

The data warehouse consists of information from the various operational areas of the company and some external systems. The data warehouse architect team understands all these data feeds and weaves them into a single integrated data reservoir. In a successful data warehouse implementation, the various business units will gain access to all the necessary information they need to stay competitive.

An architect who understands the business needs and implements them into a functional database design has the key to success. No substitute for real-world experience exists, because this is what teaches a good data architect when to break the rules and when to follow them. What is important is that the architect has the ability to remove him or herself from daily details and to take a more global view.

Abilities/Responsibilities

- Must take ownership of the entry relationship diagram and all the corresponding documentation. An example of other documentation the person should be responsible for is a corporate data dictionary, which contains all the attributes, table names, and constraints.

- Must be able to articulate the overall architecture and establish and maintain standards.

- Must possess a thorough knowledge of database design and associated tools.

- Must have good peer-to-peer communication skills. Does not require corporate political skill—but it doesn't hurt either.

- Must be fluent in evaluating and selecting appropriate hardware.

- Must be fluent in evaluating and selecting appropriate networking facilities.

- Must be fluent in evaluating RDBMS software.

- Must have good business analysis skills.

- Must be able to evaluate new software from middleware, reporting tools, and front-end software to data mining "OLAP" software.

- Must be able to educate users and technical staff on data warehouse capabilities.

- Should be monitoring industry trends and identifying technologies that should be adopted.

- Must be responsible for managing the data warehouse metadata, which is data about data. The data warehouse architect is king or queen of the data.

- Must be the watchdog of data warehouse standards. It is his or her responsibility to maintain all the documentation about the warehouse database design. The data warehouse architect is responsible for adopting database design and naming standards; he or she must also make certain these are followed. These standards should be used in all future application development.

Database Administrator

A description for the perfect database administrator would be a benevolent king or queen. To achieve success at this job, the database administrator must have a tight reign over his or her database kingdom. He or she must surround the database castle with a moat, lowering the drawbridge only to those who have earned the right to use the database. Only friends—not foes—can enter the database. Like a benevolent king or queen, the ideal database administrator is concerned with the safety and security of the castle. This means appropriate measures are taken and procedures are established to make certain the database is backed up and secure. He or she measures the response of the database and takes corrective action to ensure response time is adequate.

This is a critical role, which should be present early in the process. Many organizations make the mistake of not keeping a full-time DBA in the process. The database administrator should be a normal extension of the team from the beginning for complete effectiveness.

Abilities/Responsibilities

- Must have some political skills. For example, the database administrator might not want to upgrade the system on the busiest business day of the year. Common sense is a requirement.

- Must ensure appropriate backup and recovery procedures are in place to meet the business requirements. If a project is not backed up and a database is lost, a month of the project team's work could be lost.

- Must be fluent in how to design the logical database, then take that logical database and implement the physical model.

- Must be responsible for putting security in place to make certain only the right people can look at the right data. In other words, the DBA uses Oracle mechanisms to control all access to the database as discussed in Chapter 12. The database administrator works closely with the data architects to implement the database design. In addition, he or she must be able to set up a procedure that logs usage of the warehouse.

- Must be able to implement processes that monitor query and database performance.

- Must work closely with the technical team to ensure they adhere to corporate policies and procedures pertaining to the database. This includes development of policies to control the movement of applications onto a production database.

- Must monitor the growth of the database to ensure the smooth running of daily activities.

- Must monitor performance. This is a critical function of the DBA. He or she must establish baselines and compare the database performance against the baselines to ensure it is performing adequately.

- Must tend to daily administration of the database.

- Must be able to tackle issues as soon as they spring up. The database administrator position is one of the most technically challenging roles that exist within all the teams.

- Must have minimum writing skills, although email etiquette is a plus.

- Must be available to work 24x7. This is not a 9 to 5 job.

- Must work closely with the system administrator to install all database software and patches.

- Must be able to establish procedures that monitor the loading of the database. These procedures should ensure that adequate database space is available. The procedures should make sure that data is loaded in the most efficient manner. Data loading is discussed in Chapter 8.

■ Must be able to monitor data quality. The DBA is concerned with data quality.

■ Must be able to select and size hardware platforms.

■ Must be able to select and implement middleware.

System Administrator

The system administrator (SA) must understand the ins and outs of the chosen data warehouse environment. The SA is responsible for administering the computer systems, whereas the DBA is responsible for administering the databases. The SA is responsible for system backups, installation of new hardware, upgrading the hardware, system software, firewall creation, and any other daily activities concerning the computer system. A *firewall* is a set of computer programs restricting network access to the data warehouse. Think of how much project time would be lost if your development environment were destroyed.

In today's world, the system administrator is the cowboy or cowgirl of computers. Many times they work alone and on off-hours. They are constantly on call and dealing with show-stopping problems. This gives them an attitude and tends to make them stand alone. You can spot many a SA, by the ponytail—that's why I call them the cowboy of computers.

Abilities/Responsibilities

■ Must have some political skills. For example, the system administrator may not want to upgrade the system on the busiest business day of the year. Common sense is a critical requirement.

■ Must be available 24x7. When things happen, the system administrator must respond immediately.

■ Must ensure appropriate backup and recovery procedures are in place to meet the business requirements.

■ Must take responsibility for putting security in place to make certain only the right people can look at the system. In today's environment, the SA typically gets involved in firewall creation.

- Must work closely with the technical team to make certain they adhere closely to corporate policies and procedures pertaining to the system. This includes development of policies to control the movement of applications onto a production system.

- Must be able to do performance monitoring; this is another critical function of the system administrator. He or she must establish baselines and compare the performance of the system against the base to ensure it is performing adequately.

- Must have minimum writing skills, although email etiquette is a plus.

- Must be able to access the system remotely. When something happens after hours, the SA must be able to respond.

- Must be fluent at administering user access and security.

- Like the DBA, they must be able to account for users' activities.

- Must be capable of evaluating and selecting hardware and software—that includes the network hardware and software.

Data Migration Specialist

This is a cornerstone position. If you can't get the data out of the legacy system, your warehouse project will fail. The data migration specialist is responsible for the development and acquisition of software that enables your organization to move data from legacy systems and external data sources into a staging area for the transformation effort. The *staging area* is a holding area for some data before it is moved into the Oracle data warehouse repository.

The data migration specialist must understand the relationship and the differences between the legacy system and the warehouse. The role of the data migration specialist is to transfer the knowledge and data from the legacy system into a format with which the data transformation team can work. The goal of *data migration* is to move this data into a new format without compromising data integrity and to maintain all the business rules. This is such a critical task, with so many intricacies, that it is useful to break it into a separate effort from transforming the data. Many times, a major role data migration plays is getting the data into an Oracle table or an ASCII file.

An *ASCII* file contains text data. These formats make it easy for the new technology tools to manipulate the data.

If you were looking for a data migration specialist, you should look within your organization for a long-time player who possesses an intimate working knowledge of the legacy systems and a strong desire to learn the new technology. This is typically a person within your organization who has chosen the technical route vs. the management route. In this position, technical prowess is king.

You need to write or develop internal tools to facilitate migration because this is an evolving area within building a warehouse. The data migration specialist must be open to third-party solutions. There are many new solutions coming to market every day. This individual should be able to evaluate these tools and be able to make a reasonable business decision, to determine, for example, if buying a solution is better than building it in-house.

Abilities/Responsibilities

- Must have intimate knowledge of the current legacy system and understand the data stored within the system. This knowledge must include the internal structure of the existing legacy systems or the ability to analyze the legacy system to learn the data structures. This is a highly technical area where strong programming skills are a must.

- Need not be political. Like the rat mentioned earlier, the data migration specialist must know how to navigate through the maze to find the cheese. His or her nose and wits are all they need—political savvy is just plain not needed.

- Must be competent with legacy tools. Communication or writing skills is not important. This is a highly technical slot.

- Must work closely with the legacy technology specialist to learn necessary information.

- Must be proficient at developing data cleaning and data migration programs.

- Must be proficient at identifying data sources. Like a bird dog, he or she needs to be able to follow the scent and bring home the bird.

- Must be able to automate the entire migration process. Many times, these programs will be running for quite some time. This includes procedures to ensure the process works correctly.

- Must be able to develop test plans.

Data Transformation/Grooming Specialist

People in this position are concerned with migrating the data into the appropriate Oracle tables with their associated attributes. Many times, this includes cleaning the data, making certain all the codes are standardized. One record in the legacy system can become split into multiple table rows, which can quickly become very complicated. What sounds like a simple task is not. This effort will consume a major portion of the project. In essence, the data transformation specialist makes an apple into an orange or tries to fit a round peg into a square hole.

Unlike many of the existing legacy systems, Oracle is not as forgiving of inconsistencies. For example, if an attribute is defined as "not null," you must supply a value. There is an old saying "garbage in, garbage out" (GIGO) that applies here. If you don't take the time to convert and load the database correctly, then don't start the project. The bottom line? The data transformation/grooming specialist is concerned with the actual transformation of the data into the new database design. This is where the old system becomes the new one.

Abilities/Responsibilities

- Must be highly technical. The data transformation/grooming specialist position requires a strong working knowledge of SQL*Loader (discussed in Chapter 8) and PL/SQL.

- Must be a perfectionist. The data transformation specialist position contains the "bean counters" of the technical world. If they are not perfectionists, you will be in trouble. Dirty data is worthless data. The value of the warehouse correlates directly to the quality of the data.

- Need not be political.

- Must develop the code needed to groom the data into the new data structure, meeting all the new standards.

- Must work closely with the data architect and data provision specialist to make certain all business needs are met.

- Should be proficient at being able to search for causes of incompatibility of data. If you want a warehouse to be successful when you first turn it on, don't expect your users to find data problems. If you do, they will quickly not trust or use the warehouse.

- Responsible for developing and implementing the software that will clean and scrub the data.

- Must be able to develop and implement test plans.

Data Mart Development Leader

A *data mart*, by definition, is a subset of the data warehouse. The required skills for the data mart development leader closely mirror those of the data provision specialist. The only difference is the effort of a data mart development leader concentrates on a particular business area. For example, the data mart development leader might be working on the marketing data mart. His or her effort is focused on how to present the key components of the warehouse in which the marketing group is interested, no more and no less.

Abilities/Responsibilities

- Must know how to phrase questions to determine the end users' needs.

- Must have excellent writing skills and the ability to convey the end users' needs to the technical teams.

- Should be proficient in the business area the data mart is being built for.

- Must be able to develop the data mart schema and be familiar with data concepts like the star schema.

- Must take responsibility for defining the scope statements. Must work with the technical teams and the user community to obtain the necessary consensus so the project moves forward.

- Must have excellent people skills. Data mart leaders not only must be diplomats, they must also be eloquent communicators. Much of the success of a particular data mart hinges upon the ability of the data mart leader to work well with the user community.

- Must have enough political savvy to identify key decision makers. He or she must then know how to make the best use of the key decision makers' time.

- Must be able to assist the end users in how to find the information they need from the data mart. He or she must also structure the data mart so that it makes sense for end users to navigate.

- Must be able to help train the end users.

- Must be able to develop EIS and decision support systems.

- Must be able to develop and implement test plans for new applications. This includes monitoring data quality. Dirty data will destroy a data mart very quickly.

- Must be able to gain consensus among different users' departments for the good of the warehouse. This means helping to develop and implement common data definitions and key performance indicators.

- Must be able to identify and document the inflows and outflows of data to the mart. This includes identifying possible incompatibility of data in the warehouse to other systems. For example, he or she must ensure that the financial data in the warehouse reconciles to the source financial systems.

- Must be able to evaluate new software from middleware, reporting tools, and front-end software to data mining "OLAP" software.

- Must be able to deploy the data mart quickly. In today's world, users must see results every 60 to 90 days.

Quality Assurance/Testing Specialist

"A job worth doing is a job worth doing well!" Quality is something you achieve the old-fashioned way—you work at it. Someone within the team must be focused on quality. If the culture of your warehouse team has strong roots in quality, then the product built will be one of quality. One way to obtain a high-quality product is to have a thorough testing process. The quality assurance team is established to play the role of "gatekeeper" who is responsible for quality.

The quality assurance/testing specialist works with stakeholders to make certain everyone works together to deliver a finished product. Typically, this function is responsible for creating and approving testing plans. This specialist is responsible for reviewing test results, which may mean making certain the code compiles cleanly before it moves into production or comparing the legacy system results to the warehouse results. He or she must be adept at tracing problems back to their source and have enough political savvy to get source systems to correct the problem at the start and not make the warehouse have the horrendous job of fixing all data problems within the warehouse.

Abilities/Responsibilities

- Must be responsible for creating and reviewing all test plans. This includes identifying the appropriate warehouse team members and members of the user community who should participate in the quality/testing process.

- Must be aware that this is a cooperative effort of all the stakeholders. To obtain a quality product, the quality assurance/testing specialist and all the stakeholders must make a concentrated effort throughout the project. A quality product will not be obtained if the effort occurs only at the technical end.

- Need not be political, except team members will always have good reasons why they do not have to comply with the rules. We suggest you have the quality team report to the project manager. Otherwise, they will not be effective.

- Need not be a highly technical role. The position of quality assurance/testing specialist is primarily one of user testing.

- For this process to work, a plan must exist. Without proper preparation, you will not achieve the results you want.

Infrastructure Specialist

The infrastructure specialist is the person responsible for crossing all the "T"s and dotting all the "I"s. This person or team makes certain all the pieces are in place. Do all new users have appropriate hardware? Do they have proper system accounts? Are all the database access roles defined? Do they have the appropriate training to do the job? As you can see, a successful data warehouse has thousands of intricate details, each of which must be attended to for a successful project. The infrastructure specialist is the person responsible for all the nitty-gritty details.

The infrastructure specialist must be a good technical coordinator to be successful. He or she must be able to develop an implementation plan and track its progress throughout the organization. The infrastructure specialist must know when to raise that alarm bell and when to do careful prodding. You can build the greatest system in the world, but if your users can't access it, your work was for naught.

Abilities/Responsibilities

- Must be able to see the bigger picture. For example, you don't want to order a personal computer (PC) for the field a year ahead of time. And you don't want to give end users a PC without making certain they know how to use it.

- Must be moderately technical. It helps if the infrastructure specialist can talk the terminology.

- Must have excellent organizational skills. He or she must be able to hold people's feet to the fire. If the network specialist promises to have network software installed on Thursday, then the infrastructure person needs to make certain it happens.

Power User (Legacy System Specialist)

No one understands the application better than end users. They are the ultimate customers. If you want to be successful, keep the end users happy and involved. They have a much better understanding of the business than the technical team. Look for those power users who typically love technology and will work with you, quickly embracing the new system. A system must be used if it is to be accepted. The sooner you can get users using and embracing the system, the sooner the warehouse will be accepted.

These power users typically help your team bridge the gap of knowledge between the old system and the new system. You need them to help you understand the current operation systems.

Abilities/Responsibilities

- Must have an intimate working knowledge of the current legacy system.

- Must have a strong working knowledge of application, but technical ability is not a requirement.

- Must have strong communication skills, because you want them to help teach the new system to other end users.

- Must have political savvy and connections. You want them to spread the good news. A classic trait of a power user is someone the rest of the organization uses for information. He or she becomes the answer person within the department.

- May or may not be technical, yet power users are adept at making the system work for them.

- Must love technology.

Trainer

A big mistake many organizations make is to put technology on the desks of users without formal training. If you want to be successful, you must teach the community how to use the warehouse. The best trainers are typically in-house power users that know and understand the business. We recommend you have a trainer who develops strong training material and give him or her to the power users to teach their department. In other words, train the trainer. This way, power users reinforce their own knowledge and enhance their standing in the department. You want to help strengthen their power base because they are on your side. Power users know their peers better than anyone. The more they spread the good news, the better.

Abilities/Responsibilities

- Must have excellent communication skills and infinite patience.

- Must have excellent user knowledge of the warehouse and its tools.

- Must have excellent writing skills. A difference exists between good technical documentation and good training materials.

- Must have the ability to laugh. A good smile is a plus.

Technical Writer

What if a developer gets hits by a truck on the way to work? Would the necessary documentation exist to protect the interests of your company? Many times, the answer to this question is "No!" Most developers do not want to write technical documentation. This is a fact we must face. You need good documentation to help get the word out about the work you are doing. Does it make sense to have a programmer writing documentation or to have a technical writer doing the documentation? Which choice leads to better job satisfaction and a better product? The answer is the technical writer; let the writer write.

The position of technical writer is frequently overlooked. A data warehouse is a complex application. Having good standardized technical documentation is helpful. This is one of the ways your user community will judge the effort.

Abilities/Responsibilities

- Must have excellent communication skills and infinite patience, because the technical writer is dealing with developers with little to no program documentation.

- Must have good working knowledge of the warehouse.

- Must write clearly and concisely; must employ good standards within the documentation.

- Need not be political.

- Must have a working vocabulary of data warehousing.

- Must have the needed credentials. This is a professional skillset and you want it done right.

Public Relations Person

The public relations (PR) person should have a quick wit and a great smile. Typically, he or she must know how to play golf. You want the PR person to get the word out to senior management wherever possible. He or she must understand the business and how the warehouse will impact it. The idea with this role is for the PR person to provide management with the status of the project in a controlled manner. He or she needs to know how to distribute bad news softly and good news with a bullhorn. The PR person is responsible for corporate-wide communication, which includes overseeing such activities as newsletters, power user meetings, senior management meetings, and participating in key presentations.

Abilities/Responsibilities

- Must know how to let senior management win the golf game.

- Must have excellent communication and presentation skills.

- Should have attended a "dress for success" seminar.

- Should know how to turn a challenge into an opportunity.

- Must know how to turn a project delay into a respite.

- Must be a great politician, with an ear constantly against the wall.

- Must be loyal to the cause.

- Must like to travel, to get the good word spread.

- Must never talk technical. This frightens the nontechnical community.

Corporate Sponsors

If the project is to be successful, you must know who backed the project in senior management. Then, you can use the backers to break down the large barriers in your way. Look for ways to enhance their standing in the company. Know who your strongest ally is and what his or her agenda is. Make certain the PR person works closely with your strongest ally. This will help you understand how to keep the project healthy and happy. Beggars can't be choosers. Corporate sponsors come in all sizes and shapes, and you get what you get.

Help Desk Functionality

An undertaking of this magnitude will have problems. Your ability to get users working painlessly with the warehouse is critical. A help desk is a great way to diffuse anxiety. If users know someone is listening and cares, they will give you the needed break. Don't go live until you have a functioning help desk—a one-stop place for answers. Monitoring the volume and types of calls is critical so that the quality team is aware of trouble points and can address them early in the process.

TIP
Do not turn on your warehouse until you have figured out how your help desk function will be handled.

Abilities/Responsibilities

- Must have a trained person who understands how to use the warehouse properly.

- Must have infinite patience and understanding.

- Should have good technical knowledge so he or she can communicate the problem to the team.

- A help desk must be organized.

- Must have excellent communication skills and know the terminology of the community of users. Don't have propeller heads answering the phones.

Tools Specialist

A successful data warehouse implementation consists of many sophisticated tools. You need good application developers who understand the tools you are using to build and deploy the warehouse. The tool specialist's ability to use these tools will help minimize the risk of the project.

Abilities/Responsibilities

- Must be highly technical.

- Should be aware and have a good working knowledge of the core third-party tools in the marketplace.

- Should have the ability to choose the right tool for the right job. For example, in the Oracle arena, this person would know when it makes sense to use PL/SQL compared to SQL*Plus.

- Must be a worker rat. The tool specialist builds the maze and, thus, needs no political skills.

Vendor Relations Person

Building a data warehouse in today's world requires the use of many key vendors. No one vendor yet—not even Oracle   can supply you with one-stop shopping. Your ability to manage your vendor relationship is critical. You need vendors who bring real solutions to the table and who do not waste your time with immature products that someday may be ready. This position requires a dedicated eye to the problem. If this position is filled correctly, you will be successful much quicker.

Abilities/Responsibilities

- Must have good technical skills and understand the warehouse requirements.

- Must be able to develop criteria that can be used to determine if a vendor product makes sense. From day one, the vendor relation's person should be aware of the core data warehouse products.

■ Must have good communication skills.

■ Must have good writing skills.

■ Must have good negotiation skills, which includes the ability to review the contracts.

■ Must understand the political relation between the vendors and your company.

Web Master

Face it, we live in an Internet-enabled world already. Many people consider the pace at which PC usage has grown around the world frightening. Well, Internet technology is growing at a rate three times faster than the PC. An Internet year is like going from the 80386 chip to the Pentium Pro in just one year. Recently at an industry show, the president of the United States' adviser on Internet technologies stated that by the year 2002, the industry expects $400 billion USD to be spent online. It's no wonder, the Internet age is heating up so fast—the private sector of the world smells opportunity and is gravitating to it very quickly.

The Internet is also revolutionizing how we deploy software. With software based off of a universal browser, you have a very easy way to deploy and maintain application. With all this in mind, the Internet landscape is changing every day and requires someone who is responsible for paying attention to it and how it should impact the data warehouse.

Abilities/Responsibilities

■ Responsible for being quickly abreast of emerging Internet technologies as they apply to the warehouse.

■ Should be familiar with key vendors' Internet strategies.

■ Must be able to evaluate and install Internet technologies.

■ Must be able to install and implement the network. This includes firewall technologies and developing processes to identify performance bottlenecks.

Consultant

Face it, you can't be all things to all people. Sometimes you need to reach outside your organization and bring in the experts. Just be smart about it. Check résumés and check references.

As you can see, many roles and individuals are necessary for a successful data warehouse project. In this chapter, we took time to highlight some of the key roles. Since many of the roles overlap each other, we did not describe in detail all the roles—only the key ones. Don't get hung up on titles, since they are constantly changing and many titles mean the same thing. For example, to many people a system administrator is the same as a system manager, which is the same as a network administrator. Focus in on what jobs you need done and make sure you cover as many bases as possible. This chapter should have given you the information you need to put a successful team in place. Chapter 4 discusses managing the data warehouse team. Suggestions will be offered on some sound and proven project management techniques. The techniques presented helped us deliver projects on time and on budget.

CHAPTER
4

Managing the Data Warehouse Project

hat are the correct expectations for managing a data warehouse project? Simply stated, no data warehouse project will ever stay on target as originally planned. Anyone who tells you it will stay on target has never managed such a large undertaking. It has been the author's experience that no large project is ever accomplished on plan or on target. The goal to good project management is to pick goals and targets you can manage. We all know problems will arise, so you must set up policies and procedures to deal with the rough spots. You must make sure you set proper user expectations. If you do all this correctly, you will have a successful implementation of your data warehouse or data marts. You will see the yellow warning flags coming up the pole long before a red flag appears and stops the entire project.

The key to successful project management is to develop standards by which you can judge the success or failure of the project and all its undertakings or individual tasks. By establishing these standards down to the task level, you will very quickly be able to determine problems at a micro level as they arise and make the needed adjustments quickly.

The best analogy to this is how a doctor or nurse works with a patient in the hospital. No two patients are the same. Likewise, no two projects are the same. Because each project is unique, you know the techniques you choose to apply may not always work as expected.

When a doctor or nurse works with a patient, he or she is constantly reviewing the patient's progress against predetermined milestones and benchmarks. Based on the measured results, appropriate changes are made to the care given. Many times this includes changing the dose of medicine, or even the type of treatment given. This chapter will discuss some project management techniques you can apply to ensure the success of your data warehouse project.

What Is Project Management?

As part owner of a consulting company in Massachusetts doing larger and larger projects, one thing has become clear to the firm: good project management is essential. Our proficiency at being able to manage a project will make or break us. Even though we have a successful track record, it was clear that as a company we could improve upon the process. So, we went in search of project management experts who would take our combined project management skills in the company to the next level. In the quest for experts, we engaged the services of a company called Duncan Nevison in Lexington, Massachusetts. They taught a course for us entitled "Mastering Modern Program Management." Much of the following material is based on years of practical experience and the guidance of a project management expert from Duncan Nevison.

During this project management course, a slide was held up with a quote from the *Harvard Business Review*: "High performing companies boast . . . we've got the best project managers in the world." This quote certainly reflected how we felt. Our track record of meeting or exceeding customers' expectations has been excellent but, as the data warehouse initiatives we were undertaking became more and more complex, we knew we must improve our project management capabilities.

In the past, we had committed to, and delivered, a high level of service to our customers. To continue this level of service, we felt we must improve our project management skills. Having the best talent is not enough. If having the best technology meant you would always be successful, would we be using Windows 95 today? Having the best technologist was also not enough. We had to become the best project managers. At my firm, we agree completely with the quote from the *Harvard Business Review*: high-performing companies have the best project managers in the world.

Failure on the project management front could put the firm at risk on two fronts: with our customers and with our employees. As a company, we have an obligation to communicate in an open and honest manner with our customers concerning the status of their projects and the likelihood of coming in on time and on budget. To be successful, we needed to apply good project management techniques. At the same time, we have an obligation to our internal staff to work hard at fine-tuning necessary resources so we will be neither overstaffed nor understaffed.

Companies around us who did not manage projects correctly either burned out good staff members or overcharged customers for resources they did not need. In addition, an overstaffed project meant a waste of good talent, which, if not challenged, would leave the company. As we are all well aware, with the shortage of good Oracle talent in the marketplace, we cannot afford to overstaff a project. If we wanted to continue as a high-performing company, we had to improve our project management skills. Our desire to be the best was used as an opportunity to reevaluate how we managed our projects. This chapter represents an overview of some basic project management techniques. We encourage you to use this as a test to see if you are on the right track. If the answer is "NO," then take the time to learn more.

VIP

Failure on the project management front could put you at risk on two fronts: with your customers and with your employees.

Exactly what is project management? *Project management* is the application of knowledge, skills, tools, and techniques to project activities to meet or exceed stakeholders' needs and expectations.

What we especially like about this definition is the use of the term "stakeholders." Yes, stakeholders. Like all corporations, we have a fiduciary responsibility to our stockholders, just as a project manager has a fiduciary responsibility to those individuals and organizations affected by the project plans and their execution. So, a *stakeholder* is any group or individual affected by the project and all its activities. These stakeholders include the customers as well as all the people involved in the project internally. Yes, everyone involved has a stake on the successful implementation of the plan. The sooner you recognize this, the more likely you are to be successful.

VIP

Stakeholder is any group or individual affected by the project and all its activities.

If you want to have a successful project, you must take the time to identify all your stakeholders and to understand what impact they will have on the project. You must take the time to understand what their needs and expectations are. Without understanding a stakeholder's needs and expectations, you can never manage or influence them. If you do not take the time to understand your stakeholders needs and expectations, your project will fail. The better you understand your customers, the greater chance you have at being successful. Like all choices you make in life, there are trade-offs; successful project management is about making trade-offs.

VIP

You must take the time to understand what a stakeholder's needs and expectations are. Without understanding their needs and expectations, you can never manage or influence your stakeholders.

In many ways, the project manager needs to be a great diplomat because some of the customers' needs and expectations may be in conflict. This is not uncommon. The project manager must be someone who can look at the problem from each person's perspective and then work toward decisions that ultimately meet the needs of the organization in the most cost-effective and resource efficient manner.

Another painful lesson we have learned over the years is that no good tools exist to provide project management. Project managers provide project management. Many organizations let "the project management tool" tail wag the dog—they start to manage the project according to the strengths and weaknesses of the tool. This does not work. We have been at companies that think sending someone to a Microsoft Project class is sending them to a project management class. What these companies are doing is sending someone to a class that will concentrate on how to use the tool, not on good project management techniques. These are two distinctly different things.

VIP

Project managers provide good project management. Stated in another way, project management tools do not provide project management. Many people think that if they use Microsoft Project, this will give them good project management. This is simply not true. This way of thinking will get you in big trouble. The best analogy to this is a carpenter—the carpenter builds the house, not the hammer.

What we recommend, and also implement, in our company is that you concentrate on giving everyone within your firm an understanding of good project management techniques. Create special project management courses for each employee within the company. Some people receive a course that introduces them to the terminology, while others receive a course that teaches them critical skills like understanding the critical path. We do this to make sure we have a team of cathedral builders.

There is a very old story about a gentleman who walks up to two masons hard at work. He asks the first mason, "What are you working on?" The mason replies, "I am building this walkway." He asks the second mason, "What are you working on?" The mason replies, "I am part of a team building this cathedral." Which mason would you want on your team? Well, at our firm, we want a team of cathedral builders. The more they understand project management, the smoother the process will work and the happier everyone will be.

What we are not doing is getting people hung up on how to use the tool. Many times, good project managers fail because they are too busy trying to make a project management tool do the job. Instead, they should be spending their time managing the staff, customer expectations, and communication. Trying to make a project management tool do the job is like trying to make a round peg fit into a square hole. As a company, we also have decided to hire a management tool expert and to leave the project managers free to manage the projects. This brings us back to the key point: don't let the project management tool tail wag the dog. Develop internal staff members who are "tool du jour" experts. This leaves your project managers free to be doing what they should do best:

- Appraising each stakeholder and determining his or her needs
- Influencing stakeholders to move the project forward
- Setting the right customer expectations
- Looking for the yellow warning flags and dealing with them
- Taking the time to manage the project and not letting the project manage them
- Managing the team members tasks to make sure they are not overutilized or underutilized

Let's back up a bit now and talk about a project, the atomic commodity of the management initiative.

What Is a Project?

Here we are talking about project management when we haven't yet defined the term "project." For this definition, we go to the source—the Project Management Institute. The Project Management Institute is a nonprofit professional organization dedicated to advancing the state of the art in the management of projects. Membership is open to anyone actively engaged or interested in the application, practice, teaching, and researching of project management principles and techniques. (One of the best ways to contact the institute is on the World Wide Web at *www.pmi.org*.)

According to the book, *A Guide to the Project Management Body of Knowledge*, published by the Project Management Institute standards committee, a *project* is a temporary endeavor undertaken to create a unique product or service. One key point here is *temporary endeavor*. This means the project must have a defined start and end. If you are unclear about what must be done to complete the project, don't start it. This is a sure path to disaster. In addition, if at any point in the project it becomes clear that the end product of the project cannot be delivered, the project should be canceled. This also applies to a data warehouse project.

 VIP
A project is a temporary endeavor undertaken to create a unique product or service. A project must have a defined start and end.

Another key point of the definition is to create a *unique* product or service. You must have a clear idea of what you are building and why it is unique. It is not necessary for you to understand why your product or service is unique from day one, but through the process of developing the project plan you will uncover the unique attributes of this project. Once you understand the uniqueness of the project, you will then be able to determine what constitutes a completed project. Only with a defined end do you have a project that can succeed.

The Scope Statement

One of the major proven techniques we can use to help us with this discovery process is called a scope statement. A *scope statement* is a written document by which you begin to define the job at hand and all its key deliverables. In fact, we feel it is good business practice not to begin work on any project until you have developed a scope statement. These are the major elements in the breakdown of a scope statement:

1. **Project title and description** Every project should have a clear name and description of what you are trying to accomplish.

2. **Project justification** A clear description of why this project is being done. What is the goal of the project?

3. **Project key deliverables** A list of keys items that must be accomplished so this project can be completed. What must be done for us to consider the project done?

4. **Project objective** An additional list of success criteria. These items must be measurable—a good place to put any time, money, or resource constraints.

VIP
Every project must have a scope statement.
A scope statement is a written document that
defines all the deliverables.

Think of a scope statement as your first stake in the ground. What's important is that a scope statement provides a documented basis for building a common understanding among all the shareholders of the project at hand. It is crucial that you begin to write down and document the project and all its assumptions. If you do not do this, you will get burned. All a stakeholder remembers about a hallway conversation is the deliverable, not the constraints. Many project managers have been burned by making a hallway statement, such as: "If the new network is put into place by July 1, I feel comfortable saying we can provide you with the legacy data by July 10." All the stakeholder will remember is the date of July 10, not the constraint associated with it.

Don't be alarmed as you continue down the scope statement path if it is reworked. That's a good thing, because through the process of discovery, the project plan and associated scope statement will change. This is a discovery process.

To illustrate this point better, let's say you were approached by a major publisher to write a book on data warehousing for the Oracle Press series. Let's see what a starting scope statement might look like, as shown in Figure 4-1.

As you can see from Figure 4-1, we have created a document that attempts to articulate the job at hand. This is our first stake in the ground. In the project justification statement, we try to say why we are doing it. If we can't state this in clear terms, we should question even doing the project. In the project deliverables section, we try to identify major components that must be completed for us to say the job is done. In the project objectives, we try to discuss additional success criteria, which includes any time constraints. For example, we now know it would not be acceptable to deliver a document of 100 pages in length.

VIP
*If you can't state in clear terms a project
justification statement, you should question
even doing the project.*

This becomes a powerful tool when working with the stakeholders. It becomes a common point of reference for all stakeholders. The scope statement should be written so anyone can understand it. You should have one scope statement for all users. You do not create different scope statements depending on the audience.

Work Breakdown Structure

Once you have completed your project scope statement, another technique we find useful is called a work breakdown structure. We use this technique to help fill in any gaps or missing items. In *A Guide to the Project Management Body of Knowledge,* a *work breakdown structure* is defined as "a deliverable-oriented grouping of project elements, which organizes and defines the total scope of the project. Each descending level represents an

Oracle Data Warehousing Project Scope Statement

Overview

A 300-400 page book that will explain to the reader what a data warehouse is, provide an overview of how you manage the effort, and discuss in detail how you use Oracle RDBMS and its associated software to implement a warehouse.

Project Justification

■ It is clear that to implement a data warehouse is a very complex process and there is not an existing book today that teaches Oracle users how to do this taking full advantage of the Oracle software.

■ It is clear that this book will enable the Oracle community to better understand how to correctly use Oracle tools when building a data warehouse. This will generate additional software sales and improved customer satisfaction.

■ There is a hot market for data warehousing material. It is critical that the Oracle Press series develop a warehouse offering or run the risk of losing the business to competitors.

■ Without a data warehouse offering, the credibility of the Oracle Press series is at risk.

Project Deliverables

■ A technical editor must be chosen.

■ A work breakdown structure must be completed.

■ A signed contract must be delivered.

■ A finished manuscript must be delivered.

■ A draft of all artwork must be finished.

Project Objectives

■ The finished manuscript must be at least 300 pages.

■ The finished manuscript must be delivered by July 31, 1998.

■ Each chapter should be at least 20 pages in length.

■ The book should teach people how to effectively implement a data warehouse using Oracle's technology.

FIGURE 4-1. *Sample scope statement*

increasingly detailed definition of a project component. Project components may be products and services."

A work breakdown structure is exactly as it sounds—a breakdown of all the work that must be done. This includes all deliverables. For example, if you are expected to provide the customer with weekly status reports, this should be in the structure. If you expect to hold a kickoff meeting, this should also be in the structure. Both these items would fall under the category of project management.

When we create a work breakdown structure, we show it to our customers and say, "If you don't see it in here, don't assume it's being done." To illustrate this point better, Figure 4-2 shows a high-level view of a work breakdown structure.

How to Create a Work Breakdown Structure

One of the easiest ways we have seen to create a work breakdown structure is to find a blank wall and a pack of sticky yellow notes. Put the project

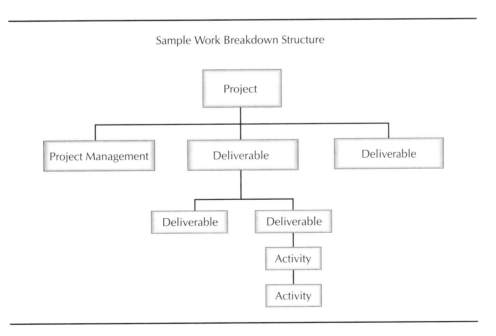

FIGURE 4-2.   *High-level work breakdown structure*

name on a note on the wall. Next, from the scope statement, write each major deliverable on a note and add them to the wall. Write "project management" on a note and add it. Then, under each of these areas, start to decompose all the deliverables (i.e., split them up into smaller pieces). Figure 4-3 shows the start of a work breakdown structure based on the sample scope statement shown in Figure 4-1.

As you can see, this exercise quickly makes you think about all the required steps. When you review this document with the stakeholders, you are well on your way to having enough detail to estimate the project. In addition, you can now start to apply some resources to each of the items in the work breakdown structure. This work breakdown structure should be at a level where any stakeholder can understand all the steps it will take to accomplish each task and produce each deliverable.

After you have completed the work breakdown structure on the wall, we find it helpful to write it down in outline form. Look at this work breakdown structure in outline form, as shown in the next listing:

```
Oracle Data Warehousing Project—Work Breakdown Structure
                        Outline Form

1.   Project Management
     1.1    Administrative
            1.1.1   Daily Management
            1.1.2   Daily Communication
            1.1.3   Issue Resolution
     1.2    Meetings
            1.2.1   Client Meetings
            1.2.2   Staff Meetings
            1.2.3   Kickoff Meetings

2.   Technical Editor
     2.1    Choosing the Technical Editor
            2.1.1   Determine Skillset
            2.1.2   Screen Candidates
            2.1.3   Determine Appropriate Candidate
            2.1.4   Choose Candidate
     2.2    Technical Editor Compensation
            2.2.1   Sign Contract
            2.2.2   Send Check
     2.3    Working with Technical Editor
            2.3.1   Establish Procedure
            2.3.2   Agree On Rules Of Engagement
```

```
3.  Writing The Foreword
    3.1   Choosing Writer For Foreword
```

Once you have this work breakdown structure in outline form, you should then start to describe each item and create a description of what must be done. These descriptions should be at a level any stakeholder can understand, as illustrated in the next listing:

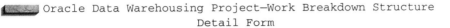 Oracle Data Warehousing Project—Work Breakdown Structure
                        Detail Form

1. Project Management

```
This activity is not normally thought of as a deliverable but,
because it consumes up to 25 percent of the total project budget,
we recommend you include it.
```

1.1 Administrative—
```
        This includes the overhead items associated with a project.
```
1.1.1 Daily Management—
```
        This includes gathering time cards, status reports,
        dealing with vacations, project costs, attrition, and
        training.
```
1.1.2 Daily Communication—
```
        This includes a combination of ongoing formal and informal
        discussions. The communication with the client is vital to
        the project delivery and will be the primary vehicle for
        potential problem resolution.
```

After you have completed the work breakdown structure, you should review it to make certain any stakeholder can understand it. With the proper level of description, this should not pose a problem. Make sure the work breakdown structure contains enough detail so you can begin to make educated guesses on the resource requirements. Ensure the work breakdown list is as complete as possible. For example, many times people forget to include meetings, documentation, training, demonstrations, equipment setup, time for review, time to learn new tools, weekly status reports, and many other tasks that are implied yet take significant time and resources to accomplish.

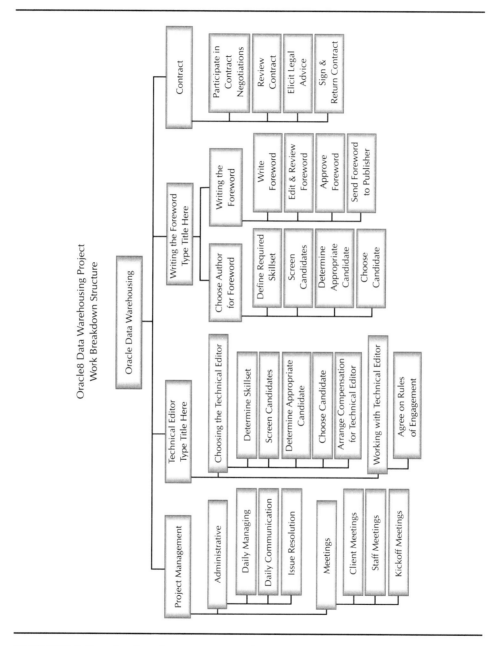

FIGURE 4-3. *Further decomposition of work breakdown structure*

Project Estimating

Now that you have a breakdown of what needs to be done, you can begin to estimate how long it will take and how much effort it will require. Clearly, your customer will want you to determine the cost—this means you need to know how long each activity will take so you can accurately price it. Recent studies show that approximately 47 percent of all consulting jobs performed were fixed-price bids. With the trend for consulting services moving rapidly toward fixed-price bids, we may soon be building software systems the way we build a house. There will be a detailed project plan and severe penalties when we are late. In the field of project management, the construction industry is way ahead of the software industry. When you decide to build a house, they can give you great detail on how much and how long it will take.

By using good project management techniques today, your organization can gather the necessary information to price and predict jobs correctly in the future. Here are two types of activities you can estimate:

1. Activity estimates are low-level educated guesses at how long a particular task will take within a given project. They are your primary tools when gauging the progress of a project.

2. Project estimates are high-level guesses to help you make funding decisions. Many times, your initial project estimates have no bearing on how long it will take to accomplish the project or how much it will cost.

This leads to an important point: *activity estimating is not a negotiation.* If it takes two hours to create a database, it takes two hours. Never lower your estimates. If your manager or another team member thinks your estimate is too high, find out why they think it is too high. They may have a good reason and you may agree.

VIP

Activity estimation is not a negotiation. If it takes two hours to build a database, it takes two hours. Don't be persuaded into agreeing to time frames that are not realistic.

If your time line is too long, look at other ways to get around this obstacle. Perhaps having two people working on the task will bring it in by the needed date.

Probability and Risk

In life, most things result in a bell curve. Figure 4-4 shows a sample bell curve that measures the likelihood of on-time project delivery. The graph measures the number of projects delivered late, on time, and early.

As you can see in Figure 4-4, the most likely outcome falls to the center of the curve. This type of graph is skewed in the center; hence, the terminology *bell curve* is taken from the shape. Table 4-1 summarizes the data presented in Figure 4-4.

What this teaches us is that we currently do time estimates incorrectly. That is, trying to predict a single point will never work. The law of average works against us.

We should predict project time estimates like we predict rolling dice. Experience has taught us that when a pair of dice is rolled, the most likely number to come up is seven. When you look at alternatives, the odds of a number other than seven coming up are less.

A craps table is an excellent way to observe this. When you play at a craps table, you can place a bet on what the next number rolled on the dice will be. Based on the number you pick, you will get a corresponding payoff based on the casino's risk. For example, if you predict the next number rolled is seven, that prediction will pay far less than if you bet the next number rolled is twelve. The casino has looked at the probability of any outcome and determined its associated risk. Why not do this with project

Percentage of Projects Delivered	Days from Expected Delivery
25	33 days early or 35 days late
50	25 days early or 25 days late
75	8 days early or 13 days late

TABLE 4-1. *Bell Curve Data Summary*

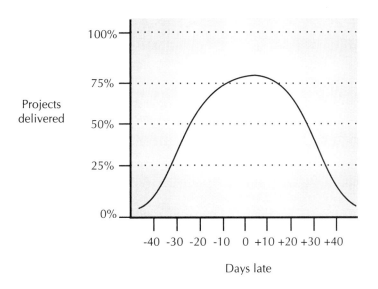

FIGURE 4-4.   *Project delivery bell curve*

managing? For example, why not get a three-point estimate—the optimistic view, the pessimistic view, and the most likely answer? Based on those answers, you can determine a time estimate. Table 4-2 shows an example of a three-point estimate worksheet.

As you can see from Table 4-2, just the task of choosing the technical editor has considerable latitude in possible outcomes, yet each one of these outcomes has a chance of becoming reality. Within a given project, many of the tasks would come in on the best-case guess, and many of the tasks will also come in on the worst-case guess. In addition, each one of these outcomes has an associated measurable risk.

We recommend you get away from single-point estimates and move toward three-point estimates. By doing this, you will start to get a handle on your true risk. By doing this exercise with your team members, you will start everyone thinking about the task and all the associated risks. What if a team member gets sick? What if the computer breaks down? What if someone gets pulled away on another task? These things do happen, and they do affect the project.

Task	Subtask	Best Case	Most Likely	Worst Case
Choosing the technical editor	Determine skill set	1.0	3.0	5.0
	Screen candidates	1.0	2.0	3.0
	Choose candidate	0.5	1.0	2.0
Total		2.5	6.0	10.0

TABLE 4-2. *Three-point Time Estimate Worksheet*

VIP
Get away from single-point estimating. It is better to establish a pessimistic and optimistic range for a task to be done.

You are now also defining the acceptable level of performance. For example, if a project team member came in with 25 days to choose a technical editor, we would consider this irresponsible. We would require a great deal of justification. Another positive aspect to the three-point estimate is that it improves the stakeholders' morale. The customer will start to feel more comfortable because he or she will have an excellent handle on the project. At the same time, when some tasks do fall behind, everyone realizes this should be expected. Because the project takes all outcomes into consideration, you could still come in within the acceptable time lines. An entire science exists within project management that allows you to take three-point estimates and improve the level of accuracy.

Let's take a closer look at risk. When you do get caught, this is typically due to one of three situations:

1. **Assumptions**   You get caught by unvoiced assumptions. They were never spelled out.

2. **Constraints** You get caught by restricting factors, which were not fully understood.

3. **Unknowns** Items you could never predict, be they acts of God or human error.

The key to risk management is to do your best to identify the source of all risk and the likelihood of its happening. For example, when we project plan, we typically do not take work stoppages into account. But if we were working for an airline that was under threat of a major strike, we might reevaluate the likelihood of losing valuable project time.

Calculate the cost to the project if the particular risk happens and make a decision. You can decide either to accept it, find a way to avoid it, or try to prevent it. Always look for ways around the obstacles. For example, on one particular client site, we have a complicated transformation process running every weekend on Tandem hardware. Because we are running on a Tandem, we have decided the likelihood the system will not be available is nil. At the same time, we have a staff member who covers this job all weekend to make certain it is successful. Duncan Nevison lists the following types of *internal* risks:

1. Company politics
   - Corporate strategy change
   - Departmental politics

2. Project stakeholders
   - Sponsor
   - Customer
   - Subcontractors
   - Project team

3. Project characteristics
   - Schedule bumps

- Cost hiccups

- Technical surprises

They also list the following *external* risks:

1. Environment

    - Fire, Famine, Flood

    - Pollution

    - Raw materials

2. Government

    - Change in law

    - Change in regulation

3. Economy

    - Currency rate change

    - Market shift

    - Competitor's entry or exit

    - Immediate competitive actions

    - Supplier change

By looking at these risks, you get a sense of all the influences that may impact your particular project. You should take the time to assess and reassess these. For example, if your project is running severely behind schedule, is there another vendor waiting to try to take the business? If your project is running way over budget, is there a chance the funding may get cut? We must always be aware of the technology with which we are working. Familiarity with technology is important; we need to know, for example, if what we are working with is a new release of the software or a release that has been out for a long time.

After you determine what must be done and how long it will take, you are ready to start looking for your critical paths and dependencies. These critical paths are yet another form of risk within a project. For example, there are inherent dependencies among many project activities. A chapter must be written before it can be reviewed. A technical editor must be selected before the editing cycle of a chapter can be completed. These are examples of dependency analysis.

Let's say we are working on a project with three unique lists of activities associated with it. Each unique path (A, B, C) of activities is represented based on its dependencies. Each cell represents the number of days that activity should take. By adding all the rows together, you can tell the duration of each path. This is shown in Table 4-3.

Start A represents a part of the project with three steps, which will take a total of eight days. Start B represents a part of the project with three steps, which will take a total of six days. Start C represents a path with two steps, which will take a total of 20 days.

The critical path is *Start C*. You must begin this as soon as possible. In fact, this tells us the soonest this project can be done is 20 days. If you do not start the activity that takes 15 days first, it will delay the entire project ending one day for each day you wait.

NOTE
Be aware that as any project continues, the critical path can change over time.

Project Management Summary

A data warehouse initiative could be one of the toughest projects you will ever work on—without good project management, you will fail. We have

Unique Task	Part #1	Part #2	Part #3	Total
Start A	1	3	4	8 days
Start B	1	2	3	6 days
Start C	15	5		20 days

TABLE 4-3. *Critical Path Analysis*

given you an overview of the major concepts of project management and some good project management techniques to follow, but this chapter was not intended to replace the need for good project management training or experience. Its purpose was to provide a good framework by which to begin the complexities of managing a data warehouse initiative.

All projects have stakeholders. Stakeholders are the individuals or organizations affected by the project and all of its activities. You must take the time to understand their needs or you will never be able to manage or influence them. Without understanding your stakeholders, your project will fail.

Project managers—not project management software—manage projects. Do not expect Microsoft Project to manage your project, because it is just one of many tools you might use to help you succeed. A project is a temporary endeavor; it must have a defined start and end.

A scope statement is an excellent starting point for any project and a common technique to help you identify and scope the tasks to be done. In the process of discovery for the scope statement, you will identify what must happen for a project to end. Following the initial scope statement, we recommend you develop a work breakdown structure to help you find any missing components in your project. During the process of developing a work breakdown structure, you will discover any existing holes. When you develop the work breakdown structure, list all activities that must happen for the project to be a success. The example we used to illustrate this was the project management activity. This activity alone can account for as much as 20 percent of a team member's time, yet it is commonly overlooked.

Once you have identified all the activities, it's time to start placing resources and estimates against them. Our experience has shown that three-point estimates work, but single-point estimates do not work. Single-point estimates do not reflect the real world because they do not take risk into account. By applying all the techniques covered in this chapter, your data warehouse project will run smoother.

Time to move on. Let's get into the meat of the data warehouse design. Many cringe when they hear that word—DESIGN. Design is the nature of the beast, no matter where or how you spend your regular 9-to-5 day in information technology.

CHAPTER

5

Data Warehouse Design

he design of a data warehouse is a paradigm shift from the way that operational systems are designed. Data warehouse designers must now contend with not only designing a database and a user interface; they must also design data loading strategies, data access tools, user training, and ongoing maintenance issues. The data warehouse requires a strong database design with many facets. When embarking upon a data warehouse design, you must now consider numerous issues that did not have to be considered in operational design. This chapter is intended to help you gain a better understanding of how the warehouse is built and the issues that you must consider in achieving a complete data warehouse design.

One may even say that data warehouse designers are not as "normal" as operational system designers. In this chapter, we will provide you with the guidance necessary to design a data warehouse. We will focus on design theory and dimensional modeling, and provide a proven approach to designing a robust data warehouse.

Design—The Next Logical Step

Most definitions of data warehouses start with a few baseline concepts of what they are supposed to do, and who uses them for decision making. Ask the question: What is a warehouse? Depending on who you ask, you will probably get an equal number of different answers. The data warehouse is not just a database; it is an entire system. From the extraction of data from operational systems, to the loading and management of data within the warehouse, to end-user data access, the warehouse is a system to help people better understand and analyze their organizations. In Chapter 1, we looked at how we see the data warehouse within your organization. Now that we are designing the warehouse, we must be sure to design a system that meets the needs of both users and developers.

At its most granular, atomic level (we will get to this later), the *warehouse* is a repository for detailed, nonvolatile, time-based information. The warehouse must also serve as a tool to perform summary-level, strategic analysis of this information. The warehouse may also act as the source for high-performance query structures such as specialized data marts or multidimensional databases such Oracle Express. Achieving both purposes in an effective manner is the focus of this chapter.

Building an enterprise data warehouse or a focused data mart is a process that merges the business users directly to the corporate data they need to make informed strategic, effective, and detailed business decisions. The design of the warehouse must therefore be easily understood and manipulated. Because end users will be directly querying the warehouse, this design must be simple to understand and navigate. When you create a complex data warehouse that contains structures that are difficult to navigate, you expose your warehouse to being misunderstood. This can result in invalid assumptions and misinterpretation by decision support system (DSS) users and, ultimately, incorrect and even dangerous business decisions.

The warehouse, when designed in an intuitive manner, allows business users to easily understand the data that they are viewing and interrogating. These users intuitively understand the data that helps them run their business—items such as product numbers, corporate regions, product lines, customer types, and so on. This information is the window into the data that the users can quickly incorporate into their information analysis. Data warehouses that are created in isolation of end-user requirements are doomed to failure. By creating your data warehouse with end users in mind, you help them to quickly embrace the new technology and ensure the success of your data warehouse design and implementation.

Ongoing Interaction with the Users

Building an enterprise data warehouse is a full-fledged development project—one that requires a focused group of users and developers to come together in the development process. In many ways, it is more difficult than developing an operational system. The requirements are more ambiguous, given the necessity of ad hoc analysis. Designers must contend with uncertainties in the major components of data to be stored and the methods of accessing that data.

Understanding the requirements is imperative. We must understand a number of areas, including the following:

- User reporting requirements

- Historical data retention

- Nature of the data to include

■ Nature of the data to exclude

■ Where to get the data

■ How to get the data from point A (its source) to point B (the warehouse), and possibly onto point C (a high-performance query structure)

■ How to ensure that the data is properly replicated (*replication* is one of the approaches used to ensure a change to operational system data is reflected in data warehouse data)

■ How to provide enough flexibility so we do not limit the long-term viability of the warehouse

In analyzing requirements, we need to ask users to provide examples of the reports they currently use. Analyzing these outputs gets you well on your way to identifying the data that must be in the warehouse. In addition, if you can replace these, you may be able to eliminate the subsystem that produces them, thus enhancing the return on investment (ROI) of your warehouse. Questions we frequently ask users when designing a data warehouse include the following:

■ What is your department's role within the enterprise?

■ What is your role within the department?

■ What reports do you use to fulfill that role?

■ Where do you currently get this information?

■ What do you do with this information after you've obtained it?

■ Is this information typically produced at your request or is it found on some periodic report?

■ Do you ever type this information into a spreadsheet to analyze it further?

■ How timely must this information be?

The design of a data warehouse is not simply the design of a data repository; it's the design integration of many components. There is the consideration of the operational data sources, the staging area, and the data repository and aggregation structures when designing the data warehouse. The other item that must always be considered when designing and implementing the warehouse is the types of reporting that the system will be required to perform. In our experience, we have seen many data warehouses that have failed to provide the necessary performance and flexibility, since they were built in isolation from the reporting requirements. In addition, it is rare that a single reporting tool can satisfy all reporting uses of the warehouse. In general, most warehouses are accessed by a variety of different users and tools, each optimized for a particular reporting purpose: report writing, batch file creation, online analytical processing, data mining, and others. To be successful in designing your data warehouse, you must ensure that all factors affecting your design are considered. Better to overdesign than to find that you have missed some critical information once the system has been implemented.

Designing the data warehouse is an iterative experience. The design team is not your typical operational system design team. When building the data warehouse team, the most important members of the design team are the target users and business analysts. In Chapters 3 and 4, we looked at the data warehouse project team and managing the project. The target users provide us with the details on the purpose of the warehouse. These users have an important perspective on the way that the warehouse will be used.

NOTE
The user community must be an active participant in the warehouse design process. Without user involvement, the warehouse will cough, sputter, and die!

A successful warehouse effort teams users and designers from the start. These user teams perform a number of roles, including the following:

■ Providing user requirements

■ Signing off on the development team's interpretation of user requirements

■ Acceptance-testing the completed system

■ Suggesting enhancements after the warehouse is released into production

The designers must act as the facilitators in the design effort. An experienced data warehouse designer who has a variety of experiences building data warehouses can be a major asset to the overall success of the project. The designer acts as a facilitator, ensuring that all aspects of the warehouse are analyzed and that the design is accurate and complete. The business analysts should be people from your organization who understand how your business is run and the processes that are in place to collect information. They may have been part of your operational systems design team or may be business users of your warehouse. These people will contribute an interesting perspective for the design team. They understand the business processes and business rules that will be stored by the warehouse and how and where operational data required for the warehouse resides.

The design team can be quite large; make sure that your team does not grow too large where useful discussions are difficult to carry out. We have been working in design teams as small as three individuals (facilitator, business analyst, and end user) and as large as 20 people. When forming the team, focus on a complete team since everyone must come together to create a dynamic and robust data warehouse.

Data Warehouse Databases Vs. Operational Databases

Since the introduction of relational databases, data modelers have been trained to build normalized databases for operational information systems. Normalized structures store the greatest amount of data in the least amount of space; hence, we define *normalization* as a method of designing a database. At its simplest level, normalization is a process of decomposing data structures into their smallest components. The emphasis in normalization is on flexibility and efficiency of storage. Normalization also supports data-driven systems that can frequently be enhanced with changes only to data, not to data structures and programs. These systems need to be shared and nonredundant within the corporation. For years, we have been building our operational systems with the idea of normalization as our only goal. The warehouse is a paradigm shift in database design. While flexibility and efficiency are lofty goals in a warehouse, they are not the ultimate goal.

NOTE
The ultimate goal in the data warehouse arena
is rapid access to large amounts of data.

In fact, warehouse designers will frequently trade off flexibility and efficiency for query performance. Warehouse table structures can take on a number of forms. Pilots frequently state, "If a plane looks good, it flies good." The sad truth of warehousing is that, frequently, the uglier the structure (in terms of maintenance and space required), the better the performance. Table 5-1 shows you that the different characteristics between data warehouses and operational systems are great enough that they must be designed uniquely. So if it smells like an operational system and barks like an operational system, then it must be an operational system, not a data warehouse.

Operational transactions become historical events in the warehouse. In many operational systems, simply retaining the expired operational data permits strategic reporting from the operational database. This arrangement sounds good in theory, but has proven to be impractical—the real-world performance, capacity, and technology limitations cannot be ignored. Therefore, building the warehouse becomes an integral part of your organization's data strategy.

Realistically, few operational systems can provide truly ad hoc data access or at least queries that perform well (i.e., run to completion in a short

Data Warehouse Data	Operational System Data
Long time frame	Short time frame
Static	Rapid changes
Data is usually summarized	Record-level access
Ad hoc query access	Standard transactions
Updated periodically	Updated in real time
Data driven	Event driven

TABLE 5-1. *Data Warehouse Data Vs. Operational System Data*

amount of time). The warehouse asks you to provide the access. Data warehouse designers must generally understand the access needs and specifically understand the data to be used as a basis of that access. Users may have some chance of making up a query on the fly, but they have no chance of making up the data from which the query is derived. In many ways, the data model is more important than the data analysis.

Types of Data in the Warehouse

We think of the data warehouse as a collection of historical transactions and summarizations. It may be thought of as the giant spreadsheet that sits on that big computer. The warehouse is much more than just a simple collection of information. It can hold many different flavors of data. The following is a common sampling of the types of data that are contained in the warehouse.

- Transactions downloaded from operational systems—this data is time stamped to form a historical record.

- Dimensional support data (customers, products, time).

- Table to support the joining of dimensional data and numeric facts relating to this data.

- Summarization of transactions (e.g., daily sales by department). These are really preemptive queries; the data is aggregated when it is added to the warehouse rather than when a user requests it.

- Miscellaneous coding data.

- Metadata, the data about the data. This category might include sources of warehouse data, replication rules, rollup categories and rules, availability of summarizations, security and controls, purge criteria, and logical and physical data mapping.

- Event data sourced from outside services, such as demographic information correlated into the geographic areas in which your company operates.

These types of data that we have just described are all contained in the warehouse. It shows us that the information that we hold in the data warehouse is vastly different from the information that is contained in an operational system. When looking at designing a data warehouse, you must keep in mind that "I am not designing an operational system! I am not designing an operational system!" This mantra will be your guide: do not design a "normal" database for your warehouse without understanding the end use of your information. By the end of this chapter we will have shown you the concepts behind database design, data warehouse design, and a proven approach to warehousing; you will see that "You're not in Kansas anymore!" and that designing the warehouse is a paradigm shift from operational system design. Let's then move forward so we can change your way of looking at data. This process could be irreversible—look both ways before crossing.

"Normal" Operational Design

Operational system design and creating databases to serve operational purposes differ significantly from the goals of data warehouse design. When creating a database for an online operational system in a relational model, the concern is with quick response time and efficient data storage. Therefore, when designing with these goals in mind, we create a data model that is in third normal form. There are other higher forms of normalization, but the description to the third level suffices for describing the differences between operational and data warehouses. Nowadays many operational systems are designed to levels higher than third normal form. Normalization of a database is a concept developed by Dr. Codd and a number of other database theorists to design databases that achieve the goals necessary to deploy efficient operational systems. Each step in the normalization process addresses a single issue. The following sections will help you better understand what has come to be called normalized relational design.

First Normal Form

The first step of the normalization process is the removal of repeating groups. The resultant tables are said to be in the first normal form. First normal form has the following attributes:

- All attributes are atomic.

- They cannot have a set of values.

- They cannot have any nested relations.

The structure pictured in Table 5-2 is in first normal form. As you can see, all the items are at their lowest form—this is placing items at the atomic level. As well, there are not repeating groups. For example, you could think of listing all of this person's projects in one record. This would then limit the flexibility of your information, so we ensure that we do not have any repeating groups. First normal form is a place to start, but it is only one stop on our normalization adventure.

Employee ID

First name

Last name

Street address

City

Province

Country

Home telephone

Office telephone

Cellular telephone

Job description

Salary

Project number

Project name

Budget

Duration

Start date

Projected end date

Manager

TABLE 5-2. *First Normal Form*

Second Normal Form

The first normal relations are then decomposed stage-wise by addressing each of the normalization criteria. When dependencies on part of the key are removed, the relations are said to be in the second normal form. Second normal form ensures that the relations of all nonprimary attributes are fully dependent on the primary key. Table 5-3 illustrates a few relations in second normal form, with the primary key attributes underlined.

Let's dissect the relations pictured in Table 5-3 and show how the nonkey attributes are fully dependent on each relation's primary key.

In the Employee Data entity, all of the nonkey attributes are dependent on the Employee ID. For example, picking on employee number 100720, that person's name is directly hooked to the ID, as is that person's address of 60 Cocksfield.

The EMPLOYEE and PROJECT tables have now been separated such that all nonkey attributes are now fully dependent upon their respective primary keys. We have therefore created three data sets: one for the employee; another for the project; and, finally, a table that relates the two, the

Employee Data	Project Data	Assignment Data
Employee ID	Project number	Employee ID
First name	Project name	Project number
Last name	Budget	Duration
Street address	Manager	Start date
City		Projected end date
Province		
Country		
Job description		
Salary		
Home telephone		
Office telephone		

TABLE 5-3.   *Second Normal Form Table (Removal of Key Dependency)*

assignment data. As you can see, all nonprimary attributes are fully dependent on the primary keys.

Third Normal Form

The transitive dependencies (dependencies on nonkey attributes) are removed by further decomposition. The result is the third normal form, or the so-called Boyce-Codd normal form. Third normal form is characterized by the following:

- All nonprime attributes are fully dependent on every key.

- All prime attributes are fully dependent on the keys that they do not belong to.

- No attribute is fully dependent on any set of nonprime attributes.

The entities shown in Table 5-4 are in third normal form, again with the primary key attribute(s) underlined and the foreign keys underlined and bolded. Let's dissect the relations pictured in Table 5-4 and show how the nonprime attributes are now fully dependent on every key:

- In the Employee Data entity, the nonprime attribute Job type is now dependent upon the Job type data entity. For example, people who all are consultants will have their job type being defined in the Job type data entity.

- In the Project Data entity, we have defined a link to the Manager Data entity. So, if a manager manages multiple projects, this information can be linked via this common key.

The data objects have now been brought into third normal form. The exercise to go from first to second, and then on to third normal form, shows how we must focus on the following steps:

- First normal form: remove all repeating groups

- Second normal form: link all entities by primary keys

- Third normal form: link nonkey attributes by keys to supporting foreign keys

Employee Data	Pay Data	Project Data	Manager Data	Assignment Data
Employee ID	Job type	**Project number**	Manager ID	Employee ID
First name	Description	Project name	Name	Project number
Last name	Salary	Budget	Location	Duration
Street address		**Manager ID**		Start date
City				Projected end date
Province				
Country				
Job type				
Home telephone				
Office telephone				

TABLE 5-4.   *Third Normal Form Data Structure*

Further decomposition to remove multivalued dependencies may then be used to produce a set of relations in the fourth normal form. Some designers recognize a domain key normal form (or DKNF: Fagin 1981) in which every constraint on the relations is the result of only two variables—the key and the domains of the nonkey attributes. No generalized method for achieving this state has been proposed.

Operational database design, by convention, will be based in a normal form. The data warehouse, by comparison, will usually be denormalized for efficient retrieval of information. By denormalizing the structures contained in the data warehouse, we improve performance and usability of the information. The design of the warehouse is a paradigm shift in the way that we design and implement a database.

Dimensional Data Warehouse Design

Since we have looked at operational system design at a high level, we can now look more closely at the components that constitute the data warehouse. The data warehouse database is a combination of many different components, including the following:

- The staging area

- The data warehouse

- The focused data marts

The staging area is a set of database tables that will be used to receive the information from the operational data sources. The information will be populated with data from the operational systems. Often, we get flat files containing the data. The staging area mirrors these structures. By creating a staging area, we can then accelerate the data loads and more easily manipulate the data within the Oracle database. The staging area provides a simple environment from which we can create the data transforms and load the data into the warehouse. The data warehouse is a set of data tables that will contain all of your data. The structures in the warehouse simplify the enterprise's data while still retaining a nonprocess-oriented database structure. The data here is time stamped to allow for time-based analysis. The level of normalization or denormalization within integrated warehouse database structure is determined based upon the requirements for this database. How these structures will be used will drive the structure to the warehouse. The final data storage format is a high-performance query structure such as a data mart or a multidimensional database. Data marts are normally created using a star schema to enhance data retrieval by end users. This concept will be detailed in Chapter 6, "Data Marts."

Each component is built in the warehouse based upon user requirements. If the user is looking at creating a complete enterprise-wide data warehouse, you should plan to build all three parts. However, in the case of the creation of an individual data mart, you may be able to satisfy the user's requirement with a stand-alone data mart. The truth is usually somewhere in the middle of all this. Figure 5-1 illustrates at a high level how all of the components within the data warehouse are integrated, and shows you how the data will flow through an enterprise data warehouse.

The topology of the warehouse is a varied affair. The data is extracted from sources such as operational systems and flat files. This data is then loaded into the data warehouse using a number of methods, such as SQL*Loader and data warehouse loading tools. The warehouse will be created at the highest detail level of information required by the users. The data warehouse is then used to populate the various process-oriented data marts. These data marts will be structured in a star schema topology to achieve maximum retrieval performance. The entire data warehouse then forms an integrated system that can serve the end-user reporting and analysis requirements of the user community.

We now move on to discussing the famous star schema. You can't spend more than a few minutes looking at data warehouse design or conversing with your colleagues without running across these two words. The star schema can

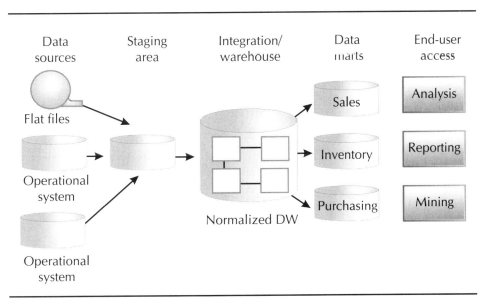

FIGURE 5-1. *Data warehouse topology overview*

help you to optimize data warehouse performance, so leverage this knowledge when designing your overall data warehouse implementation.

The Star Schema

The *star schema* is a concept that provides superior data retrieval power to the data warehouse and the deployment of decision support systems. Companies like A. C. Nielson and IRI (the company acquired by Oracle in 1995 that led to the Oracle Express line of products) have shown over time that the concept of the star schema is necessary to top-performing data warehouses. The design idea of the star join schema has allowed us to better empower the data warehouse to more directly meet the needs of the end users. The name "star schema" is derived from the appearance of the data model, with a large central table surrounded in a star formation by subordinate tables. The central table, known as the *fact* table, is surrounded by many *dimension* tables. This type of modeling is known as *dimensional data warehousing*.

Fact tables contain measures that are used to perform analysis, and also the keys that link the dimensions. *Measures* are the numerical information that is used to perform analysis; they are often used in functions like sum, average, median, and standard deviation. Measures include items such as total sales, monthly bank balance, quantity shipped, and so on. The dimension tables contain the attributes that describe the data components and provide the information to do comparative analysis. The star schema is another way to model transactions. For example, *performance measures* are some of the ways to judge how the organization is performing. The schema describes those measures. For example, dollar sales are a measure of how well the organization is performing. Sales can also be described or measured according to the following:

- Where they took place (location)
- Who they were made to (customer)
- When they occurred (time of year)
- What was sold (product)
- Who sold it (sales personnel)

The star schema is designed with a great deal of redundant dimension data, which is provided in this manner only to improve performance of information retrieval. By creating a data model in the star schema design, we prejoin the dimension information for the users and simplify the relationships that will need to be analyzed by the users. The following describes facts and dimensions and helps you to relate these in your own data warehouse.

The Fact Table

The fact table is a table that may be viewed in two parts. The first part defines the primary key; the other holds the numerical measurements on the warehouse. These measures are defined and calculated for each derived key and are known as facts or measures. Measures should have the following characteristics:

- Numeric

- Additive (usually)

However, at times you may find that a measure is required in the warehouse, but it may not appear to be additive. This is known as *semiadditive facts*. An example of a semiadditive fact would be room temperature in different parts of an office tower. If we would add together the temperatures in all the locations in the building, a completely meaningless number will be derived. By averaging this number, a more meaningful conclusion will be reached. Another example is inventory balances, which are not additive over the dimension of time. This value again lends itself to aggregation using an SQL function other than **sum**, such as **average**.

Dimension Tables

The dimension tables can be viewed as the windows through which users will analyze their data. They contain the text descriptions of the items that support business operations. The design of the dimensions provides for the definition of the dimension's attributes. These attributes should be plentiful. A product dimension could easily contain 50 or more attributes. These attributes should have the following characteristics:

- Be textual

- Be discrete

- Define constraints

- Provide row headers during analysis

When looking at the dimensions, the attributes of a dimension can be seen as information to describe the item. So, for a product information dimension, we may say that it can be described as having a certain color. This attribute would be textual, such as "blue." Each product with a different color would have its own record within the dimension, making it discrete. This attribute for color could then be used to define your comparative analysis—such as give all the sales for blue products—thereby defining your constraints. Finally, the attribute can be used as a heading during analysis, so we could use the attribute name of color, or we may use the name of each distinct color. Attributes are very powerful for analysis of your data within the data warehouse. Some may say that the attribute is your window into your data.

As we have discussed previously, the following example shows the power and depth of attributes. If we want to determine the number of sales of blue-colored ice creams, we would enter the data structures via the product dimension, which contains the color attribute for our products. This dimension provides users with a number of analysis windows, which are opened by accessing the attributes in a conditional manner.

Let's look at what types of data components will more than likely become a dimension versus a fact or a dimensional attribute:

- When a component is a number, and is additive or semiadditive, it will likely be a measure.

- When a component is a description, it will likely be a dimensional attribute.

Table 5-5 shows some examples of dimensions and the types of attributes that would form the dimension definition, again with primary key columns underlined.

As you can see in Table 5-5, every dimension has a surrogate key. A *surrogate key* is a system-generated primary key used to designate individual

Time Dimension	Product Dimension	Customer Dimension
Time key	Product key	Customer key
Date	Operational ID	Name
Month	Product name	Street address
Day	UPC code	City
Year	Product class	State/province
Quarter	Color	City
Fiscal year	Flavor	Country
	Product size	Type

TABLE 5-5.   *Sample Dimensions*

records in each dimension of the data warehouse. The surrogate key removes any requirement to use an implied key from your operational systems. This is required so that when we determine how we will manage changes within a dimension, we are not confined by a key implied from an operational code. Also, by removing the dependence on operational keys, heterogeneous codes from multiple operational systems can be collected in common warehouse coding structures. Surrogate keys also have better performance: they are limited to one column rather than concatenations of columns and they are generally integer data types, which are processed more quickly than character data types. The power of the star schema comes in its simplicity.

Table 5-6 describes how these keys (underlined as usual) are linked in a fact table, along with some measures that can be used during data analysis.

So, as you can see, the fact table is composed of two distinct sections: the primary key, comprised of the keys from the dimensions, and the numeric measures. This simple structure allows for very interesting and detailed data analysis.

Figure 5-2 illustrates how users can easily navigate and understand the model to create interesting queries. The schema that we provide you with is a simple one to understand, and with simple training can be used by all

Time key

Product key

Customer key

Sale amount

Quantity

Discount

TABLE 5-6. *Sample Fact Table*

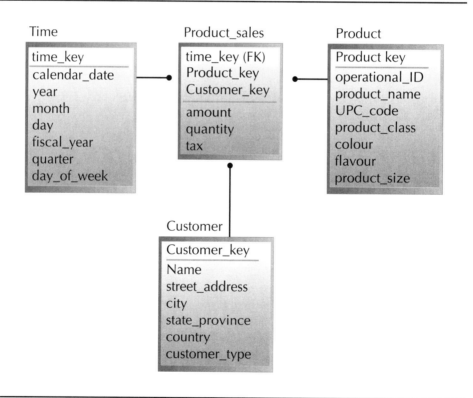

FIGURE 5-2. *Sales star schema*

users in your organization. The database schema described shows a PRODUCT_SALES fact table and TIME, PRODUCT, and CUSTOMER dimensions. The dimensions are joined together in the fact table by foreign keys defined for each dimension. The foreign keys ensure that we create a consistent view of the data, with all records related by our generated surrogate keys. We will discuss how to guarantee that when you load data into the warehouse, the data consistency is retained.

NOTE
The primary key of the fact table is comprised of foreign keys to the dimension tables and numeric measures.

NOTE
The fact tables are actually highly normalized (except in unusual situations where the fact tables might be denormalized by a dimension like time). Dimension tables are highly denormalized.

Let's continue the design discussion by looking at granularity.

Granularity

Granularity is defined as the level of summarization that will be maintained by your warehouse; however, a warehouse will usually contain many levels of granularity. When creating your data warehouse or data mart, you must define the granularity of the data as part of your warehouse definition. Table 5-7 provides a quick reference on the relationship between granularity and data detail.

Grain can be defined as the highest level of detail that is retained in the warehouse, such as the transaction level. This data is highly detailed and can then be summarized to any level required by your users. It is imperative when designing your data warehouse that you define the granularity of the data at the outset of your analysis effort, since it will affect your database design. If you define the grain improperly, you can handicap your

Grain	Data Detail
Low (e.g., transactional)	Very high
High (e.g., summarized)	Medium to low

TABLE 5-7. *Granularity Summary*

warehouse and defeat the purpose of creating it. When defining granularity within the warehouse, consider the following factors:

- Type of analysis you will be performing

- Acceptable lowest levels of aggregation

- Volume of data that can be stored

The types of analyses you plan to perform with the warehouse will directly affect your warehouse's granularity. If you plan to use the warehouse to perform analysis based on information summarized at the daily level, then you would not want to define the grain at the weekly level.

NOTE

If you define your level of granularity too high, you may not be able to perform some more detailed operations within your warehouse.

The data warehouse will usually have multiple levels of granularity within the same schema. You may have one level for data that was created within the current year and another for data in the previous two- to five-year window. This is based upon the lowest level of aggregation required in the warehouse. You may find that your users will need transactional data in the warehouse, but this data is only applicable during the current year; after that period, the data can be summarized at a weekly or monthly level. These decisions are critical to your overall data warehouse design and must not be taken lightly.

Finally, the last contributing factor to defining your warehouse's granularity is the amount of disk space that you can make available to the warehouse. If you have limited resources, you may find that you can only handle data volumes if your data is summarized at a weekly level. This analysis must be performed based upon your knowledge of your data requirements and the amount of space that this information will take up within the database. We find that if you design your warehouse based upon hardware limitations, you will impose artificial limits on the warehouse, which could defeat the long-term viability of the system. Today, the price of disk space is cheap, so make every attempt to define your level of granularity based on information requirements.

Now that we have defined the components of a data warehouse, we must put it all together. To that end, we provide you with an approach that has proven successful in designing data warehouses.

Data Warehouse Design Approach and Guide

We have discussed the components of the data warehouse and some of the concepts that we will use during the analysis and design of a warehouse. The most important step towards the design of the warehouse is to create a design team that represents all parties concerned with delivering and using the data warehouse. For years we have been developing systems with little or no user representation. The data warehouse embraces the users and their requirements.

The design of the data warehouse is iterative and requires careful planning and analysis. The following is a methodology that has proven successful in designing and deploying data warehouses. Through this process, you will design and develop your data warehouse topology. This will include the database structure, the extraction methods and procedures, the data loading and transformation techniques, and the end-user reporting and retrieval strategy.

Project Analysis and Planning

This phase of the project is crucial to successfully delivering data warehousing solutions. Analysis and planning are often the least appreciated phase of any project.

We prefer the use of joint application development (JAD) sessions as the vehicle to bring the team together to qualify and quantify the details for the project. In commencing the process, we (along with the design team) will identify the goals and direction for the data warehouse. We will confirm the warehouse's focus, its target audience, and its purpose within the corporation. This will then lead into defining the project, scope, and tasks. The definition of the scope allows the team developing the plan to review and analyze the details of the project to identify the tasks, deliverables, dependencies, and assumptions of the project. We first looked at scope in Chapter 2, when looking at the data warehouse project team. When defining your project scope, you need to capture the following information:

- Subject areas

- Number of tables

- Amount of history

- Number of target users

- The summarization level of the warehouse

- Management of individual data changes within the warehouse

- The window available for data warehouse extraction and cleansing

Two streams of thought that are pursued during the JAD sessions will satisfy distinct components of the complete data warehouse solution. The first stream will focus on the data storage side of the solution, and the second will focus on the reporting requirements. It is imperative to the success in architecting a sound data warehousing solution that a high-level understanding of the reporting requirements be achieved.

During the analysis phase we determine the processes within the business that we are trying to model with the data warehouse or data mart. Initially, one must define the processes that will be satisfied by the warehouse. The process could be any of the following or another as defined by your own business:

- Point of sale transactions

- Pay-per-view subscriptions

■ Manufacturing analysis

■ Insurance claims

■ Bill of materials

■ Purchase orders

■ Plant logistics

As you can see, there is no limit to the types of analysis you will need to support with the information contained in your data warehouse. Now that you have started to define the business foci of your warehouse, you are ready to start defining your supporting details. The dimensions of your data model will form this supporting information for your warehouse. Now that we have defined the processes, we can take an initial run at defining the required dimensions.

A very useful tool in performing this analysis is the process/dimension matrix. This matrix defines the processes that will support the business processes and specific information that will be required to satisfy the reporting needs. Table 5-8 is a sample matrix developed for a banking system, with dimensions across the top and processes down the leftmost column.

A review of the operational information systems will be performed. This review will allow the design team to better understand the current data sources and data flows. These systems form the operational foundation of the business, and this review will identify the data that is being used within

Dimension /Process	Time	Account	Product	Customer rep.	Branch	Securities	Customer
Track customer account	X	X	X	X	X		X
Security transaction	X	X	X		X	X	X
Monthly account balance	X	X	X		X		

TABLE 5-8. *Process/Dimension Matrix*

the company. The understanding of these processes allows us to define a clear vision of the current business processes related to the collection and dissemination of information required for the data warehouse. Based upon the scope and requirements that you have defined, time and resource estimates for delivering the required solution are established. The entire data warehouse team reviews the scope and systems requirements, and any missed items are then included for completeness. This review also serves as a way of further enhancing user involvement in the project by allowing users to understand the direction that the project is taking and ensuring that all their requirements are being addressed.

High-level Design

The high-level design phase of the methodology builds towards the goal of delivering the Data warehouse. This phase focuses on integrating the business processes and business needs that will drive the construction of the data warehouse and the related decision support system.

Merging the information related to your current business process and the goals intended for the data warehouse, the data warehouse architect will create a high-level entity relationship diagram (ERD). The *ERD* is a diagram that shows us all the objects in the database. It describes all the tables (entities) and how each one relates to the other. By creating your ERD in a CASE tool, you can provide a graphical description of your database. This ERD will start to form the database road map of the data warehouse. It will show the major objects and their relationships to each other. It will document the data transformations from operational systems to the data warehouse. The ERD will form the starting point for creating the staging area and/or operational data store (ODS) and the data warehouse dimensional models. These will be refined in future phases of the life cycle.

Once your entities are defined, you must also define the level of granularity of your warehouse. This definition will then help in defining your objects. Figure 5-3 shows the high-level version of such an entity relationship diagram.

As you can see from Figure 5-3, we have defined the major objects and the relations between them. This will form the initial database structure. This step allows us to see that we have identified the major objects in our data warehouse. We would also define the major objects required by any staging objects in the database. The initial design allows us to validate the design

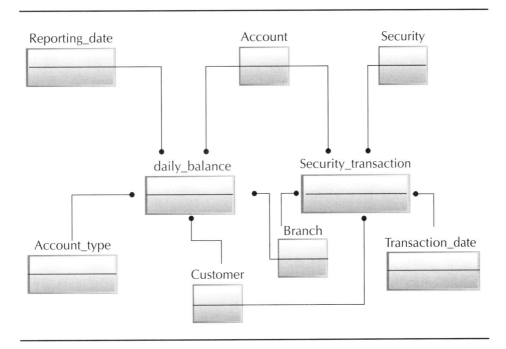

FIGURE 5-3. *High-level entity relationship diagram*

direction that we have chosen with our data warehouse. Together with the target user group, we will review and ensure that we have created a design that collects and collates the information in a simple and efficient manner.

Defining a staging area within your data warehouse topology depends upon the detail requirements of the end users. The staging area can be a time-based data structure that holds the information from your operational systems in common structure and coding standards. The time component of the staging area allows you to track the changes in the data over time, allowing for very detailed analysis and trending of your operational data. It will be structured in a manner similar to the operational system; this structure can be used for quick loading of information into the database and allows you to work within a simple environment from which to populate the warehouse and standardize the data. The staging area allows for a simpler method of loading the data, since loading a normalized schema that contains a minimum of information requires a minimum amount of reformatting. This will reduce the amount of user programming to guide the load before the data is moved into the data warehouse. If you do not want to refer back to your operational database platform, then storing detailed data in your staging area would be the valid direction to resolve this issue. If you do not require this level of detail or do not have the resources to support it, then a simple staging area will suffice and data would be purged after that warehouse's high-performance query structures are populated. If you create a time-based staging area, you will then have a platform from which your data warehouse will be populated. Regardless of how you stage and store your raw data from your operational systems, you must first consider how this information should be integrated into your overall data warehouse strategy. Although this method offers a more robust data warehouse architecture and a more flexible data mart strategy, how users plan to access and manipulate the data must be considered. When you retain the data within the staging area, you then have available to you an area of the warehouse that can be used to populate historical information into the warehouse as the mandate of the warehouse changes.

At the conclusion of your high-level design, you will be able to show a low-detail version of your data warehouse. This will then serve as a vehicle to confirm that you have collected the requirements correctly and that your model can satisfy the information requirements of the warehouse's users. At this point, we should also confirm that we have satisfied our reporting requirements at a high level. In cooperation with the end users, the model should be reviewed against the reporting requirements that were defined during the early stages of the design process.

NOTE
The high-level design is concerned with understanding the business. This level ensures that all the business process of the data warehouse are documented and that we get a basic understanding of the information that will need to be collected.

Mid-level Design

The mid-level design refines the information collected during the previous phases of the project. The mid-level design will create a more detailed definition of the data warehouse. The focus at the mid-level is detailing the data.

The review of your operational systems will continue. It will now focus on the detailed data attributes that these systems provide. The ERD will be further refined to include the individual attributes in the data model. As well, the review will include the definition of standards that will be adhered to for the data attributes. Since information sources have diverse information standards that need to be coalesced into a common information repository, the definition of standards is imperative.

During refinement of the ERD, the data warehouse architect will map the data sources to their respective data warehouse destinations. He or she will also identify information that may be required in the data warehouse that is not currently available in the operational sources and must be derived from other information sources.

At this point, we can now start to integrate some aggregation and focused dimensional modeling into the ERD. This design consideration will be based on the high-level business intelligence requirements that were captured and compiled within the project analysis and planning phase.

At the conclusion of the mid-level design, we will once again present the results to the user community. This will ensure that the business requirements are being met by the design. At this point we will also encourage feedback on the direction the data warehouse is taking. It is imperative that we continue to inform and discuss the data warehouse design with the parties involved to ensure that we are building a warehouse that meets the users needs. Figure 5-4 shows a mid-level design diagram.

Figure 5-4 documents the results of the mid-level design. As you can see, the dimensions and facts now have a number of attributes. These attributes are developed based upon user input, reporting requirements, and operational data sources. This model is moving us closer to the physical model that we will need to then implement the data warehouse.

NOTE

The mid-level design is concerned with structure and completeness. This level ensures that all the data elements required by your business warehousing needs are now included in the model. We are less concerned with how and where the data will come from, and more interested in satisfying information requirements.

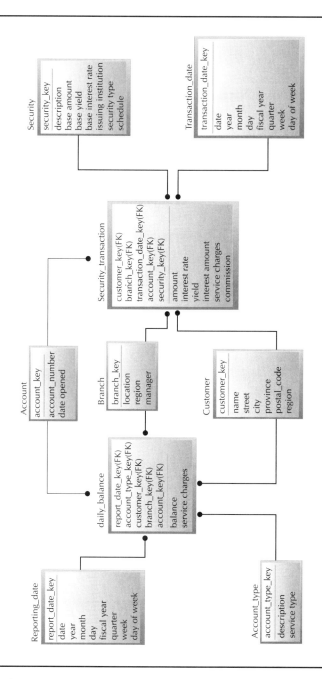

FIGURE 5-4. *Mid-level design diagram*

Low-level Design

This phase of the project focuses on creating the physical database design and the processes required for creating and populating the data warehouse. Based on the results of previous project phases and feedback acquired during each phase review, the physical data model will now be completed. The model will include all entities, relationships, attributes, and attribute definitions. The model will identify all data sources for each attribute and the extraction and construction methods for information that is being transformed from its original format or derived from other sources.

The processes required to load and transform the data from the operational data sources will be defined. The process definitions will identify the source and target hardware platforms, the methods for transmitting data across the network, the data loading methods, the data cleansing methods, and data transformation methods and techniques.

We will then create an implementation plan that will address and schedule the implementation and development of the system. This will be the final checkpoint before full development commences. The database design will be completed, the storage requirements defined, the data growth predicted, the hardware configured, and user approvals obtained. The implementation plan will describe the system in its entirety, documenting all data, interfaces, and methods that will be used to create the physical data warehouse solution. This plan will serve as the baseline for the development phase of the project.

A complete review of the database, the data interfaces and the planning will be carried out at the end of this phase to ensure that the users understand the system that they have helped to design. Any changes that are required will be incorporated before development is initiated, thus maximizing the development team's productivity. With our data warehouse design, we are now ready to move forward into the development and deployment of the data warehouse.

Speaking of deployment, let's move on to discussing data marts. In the first version of this work, we struggled over calling them "datamarts" or "data marts." Now that we have come to a unanimous decision that they are "data marts," we feel we have been able to gain a consensus among the four of us. Hopefully this will inspire the players in the potential warehouse vs. data mart struggle to reach a quick agreement as well. After all, life is a series of concessions—being willing to listen to others when they make sense, and being willing to listen to others when they don't.

CHAPTER
6

Data Marts

his chapter is dedicated to data marts—the dimensional solution that holds the information key to the decision-making process. Unlike the enterprise data warehouse, the data mart supports specific processes in segments of a corporate suite of decision support systems; however, by linking data marts we can achieve a detailed view of our business and find trends that may have been previously unknown.

We first defined a *data mart* as a subject-oriented business view of the warehouse. It contains significantly smaller amounts of data than the warehouse and it is the object of analytical processing by the end user. In a corporate data warehouse solutions environment, there may be marts set up for pockets of the company, such as sales, manufacturing, and billing. Data marts enable pockets of a company's organization to make better-informed and more accurate strategic business decisions. Data marts commonly are less expensive and much smaller than a full-blown corporate-wide data warehouse. Organizations that intelligently implement a number of data marts find it provides their users with a quick introduction to warehousing. By allowing users to use and understand the power provided to them by the data mart, they can then embark on a more complete corporate warehouse. As the corporate enterprise data warehouse is built, the user community always has access to their own data marts, which evolve over time. The old saying of "If you build it, they will come," is very true during data warehouse development—by having users better understand the analyses that they can perform on their data, the more complete the warehouse will evolve into. So, get your users involved in a data mart initiative, building toward the enterprise data warehouse.

The current industry trend is to build the enterprise data warehouse with an "architected solution approach," which means to build each data mart taking into account corporate information issues. As a result, we create the true customer list at the true atomic level; thus, as more marts come online, their dimensions are consistent and reusable, and the mart is more easily modified over time. The atomic level of data—the data staging area—makes it possible to join across marts, and your collection of marts become the enterprise data warehouse—never evolving and no single mass project is ever embarked on.

Classic operational systems concentrate on high-level requirements that cater to the needs of all the users. When the global system is ready, the lower-level detailed needs of segments of the user community are met. This type of implementation is called *top-down*. A common example of top-down development is a financial management application. Specific modules are planned to deal with transactions as they move through the life cycle from budgets to expenditures. All the needs of all the users are attended to and the final product is delivered according to the Big Bang theory of system development. Data marts are usually developed in the opposite way, which is called *bottom-up*. The specific needs of small focused locations within a business are addressed using the bottom-up approach.

Trade-offs is an interesting word when you think of designing data marts. Visions of a multiterabyte (a terabyte is 1,024 gigabytes) warehouse conjures up scenarios where end-user queries take forever to complete and cause endless frustration in the community. Because the data mart can check in at a fraction of the size of the enterprise data warehouse, analysts, development staff, and users may feel this is definitely the way to go based on size and size alone. This approach may be an easy sell to management in the short term, but, as all our experience has shown, it is not the way to proceed. Granted, current and future hardware acquisitions may be driven by the plans for data mart/warehouse rollout, but the business needs of your organization's decision makers outweigh all other factors. The data mart is developed using the Dimensional Modeling methodology as discussed in Chapter 5, "Data Warehouse Design," but focuses on only a single business process.

Data Marts

Data mart—this word evokes visions of a 24-hour convenience store with specific goods that are tailored to meet consumer needs. In the data mart, you could not be closer to the truth. The specialty item is data—data designed to solve the business requirements of a pocket of corporate data warehouse users. Data marts are subject-oriented dimensional databases with a normal life expectancy of three years. Unlike the enterprise data warehouse, they can check in with a figure under $250,000. Most data marts ring in at 25 gigabytes and support a user community between 10 and 25 users.

Vendors of tools that build, and then manage, data marts must provide a cost-effective rapid solution that can be used on any sized project. The results of the build effort must be made available to the user community in a timely fashion. *Timely fashion* means a time to market of two to four months. Prospective users of corporate data marts can easily lose interest when turnaround times are longer. Data mart software must leverage existing operational and other DSS repositories during their build phases. Providers of technology must be able to read data directly from a suite of legacy systems implemented on IBM mainframe servers using products such as IMS and DB2, as well as newer systems such as SAP and Peoplesoft running on UNIX servers. Data can be extracted directly from these systems using COBOL modules, and the results moved into the data mart from flat files.

The model of the data mart is driven by the ways the user needs to view and use the information. Rather than paying so much attention to the physical layout of the data, the data mart model reflects what the users want to be able to do and how they wish to have it presented. Data mart implementers interview the users and, with their input and the knowledge the implementers have about the technology, design a model that is ideally suited to the users' requirements. This is an iterative process, which sometimes goes on for the life of the data mart. An *iterative process* is one that is repeated, but this does not mean the iteration is repeated because its previous execution was flawed. An iterative process is simply executed over and over again usually in response to changing corporate uses of the data. Grocery shopping or paying the phone bill, are parts of everyday life that are iterative processes.

Stand-alone Data Marts

Pockets of some organizations have beaten a trail on their own to the data mart solution. Sometimes, in a largely decentralized company, segments of the business community have funded, developed, and deployed the data mart solution virtually without the involvement of the personnel tasked with the management of computer system solutions. These are known as *stand-alone data marts*. As the 1990s come to a close, and with the parallel-capable hardware and software products in the marketplace, these stand-alone data marts are difficult if not impossible to integrate into a larger corporate data mart or data warehouse initiative. Too many discrepancies exist between different stand-alone data marts in the way the data is structured and how the data is encoded. It is virtually impossible to merge these data marts' contents when looking for ways to share data between the corporate segments of an organization. As with data that comes from many data sources, the coalescing of the information can be difficult. The lessons that we learn from the building of data warehouses should be used when designing data marts—the data marts must form consistent views of our business. Data marts should not be built in isolation, and organizations must develop an overall data mart strategy that incorporates all lines with the business.

Many data marts are a *subset* of a large data warehouse's information, centrally designed, built, maintained, and distributed to groups of DSS users throughout a company. Today, the thrust is towards centralized management. This reduces the administrative redundancies inherent in a decentralized model. Companies are building data marts that feed on a combination of larger operational and decision support data sources. These data marts incorporate a company-wide approach to delivery of decision support systems; this is only possible in businesses that are committed to deploying systems from a central point under the auspices and supervision of a company-wide systems development and deployment group. The types of processes that lend themselves very well to data mart development include sales, purchasing, customer service processes, logistics, and manufacturing. The model shown in Figure 6-1 demonstrates how a process, such as Pay-TV Orders can form a data mart using a star schema. The data mart is a simple one, yet you can already realize the types of queries you could write, even with what at first glance appears to be a simple model.

Data marts often share information portions within the organization and an overall data mart strategy. In the banking industry, many business processes share the account dimension. These processes will include bank balances, loans, credit cards, and marketing. The account is a common concept in almost all areas of the bank's business. By creating an account dimension and then sharing this dimension among the data marts, we allow the bank to form a common view of their account holders within many business focus areas. The idea of shared dimensions has been called "conformed dimensions" by Ralph Kimball. Dr. Kimball says that through the sharing of information contained in these conformed dimensions, we can join information together in what would have been independent data marts. This idea is critical to allow data marts to exceed the information limitations that a stand-alone data mart provides. With conformed data marts, you can now analyze your data across data marts. Remember that the granularity of your data marts must be the same for this analysis to be useful. The diagram

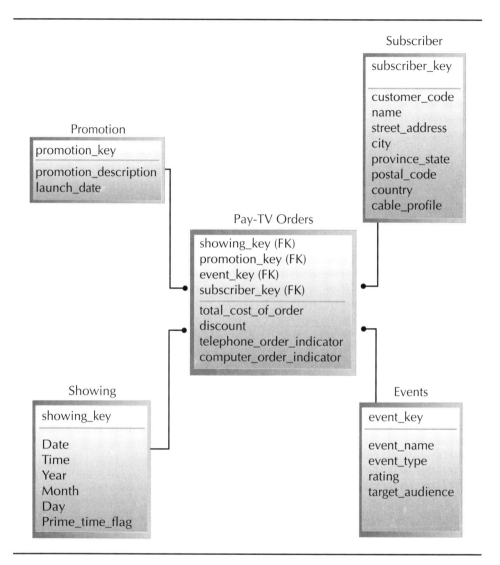

FIGURE 6-1. *Pay-TV data mart*

in Figure 6-2 shows how our original data mart of Pay-TV Orders can be related to a customer product transaction data mart. Through the subscriber dimension we perform analysis, such as how many customers with a particular cable service have ordered Pay-TV family-rated movies.

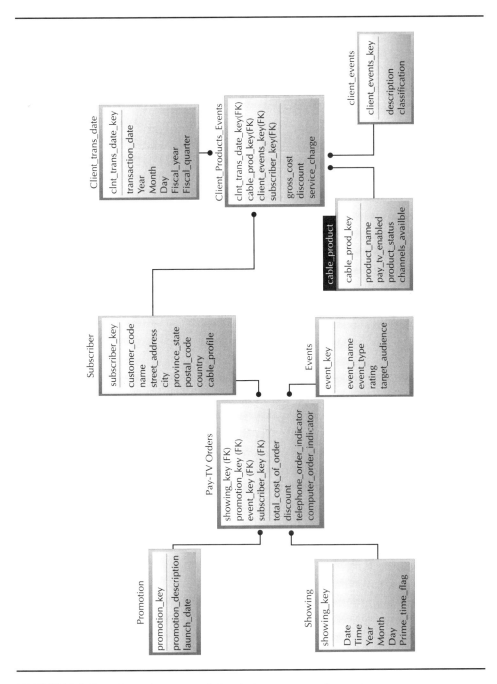

FIGURE 6-2. *Two data marts joined via common dimensions*

Dimensional Database

Data marts are dimensional. A *dimensional* database allows for decision support queries using a wide range of criteria combinations, so many queries using the data in a data mart are ad hoc. An *ad hoc query* is one whose selection criteria are chosen by the user as the query is formulated. Many queries against operational systems are canned or preprogrammed. A *canned query* is one set up to run at the user's request and to bring back data in a predetermined format; they always access the same tables. That is why it is so important to design your data mart with query efficiency in mind. The star schema provides a high degree of performance and the simplicity that power users and occasional DSS users require. As we have already discussed, the star schema is a simplistic approach to database and data warehouse design. The schema developed for a data mart appears simple to navigate to users; its power is also based in this simplicity. By creating the data mart with query in mind, we provide ad hoc users with a schema that is simple to navigate and that is tuned specifically for query performance.

NOTE
It has been shown that 90 percent of all queries are driven by canned queries in a data warehouse environment, with only 10 percent being ad hoc queries.

The data mart must support *n*-way queries with a network of indexes constructed in such a way that the operator can use an OLAP tool and:

■ Report on the information in one table in the data mart using any column as a selection criterion.

■ Assemble data from two or more tables in the data mart, joining the objects using foreign key relationships; one query may join tables X, Y, and Z, and the next minute, the same user could join A, B, and C in a way that may never happen again.

The data mart serves as a foundation for online analytical processing (OLAP) in a decision support system. As a result, the DSS architect listens to the users and collects information on factors, such as:

■ What do they wish to glean from the data mart?

■ How do they want that information presented?

■ What level of summary (granularity) do they want?

■ What tables will be commonly joined together in OLAP query processing?

Armed with the answers to these questions, the analyst begins the data mart design process and arrives at a physical model that will suit the needs of the most important commodity in the entire process—the *user*.

Dimensions Affect Design

Dimensions together with facts form the basis of the star schema. The star schema is the basic unit of design in the data mart. Please refer to Chapter 5 for a more complete discussion of star schemas. Designing the data mart utilizing dimensional modeling will enable you to maximize the effectiveness of the data mart. Often after a mart has been used for a period of time, new information is identified by users. When the original design of the data mart was developed, it was created by defining the business process and the dimensions and facts to support this requirement. Each dimension in a data mart requires storage of another column in the central fact table. So, when designing the data mart, we try and predict all the types of uses for that data mart. The initial design will address the dimensions and the facts that will satisfy the analytical processing requirements of the data mart (i.e., its raison d'être). However, there are times when you discover that a new dimension is required in the mart. A careful review of this addition must be done, since we will be changing the fact table in our star schema. Your review must include the following details:

■ Define the new dimension requirement (e.g. product, promotion, salesperson).

■ Is this a new data requirement or can we add additional attributes to an existing dimension.

■ If this can be satisfied by new attributes, the impact is that we need to add the new attributes to an existing dimension.

■ If this requires a new dimension, we must design the new dimension by defining the new table. This will include the primary key and all attributes for the new dimension.

■ How will the dimension be incorporated into the fact table? We must define how we will rebuild the data contained in the fact table, since the dimension will form a new part of the primary key.

■ Define how historical data will be reconciled with the dimension.

■ Define the impact to the loading, extraction, and population routines currently involved in the data mart.

■ Develop a plan for implementing the new dimension.

■ Implement the new dimension.

As you can see from this list, the impact of what may be considered a simple dimension to an existing data mart or data warehouse is no small exercise. Your analysis may show you that the current operational system does not allow us to rebuild the existing data, so you may be required to deploy a new data mart to satisfy this new requirement. Remember that your data warehouse is only as good as your operational data sources and the historical data that they contain. Figure 6-3 shows the star schema with a new dimension and attribute.

Drill-down Requirements Impact Design

As data is moved into the data mart, it usually undergoes some form of summarization. The statement, "The company grossed $26 million last year" does not mean much to the DSS user. When users are presented with this information, they inevitably want to get at the underlying information that rolls up to the multimillion-dollar figure. This process of digging deeper into

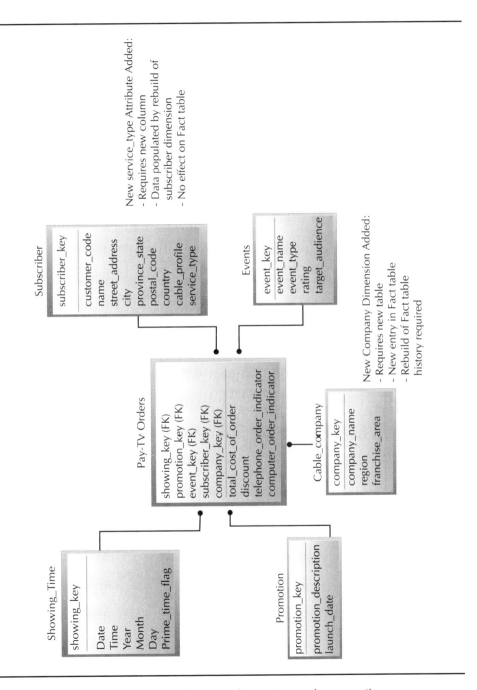

FIGURE 6-3. *Star schema with a new dimension and new attribute*

data is referred to as *drill-down*. The data mart implementation team has the responsibility to decide the following:

1. What level of drill-down does the data mart user wish to have available?

2. Based on the answer to the first question, what information will be stored in the data mart and what information will be derived at run time?

Table 6-1 illustrates how complex drill-down can get for a sales data mart.

Country	Continent	Region	State/Province	City
USA	North America	East	Florida	Miami Orlando Tampa
			New York	New York Albany Lake Placid
		West	California	San Francisco Los Angeles San Diego
		Central	Michigan	Detroit Ann Arbor Sault Ste. Marie
Canada		East	Nova Scotia	Halifax Yarmouth Hebron

TABLE 6-1. *Sales Data Mart Drill-down Example*

Country	Continent	Region	State/Province	City
			Quebec	Montreal
				Sherbrooke
				Sainte Agathe
		Central	Ontario	Ottawa
				Nepean
				Toronto
				Hamilton
UK	Europe	Central	London	London
				Ealing
				Brentford
		Northern	Yorkshire	Birmingham

TABLE 6-1. *Sales Data Mart Drill-down Example* (continued)

Design decisions impact the performance of queries against the data mart. As we can see, a simple dimension such as a location dimension can break down into many combinations that allows for a strong ability to analyze your data from many different directions. From the data shown in Table 6-1, Table 6-2 illustrates the types of analysis that can be performed.

As you can see, the types of analysis and the number of ways that you can slice and dice the data provide for a great deal of flexibility. The data mart may store summary data at the city level and roll up to the continental level as a query is processed. A point exists where the drill-down capability stops. When first contemplating where to stop the process, the DSS analyst needs to converse with the user of the data mart and ascertain when the loss of detail does not affect the ability to make informed decisions. In the design illustrated in Table 6-1, once the user has drilled down to the city level, there is nowhere else to go.

Type of Analysis	Columns to Satisfy Requirement
Sales for the entire organization	Summary of all data in data mart
Sales by country	Summarize by country
Sales in North America by region	Summarize by continent and region

TABLE 6-2. *Types of Analysis on Sales Data Mart*

Queries Against the Data Mart

Query criteria can be lumped together into four main categories:

1. Inclusion operations, where data is selected based on its passing one or more comparisons. This includes the three mechanisms shown in bold in the following listing:

```
-- Equality
select amt
  from dw_fin
 where acc_num = '555199';
-- Equality within a set
select sum(bal)
  from dw_fin
 where acc_num in ('555199','555210');
-- Bounded range
select sum(amt)
  from dw_fin
 where acc_num between '231999' and '556112';
```

2. Exclusion operations, where data is eliminated based on its not conforming to one or more comparisons. This operation usually uses some form of negation construct. These are shown in bold in the next listing:

```
-- Not equal
select sum(amt)
  from dw_fin
```

```
 where acc_num <> '555199';
-- Not in a set
select sum(bal)
  from dw_fin
 where acc_num not in ('555199','555210');
-- Not within a bounded range
select sum(amt)
  from dw_fin
 where acc_num not between '231999' and '556112';
```

3. A combination of inclusion and exclusion operations, where some data is eliminated and qualifying data become part of the result set. The following listing illustrates this type of query:

```
select sum(bal)
  from dw_fin
 where acc_num <> '552123'
   and acc_num between '550992' and '568903';
```

4. Arithmetic functions, such as MIN, MAX, or AVG, where a function is applied to numeric fields in the query, coupled with any combination of inclusion and exclusion operations. Usually, character fields are either left as is or become the sources of grouping operations. Examine the following two SQL statements for examples of this type of query selection criteria:

```
select sum(bal)
  from dw_fin
 where substr(acc_num,1,3) <> '555'
   and to_char(trans_date,'Mon') = 'Feb';
select count(*)
  from dw_fin
 where avg(tran_amt) < 1000
   and to_char(trans_date,'Mon') in ('Feb','Mar');
```

The data mart is heavily indexed, with the anticipation that the users will base query results on large amounts of data using a wide range of selection criteria. Chapter 20 offers some guidelines of what columns to index in the data warehouse.

Sum of This, Sum of That

Aggregates play a vital role in the decision support data mart. *Aggregation* is a process whereby multiple detail records are combined into a single data mart record. The numeric data stored in each aggregate record represents the sum of the corresponding fields from all the operational records it summarizes. The rows in a data mart can be thought of as a slice of operational data, with an added dimension involving time and a level of summarization. Data is no longer atomic, where each row contains information related to one and only one transaction. In Chapter 5, we discussed granularity and how highly granular data equate to highly summarized—that is, low-detail data—and vice versa. As data is brought into the data mart, the analyst decides with what level of granularity to begin. The **sql sum** function accomplishes the aggregation operation, coupled with the **group by** statement as the data is moved into the data mart. Additional types of aggregation are identified once the end users start to work with the data marts.

Data Warehouse Vs. Data Mart

One of many intriguing factors about data warehousing in general, and data marts in particular, reminds us of the saying, "You can't see the forest for the trees." In this context, this familiar metaphor illustrates how data mart data can reveal remarkable similarities among previously unrelated data. The trees are represented by the seemingly isolated occurrences of data, and the forest is the total set of data, which has previously unforeseen similarities. Just remember that although you can find a correlation between two previously unrelated facts, this does not mean that the facts are related. You may find that the sales in your organization are affected by the season, but the relationship between the ambient room temperature and the sale of gum may not be a true relationship. So, when relating two or more factors in a DSS system, remember that you may be able to relate apparently unrelated attributes and come to a conclusion. However, this conclusion may be coincidental, so care must be taken in defining the types of analysis you plan to perform.

The data mart is the target of a number of data warehouse steps; it is where the DSS end user will spend most of the day. The sheer size of an enterprise data warehouse can make some decision support tools balk. Also, the navigation of the enterprise data warehouse may be difficult, which may intimidate a certain portion of your users. The smaller data mart, containing less data, is set up to optimize the analyst's access to information. Many vendors exist who market data mart software that is designed to help complete the journey that data make out of operational systems into the warehouse environment. Figure 6-4 shows the major components in this journey.

Some data mart providers read operational system data dictionaries, make sense out of the relationships, wade through the inherent complexities, and provide the analyst with choices on how the data can be loaded into the data mart. Assistance with this time-consuming activity is fundamental to a mature data mart solution provider.

An interesting benefit of sinking time and money into developing data marts is they can cost a fraction of the money needed to implement a full-blown enterprise data warehouse. Analysis dollars are eaten up quickly when companies embark on a project, insisting that the be-all, end-all warehouse is the only acceptable output. Experience has shown that

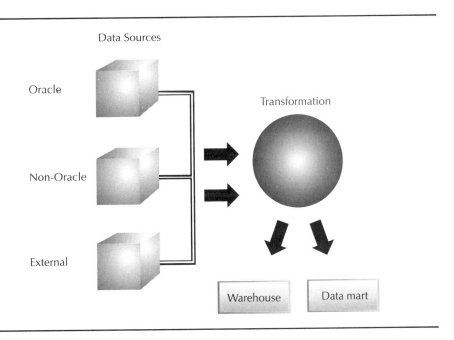

FIGURE 6-4.   *The incredible journey*

warehouse development checks in with a three to five million dollar price tag and up to three years for delivery. Figures like these are within the grasp of large corporations, but data marts help provide solutions for smaller businesses as well as focused segments of a company's decision makers. The enterprise data warehouse may be a longer-term goal for some smaller companies but, as previously mentioned in this chapter, data marts are rapid development outputs that implement a bottom-up approach. They get the information required for smart business decisions out to the consumer in shorter time periods.

Data marts are the new breed of data warehouse solutions. Being bottom-up, they are driven by consumers in cooperation with a team of information technology (IT) experts. Many enterprise data warehouse projects have floundered, just as many of their operational system predecessors have. Companies end up biting off more than they can chew; the initiative comes in way over budget, coughs, and dies. This is a reality of data warehousing; they are often developed, and when they are finally launched to the user community, they do not meet the user's information needs. This could be a result of changes in requirements during the long time needed for development. Data marts address this concern directly by ensuring that users are involved from the inception of a data mart project. The users drive the process, since they are the business users and the owners of the data. However, remember, as we previously stated, data marts need to be built with the enterprise in mind as well. Stand-alone data marts do not play nice with the other data marts which can lead to difficult and costly integration efforts.

Recently a number of sophisticated tools have been developed to access the data mart. Previously, data warehouse projects made use of a hodgepodge of 3GL and 4GL tools. *3GL* refers to the family of computer languages (or generation of languages) such as C, COBOL, Pascal, and PL/1. *4GL* refers to a later breed of languages such as PL/SQL used in tools such as Developer/2000 and PowerBuilder. Data warehouse teams were tasked with building their own management mechanisms, and could be said to be "reinventing the wheel" with every step (just as was said of their operational system counterparts). How many times have organizations decided to develop their own custom solution, only to realize in several years that they should have purchased commercial off-the-shelf (COTS) software? In the late 1980s, we were looking at some COTS for a client to solve their financial management requirements. Now, in 1998, they are still kicking themselves for doing their own solution, which is riddled with unnecessary complexities. As we will discuss, these tools for managing and populating your warehouse are reaching a level that allows data warehouse and data mart designers to leverage them during their implementation process.

The data warehouse industry is exploding, especially in the area of managing data marts. A next-generation set of tools is so data warehouse sensitive that it automates collection of metadata as the project progresses. *Metadata* is data about data; it describes what type of data is stored where in the warehouse, and it leads you through the network of relationships that exist within the data.

Referential Integrity

Referential integrity (RI) plays a big role in the data mart and the data warehouse. RI is a mechanism used in relational databases to enforce relationships between data in different tables. RI also enforces business rules, such as:

- No building address may be entered into the client address table until the street on which that building resides has been recorded.

- No part number may be recorded in inventory until the manufacturer of the part has been recorded.

- No small business may use the quick method for filing the goods and services tax until it has received notification from Revenue Canada Taxation.

Star schema was first discussed in Chapter 5. This special schema takes advantage of Oracle's referential integrity mechanisms for the optimizer to correctly plan its execution path. The data mart builders pay special attention to this schema because it provides the optimal access to data in many data marts or full-blown data warehouse repositories. For the schema to be set up, you must define primary and foreign keys in the Oracle source data before the schema can be designed and implemented. Let's discuss setting up primary and foreign keys in your data mart.

Primary Keys

You have probably heard of primary keys, but many developers and administrators have little or no experience with how they are defined in Oracle. A *primary key* is one field or a combination of fields in a table that can uniquely identify each row in that table. The SQL to set up a primary key can be done when a table is created, as shown in the next listing:

```
create table dw_finsumm
(dwf_id number constraint dwf_pk primary key, …
```

or after a table is created, using the *alter table* construct:

```
alter table dw_finsumm add constraint dwf_pk primary key (dwf_id);
```

Oracle creates a unique index on the combination of one or more columns defined as the primary key. Some additional specifications can be used when creating primary key constraints; these are documented in the *Oracle8 Server Administrator's Guide,* as well as in the *SQL Language Reference Manual.*

Foreign Keys

When a column has been defined as a primary key in one table and is included in a different table, that column is called a *foreign key*. Note that foreign key columns can only reference columns in other tables that have already been defined as part of that table's primary key. The syntax for defining a foreign key is

```
alter table dw_finsumm add constraint dw_acc_fk
      foreign key (acc) references account;
```

To put it another way, a foreign key is the primary key from one table stored in another table. In the relational database model, foreign keys define relationships between common columns in different tables. Figure 6-5 shows two relationships based on foreign keys.

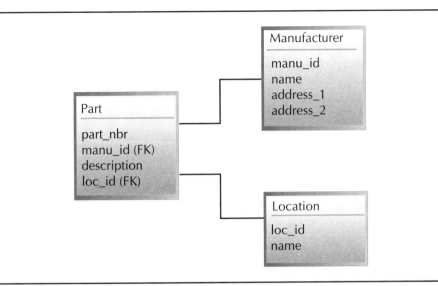

FIGURE 6-5.   *Foreign key relationships*

TIP
The SQL statements shown for setting up primary and foreign keys are the tip of the iceberg on a large topic, which you should study before setting up a system of RI in a data mart or data warehouse.

Once primary and foreign keys are defined, the DSS architect can begin to map the tables in the data mart, leveraging the existence of primary and foreign keys as the way data are related to one another.

Best-of-Breed Data Mart Tools

With the onslaught of data mart solutions providers, consumers are looking for the following before deciding which set of tools is for them:

1. Consumers want a cost-effective toolset that can deliver solutions in less than six months, with a price tag of less than $250,000.

2. Consumers want a toolset that is an example of "one-stop shopping." Consumers insist that whatever vendor they do business with must bundle the core data mart functions into a single engine. These functions are discussed in the following section.

3. Consumers want a tool that can facilitate rapid inclusion of existing metadata, which already resides in operational systems.

4. Consumers want a toolset that can take advantage of the gains in parallel processing facilitated by multi-CPU computers, which serve as the host for many large data warehouse and data mart implementations.

5. Consumers want a tool that can grow to be used in an enterprise DWH.

Core Data Mart Tool Functions

Consumers are looking for a set of core modules when evaluating vendors whose products provide a data mart solution to the marketplace. The next few sections cover some of these core modules.

Extraction

Data mart software providers must play a role in facilitating this extraction process. *Extraction* is closely related to transformation because data representation can be so radically different in unrelated systems that serve as source data for the data mart. The simplest way to move data into the data mart is to use the standard SQL **insert** statement. For some small data marts, you may be able to get away with SQL because of very low volumes, but a loading tool that can also do bulk loads is far more valuable and flexible. Disabling the generation of redo information while moving data into the warehouse will be discussed in Chapter 8. The source of the data mart data must be a database management system that can be read using standard SQL commands.

Transformation

Transformation ensures that as data is moved into the data mart, it conforms to a standard system of codes and abbreviations. Decisions are made on which way to indicate code fields and which descriptions to use if the code data is extracted from tables in different systems that use the same code but use a different method of representation. Many transformations can be handled by straight SQL functions and operations, but some data mart vendors have decided to complement the SQL functionality with their own proprietary mechanisms. We find that we are often required to program very complex transformation with a variety of tools to meet the requirements of the data mart. Tools from suppliers such as Sagent, Vmark, and Informatica are used to complement transformation requirements. These tools usually have proprietary languages that are used to program complex transformation rules. Remember that you will spend most of your development time creating your data transforms. It is not a small or a simple task, so plan this step wisely and evaluate the various programmatic alternatives available to you.

Load

Moving the data into the Oracle repository can be a challenge. As the size of your data mart increases, the problem's complexity is magnified. Chapter 8 will speak about moving data between other Oracle systems using export and import and other systems using SQL *Loader or the Oracle Transparent Gateways, as well as a handful of third-party products. Adopters of data mart tools are looking for assistance with this load process. They want the ability to schedule loads, and to specify what data should be replaced, and where the data resides in the data mart.

When loading data into the Oracle data mart, the data can be put directly into the target tables or moved into intermediary tables; then, the data can be further processed as they are moved into the actual target tables. Using a set of intermediary tables can be the most efficient way to load information into the data mart. The structure of the intermediary tables is often radically different from the target tables. Many of the current generation of loading and transformation tools create these tables as part of their implementation strategy; these tools then manage these tables.

TIP
If you do use this technique, remember to delete the data from the intermediary tables when you are done with them. To avoid generating redo when these tables are wiped, use the Oracle **truncate table** *construct rather than a* **delete** *method.*

TIP
Another possibility is that these intermediary tables stay in existence and become your atomic level, so that it keeps a historically correct data layer that can be used to rebuild or change your data marts.

A data mart tool must be able to leverage the parallel processing power of many high-end processors because so many loads involve vast amounts of data. A *high-end machine* is one that has the strong processing power coupled with fast parallel I/O operations. Machines with more than one processor (referred to as MPP or SMP, depending on how they are configured) are ideal candidates for housing the data mart and warehouse.

Data Mart or Data Warehouse

Should we build a data warehouse or a data mart? This question has been asked many times, and it has many different answers. Often, those two words that serve as a catch answer to many difficult questions creep up in response to this query: *good question.* Our experience has shown you should not begin a turf war—the "must be a data warehouse" on one side and the "must build a data mart" on the other side. We like to use the term "datahouse" or "waremart." In other words, it does not matter what you build, but decide now and do it, or create an enterprise warehouse over time from an architected set of marts with a common atomic layer. We have developed a set of questions to ask customers when they are seeking guidance on making this hard decision. This is actually a score sheet. As indicated in the right column of Table 6-3, mark "1" for each YES and "0" for each NO (except in questions 7 and 10, as noted). Tally up your score; then we will discuss the outcome.

So, how did you do? Tally your score. If you got 10, you are definitely data warehouse bound. If you scored 0, you are definitely data mart bound. A tally between 2 and 6 indicates that the data mart way is the best way to proceed. A tally between 7 and 10 suggests data warehouse. If you threw your hands into the air, waffling about some yes and no answers, if you

	Question	**YES = 1** **NO = 0**
1.	Is your business able to commit to a multimillion-dollar project that will span many fiscal years?	
2.	Are your business units selling or servicing customers who fall into similar profiles?	
3.	Do management personnel in the business units normally agree on data definitions of your business commodities?	
4.	Are your corporate decision makers capable of sitting and waiting for their turn, or do they have a "me first" attitude?	
5.	Is your organization centralized?	
6.	Is there a consensus on the amount of historical data that your organization needs to maintain?	
7.	Are there certain business areas that are much more interested in starting a focused DSS initiative? (YES = 0 and NO = 1)	
8.	Does your organization have the hardware in place to support a very large data warehouse?	
9.	Do the decision makers agree on the level of summarization that they need to make decisions?	
10.	Are there any data marts currently in use in the organization? (YES = 0 and NO = 1)	

TABLE 6-3.   *Data Mart Vs. Data Warehouse Checklist*

have more yay's than nay's—data warehouse; if you have more nay's than yay's—data mart. Also, review how you answered certain questions. For example, if your business users are not dedicated to developing a data warehouse or a data mart, you must first get them involved for any initiative. If you find that there is an individual or group of individuals within your organization that have read the magazines and believe the gospel of the data warehousing singers, then a focused data mart for this group may provide the best payoff. This group will be motivated to work with you to develop their data mart solution. This group can then be used as a strategic vehicle to educate the rest of your organization on the power of a data mart and data warehouse. Sometimes, until the users can look at it and touch it, they cannot see the benefit. Providing a concrete solution and a review of how the data mart has been leveraged by the group can help to launch an enterprise warehouse project. Data marts are often used to provide companies with a proof of concept when they are first embarking into the data warehouse world.

Key to the successful building and deployment of data marts is the users' ability to understand what data it contains and how the objects are related to one another. Integrating data marts within the data warehouse allows users to more quickly grasp the benefits of data warehousing. These data marts can be used to leverage and market your overall data warehousing strategy.

The data mart is focused on providing a solution to a business process while providing high-powered analysis support. It primarily deals with satisfying a single business process. It is a more inexpensive alternative to an enterprise data warehouse. Finally, it can serve as a vehicle for an organization to launch a full data warehousing strategy. Although they may appear to be small, the data mart is anything but small when it comes to delivering strategic power within your organization. We think it would be good to point out that the warehouse project does not have to be a data mart or a warehouse with no middle ground. A process for going from an initial data mart strategy to an eventual warehouse is a key competitive strategy for many large and small organizations during the construction of a data warehouse and data marts.

You are now leaving the data mart…ensure the checkout person looks under the cart for some of the bulkier items. You also may want to keep a close eye on the prices being rung up on the cash register. There have been known to be glitches in the bar code to price programming in some large data marts. Pay attention to the sign at checkout #6—"Data warehouse solutions ONLY!". The next chapter looks at the Oracle8 specifics with setting up the data warehouse. Much of the material covered throughout this book is theoretical and, regardless of the database of choice, offers suggestions of what to accomplish when. Chapter 7 starts to marry a great deal of the theory to the Oracle8 Server, introducing some jargon specific to Oracle's solution.

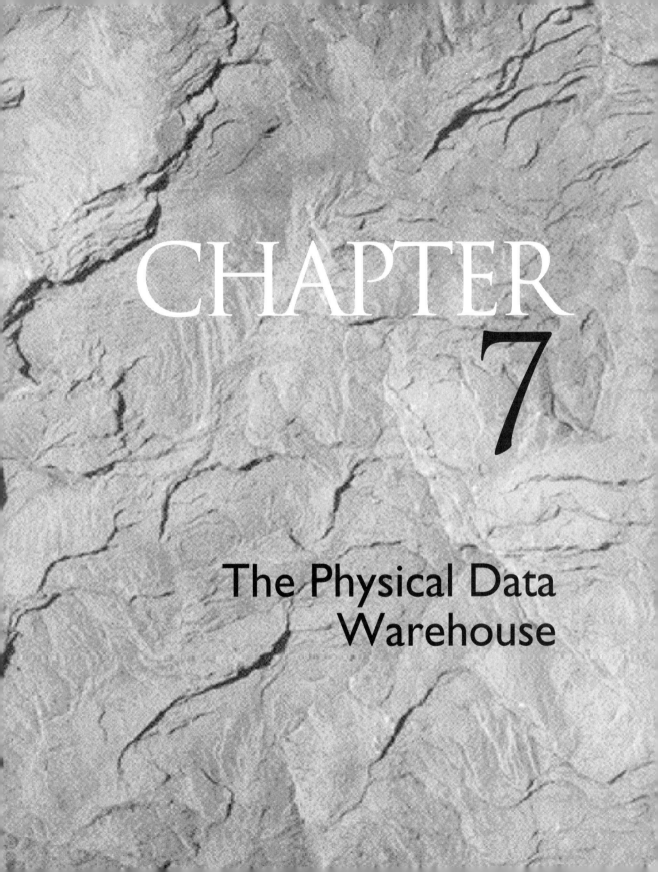

CHAPTER
7

The Physical Data Warehouse

t seems that the typical data warehouse checks in at a size substantially larger than the databases we support underneath our operational systems. This chapter looks at setting up the data warehouse using the Oracle8 Server as its repository—that is the physical layout of the warehouse. We'll take some of the material we discussed in Chapter 5 and translate it into a living/breathing Oracle8 set of tables. Some of the material is aimed at technical administrators, but the ideas presented will assist all readers when asked to participate at some level in setting up the physical data warehouse. Many readers have managed large databases over varying periods of time. This chapter will look at some additional issues that come up in a DSS repository, related to issues such as warehouse population, managing historical data, and optimal placement of database files to support the warehouse. Let's start out by looking at the very large database (VLDB), then start discussing setup issues for these large information repositories.

The VLDB

VLDB—four letters one hears everywhere in one's travels around the Oracle technical community. The classification of a very large database usually starts based on size. People speak of managing a 30 gigabyte (3,072 megabytes or 32,212,254,720 bytes), calling it a VLDB, then other people turn around and say they manage a 10 terabyte database (10,995,116,277,760 bytes) and the 30 gigabyte is not a true VLDB. Our definition for a VLDB is a lot simpler, and is applied regardless of the size of your database.

Window of Opportunity

This *window of opportunity* is the amount of time in a 24-hour period that the database is quiet within which it can be backed up. With high-speed tape drives, many installations need a window of only a few hours (if that) to copy their database to tape nightly. As the size of the database increases, many sites require more time to write these backups. Now that most tape hardware and software technology copies files at speeds well in excess of dozens of gigabytes per hour, many multigigabyte databases can be backed up in a window of opportunity of less than two hours. Simply put, one way we define a *very large database* is one that cannot be backed up to tape in its entirety during the nightly window of opportunity.

Based on that definition, if one needs 2½ hours to copy an Oracle8 database to tape and the window is only 1½ hours, that person is managing a VLDB regardless of the total database size. The layout and management techniques that come into play with the VLDB have to be followed for the 100-gigabyte database that cannot be backed up during its window as well as the 900-megabyte database that does not fit into its window.

Based on this discussion, let's look at our definition of a VLDB. A *VLDB* is

■ A database for which a consistent backup cannot be written in a DBA-defined window of opportunity. A *consistent backup* is one that can be used to restore all or part of an Oracle8 database.

■ A database whose size requires it to be broken into smaller, more manageable chunks that permit DBAs to work with portions of the repository at a time.

Care and Feeding of a VLDB

A VLDB must be handled with care. Sometimes it gets a little cranky and does not behave as expected. The same management approach you use with smaller information repositories may not work with a VLDB. The single most effective way to manage the VLDB is by breaking it up into smaller pieces and exercising care when allocating space. We are fortunate, in a way, with the VLDBs we build for data warehouses. Many warehouses are huge the day they come to life, rather than starting as a moderate repository and swelling over a period of a few months into a monster. Let's look at one space management issue and how our habits may have to change to succeed with the VLDB.

Rebuilding a Table in a VLDB

Rebuilding a table in the VLDB can be a difficult task due to the sheer volume of data. Sometimes, the rebuild is to defragment some tables. *Defrag* is the activity of taking unconnected chunks of space allocated to a table and placing all the data in one contiguous space on the disk. With small tables, the defrag exercise is pretty straightforward and simply involves making a copy of the table data using export, dropping the table, then bringing the data back using import. *Export* is an Oracle utility that writes a compressed binary copy of data, readable by the Oracle import program. With objects in the VLDB, it is an entirely different story.

Table 7-1 outlines the parameters under which a very large table defragmentation will be carried out. Before doing the defragmentation, say we decide to use four datafiles to make up the tablespace that holds the rebuilt table, such that each datafile will be 2Gb. In Oracleism, a *tablespace* is simply a collection of one or more physical datafiles that holds the data you store within the database. This will permit the table to grow over the next few months, as is anticipated. The table currently sits in a tablespace made up of eight datafiles.

NOTE
The discussion of defragmenting a large table is deliberately stripped of all the gruesome technical details of the task at hand. The list of steps is intended to give you a high-level overview of what can be a difficult job to be carried out by personnel familiar with the task.

Item	Current	Planned
Extents	108	4
Extent size minimum	30MB	1.5Gb
Extent size maximum	600MB	1.5Gb
Datafiles holding data	8	4

TABLE 7-1. *Before and After Defrag Statistics*

The work, with the Oracle8 database, involves seven steps:

1. **Get the data out of the table**   This is done using the Oracle export utility, instructing the program to just get the data, the definition of the table, and the grants on the table, and nothing else. *Grants* are privileges given out by table owners that allow other users to work with their data.

2. **Get the index definitions for the table**   This is accomplished as well with the export utility. This step requests that an export file be written but asks export not to make a copy of the data. When export runs with no rows, it simply writes the SQL statements required to create the table, indexes, and constraints, as well as any grants on the table.

3. **Get the constraint definitions for the table**   This is done at the same time as the export file is written in step 2.

4. **Preserve the grants on the table**   This is done at the same time as the export file is written in step 1.

5. **Drop and re-create the table**   The table is re-created using a SQL*Plus statement that can be extracted from the export file written in either steps 1 or 2.

6. **Move the data and grants back into the table**   This is done using import, reading the export file created in step 1. Choice of this export file is deliberate, since the one created in step 2 had no data.

7. **Rebuild indexes and implement the network of constraints**   This step is run in SQL*Plus, using a group of SQL statements that can be extracted from the export file written in step 2. Again, the step choice for the export file is crucial. In Chapter 10, specifically the "Disabling Undo for Index Creation" section, we look at ways to optimize this step.

NLS—National Language Support

In the midst of implementing a multinational data warehouse, you need to pay attention to some issues related to the storage and display of extended characters in the Oracle8 database. Some of this must be done on the client, some on the server. Without taking the time to set this up properly right from the start, characters such as "éâæôöòûùÿÖÜ£¥áíóúñÑ¿" will be displayed as "ibftvr{y#%amszqQ?". Better believe it—if Rolf Gröenveld's name is displayed as "Rolf Grvenveld", you will certainly hear about it (not to mention that if it is displayed properly, you won't hear from anyone).

NLS on the Client

When a query or OLAP tool on the client is used to access the warehouse, the Windows setup file must properly reflect the desired character set to display information correctly. On a Windows 3 or Windows NT 3.5 (16-bit) client, the following text will be displayed in the win.ini initialization file to indicate the desired setup:

```
[Oracle]
NLS_LANG=AMERICAN_AMERICA.WE8ISO8859P1
```

On these clients, you may see the text WE8DEC instead of WE8ISO8859P1; this is tantamount to the same setting. On a Windows 95, Windows NT 3.5 (32-bit), or Windows NT 4.0 client, a special Registry entry must be set properly, as shown in Figure 7-1.

TIP

Regardless of the client software, the setting of NLS_LANG is the first place to look when trying to figure out why extended characters are not being displayed properly.

NLS on the Server

This falls onto the shoulders of the database administrator responsible for the setup of the Oracle8 repository. Oracle offers a robust multilingual solution as long as the database is set up right from the start. When an Oracle8

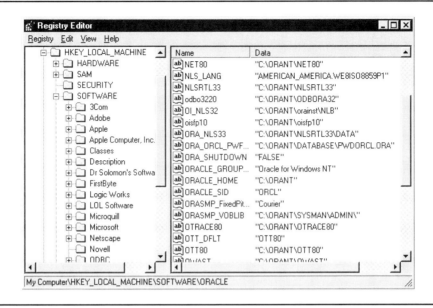

FIGURE 7-1. *Windows NT/95 Registry setting for extended characters*

database is first created, you specify a character set when running the SQL **create database** command. Database creation is done in one of many ways:

1. By answering yes when running the Oracle8 installer program. One of the options permits the installer program to create the starter database. We talk a bit more about this starter database in the "Tablespace Segregation" section later in this chapter. Most seasoned database administrators still have to think twice when selecting a language for the database. The character set of the database is determined based on the language chosen as the installer program commences its work. This dialog is shown in Figure 7-2; notice some of the language choices, including English, Danish, Dutch, German, and Greek.

NOTE
English is usually the default language displayed, and most installations can successfully store and display extended characters using this selection. If you ever want to install another language, return to this screen and reinstall the product.

2. By selecting a character set from the dialog box displayed by the Database Assistant, one of many programs delivered with the Oracle8 Server for Windows NT. The Database Assistant icon sits in the Oracle8 for Windows NT folder. Figure 7-3 shows the screen where the character set of choice is selected. Notice the wealth of character sets available; the message files for each contain characters such as variants of Chinese (CH), Japanese (JA), or Russian (RU), or any of the characters shown in the figure.

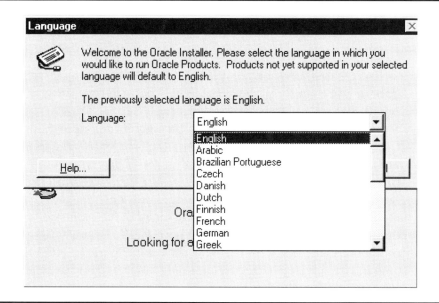

FIGURE 7-2. *Picking a language as the installer starts its work*

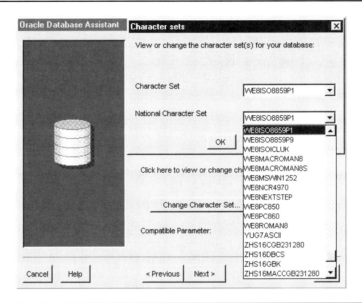

FIGURE 7-3. *Selecting a character set with the Database Assistant*

3. By changing the value of a column in a data dictionary view. Suppose a database was created with the US7ASCII character set. This used to be the default character set, but this changed somewhere around Oracle release 7.3. The PROPS$ view owned by Oracle user SYS is shown in the next listing. The column we are concerned with is VALUE$, and following the list of the columns in the table is the SQL **update** statement that will change the database character set.

```
SQL> desc sys.props$
 Name                                    Null?    Type
 --------------------------------- -------- ----
 NAME                                    NOT NULL VARCHAR2(30)
 VALUE$                                           VARCHAR2(4000)
 COMMENT$                                         VARCHAR2(4000)
update sys.props$
  set value$ = 'WE8ISO8859P1'
where name = 'NLS_CHARACTERSET';
```

NOTE
The value you set for this column must be recognized by Oracle8 or you will not be able to get the database open again. We cannot stress enough the importance of this! It's not a matter of "maybe" not being able to reopen the database—it's a fact—you will lose the database and have to rebuild from a backup.

Initialization Parameter File

As the Oracle8 database is started, it reads an initialization parameter file some people call "init.ora." We discuss this parameter file later in this chapter under the "Parallelism" section, as well as in a few sections of Chapter 20. There are a few national language support parameters that you may want to set in the initialization parameter file to control the sorting approach used by the database as well as the display approach used for date and numeric fields. Let's cover the two parameters most commonly set, then move on to the topic of parallelism.

NLS_DATE_FORMAT

Oracle displays dates by default as DD-MON-YY, so January 12, 1999 would show as 12-JAN-99 unless you tell it something different. Different geographical and linguistic areas of the world may want the date displayed using another format; DD/MM/YY (i.e., 12/01/99) and YY/MM/DD (i.e., 99/01/12) are common. This feature may be especially useful in situations where your warehouse user community is coming from an environment where the date is always displayed as YYYY/MM/DD. The following entry in the initialization parameter file will make this happen:

```
nls_date_format = YYYY/MM/DD
```

NOTE
This parameter is used most to override the DD-MON-YY date format in the warehouse where users are coming from a non-Oracle background.

NLS_TERRITORY

A number of characteristics of how data is displayed are controlled by this entry.

- **Decimal character and group separator**   Whether the characters 123456.99 are displayed as 123,456.99 or 123456,99.

- **Week start day**   In some countries the week starts on Monday, some Sunday. For example, when NLS_TERRITORY is set to "France", Monday is called day number one and when set to AMERICA, Sunday is called day number one.

- **Local currency symbol**   In the United Kingdom the symbol "£" represents the British pound, and "¥" is used for the yen in Japan.

We recommend visiting language and character display issues along the way with the users of the warehouse. It can be a real nuisance, not to mention a political nightmare, to deploy the warehouse to the user community only to have them discover character set problems that you missed.

Parallelism

Parallelism involves the ability of software to take advantage of multi-CPU machines to reduce response time when queries are passed to the database engine for processing. Let's look at the two most common types of multi-CPU machines, the features Oracle uses for parallel processing, then discuss why parallelization is such a big deal in the realm of the data warehouse.

MPP and SMP

Massively parallel processor architecture has many separate nodes hooked together by a high-speed interconnect mechanism. An MPP node consists of one or more processor(s), local memory, and, sometimes, local disk. The operating system runs separately on each node. *Symmetric multiprocessor* architecture involves more than one CPU utilizing common memory and disk. The operating system runs concurrently as one image across multiple

CPUs. The operating system provides scheduling so that tasks execute on all CPUs in a symmetrical fashion.

MPP machines are typically more scalable—as you add nodes to the existing network of machines, each comes with additional memory, additional I/O bandwidth (i.e., disk drives of its own), and added computer horsepower. We now look at Oracle's parallel query feature and how it is implemented.

NOTE
The parallel query feature is ONLY intended for machines with more than one processor. Implementation of the feature on a single-CPU machine will backfire, as the performance of queries will deteriorate.

Parallel Query

Each session that accesses an Oracle database does so by server process. This *server process* communicates on the user's behalf with the memory allocated to the operation of the Oracle instance. Remember, an *instance* is a set of support processes and memory structures put in place to facilitate communication with an Oracle database. Figure 7-4 illustrates the server processes allocated for a number of user sessions accessing an Oracle data warehouse. The arrows indicate a dedicated server process. When a session passes a SQL statement to Oracle for processing, the work is done, the results assembled, and then passed back to the user session. It is all under control of the dedicated user server process.

The magic of parallel query involves bringing up a number of extra server processes, correctly referred to as *parallel query server processes*, that share the work of processing queries. These query processes are controlled by a dispatcher; in a nutshell, the dispatcher is responsible for:

- Splitting the work to be performed among the pool of available query processes.

- Load balancing—ensuring that query processes that finish their work early share work with other processes who have not yet completed theirs.

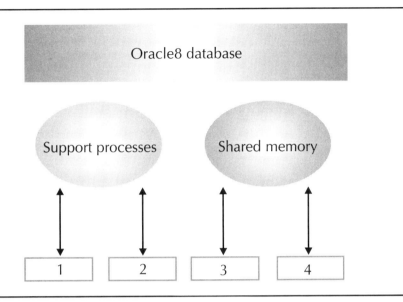

FIGURE 7-4. *Server processes without parallel query*

■ Assembling the results from the query processes into one set of data and returning it to the user.

Figure 7-5 illustrates the use of the dispatcher; notice the additional layer and how the user sessions pass their requests to the database through the dispatcher.

Parallelization and the Warehouse

A handful of operations can be parallelized using Oracle8, some of them crucial to the loading, transforming, and population of the data warehouse. Oracle8 can parallelize over 20 operations, including the following that will be done time and time again as the data warehouse is loaded and analyses performed:

■ **Table scan** The act of reading a table sequentially from start to finish.

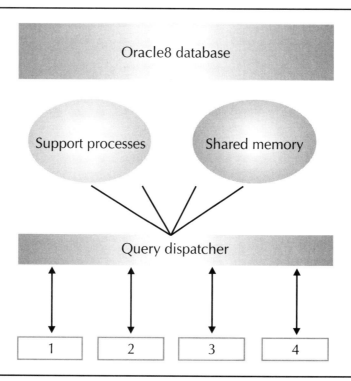

FIGURE 7-5. *Server processes with parallel query*

■ **Not in** Executing a query where the selection criteria includes a set exclusion statement where the result set's column values do not match the set. The *result set* is the set of rows that qualify for a query based on the selection criteria; this is the data returned to the user session. The segment from the following query illustrates this:

```
select manu_name, …
   from …,…,…,…
 where manu_id …
     and …
     and month not in ('Jan','Feb');
```

■ **Group by** Grouping of rows in the result set by one or more column values, commonly seen towards the end of a SQL statement that aggregates information as shown in the next listing:

```
select sum(sale_stat1),sum(sale_stat2),month, region, quarter
  from …
where …
   and …
   and …
group by month,region,quarter;
```

■ **Select distinct** Queries that look for uniqueness within rows in the result set.

■ **Aggregation** The act of producing summary information from detail data.

■ **Order by** The act of sorting data as it is returned as query results based on the columns mentioned in the query's **order by** clause.

■ **Create table as select** The creation of a table by feeding information from the join of other tables. This is a very common activity as data is being prepared for the warehouse. The skeleton of this type of operation is shown next:

```
reate table region_summary storage (initial 80m next 80m
                                     pctincrease 0)
tablespace region_data unrecoverable as
select region_code,month …
  from region,sale, …
where …
group by region_code,month, …;
```

■ **Index maintenance** The SQL statements **create index** and **rebuild index** are candidates for parallelization. Chapter 10 is dedicated to indexing the warehouse and discusses index operations.

■ **Inserting rows from other tables** Using the **insert into … select** construct is used to move rows from an existing table into a new one.

- **Enabling constraints** Constraints determine rules on relationships between tables in the warehouse and rules regarding column values in individual tables. As constraints are defined and enabled, Oracle needs to scan the table to allow itself to enable the constraint. This operation can be parallelized.

- **Star transformation** The optimization technique used when processing queries against a star schema, first discussed in Chapter 5 and mentioned in many places throughout this work. We look at star schemas again in this chapter in the "Star Schema Implementation" section.

The performance gain from parallelization is awesome. With the appropriate infrastructure in place to facilitate parallel processing, queries that may take upwards of 10 hours can run to completion in a matter of minutes.

NOTE
Turning on the parallel query feature alone is NOT enough to achieve optimal gain. There is some work that has to be done to support parallel query. Some of this is discussed in this chapter, some in Chapter 20.

Degree of Parallelism

The *degree of parallelism* is the number of query processes associated with a single operation. It can be set at the statement level or the object level. Let's look at setting this degree using both approaches.

At the Statement Level

This can be accomplished during any phase of data warehouse activity by using hints. *Hints* are special keywords used to influence the way the optimizer processes queries. The *optimizer* is a set of routines enlivened when a query is passed to Oracle; the optimizer ensures the most efficient processing is performed on the query based on the nature of the data in the tables the query references. Using hints, the developer can influence the degree of parallelism to be used on a query and what structures should be parallelized to what degree.

At the Object Level

This is the best place to define degree of parallelism. The familiar **create table** statement is changed to include a **parallel (degree n)** clause, where **n** refers to the optimal number of query processes that will be used to process queries against the object. Based on the points highlighted in the next section, we will make some recommendations upon setting this degree of parallelism.

Choosing a Degree of Parallelism

There are a number of factors that influence the choice for degree of parallelism. Oracle is limited by a combination of the available hardware on the machine, the degrees of parallelism defined for the objects, and the number of query server processes the instance has available.

The number of CPUs on the machine and the number of disk drives over which the objects (referenced in the query) are spread are obtained from the operating system before query processing commences. Oracle will choose a number equal to the number of CPUs available or the number of disks, whichever is less.

NOTE
The order of choices made to select the degree of parallelism is not as straightforward and simple as this discussion suggests. The text is designed to give you a taste of parallel processing opportunities à l'Oracle.

This rule alone explains why parallel query does nothing on a single-CPU machine, and can be summed up according to the following logic:

```
if number of CPUs = 1 then   -- On a single-CPU machine with parallel query
    process query serially -- this would NOT be wise as we have stated.
elsif number of CPUs > disk drives upon which object(s) stored then
        first degree = number of disk drives as degree
else
        first degree = number of CPUs
end if
```

Armed with this "first degree" figure, Oracle then looks at the number of query processes running in the instance and makes a second choice as follows:

```
if first degree > minimum degree of parallelism for all objects then
    second degree = minimum degree of parallelism for all objects
else
    second degree = first degree
end if
```

The final choice is made based on the number of query processes spawned when the database was started, and is shown next:

```
if available query processes > second degree then
    choice = second degree
else
    choice = available query processes
end if
```

Table 7-2 illustrates the application of this logic. It appears as though you can simply take the smallest number (underlined in the table) from the first four columns in each row and apply that as the chosen degree of parallelism. Note that the "minimum degree" can be defined by the object or by hints imbedded in the query passed to the parallel query processor for execution.

CPUs	Disk Drives	Minimum Degree	Query Processes	Chosen Degree
2	1	4	8	1
4	2	4	16	2
256	512	32	128	32
16	16	16	8	8

TABLE 7-2. *Choice of Degree of Parallelism*

This discussion so far is fine and dandy—it reminds us of those dogs that Pavlov experimented with—salivating over the reward. We don't know about you, but we are doing just that for the details about turning on parallel query. Let's look at how this is done in the next section; there will be more discussions of parallelism in Chapter 20, where we look at tuning the warehouse. Other works of note to consult for parallelism material include Chapter 5 of one of our other books, *Oracle8 Tuning* (Corey, Abbey, Dechichio, and Abramson; Oracle Press, 1998).

Turning on Parallel Query at the Instance Level

This is the part for the database administrator. The work is done in the instance initialization parameter file, placing entries therein for some of the entries that start with PARALLEL. The following listing was obtained using the **show parameters para** in Server Manager. We are going to look at the three entries in bold.

```
NAME                                 TYPE      VALUE
------------------------------------ -------   --------
optimizer_percent_parallel           integer   0
parallel_default_max_instances       integer   0
parallel_instance_group              string
parallel_max_servers                 integer   5
parallel_min_message_pool            integer   48330
parallel_min_percent                 integer   0
parallel_min_servers                 integer   0
parallel_server                      boolean   FALSE
parallel_server_idle_time            integer   5
parallel_transaction_resource_timeo  integer   300
recovery_parallelism                 integer   0
```

PARALLEL_MIN_SERVERS

This entry determines the number of query processes to spawn when the database is started. There is an additional requirement in memory to initiate and keep these processes running. When we tried it on a Windows NT 4.0 server, a setting of **2** requested an extra 1,200Kb of memory. When running on a UNIX machine, the query server processes will be identified by P000 to

P00XX where XX equals the setting for the parameter minus one. Thus, a setting of **12** will spawn query processes P000 to P011.

PARALLEL_MAX_SERVERS

This determines maximum number of query processes that can be initiated if extra processes are required over and above that set by the previous parameter. PARALLEL_MAX_SERVERS is a cumulative number, such that it specifies the total number to run, not the number of extras to start. Oracle will spawn processes over the minimum setting up to the maximum setting if query processing requires more than the minimum. Suppose the former is set to **12** and the latter to **24**; Oracle will spawn up to **12** additional processes when needed.

PARALLEL_SERVER_IDLE_TIME

This parameter sets out a time, at the expiration of which the extra query processes up to and including PARALLEL_MAX_SERVERS will be killed off by Oracle. It is measured in minutes, and it is very possible that in a warehouse with sporadically heavy usage, the number of P0XX processes could vary during different monitoring times of day.

This brief introduction to parallel query processing should suffice for the initial look at the physical data warehouse. Naturally, as the number of CPUs and available disk drives change, so will the approach used to define the parallel query environment. We are now going to have a look at the approach Oracle uses to optimize queries. During the physical setup of the warehouse, you need to design an approach to collect statistics to feed to the optimizer.

Gathering Statistics for Cost-based Optimizer

The SQL **analyze** command is how statistics are gathered for the objects in your Oracle database. The *cost-based optimizer* (CBO) is a set of routines that assist the selection of the best access path to the data required to satisfy a query passed to the Oracle SQL engine for processing. An *access path* is the method Oracle selects to assemble results for a query, which is selected based on the indexes on the objects and relevant statistics.

NOTE
Readers familiar with the rule-based optimizer need to become fluent with CBO. It is the only way to optimize queries dealing with the potentially large volumes of data in the warehouse. This is especially true when running ad hoc tools where the administrator has no control over the SQL passed to the database.

Regardless of how Oracle decides to get at the data, it needs these statistics to intelligently choose the optimal path. The cost measured by Oracle when choosing the access path is a measurement of the expected resources that will be used to process the desired information. The data distribution and storage characteristics influence the choices the optimizer makes. It develops a short list of candidate execution plans, then selects the one with the least cost.

The SQL Analyze Command

Four types of objects can be analyzed using the **analyze** command: tables, partitions, indexes, and clusters. We will focus on tables, indexes, and partitions. *Indexes* store column values for rows in a table and can be used to provide a quick path to the data in your tables when CBO chooses to read an index before going out and getting the rows from a table. There are four parts to coding the analyze statement:

1. The keyword **analyze** followed by the type of object being analyzed.

2. The name of the object being analyzed.

3. The method with which the object is to be analyzed. The choices are **estimate** or **compute**.

4. When using the **estimate** method, directions about the sample of rows to be used to estimate the object's statistics. That sample can be specified as a percent of rows to be included using the keywords **sample n percent**. The character **n** stands for a number between 1 and 99. Alternatively, the sample can be specified by specifying a number of rows using the keywords **sample n rows**, where **n** stands for the number of rows to use in the sample.

A few words on estimating statistics. The sample of rows selected is based on the following logic:

```
if estimate is specified using the percent option then
    estimate statistics using the specified % of rows
elsif estimate is specified using the rows option then
    if the number of rows mentioned >= half the rows in the object then
        compute statistics for the desired object
    else
        estimate statistics using specified number of rows
    end if
elsif estimate is specified with no options then
    estimate statistics using a 1064 row sample
end if
```

To illustrate the listing, examine the information in Table 7-3 for a fictitious 5,700,000-row ACCOUNT table.

Statement	Gathering Done	Reason(s)
analyze table account estimate statistics;	Statistics are estimated using a 1,064-row sample	No sample (percent or row count) specified
analyze table account estimate statistics sample 20 percent;	Statistics are estimated using a sample size of 1, 140,000 rows	20 percent of rows specified
analyze table account sample 2000000 rows;	Statistics are estimated using the specified row sample	Row sample is used because it is < 50 percent of rows in table
analyze table account estimate statistics sample 4000000 rows;	Statistics are computed	More than 50 percent of the rows mentioned in the sample

TABLE 7-3. *Samples of Estimating Statistics*

Estimate Vs. Compute

For most applications, the **estimate** method will suffice because it:

■ Provides a random sample of rows whose statistics can be projected onto the remaining rows in the table

■ Is significantly less time-consuming than using the **compute** method

■ Requires a less restrictive lock and will, therefore, run to completion uninterrupted by Oracle errors

Oracle uses *locks* to protect data and to ensure that one and only one user can manipulate a row of data in the database at one time. The analysis of a complete set of tables and indexes can take from four to six times longer for the **compute** option than **estimate**. We unequivocally recommend you **analyze** tables with the **sample 20 percent** option; **analyze** indexes using the **compute** option. Interestingly enough, the **analyze** command using the **compute statistics** option tries to issue a **lock table** statement implicitly and, if someone is using the table, may raise this error.

NOTE
*Tables and indexes should be analyzed during the quiet hours to avoid lock problems when using the **compute** method of collection.*

How to Analyze Objects

Two ways exist to **analyze** objects with Oracle8: one uses SQL*Plus; the other is a procedure from the DBMS_UTILITY or DBMS_DDL package.

Using SQL*Plus

A familiar trick is using SQL to write SQL. Examine the following listing; the first two SQL statements create code to **analyze** indexes and tables; the last two do the same for partitioned tables and indexes.

```
/* ------------------------------------------------------- */
/*   Oracle8 Data Warehousing      Oracle Press 1998         */
/*                                                           */
/*   analyze.sql                                             */
/*                                                           */
/*   Corey, Abbey, Abramson, Taub                            */
/* ------------------------------------------------------- */
set pagesize 0 echo off verify off feedback off
set linesize 200 trimspool off
spool all_ana.sql
select 'analyze table '||owner||'.'||table_name||
       ' estimate statistics sample 20 percent;'
  from sys.dba_tables
 where owner not in ('SYS','SYSTEM');
select 'analyze index '||owner||'.'||index_name||
       'compute statistics;'
  from sys.dba_indexes
 where owner not in ('SYS','SYSTEM');
select 'analyze table '||table_name||' partition ('||partition_name||
       ') estimate statistics sample 20 percent;'
 from sys.dba_tab_partitions
where owner not in ('SYS','SYSTEM');
select 'analyze index '||index_name||' partition ('||partition_name||
       ') compute statistics;'
  from sys.dba_ind_partitions
where owner not in ('SYS','SYSTEM');
spool off
set feed on echo on
```

Note the following points about the previous listing:

1. The first group of set commands ensures the text selected from the query has no headings, the size of each print line is large enough to accommodate output longer than the normal 80 characters, and the message about how many rows selected is suppressed.

2. It is assumed the user running the script has **select** privileges on the data dictionary views DBA_TABLES, DBA_INDEXES, DBA_TAB_PARTITIONS, and DBA_IND_PARTITIONS. This privilege must be granted by Oracle user SYS.

3. The user running the script must have the system privilege **analyze any** or the DBA role. System privileges allow certain users to perform common tasks normally associated with users having the DBA role. With these privileges (for example, **analyze any**) some, but not all, of these DBA-type commands can be issued by specified users.

4. The file all_ana.sql is produced when this program is run. The next step is to invoke that script to collect the statistics.

5. The users SYS and SYSTEM are deliberately excluded from the code because, according to recommendations made by Oracle Corporation, one is not supposed to **analyze** tables in the data dictionary.

Using a Procedure

The two packages mentioned previously must be installed in the database within which your data warehouse resides. Table 7-4 shows the expected parameters and their meanings for the DBMS_UTILITY.ANALYZE_SCHEMA procedure.

To estimate statistics for the CVAN schema using a 20 percent sample, the procedure would be invoked from SQL*Plus using the syntax:

```
execute dbms_utility.analyze_schema ('CVAN','ESTIMATE',null,20);
```

Parameter	Default Value
Owner of objects to analyze	None—must be supplied
Method for collection	None—must be **estimate** or **compute**
Rows in sample	Optional—defaults to null
Percent of rows in sample	Optional—defaults to null

TABLE 7-4. *Parameters for ANALYZE_SCHEMA*

Table 7-5 shows the expected parameters passed to DBMS_DDL.ANALYZE_OBJECT.

To compute statistics for the index PLANNER_EX owned by CVAN, the procedure would be invoked from SQL*Plus using the syntax:

```
execute dbms_ddl.analyze_object ('INDEX','PLANNER_EX','COMPUTE');
```

NOTE
Because the last two parameters have defaults, they need not be included on the command line.

When to Analyze Objects

Essentially two types of objects exist in the data warehouse—static and dynamic. *Static objects* need to be analyzed as soon as they are created in the warehouse, as well as any time the data changes. Regardless of how infrequently a table's contents change, the data is not 100 percent static. *Dynamic objects* need to be analyzed regularly; the frequency is determined by the frequency of change in the data, coupled with the percent of information that actually changes.

When propagation of changes to data from the operational system is part of a data warehouse implementation, you may need to analyze objects more often than if the changes were done by wiping previous data and inserting a completely new set of data.

Parameter	Default Value
Type of object	None—must be table or index
Owner of object to analyze	None
Method for collection	None—must be **estimate** or **compute**
Rows in sample	Optional—defaults to null
Percent of rows in sample	Optional—defaults to null

TABLE 7-5. *Parameters for ANALYZE_OBJECT*

NOTE
Analyze static objects in the warehouse when their contents are refreshed. Analyze dynamic objects in the warehouse after assessing the frequency of change in the table data alongside the amount of the table data that changes.

We start by analyzing tables weekly, every Friday morning. Keep in mind the sheer volume of warehouse data may require analyzing portions of the data on one day and other parts on other days. The data mart serves as a nice way to break up the statistic collection process. A collection process could be put in place to do one or two data marts per night, depending on their number and size.

Where to View Statistics

When you analyze your tables, partitions, and indexes, Oracle places statistics in a handful of data dictionary views. Table 7-6 highlights some columns in these views, whose contents are used when CBO is selecting an access path.

View	Column Name	Contents
user_tables	num_rows	Total number of rows in the table when analyzed
user_indexes	distinct_keys	The number of distinct values in the indexed column
user_part_col_statistics	num_distinct	The number of distinct values in the column
user_tab_col_statistics	num_distinct	The number of distinct values in the column

TABLE 7-6.   *Columns Pertinent to Viewing Statistics*

Stale Statistics

Often people report dismal performance from the cost-based optimizer. Through our travels around Oracle since CBO was introduced (version 7, circa 1993) the biggest problem is caused when people have stale statistics. In other words, it's not CBO that is the problem; it's the statistics—another version of the saying, "Poor workers blame their tools." Picture the following scenario:

■ During the programming exercise on a new set of queries, development staff had their own set of tables that they collected statistics for whenever they felt it necessary.

■ Many systems in production used the rule-based approach, the alternative method to query optimization. Using this method, Oracle weighs the access paths based on a set of rules, and chooses the path with the lowest ranking. As a result, DBA personnel were not stringent on analyzing tables when their systems moved into production.

■ The tables in the development schema were delivered to production and analyzed using **estimate** for tables and **compute** for indexes. On two of the largest objects, a query against USER_TABLES produced the following output:

```
SQL> select table_name,num_rows
  2    from user_tables
  3    where num_rows is not null;
TABLE_NAME                      NUM_ROWS
------------------------- ---------
SALE                                19009
ITEM                                 2199
```

When these two objects went to production, they did have 19,009 and 2,199 rows respectively.

■ Six months later, after significantly more data was being transported to the warehouse, there was dissatisfaction with performance of CBO. The same query as shown in the previous listing was issued with the same results! The following query showed the actual row counts:

```
SQL> select count(*) from sale;
      COUNT(*)
    -------------
        894981
SQL> select count(*) from item;
      COUNT(*)
    -------------
          53219
```

Here is where the heart of the problem lies—the statistics are stale and, when used by CBO, lead to the choice of an access path far less than the most optimal.

Consistency with Statistic Collection

You must ensure all the tables in your schemas get analyzed. If Oracle finds a table with no statistics, it will estimate them on the fly as a query access path is being selected. This is an undesirable situation for three reasons:

1. It takes processing time to build statistics.

2. The statistics are thrown away when the access path has been selected.

3. By letting the query engine gather statistics on the fly, your plans for the objects (i.e., **compute** for indexes and **estimate** for tables) is not followed.

Check your schema as part of some nightly routine and pass table, index, or partition names to the engine to gather statistics for those missing information. The next script does this dynamically. Afterwards, we move on to a discussion about tablespace segregation.

```
/* ---------------------------------------------------------- */
/*  Oracle8 Data Warehousing      Oracle Press 1998           */
/*                                                            */
/*  no_stats.sql                                              */
/*                                                            */
/*  Corey, Abbey, Abramson, Taub                              */
/* ---------------------------------------------------------- */
set pages 0 echo off feed off pages 0 ver off lines 200 trimsp on
spool missing.sql
```

```
select 'analyze table '||owner||'.'||table_name||
       ' estimate statistics sample 20 percent;'
  from sys.dba_tables
 where last_analyzed is null
   and owner not in ('SYS','SYSTEM');
select 'analyze index '||owner||'.'||index_name||
       ' compute statistics;'
  from sys.dba_indexes
 where last_analyzed is null
   and owner not in ('SYS','SYSTEM');
spool off
set echo on feed on
spool missing
start missing
spool off
```

Tablespace Segregation

The sheer volume of information in many data warehouse repositories warrants planning of where the data will be physically placed in the Oracle database. There is a logical rather than physical association between the files making up each tablespace. There are two types of tablespaces we see required in the warehouse. Let's start by discussing the two types and make some recommendations about segregation.

System Support Tablespaces

This section will highlight the operations performed by the Oracle8 installer on Windows NT 4.0. If you accept the starter database when installing Oracle, it will create the following five support tablespaces:

- **SYSTEM**   The heart of the database, containing the data dictionary and the objects owned by the special users SYS and SYSTEM.

- **ROLLBACK** This is where the installer builds rollback segments, which are used to save pre-updated copies of rows massaged by users of the database before they commit or rollback a transaction. *Commit* is the activity of saving changes to the database, and *rollback* is the act of rolling changes back to a state before the changes were initiated. Table 7-7 illustrates this concept. See how the value SMITH is kept in the rollback segment until the commit is issued.

- **TEMPORARY** This is Oracle's scratch pad, where temporary tables are created for the life of the processing cycle of each query, then cleaned up when no longer required.

- **TOOLS** This is where Oracle places tables that are used by its own tools delivered with the database; they suggest you place other vendors' objects here as well, rather than in the SYSTEM tablespace.

- **USERS** This area is set aside for any nonsystem objects required by applications.

Activity	Old Value	New Value	In Database	In User Session	In RBS
update	SMITH	JOHNSON	SMITH	JOHNSON	SMITH
commit	****	JOHNSON	JOHNSON	JOHNSON	****
update	JOHNSON	COHEN	JOHNSON	COHEN	JOHNSON
rollback	****	JOHNSON	JOHNSON	JOHNSON	****

TABLE 7-7. *Update with commit and rollback*

The next listing shows how these tablespaces are named and sized, with the tablespace name and file size following each in bold:

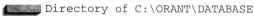

```
Directory of C:\ORANT\DATABASE
12/09/99  11:14a   20,973,568 RBS1ORCL.ORA   ROLLBACK        20MB
12/09/99  11:14a   62,916,608 SYS1ORCL.ORA   SYSTEM          60MB
12/09/99  11:14a    2,099,200 TMP1ORCL.ORA   TEMPORARY_DATA  2MB
12/09/99  11:14a    8,390,656 USR1ORCL.ORA   USER_DATA       8MB
```

From our experience with large information repositories, the two recommendations highlighted in Table 7-8 should be implemented to make these support structures capable of handling the bulk of data placed in the warehouse at the start of and any time during its life cycle.

NOTE
For readers who are "scared" by recommendations in the 2 to 4 gigabyte area for sizes of tablespaces for the warehouse, keep in mind that we are talking about very large databases. It's better to know now than somewhere down the road when you find out you need an additional 20 gigabytes and only have 2½.

Tablespace	Size	Details
rollback	500MB	The size of the default rollback segments is not enough, and you need at least one additional rollback segment of ½ gigabyte to be used as all or part of the warehouse is refreshed.
temporary	2Gb	Regardless of how much of the warehouse is refreshed, Oracle craves lots of workspace. This is a starting amount, and you should consider doubling that in the not too distant future.

TABLE 7-8. *Sizing Recommendations on Windows NT 4.0*

The next listing displays code similar to that used to resize the TEMPORARY and ROLLBACK tablespaces as suggested in Table 7-8. If the code is cryptic due to your unfamiliarity with the task at hand, show it to someone else who will use it as a sample of how to implement the change.

```
/* ------------------------------------------------- */
/* Oracle8 Data Warehousing   Oracle Press 1998       */
/*                                                     */
/* Corey, Abbey, Abramson, Taub                        */
/* ------------------------------------------------- */
drop tablespace temporary_data;
-- Remember to delete the file that used to belong to this
-- tablespace. Oracle no longer needs it after the drop
-- tablespace command finishes, so get rid of the file as well.
create tablespace temporary_data datafile
      'd:\orant\database\tempdata.dbf' size 2048m
      default storage (initial 100m next 100m pctincrease 0);
alter tablespace temporary_data temporary;
create tablespace rollback_extra datafile
      'd:\orant\database\rollback2.dbf' size 500m
      default storage (initial 25m next 25m pctincrease 0);
create rollback segment big_rbs tablespace rollback_extra
      storage (initial 25m next 25m minextents 19 maxextents 19);
alter rollback segment big_rbs online;
```

Application Tablespaces

The tablespaces that contain the warehouse data must be created manually using an interface like Oracle Enterprise Manager or SQL*Worksheet. Regardless of how the tablespaces are created, we present the following guidelines for their physical setup:

1. Estimate the space required for your data and indexes. Formulae for these calculations are in works such as the *Oracle8 Server Administrator's Guide*. Often, the row sizes in the warehouse can be estimated based on the source of their operational system counterparts.

2. Create Oracle accounts to be the keeper of the data for each section of your data warehouse or each individual data mart on its own. Suppose a warehouse has a CLIENT, SALE, and HR business area. Create a separate schema (synonymous with the concept of *account* in the Oracle world) to hold data for those business areas.

3. Separate the data and index containers such that the owner of the information for each area of the warehouse has data in one tablespace and indexes in another. Using one of the schemas from the previous point, the tablespaces for the client information area would be called CLIENT_DAT and CLIENT_IDX.

4. Dimension tables are inevitably shared amongst star schemas belonging to different business areas. We discussed star schemas in the "Star Schema" section of Chapter 5. If you know at the start what dimensions are to be shared, you either share a copy in a central schema or, based on the nature of the data in the dimension, create the dimension in one business area and then permit sharing.

Pointing Users at Tablespaces

There are two issues here with the physical planning phase of the warehouse. The first involves ensuring that users are pointed at the correct temporary tablespace, the second making sure that owners' tables and indexes end up in the tablespace for which they are intended.

A very common error we see when working with long-running queries, especially using large volumes of data, results from Oracle running out of workspace in its temporary tablespace.

```
01652, 00000, "unable to extend temp segment by %s in tablespace %s"
// *Cause:  Failed to allocate an extent for temp segment in tablespace.
// *Action: Use ALTER TABLESPACE ADD DATAFILE statement to add one or more
//          files to the tablespace indicated.
```

Translating Theory into Practice

There are two sides to the data warehouse implementation approach—design and physical implementation. The data model for many OLTP systems has been normalized as discussed in Chapter 5. In the next section, we are going to look at the process of denormalization, an activity where normalized operational data is mapped differently to satisfy the processing and query requirements dictated by decision support systems.

Systematic Denormalization

As data is moved from operational systems into the warehouse, you go through a process called *systematic denormalization* that violates all the rules relational database architects apply when modeling most systems. Systematic denormalization is done to enhance the performance of the warehouse by reducing join operations that are resource intensive. Compared to single table **select** statements, join operations:

- Consume significantly more CPU;

- Require gobs more temporary workspace (on disk and in memory) for sorting;

- Require temporary tables for holding of intermediary results;

- Perform more I/O since at least one I/O is required per table in the query.

   In the midst of studying relational database theory, you ran (or will run) across problems with data that was not properly normalized. Storing the data in one and only one place is a fundamental requirement as normalization is performed. For example, problems can creep up when a vendor record is stored in the VENDOR table for the accounts payable application and the same vendor information is stored in the SUPPLIER table for purchasing. Suppose the company moves, and the data is updated in accounts payable but not in purchasing. Picture the difficulty (not to mention embarrassment!) if one application believes the Newport Technology Group's offices are in Crystal Beach and the other thinks they're in Ottawa! (ha, ha…)
   Picture a few small tables from an OLTP environment as shown in the next listing.

NOTE
This sample is oversimplified to allow us to lead you through the denormalization exercise. Naturally, in a real-life example, PURCHASE would trap much more information, such as customer name, and ITEM would hold the UNIT_COST and then some.

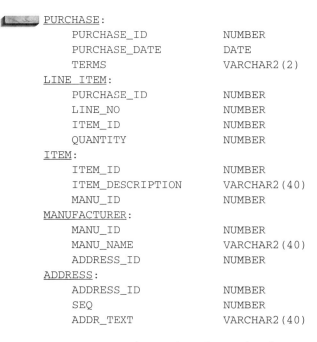

PURCHASE:
```
        PURCHASE_ID              NUMBER
        PURCHASE_DATE            DATE
        TERMS                    VARCHAR2(2)
LINE_ITEM:
        PURCHASE_ID              NUMBER
        LINE_NO                  NUMBER
        ITEM_ID                  NUMBER
        QUANTITY                 NUMBER
ITEM:
        ITEM_ID                  NUMBER
        ITEM_DESCRIPTION         VARCHAR2(40)
        MANU_ID                  NUMBER
MANUFACTURER:
        MANU_ID                  NUMBER
        MANU_NAME                VARCHAR2(40)
        ADDRESS_ID               NUMBER
ADDRESS:
        ADDRESS_ID               NUMBER
        SEQ                      NUMBER
        ADDR_TEXT                VARCHAR2(40)
```

Figure 7-6 shows the relationship between the objects in this schema.

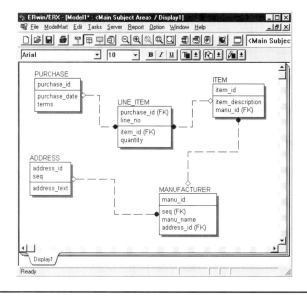

FIGURE 7-6. *Purchase order in OLTP system*

After loading a few seed rows for purchase order number 9002 into these five tables, let's look at their contents, then show the SQL used to construct the order on a data entry screen in the OLTP system.

```
SQL> select * from purchase;
PURCHASE_ID PURCHASE_ TE
----------- --------- --
       9000 12-DEC-99 CA
       9001 22-DEC-99 SX
       9002 25-DEC-99 NY
3 rows selected.
SQL> select * from line_item;
PURCHASE_ID    LINE_NO    ITEM_ID   QUANTITY
----------- ---------- ---------- ----------
       9002          1     881991          9
       9002          2     992811         10
       9002          3     221221         90
3 rows selected.
SQL> select * from item;
   ITEM_ID ITEM_DESCRIPTION                              MANU_ID
---------- ----------------------------------------- ----------
    881991 Diagonal flange B67                              90
    992811 Circular blade                                   90
    221221 Ford Fiesta                                      89
3 rows selected.
SQL> select * from manufacturer;
   MANU_ID MANU_NAME                                 ADDRESS_ID
---------- ----------------------------------------- ----------
        90 Dave's Part Mart                                9095
        89 Tamara Car                                      2355
SQL> select * from address;
ADDRESS_ID        SEQ ADDR_TEXT
---------- ---------- -----------------------------------------
      9095          1 Bay 16, 789 Flora
      9095          2 Toronto ON  M8U 7Y6
      2355          1 General Delivery
      2355          2 Chapman AB  T5Y 6Y7
4 rows selected.
SQL> select a.purchase_id,a.purchase_date,a.terms,
  2          c.item_description,b.quantity,d.manu_name
  3     from purchase a,line_item b,item c,manufacturer d
  4    where a.purchase_id = b.purchase_id
  5      and b.item_id = c.item_id
  6      and c.manu_id = d.manu_id
```

```
  7   and a.purchase_id = 9002
  8   order by b.line_no;
PURCHASE_ID   PURCHASE_DATE TERMS ITEM_DESCRIPTION   QUANTITY  MANU_NAME
-----------   ------------- ----- ------------------ --------  ----------------

     9002     25-DEC-99     NY    Diagonal flange B67        9  Dave's Part Mart
                                  Circular blade            10  Dave's Part Mart
                                  Ford Fiesta               90  Tamara Car

3 rows selected.
```

To wrap up this section, let's look at how the normalized purchase order information could be denormalized and brought together in the decision support arena. We create the denormalized table using the same type of SQL query used in the previous listing to build the purchase order image, but this time store the results in a table.

```
SQL> create table dwpurchase as
  2    select a.purchase_id,a.purchase_date,a.terms,
  3         c.item_description,b.quantity,d.manu_name
  4    from purchase a,line_item b,item c,manufacturer d
  5    where a.purchase_id = b.purchase_id
  6      and b.item_id = c.item_id
  7      and c.manu_id = d.manu_id unrecoverable;
Table created.
SQL> desc dwpurchase
 Name                                Null?     Type
 ----------------------------------- --------  ----
 PURCHASE_ID                         NOT NULL  NUMBER
 PURCHASE_DATE                                 DATE
 TERMS                                         VARCHAR2(2)
 ITEM_DESCRIPTION                              VARCHAR2(40)
 QUANTITY                                      NUMBER
 MANU_NAME                                     VARCHAR2(40)
```

After so many relational years, pursuing the nth degree of normalization, some people find it difficult getting their heads around the way tables are constructed in the decision support environment. Interestingly enough, some people find the normalization process drudgery and find the systematic denormalization exercise refreshing.

NOTE
Denormalization is not a consideration in OLTP systems; data normalization is a matter of fact for operational systems, and there is no way around it. Strict adherence to data normalization protects the integrity of the data in the operational database.

In the next section on star schemas, we will show you how to build a star schema for the Oracle8-based data warehouse using the data mart first introduced in Chapter 5. When you see the entity relationship diagram from which the schema is built, compare it against the report shown in Figure 7-7 listing some of the entities in the operational systems whose data comes together in the mart. Notice how the SUBSCRIBER entity in the data mart pulls data from SUBSCRIBER, SUBSCRIBER_ADDRESS, and SUBSCRIBER_PRODUCT in the operational and PAYTVORDER contains information pulled from PPV_RATE, PPV_ORDER, and PPV_PROMOTION_COUPON.

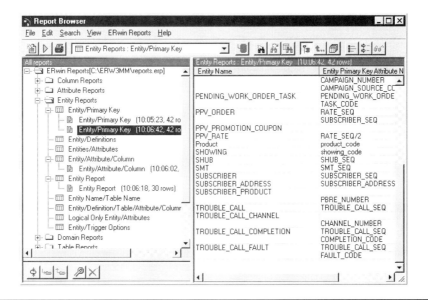

FIGURE 7-7. *Operational data model for pay TV*

Star Schema Implementation

The famous star schema—it's all fine and dandy to discuss the theory and give recommendations as to where it makes sense. Especially for organizations in the prototype phase or the early adoption of the data mart approach, the acquisition of tools may still be somewhere down the road. What we are going to do in this section is look at the building of a star schema from the ground up. The schema, first introduced in Chapter 5, is shown again in Figure 7-8. The schema is comprised of PAYTVORDER as the fact table, and SHOWINGTIME, PROMOTION, CABLECOMPANY, EVENTS, and SUBSCRIBER as the dimensions.

The next listing shows the creation of the fact and dimension tables, then the setup of the infrastructure to allow for star query processing. Regardless of whether you point and click using a GUI interface (Oracle Enterprise Manager or the like) or do it manually in SQL*Plus or SQL*Worksheet, the SQL passed to Oracle8 is similar to what you see next. When doing the physical implementation, we have made the following changes to the

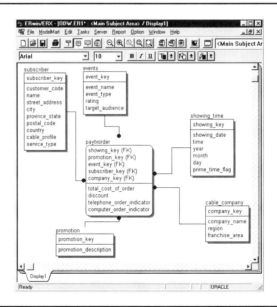

FIGURE 7-8. *PAYTVORDER fact-based star schema*

schema to satisfy one Oracle8 and one logical preference we have with table naming:

- We have changed the DATE attribute to SHOWING_DATE in the SHOWINGTIME entity, as DATE is a reserved word in Oracle.

- We have made the physical table name for the EVENTS entity singular (i.e., EVENT).

NOTE

We are partitioning the PAYTVORDER table by the SUBSCRIBER_KEY column value. Chapter 9 discusses partitioning; we partition here to be consistent with one of our recommendations throughout the book—partition large objects! The text in bold is the partitioning syntax.

```
/* --------------------------------------------- */
/* Oracle8 Data Warehousing   Oracle Press 1998  */
/*                                               */
/* Corey, Abbey, Abramson, Taub                  */
/* --------------------------------------------- */
--
-- Create the PAYTVORDER table.
--
create table paytvorder (showing_key               number,
                         promotion_key             number,
                         event_key                 number,
                         subscriber_key            number,
                         company_key               number,
                         total_cost_of_order       number(6,2),
                         discount                  number,
                         telephone_order_indicator varchar2(1),
                         computer_order_indicator  varchar2(1))
    partition by range (subscriber_key)
    storage (initial 400m next 400 pctincrease 0)
          (partition ptvo_1 values less than (2222222),
                   tablespace ptvo_pdata1,
           partition ptvo_2 values less than (4444444)
                   tablespace ptvo_pdata2,
           partition ptvo_3 values less than (7777777),
                   tablespace ptvo_pdata3,
```

```
              partition ptvo_4 values less than (8888999)
                      tablespace ptvo_pdata4),
              partition ptvo_5 values less than (maxvalue)
                      tablespace ptvo_pdata5);
--
-- Build the primary key for PAYTVORDER.
--
alter table paytvorder add constraint paytvorder_pk
      primary key (showing_key,promotion_key,
                   event_key,subscriber_key,company_key) using index
      storage (initial 400m next 400m pctincrease 0)
      tablespace ptvo_idx;
--
-- Build SHOWING_TIME, PROMOTION, CABLE_COMPANY, EVENT,
-- and SUBSCRIBER. Remember, these are the dimension tables and are
-- nothing like their OLTP counterparts. Only the columns needed for
-- analysis are included.
--
create table showing_time (showing_key     number,
                           showing_date    date,
                           time            varchar2(10),
                           year            number,
                           month           number,
                           day             number,
                           prime_time_flag varchar2(1))
      storage (initial 6m next 6m pctincrease 0)
      tablespace dim_tabs_data1;
create table promotion (promotion_key          number,
                        promotion_description varchar2(100))
      storage (initial 2m next 2m pctincrease 0)
      tablespace dim_tabs_data1;
create table cable_company (company_key     number,
                            company_name    varchar2(60),
                            region          varchar2(2),
                            franchise_area varchar2(2))
      storage (initial 2m next 2m pctincrease 0)
      tablespace dim_tabs_data1;
create table event (event_key       number,
                    event_name      varchar2(40),
                    event_type      varchar2(2),
                    rating          number,
                    target_audience varchar2(3))
      storage (initial 12m next 12m pctincrease 0)
      tablespace dim_tabs_data2;
```

```
create table subscriber (subscriber_key      number,
                         customer_code       varchar2(10),
                         name                varchar2(30),
                         street_address      varchar2(40),
                         city                varchar2(20),
                         province_state      varchar2(2),
                         postal_code         varchar2(10),
                         country             varchar2(20),
                         cable_profile       varchar2(8),
                         service_type        varchar2(3))
      storage (initial 80m next 80m pctincrease 0)
      tablespace dim_tabs_data2;
--
-- Create the primary keys for the dimension tables.
--
alter table showing_time add constraint showing_time_pk
      primary key (showing_key) using index
      storage (initial 800k next 800k pctincrease 0);
alter table promotion add constraint promotion_pk
      primary key (promotion_key) using index
      storage (initial 200k next 200k pctincrease 0);
alter table cable_company add constraint cable_company_pk
      primary key (company_key) using index
      storage (initial 800k next 800k pctincrease 0);
alter table event add constraint event_pk
      primary key (event_key) using index
      storage (initial 3m next 3m pctincrease 0);
alter table subscriber add constraint subscriber_pk
      primary key (subscriber_key) using index
      storage (initial 16m next 16m pctincrease 0);
--
-- Add foreign keys to fact table pointing at all the dimensions.
--
alter table paytvorder add constraint showing_key_fk foreign key
      (showing_key) references showing_time;
alter table paytvorder add constraint promotion_key_fk foreign key
      (promotion_key) references promotion;
alter table paytvorder add constraint cable_company_fk foreign key
      (company_key) references cable_company;
alter table paytvorder add constraint event_fk foreign key
      (event_key) references event;
alter table paytvorder add constraint subscriber_fk foreign key
      (subscriber_key) references subscriber;
```

Dual-schema Access Approach

Availability is a key issue with data warehouses. Many of us remember the need to keep operational systems up and running as much as possible each 24-hour day. The vendors, Oracle included, have gone to great ends to allow the database to be up all the time and still be backed up.

Picture the following scenario that leads to our mentioning this dual-schema access approach. One of us was working on a data mart for criminal offenders, dragging information from one main and three or four smaller operational systems. The data mart was set up to read information from one central schema—let's call it OFFINFO for offender information. Whenever the data mart was refreshed, user access had to be cut off and, for the duration of the refresh, they were out of business. One way to allow for uninterrupted access to the data mart is by having three separate schemas. Let's look at how this is put in place.

NOTE
This is the easiest of many approaches, and will enable uninterrupted access. Other approaches, which may be more complex, are used for implementing more security at the same time as this unhindered access.

Dual-schema Owners

You set up two identical schemas, going through the arduous but necessary process of always ensuring the schemas are exactly the same. Let's call these schemas OFFINFO1 and OFFINFO2. You can always check the consistency of the schema using the following SQL statements:

```
/* -------------------------------------------- */
/* Oracle8 Data Warehousing   Oracle Press 1998  */
/*                                              */
/* ckschema.sql                                 */
/*                                              */
/* Corey, Abbey, Abramson, Taub                 */
/* -------------------------------------------- */
set echo on feed on pages 0
spool ckschema
select table_name from user_tables;
```

```
select column_name,table_name from user_tab_columns;
select distinct name,type from user_source;
select table_name,index_name from user_indexes;
select table_name,index_name,column_name from user_tab_columns;
select index_name,locality from user_part_indexes;
select table_name,partition_name,high_value from user_tab_partitions;
select index_name,partition_name,high_value from user_ind_partitions;
spool off
```

Connect to the database as OFFINFO1 then OFFINFO2, running the script as both users, then compare the output. Any differences in the output should be investigated if problematic.

NOTE
*The output from ckschema.sql can be quite long; use some program similar to the UNIX **diff** command to inspect the output and report differences.*

Initial setup is done by running the schema create programs while connected to the database as each of these two users. When the data mart was first turned over to the users, the OFFINFO1 schema contained the live data and the OFFINFO2 schema was empty.

Privileges to look at the data in both of these schemas are given out to the Oracle user described in the next section. In Oracle, a *privilege* is the right to look at the data in someone else's schema.

Access Schema

This access schema provides the pass-through enabling users to look at data belonging to each of the warehouse schema data owners. This is the schema referred to in all the end-user queries; this user is granted the **select** privilege on all data belonging to OFFINFO1 and OFFINFO2. Let's call this schema OFFLOOK. OFFLOOK refers to the schema owner's tables using a private synonym. A *private synonym* is a handle or nickname used by one user to refer to data that belongs to another user. Figure 7-9 illustrates how this happens.

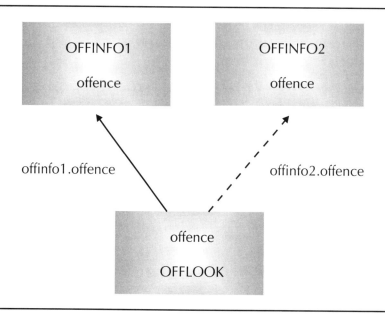

FIGURE 7-9. *Looking at data from the access schema*

Let's cover the important points from Figure 7-9.

■ OFFINFO1 and OFFINFO2 own a table called OFFENCE.

■ OFFINFO1 and OFFINFO2 have given OFFLOOK the right to look at each of their OFFENCE tables using the SQL statement **grant select on offence to offlook;**.

■ Using the Oracle convention for **owner.table_name**, OFFLOOK can refer to each schema's OFFENCE table with the name OFFINFO1.OFFENCE or OFFINFO2.OFFENCE.

■ OFFLOOK has created a synonym called OFFENCE pointing at the OFFENCE table owned by OFFINFO1. The synonym was created using the SQL statement **create synonym offence for offinfo1.offence;**.

- OFFLOOK can have its OFFENCE synonym pointing at only one schema at a time; therefore, a dotted line pointing at OFFINFO2 indicates it is not currently active.

- OFFLOOK can now issue a query against OFFENCE belonging to OFFINFO1 using the word **offence** rather than the extended account/table syntax.

Activating and Deactivating a Schema

A schema is activated by ensuring privileges are in place for OFFLOOK to look at the schema in question, then making sure the OFFLOOK synonyms point at the correct schema. This is done in two steps—giving the privilege out, then doing the OFFLOOK private synonyms.

Giving Privileges to OFFLOOK

The following SQL code can be used while connected to the database as the appropriate schema owner (we use OFFLOOK2 for the example) to ensure OFFLOOK can see the data the schema owns:

```
/* ------------------------------------------- */
/* Oracle8 Data Warehousing   Oracle Press 1998  */
/*                                             */
/* givesel.sql                                 */
/*                                             */
/* Corey, Abbey, Abramson, Taub                */
/* ------------------------------------------- */
set echo off feed off pages 0
spool givesel
select 'grant '||decode(object_type,'TABLE','select on ',
                                    'VIEW', 'select on ',
                                    'PROCEDURE', 'execute on ',
                                    'PACKAGE', 'execute on ',
                                    'FUNCTION', 'execute on ')||
       object_name||' to offlook;'
  from user_objects
 where object_type in ('TABLE','VIEW','PROCEDURE',
                       'PACKAGE','FUNCTION');

spool off
set echo on feed on
```

This will produce output similar to the following:

```
grant select on offence to offlook;
grant select on term to offlook;
grant execute on format_cell to offlook;
grant execute on yesno to offlook;
```

Creating Synonyms

The last step in enabling the OFFLOOK user to view OFFINFO2's information is setting up private synonyms. There are a number of ways to do this; regardless of which way is used, any existing synonyms have to be dropped first. The next piece of code drops synonyms while logged onto Oracle as OFFLOOK. Notice the last line of code (in bold); it is this line that runs the code to drop the synonyms.

```
/* -------------------------------------------- */
/* Oracle8 Data Warehousing    Oracle Press 1998  */
/*                                                */
/* syndrop.sql                                    */
/*                                                */
/* Corey, Abbey, Abramson, Taub                   */
/* -------------------------------------------- */
set echo off feed off pages 0
spool syndrop
select 'drop synonym '||synonym_name||';'
  from user_synonyms;
spool off
set echo on feed on
start syndrop.lst
```

Using the following code segment, the private synonyms are re-created for OFFLOOK:

```
/* -------------------------------------------- */
/* Oracle8 Data Warehousing    Oracle Press 1998  */
/*                                                */
/* syncre.sql                                     */
/*                                                */
/* Corey, Abbey, Abramson, Taub                   */
/* -------------------------------------------- */
set echo off feed off pages 0
spool syncre
```

```
select 'create synonym '||table_name||' for '||owner||'.'||
       table_name||';'
  from user_tab_privs_recd
 where owner = 'OFFLOOK2';  -- Or OFFLOOK1 if activating the other schema.
spool off
set echo on feed on
start syncre.lst
```

The Power of this Approach

The power lies in the ability to refresh one schema while users are working with the other. One schema can be worked with little or no interruption for the regular user community. The caveat about the double-schema approach lies in the processing power required to refresh one schema and how it draws resources from the users. Users normally happy with the performance of their queries can notice a dramatic drop in turnaround time when a schema refresh is running.

If you adopt this double-schema approach, we would recommend you ask yourself questions including the following before initiating a refresh during heavy user access times:

- Can the users wait until tomorrow?

- Can part of the warehouse be refreshed if they can't wait?

- Based on the way lines of authority are constructed, is the request coming from a source with the appropriate authority to make the request in the first place?

- Do you have a realistic time for the refreshed schema to be available to the users?

- How much of the refresh routine is brand new; that is, has been tested and retested in development, but not run yet against the live warehouse?

- Is the environment supporting the warehouse (i.e., the amount of memory the instance has at its disposal and the initialization parameter file used to start the database) conducive to a schema refresh? In Chapters 8 and 20, we discuss starting the database using different initialization parameter files and how one may be suited to query processing and the other mainly to loading operations.

Physical Implementation Checklist

We are going to close this chapter with a list of Oracle-specific items that need to be part of the physical data warehouse. Some relate to client issues, some to server, some to the communication between the two. Table 7-9 lists these items, in no particular order, and offers some notes on the particulars of each step. "S" stands for server, and "C" for client.

NOTE
This checklist is gleaned from our experience with warehouses, data marts, and other large information repositories. We have probably thought of some points you may not, and there is more than likely some stuff here you had not considered.

Software	S	C	Notes
Oracle8 Server installation	X		In many cases, this will involve an upgrade from an earlier release. Some functionality (e.g., partitioning with the Partitioning Option) is not part of the base product and must be acquired separately.
Load and transformation	X	X	In-house routines as well as one or more canned products used to deliver this cog in the warehouse solution need to be in place. There are many extract, transform, and load tools out there; many have a server and a client component.

TABLE 7-9. *Physical Implementation Checklist*

Communications	S	C	Notes
Net8 installation	X	X	Server portion is done as part of the Oracle8 Server installation. Usually, but not always, TCP/IP is the chosen protocol on both ends.
Net8 configuration files	X	X	The Net8 "tnsnames.ora" file is required on both the server and the client, and "listener.ora" is required on the server. The former contains a list of database aliases and connect information for the database running on the server. The latter contains information about the incoming connections and how they should be dispatched by Net8.
ODBC		X	Four letters in the industry that are a double-edged sword. Open Database Connectivity permits communication between many development, OLAP, and query tools and the Oracle8 database, as well as the offerings by other database vendors, including Informix, Sybase, and Microsoft. Many installations are not enamored with ODBC, but realize they are "stuck" with it. Some vendors, Cognos in particular, have weaned themselves of ODBC in their connectivity equation. Some people feel the choice of tools is affected by whether ODBC need be part of a vendor's solution.

TABLE 7-9. *Physical Implementation Checklist (continued)*

Space	S	C	Notes
OLAP cubes			Different vendors' products use different approaches for storing their data in their multidimensional cube. In the OLAP product selection, procurement, and rollout phase, you will have to visit this issue with the vendor(s) and ensure adequate space is available.
Data verification stage/area			This is a holding tank where data that will end up in the warehouse is inspected and further prepared for insertion in the warehouse tables.
24 x 7 availability			This will impact on the backup and refresh activities on the warehouse. The 24 x 7 issue is easily addressed with Oracle8 with the proper preparation. You should use tape backup software that is capable of backing up open datafiles if such an animal exists in your operating environment.
Hardware			
Approach to parallelism	X		Naturally, this is hardware dependent, and may end up being something you are forced to live with (i.e., the fact that the warehouse machine only has one CPU).
RAID level			RAID (redundant array of independent disks) is discussed in Chapter 13. The level, from 0 to 5, needs to be selected in the midst of the physical planning for the warehouse.

TABLE 7-9.   *Physical Implementation Checklist* (continued)

Availability	S	C	Notes
Backup			Routines related to backup and recovery need to be ironed out, tested, and put in place. Chapter 11 is dedicated to backing up the warehouse. There are hardware, software, and management issues to consider.
Loading area			Many locations place their warehouse- and analysis-bound data in a special area where it can be scrubbed, cleaned, transformed (laundered?) before it ends up in its final resting place. The amount of space is very installation dependent.
Two schemas			If using the approach we have called dual-schema access, the user accounts must be in place and the users must have appropriate space allocations in place to accommodate their version of the warehouse schema.

TABLE 7-9.   *Physical Implementation Checklist* (continued)

We now move on to the data transport piece. In the next chapter, we will have a look at extraction, transformation, and loading of information into the warehouse. There is quite the hodgepodge of solutions out there to assist the process. The key, once the source data is identified and mapped to target locations, is ensuring the feed of data from operational systems and other sources is robust and easy to set up, maintain, and change. Easier said than done? We'll see.

CHAPTER

8

Moving the Data into the Warehouse

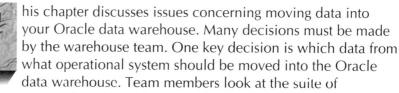

his chapter discusses issues concerning moving data into your Oracle data warehouse. Many decisions must be made by the warehouse team. One key decision is which data from what operational system should be moved into the Oracle data warehouse. Team members look at the suite of operational systems and decide which have data useful to the decision support process. Once the source data has been selected, the team moves on to decide how to get the data into Oracle. This chapter bites off quite a bit of material—we hope you're hungry—including the following:

- Moving data from flat files (regardless of the source) into Oracle using SQL*Loader

- Moving data from other Oracle systems into the Oracle8 data warehouse using export and import

NOTE
Partitioned objects can be the target of SQL*Loader and import sessions, and also the source of export sections. We will highlight the syntax for using partitioned objects with these tools; the theory and examples we use in this chapter could be easily tailored to partitioned objects.

- Moving data into the warehouse using third-party software

- Using Oracle Enterprise Manager for running SQL*Loader, export, and import

- Oracle's Data Mart Suite for NT offering

- Engine-based and code generator tools for moving data into the warehouse

- Oracle's Transparent Gateway technology—how it can be used to read data directly from some non-Oracle systems

Your business operational systems, whether they are Oracle or non-Oracle in nature, are the source repositories from which warehouse data is collected. This chapter focuses on moving data into the warehouse regardless of the source; however, the mechanisms and routines discussed in the export/import section are only applicable when the source data is stored in an Oracle database. No reason exists why Oracle source data must be in version 7—Oracle8 is available on most operating systems today.

The section on SQL*Loader and the Transparent Gateways is applicable regardless of where the source resides. These gateways allow reading of data from a handful of popular database vendors. In a nutshell, Oracle highlights gateways to the following non-Oracle databases:

- Procedural Gateway to APPC—applications that use IBM's Advanced Program-to-Program Communication

- Transparent Gateway for IBM's DB2

- Transparent Gateway for IBM's DRDA using the DRDA standard APPC/LU 6.2 protocol

- Transparent Gateway to EDA/SQL that allows transparent access to 15 IBM MVS mainframe databases

- Transparent Gateway to Informix

- Transparent Gateway to Unisys' Relational Data Management System (RDMS)

- Transparent Gateway to RMS on Digital (DEC) VAX

- Transparent Gateway to Sybase

- Transparent Gateway to Teradata

Many data warehouses use SQL*Loader as a data loading workhorse. The input to SQL*Loader is usually an ASCII text flat file produced in an Oracle or non-Oracle operational system environment. As the data is loaded into Oracle, a control file instructs SQL*Loader how to map the incoming text into columns in one or more Oracle database tables. For example, the following four lines show a sample of how the text may be mapped. The first two lines establish column positions in the input text file:

```
         1         2         3         4         5         6         7
1234567890123456789012345678901234567890123456789012345678901234567890123
0-07-882390-0Oracle8 Tuning          Corey Abbey Dechichio Abramson  1998
84-481-0337-3Puesta a punto de OracleCorey Abbey Dechichio          1995
```

Once SQL*Loader knows the book ISBN lies in columns 1 to 13, the book title in columns 14 to 37, the author names in columns 38 to 69, and the year of publication in columns 70 to 73, it can place the data in the correct column in the corresponding Oracle table.

Database Objects

For the SQL*Loader section of this chapter, we will lead you through a few sample load sessions, using the Oracle tables shown in Table 8-1 as the target objects.

NOTE
*The sections on SQL*Loader, export, and import are going to concentrate on using these three products in a DOS window from Windows NT 4.0. They can also be run from the Oracle Enterprise Manager (OEM)/Data Manager interface. We spend a wee bit of time at the end of the chapter (in the "But I Want to Use OEM" section) showing you the Data Manager and mapping one of the DOS window activities to how it is done in OEM.*

Acc_trans		Account	
account_nbr	number(10)	Account_nbr	number(10)
day	number(2)	Account_type	varchar2(2)
month	varchar2(3)	Owner	varchar2(30)
year	number(4)	Last_activity	date
transaction_code	varchar2(2)	Status	varchar2(2)
debit_amount	number(10,2)		
credit_amount	number(10,2)		

TABLE 8-1. *Tables Used in Examples*

SQL*Loader

SQL*Loader is used to move data from operating system files into Oracle database tables. An *operating system file* contains alphanumeric text data; alphanumeric data comprises upper- and lowercase letters, digits 0 to 9, and an assortment of special characters—for example, commas, colons, and question marks. There are two main inputs to a loader session:

1. The data to be moved into the Oracle tables.

2. A set of one or more command line or control file configuration parameters that tell Oracle what the incoming data looks like (and where it can be found) and how to place data in the target tables.

These discussions of SQL*Loader and step-by-step guidelines on how it is used do not cover every situation you may encounter when moving data into the Oracle data warehouse. Based on our experience with the product, features and methods we highlight pertain to 95 percent of all SQL*Loader sessions. A thorough discussion of the bells and whistles of SQL*Loader can be found in the *Oracle8 Server Utilities User's Guide*, part of the documentation set on paper and CD.

NOTE
*SQL*Loader is generally the load method of choice for large warehouses as it offers the fastest load rates into Oracle (using the parallel/direct path).*

Features of SQL*Loader

SQL*Loader loads a variety of types of data into Oracle tables and can do the following:

- Load data from disk or tape.

- Support a wide range of data types, including date and binary data.

- Selectively load data into one or more tables based upon one or more filtering criteria.

- Load fixed- or variable-length records. A *fixed-length record* is one where the width of each single information item—for example, LAST_NAME—in each line of data being loaded is the same length. If the LAST_NAME is allocated 25 characters, then the name CHARRON would be padded with 18 blanks, and the name RUTHERFORD would be padded with 15 blanks. A *variable-length record* is one where the width of each single information item depends on its number of characters: CHARRON would be 7 characters long and RUTHERFORD would be 10 characters.

- Generate unique keys as Oracle tables are populated.

- Support a number of high-performance mechanisms crucial to large data loads.

- Produce sophisticated error reports to assist further processing required on bad or incomplete data. When records being loaded into Oracle contain data that does not conform to the restrictions of the target table, this record is said to contain *bad data*. Suppose a numeric bank balance field contains the characters "40984T"; because the letter *T* is nonnumeric, the row contains bad data. When records are missing data in items the Oracle table insists cannot be blank, the data is said to be *incomplete*. Suppose a target table contained a STATUS column specified as **not null**—that is, must not contain only spaces—and a record in the input file had two spaces where the status should be located. The record would be rejected because it is incomplete.

- Preprocess data before it is moved into Oracle. Suppose an operational system uses all uppercase text and the data warehouse needs mixed cases. As the name BARNEY LLOYD is moved into the target table, it could be converted to "Barney Lloyd."

NOTE
*We use a Windows NT 4.0 environment for all the command samples we use in this SQL*Loader session. The command is different for other platforms; for example, **sqlldr** or **sqlload** is used in UNIX.*

Invoking SQL*Loader

The command used to run SQL*Loader is **sqlldr80**. The next listing displays the help output from invoking SQL*Loader without any parameters:

```
SQL*Loader: Release 8.0.4.0.0 - Production on Thu Dec 18 9:0:58 1999
(c) Copyright 1998 Oracle Corporation.  All rights reserved.
Usage: SQLLOAD keyword=value [,keyword=value,...]
Valid Keywords:
    userid -- ORACLE username/password
   control -- Control file name
       log -- Log file name
       bad -- Bad file name
      data -- Datafile name
   discard -- Discard file name
discardmax -- Number of discards to allow        (Default all)
      skip -- Number of logical records to skip   (Default 0)
      load -- Number of logical records to load   (Default all)
    errors -- Number of errors to allow          (Default 50)
      rows -- Number of rows in conventional path bind array or
              between direct path data saves
                (Default: Conventional path 64, Direct path all)
  bindsize -- Size of conventional path bind array in bytes  (Default 65536)
    silent -- Suppress messages during run (header,feedback,errors,
              discards,partitions)
    direct -- use direct path                    (Default FALSE)
   parfile -- parameter file: name of file that contains parameter
              specifications
  parallel -- do parallel load                   (Default FALSE)
      file -- File to allocate extents from
skip_unusable_indexes -- disallow/allow unusable indexes or index
                      partitions (Default FALSE)
skip_index_maintenance -- do not maintain indexes, mark affected indexes
                      as unusable  (Default FALSE)
commit_discontinued -- commit loaded rows when load is discontinued
                      (Default FALSE)
PLEASE NOTE: Command-line parameters may be specified either by
position or by keywords.  An example of the former case is 'sqlload
scott/tiger foo'; an example of the latter is 'sqlload control=foo
userid=scott/tiger'.  One may specify parameters by position before
but not after parameters specified by keywords.  For example,
'sqlload scott/tiger control=foo logfile=log' is allowed, but
'sqlload scott/tiger control=foo log' is not, even though the
position of the parameter 'log' is correct.
```

In the listing, the usage line tells the operator to enter keywords followed by their values. A *keyword* means something to SQL*Loader; it behaves in a certain way based on the keywords it finds and the values placed after each keyword.

SQL*Loader can be invoked in two ways—using a series of command-line parameters to control the behavior of the session or using a minimal set of command-line parameters and specifying the session parameters in the control file. Look at the following command used to invoke SQL*Loader:

```
sqlldr80 userid=/ control=regional bad=regbad.dat discard=regdsc.dat
```

would accomplish the same as using the command:

```
sqlldr80 userid=/ control=regional
```

and placing the following keywords in the control file beside the name of the input file:

```
infile 'regional.dat' badfile regbad.dat discardfile regdsc.dat
```

Inputs to and Outputs from SQL*Loader

The SQL*Loader control file is responsible for directing what goes where—that is, what Oracle table or tables receive data—and for describing the environment within which the loader session operates. Regardless of what is in the control file, SQL*Loader creates a number of output files by default. In this section, we refer to a control file named "accload.ctl". The file extension ".ctl" is assumed by SQL*Loader unless you manually use something else.

Log File

With the control file "accload.ctl", SQL*Loader writes a log file named "accload.log". This file contains a wealth of information about the load. A log file can be specified when SQL*Loader is invoked using the following convention:

```
sqlldr80 userid=/ control=accload log=accload
```

although usually we let it write a default file name.

CAUTION
SQL*Loader will overwrite a log file without asking if it finds one by the same name specified in the current directory. To avoid this, you might have to use the "log=" entry when invoking the loader. Be careful!

Bad File

By default, SQL*Loader will write a bad file with the extension ".bad" and the same name as the control file; in this case, it would be "accload.bad". SQL*Loader writes records to this file when it is unable to insert a record into a table. This could be caused by a data type inconsistency if nonnumeric data is found where a numeric is expected. SQL*Loader always writes a bad file and, in most cases, the existence of a bad file with a nonzero length indicates something probably went wrong with the run.

Discard File

Some loader sessions do different tasks with the records in an input file, depending on what is found in each record. As data is read, it is tested using the SQL*Loader **when** evaluator. If a condition specified in a **when** clause is true, a row is loaded according to the column specifications after the **when**. Say you want to load only the record whose third column has the letter "A." The **when** clause to accomplish this is

 when (3) = 'A'

If one or more **when** keywords are used and a record fails all the tests, it is written to the discard file, not the bad file. The extension for the discard file defaults to the text ".dsc" unless otherwise specified. If no **when**'s exist in a control file, a discard file is not created.

The Control File

This file controls how SQL*Loader will behave during a load session, hence, the name "control." The control file has a number of sections—some mandatory, some optional—depending on the nature of its loader session. The control file usually begins with the text:

```
load data
```

though the keyword:

```
options
```

with a number of parameters and parameter values can precede load data.

Specifying the Input File(s)

The input file is specified next starting with the keyword:

```
infile
```

followed by the name of the file. The file extension ".DAT" is assumed, such that the syntax:

```
infile = 'ACCOUNTS'
```

would assume the input datafile name was ACCOUNTS.DAT. Multiple input files are specified by successive infile keywords, each followed by the file name.

TIP
Enclosing the file name in single quotes is recommended. Some characters—for example, the "$,"—mean something special to some operating systems, such as UNIX. If one of these types of characters is imbedded in the input file name, the quotes help ensure SQL*Loader will be able to open the file.

Using UNIX as an example, if the file name is specified as IN$ACCDATA without the quotes, SQL*Loader will complain that it cannot open a file named "IN.dat"!

Processing Options for the Input File(s)

After the input file specifications, its processing options can be listed. These options instruct SQL*Loader what to do with the bad and discarded records. If a session read the input file "mytown.dat", the control file could override the bad and discard file defaults (mytown.bad and mytown.dsc, respectively) by specifying the input file and its processing options:

```
load data
infile 'mytown.dat' discardfile mtdisc.rec
                    badfile mtbad.rec
```

Most control files do not list input file processing options. Imagine the following scenario that would warrant coding these options: Regional data has been deposited in four directories, called "d:\usr\apps\region\north", "d:\usr\apps\region\east", "d:\usr\apps\region\south", and "d:\usr\apps\region\west". Each directory contains a text file called "reg_dat.dat" and SQL*Loader and its regional control file sit in "f:\sys\dba\region\load". The load process is four phases, with one run per region. To make things easier to manage, the load has eight steps:

1. Copy north data to d:\usr\apps\region\load directory (this is required because the person running the load sessions cannot create the log and bad files anywhere other than f:\sys\dba\region\load).

2. Run SQL*Loader using reg_dat.dat as input and regional.ctl as the control file.

3. Copy east data to the d:\usr\apps\region\load directory.

4. Run SQL*Loader using reg_dat.dat as input and regional.ctl as the control file.

5. Copy south data to the d:\usr\apps\region\load directory.

6. Run SQL*Loader using reg_dat.dat as input and regional.ctl as the control file.

7. Copy west data to the d:\usr\apps\region\load directory.

8. Run SQL*Loader using reg_dat.dat as input and regional.ctl as the control file.

Guess what? Each run of SQL*Loader created the same log file (regional.log) and the same bad file (regional.bad). It gets worse! The west region data load's log and bad files are what sit on the disk when the eight steps are completed. Where are the files for the other three regions? They are lost—overwritten by the west load session. Can you determine how successful (or even worse, unsuccessful) the other three regions' loads were without their log and bad files? Probably not. This is a situation where naming log and bad files may be useful.

Target Object(s)—Tables

The target table name is specified next, preceded by the keywords **into table**. The table must exist before the load process commences, and its record count before the load must synch with the keyword specified for the record creation mode in the next section. The user ID running the SQL*Loader session must have sufficient Oracle privileges to insert rows into the destination table.

If more than one target table exists, each has its own **into table** clause. The following listing illustrates how this is worded in the control file:

```
into account_trans
    when day between '01' and '31'
. . . .
into account_nbr
    when account_type between 'AA' and 'ZZ'
. . . .
```

Target Object(s)—Partitioned Tables

This is no big deal; the target can be a partitioned table or one specific partition within that table.

> **NOTE**
> *We discuss partitioning in Chapter 9; please consult the material there for a discussion of the partition key and general concepts related to the Partitioning Option with Oracle8.*

There are two points to cover when working with partitioned objects in SQL*Loader:

1. When the target of a load session is a single partition within a partitioned table, you use the table extended partition syntax as shown in the next listing. Notice the table name with the partition receiving the data in parentheses after the table name:

```
load data infile 'reg_east.dat'
into table sale partition (east_data) . . . .
```

If data in the input file cannot be loaded into the specified partition, you will receive the Oracle error shown next and a piece of the log file similar to that shown after ORA-14401. The log file will highlight the errors and relate them to the partition being loaded. The rows that fail based on their partition key will be written to the loader session bad file.

```
Record 122199: Rejected - Error on table SALE, partition EAST_DATA.
ORA-14401: inserted partition key is outside specified partition
Record 123270: Rejected - Error on table SALE, partition EAST_DATA.
ORA-14401: inserted partition key is outside specified partition

Table SALE, partition EAST_DATA:
  134213 Rows successfully loaded.
  2 Rows not loaded due to data errors.
  0 Rows not loaded because all WHEN clauses were failed.
  0 Rows not loaded because all fields were null.
Space allocated for bind array:                    256 bytes(64 rows)
Space allocated for memory besides bind array:       0 bytes
Total logical records skipped:          0
Total logical records read:        134215
Total logical records rejected:         2
Total logical records discarded:        0
```

2. If all the partitions are being loaded at once (i.e., as if the table were not partitioned), the same syntax is used for the table name as shown in the "Target Object(s)—Tables" section.

Record Creation Mode

You have one of three choices for this section of the control file:

1. **insert** This is the default, which is assumed if this keyword is not in the control file. The table must be empty before the load.

2. **replace** The table is emptied of rows prior to the load and the successful rows are moved into the table(s).

3. **append** Data that already resides in the table is left as is and new rows are added.

If **insert** (the default) is chosen for record creation mode, the table must be empty prior to the load. If **replace** is chosen and the table has no rows in it, the rows from the input datafile are loaded. When **replace** is chosen, the person running the session must have delete privileges on the target table(s).

Processing Fixed-Length Records

Processing fixed-length records is the heart of most SQL*Loader sessions. This is where the layout of the input file is established. Three main parts exist to each entry in this section:

1. The name of the column in the target table that will receive the specified data. The first line in a series of column specifications must start with an opening parenthesis. The last line in a series must be terminated with a closing parenthesis.

2. The start and end positions of the specified data.

3. The data type of the incoming data.

   ```
   -- The double dash is how to embed comments in a SQL*Loader
   -- control file. Blank lines can be left anywhere.
   load data
   infile 'account.dat'
   into table account_trans append
   (account_nbr        position(01:10) character,  -- i
   ```

```
day                 position(11:12) character,   -- ii
month               position(13:14) character,
transaction_code    position(15:16) character,
debit_amount        position(17:26) character,
credit_amount       position(27:36) character)   -- iii
```

The following should be noted about the previous control file:

i. Note the opening parenthesis at the start of this first position line. Successive lines are separated by a comma.

ii. Using the two-digit number all the way down is cosmetic. Some large control files get hard to read when many position lines have unaligned specifications. Note how the numeric fields in the table receive what is referred to as "character data" in the input file. The number "23" for example, is simply the alphanumeric character "2" followed by a "3," even though the target table treats them as a number.

iii. Note the closing parenthesis on the last position line. No comma is at the end of this last line.

Ninety-five percent of control files resemble what is shown in the previous listing. If you need to do a run that falls into the remaining five percent, read on and consult the *Oracle8 Server Utilities* manual for issues not addressed here.

Fixed-Record-Length Examples

To round out this section of the chapter, here are two live examples of SQL*Loader sessions. The first example will load data from an input datafile into the ACCOUNT table, described at the beginning of this chapter in the "Database Objects" section. The second example will load data into either the ACCOUNT table or the ACCOUNT_TRANS table.

EXAMPLE #1　This session conforms to the specifications shown in Table 8-2.

Specification	Value
Input file	account.dat
Control file	account.ctl
Bad file	account.bad
Log file	accload.out
Table to load	account
Table status before load	preserve existing data

TABLE 8-2. *Specifications for Example #1*

NOTE
The bad file has the same name as the control file; therefore, no need exists to mention the bad file on the command line. The log file uses the file extension ".out" rather than the default ".log;" the name of the log file must be mentioned on the command line. The following listing shows the control file:

```
load data
infile 'account.dat'
into table account append
(account_nbr    position(1:10)  char,
 account_type   position(11:12) char,
 owner          position(13:42) char,
 last_activity  position(43:48) date 'YYMMDD',
 status         position(49:50) char)
```

Notice the incoming data uses the date format 'YYMMDD' for its dates. This format—for example, January 18, 1999, would be shown as 990118—is shown in the control file. As the data is moved into Oracle, it is converted to the default Oracle date mask and becomes 18-JAN-99. The following listing shows the output from invoking SQL*Loader for this run:

```
sqlldr80 userid=system/manager control=account.ctl log=account.out
SQL*Loader: Release 8.0.4.0.0 - Production on Wed Nov 12 14:02:14 1999
Copyright (c) Oracle Corporation 1998.  All rights reserved.

Commit point reached - logical record count 64
Commit point reached - logical record count 128
Commit point reached - logical record count 192
Commit point reached - logical record count 256
Commit point reached - logical record count 320
Commit point reached - logical record count 384
Commit point reached - logical record count 448
Commit point reached - logical record count 512
Commit point reached - logical record count 576
Commit point reached - logical record count 640
Commit point reached - logical record count 704
Commit point reached - logical record count 768
Commit point reached - logical record count 832
Commit point reached - logical record count 896
Commit point reached - logical record count 960
```

Now look at the log file:

```
SQL*Loader: Release 8.0.4.0.0 - Production on Wed Nov 12 14:28:59 1997
Copyright (c) Oracle Corporation 1998.  All rights reserved.
Control File:   account.ctl
Datafile:       account.dat
  Bad File:     account.bad
  Discard File: none specified

(Allow all discards)
Number to load: ALL
Number to skip: 0
Errors allowed: 50
Bind array:     64 rows, maximum of 65536 bytes
Continuation:   none specified
Path used:      Conventional
Table ACCOUNT, loaded from every logical record.
Insert option in effect for this table: APPEND
```

Column Name	Position	Len	Term	Encl	Datatype
ACCOUNT_NBR	1:10	10			CHARACTER
ACCOUNT_TYPE	1:12	2			CHARACTER
OWNER	13:42	30			CHARACTER

```
LAST_ACTIVITY            43:48           6        DATE YYMMDD
STATUS                   49:50           2        CHARACTER

Table ACCOUNT:
  960 Rows successfully loaded.
  0 Rows not loaded due to data errors.
  0 Rows not loaded because all WHEN clauses were failed.
  0 Rows not loaded because all fields were null.

Space allocated for bind array:                 4608 bytes(64 rows)
Space allocated for memory besides bind array: 56709 bytes
Total logical records skipped:          0
Total logical records read:           960
Total logical records rejected:         0
Total logical records discarded:        0

Run began on Wed Jun 12 14:28:59 1997
Run ended on Wed Jun 12 14:29:00 1997
Elapsed time was:      00:00:01.12
CPU time was:          00:00:00.17
```

Seems like everything went well. All 960 records were loaded. Suppose problems had occurred? The following listing describes the same load session, but with some bad data:

```
Record 64: Rejected - Error on table ACCOUNT, column LAST_ACTIVITY.
ORA-01839: date not valid for month specified
 Record 203: Rejected - Error on table ACCOUNT, column ACCOUNT_NBR.
ORA-01722: invalid number

Table ACCOUNT:
  958 Rows successfully loaded.
  2 Rows not loaded due to data errors.
  0 Rows not loaded because all WHEN clauses were failed.
  0 Rows not loaded because all fields were null.
Space allocated for bind array:                 4608 bytes(64 rows)
Space allocated for memory besides bind array:  56709 bytes
Total logical records skipped:          0
Total logical records read:           960
Total logical records rejected:         2
Total logical records discarded:        0
```

Record 64 was rejected because it had a month number of 15; record 203 was kicked out because its account number was expected to be numeric, but it contained at least one nonnumeric character. The offending rows were written to account.bad, which is shown in the following listing. The offending data is in boldface:

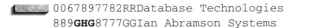

```
0067897782RRDatabase Technologies      961529TT
889GHG8777GGIan Abramson Systems       960529TT
```

What is so powerful about the bad file is that its data can be fixed; then, it can be used as input into another SQL*Loader session. By writing offending rows to the bad file, SQL*Loader gives the best of both worlds:

1. No bad data can possibly be written to the database.

2. The bad data can be fixed and fed back to another loader session, providing a significant degree of completeness checking to the operator.

EXAMPLE #2 This session conforms to the specifications shown in Table 8-3.

Because the discard file does not use the same file name as the control file, the discard file must be mentioned when SQL*Loader is invoked. The session will try to load account data into two tables; hence, the **when** keyword will be used. Records will be written to the discard file when they

Specification	Value
Input file	account.dat
Control file	accmult.ctl
Bad file	account.bad
Discard file	accmult.dsc
Tables to load	account_transaccount
Table status before load	replace existing data

TABLE 8-3. *Specifications for Example #2*

fail all the criteria defined by the **when** clause. The next listing shows the control file for this run of SQL*Loader:

```
load data
infile 'account.dat'
-- We only want to load transaction records for the year 1990
-- and records for active accounts (i.e., status of 00)
into table account_trans replace
when year = '1990'
  (account_nbr          position(01:10) char,
   day                  position(11:12) char,
   month                position(13:15) char,
   year                 position(16:19) char,
   transaction_code     position(20:21) char,
   debit_amount         position(22:31) char,
   credit_amount        position(32:41) char)

into table account replace
when status = '00'
  (account_nbr     position(01:10) char,
   account_type    position(11:12) char,
   owner           position(13:42) char,
   last_activity   position(43:48) date 'YYMMDD',
   status          position(49:50) char)
```

Because two tables receive data, SQL*Loader evaluates each **when** condition in turn, according to the following logic:

```
if positions 16 to 19 contain the text "1990" then
   if rest of data in the record does not violate the rules then
      load row into ACCOUNT_TRANS
   else
      write row to account.bad
   end if
else
   if positions 49 to 50 contain the text "00" then
      if rest of data in the record does not violate the rules then
         load row into ACCOUNT
      else
         write row to account.bad
      end if
end if
```

"Violate the rules" means the data does not raise any error conditions when an attempt to load into one of the tables is executed. Say positions 49 and 50 of a record contain the text "00" (meaning it is a candidate for insertion into the ACCOUNT table), but positions 43 to 48 (where a valid LAST_ACTIVITY date is expected) contains the text "960431" (for April 31, 1996). Because there is no such date as April 31, the row is rejected with Oracle error 1839.

The next listing shows the output from invoking SQL*Loader for this run:

```
C:\ORANT\DATABASE> sqlldr80 userid=system/manager control=accmult.ctl
discard=accmult.dsc
SQL*Loader: Release 8.0.4.0.0 - Production on Wed Nov 12 14:02:14 1999
Copyright (c) Oracle Corporation 1998.  All rights reserved.
Commit point reached - logical record count 64
Commit point reached - logical record count 128
Commit point reached - logical record count 192
Commit point reached - logical record count 256
Commit point reached - logical record count 320
Commit point reached - logical record count 384
Commit point reached - logical record count 448
Commit point reached - logical record count 512
Commit point reached - logical record count 576
```

Now look at the SQL*Loader log file:

```
SQL*Loader: Release 8.0.4.0.0 - Production on Wed Nov 12 20:54:44 1999
Copyright (c) Oracle Corporation 1998.  All rights reserved.

Control File:   ././accmult.ctl
Datafile:       ././account.dat
  Bad File:     ././account.bad
  Discard File: accmult.dsc
 (Allow all discards)

Number to load: ALL
Number to skip: 0
Errors allowed: 50
Bind array:     64 rows, maximum of 65536 bytes
Continuation:   none specified
Path used:      Conventional
```

```
Table ACCOUNT_TRANS, loaded when YEAR = 0X31393930(character '1990')
Insert option in effect for this table: REPLACE
  Column Name                  Position   Len   Term Encl Datatype
-------------------------    -----------  ----- ---- ---- ----------
ACCOUNT_NBR                        1:10   10              CHARACTER
DAY                               11:12    2              CHARACTER
MONTH                             13:15    3              CHARACTER
YEAR                              16:19    4              CHARACTER
TRANSACTION_CODE                  20:21    2              CHARACTER
DEBIT_AMOUNT                      22:31   10              CHARACTER
CREDIT_AMOUNT                     32:41   10              CHARACTER

Table ACCOUNT, loaded when STATUS = 0X3030(character '00')
Insert option in effect for this table: REPLACE
  Column Name                  Position   Len   Term Encl Datatype
-------------------------    -----------  ----- ---- ---- -----------
ACCOUNT_NBR                        1:10   10              CHARACTER
ACCOUNT_TYPE                      11:12    2              CHARACTER
OWNER                             13:42   30              CHARACTER
LAST_ACTIVITY                     43:48    6              DATE YYMMDD
STATUS                            49:50    2              CHARACTER

Record 43: Discarded - failed all WHEN clauses.
Record 213: Discarded - failed all WHEN clauses.
Record 462: Discarded - failed all WHEN clauses.
Record 2: Rejected - Error on table ACCOUNT_TRANS.
ORA-01843: not a valid month.

Table ACCOUNT_TRANS:
  254 Rows successfully loaded.
  0 Rows not loaded due to data errors.
  2 Rows not loaded because all WHEN clauses were failed.
  0 Rows not loaded because all fields were null.

Table ACCOUNT:
  318 Rows successfully loaded.
  1 Rows not loaded due to data errors.
  1 Rows not loaded because all WHEN clauses were failed.
  0 Rows not loaded because all fields were null.

Total logical records skipped:          0
Total logical records read:           576
Total logical records rejected:         1
Total logical records discarded:        3
```

```
Run began on Wed Nov 12 20:54:44 1999
Run ended on Wed Nov 12 20:54:44 1999
Elapsed time was:      00:00:00.58
CPU time was:          00:00:00.21

Space allocated for bind array:                    9728 bytes(64 rows)
Space allocated for memory besides bind array:  91245 bytes
```

The row that was rejected due to the Oracle error was written to
account.bad and the rows that failed all **when** tests were written to
accmult.dsc. The next listing shows the contents of the bad, then the discard
files, in that order; the offending data is in boldface:

```
0067897782RRDatabase Technologies           96043100
0032236177THRiver Styx                      90021205
006789778212JUN1988CR           0000034569
004329744404DEC1991DR0000234888
```

Processing Variable-Length Records

A common occurrence is to move data from a desktop application—for
example, MS Access—into Oracle for the data warehouse. "Delimited"
describes this format of input data. A *delimiter* is a character that separates
one item of information from another on the same line. For example, the
data in the next listing is called *comma-delimited*:

```
123,"OK","Michael Abbey Systems International Inc.",1828,9383,"R",908
456,"GT","IOUG Americas",342,2211,"Q",82
789,"OK","The Beatles",77,2128,"R",112
```

Most comma-delimited files place character data in quotation marks.
Herein is the reason for calling this type of information "variable length."
Notice how the first line is 69 characters long, the next line is 40 characters,
and the last line is 38 characters. Once SQL*Loader is told what delimits
separate information items, it can properly move the data into Oracle tables.
Look at the control file to accomplish this load:

```
load data
infile 'customer.dat'
into table customer append
(cust_id    char terminated by ',',
 status     char enclosed by '"',
 cname      char enclosed by '"',
```

```
acc_num    char terminated by ','
tax_class  char terminated by ',',
dsc_class  char enclosed by '"',
source     char terminated by whitespace)
```

Note the following:

1. The single quote is used to delimit the delimiting character (this reminds me of defining a "football" as a "football" when we were kids—in other words, using a word to define the word we're defining!). Some software permits using the single and double quotes interchangeably, but Oracle does not.

2. The punctuation rules—that is, comma-separated field definitions with the whole list bound in parentheses—are the same as for fixed-length record loads.

3. The trailing information item is not terminated by the comma; hence, the keyword **whitespace** is used in its place.

The options for processing variable-length records are endless. The chapter in the documentation shows a number of examples. SQL*Loader is also a topic of interest when you are browsing the World Wide Web. For example, end your favorite search engine with the text:

```
sqlldr80 loader oracle text sql
```

and see what you find. Before discussing export and import, this section will discuss two features of SQL*Loader that prove crucial to the needs of the data warehouse because they can dramatically speed up the load process.

Parallel and Direct Loading

The Oracle Parallel Loader technology is the heart of their data loader feature, so crucial to the population of the data warehouse. The feature boasts a load potential of over 100 gigabytes per hour. Prior to release 7.2, the parallel load capability required the Parallel Query Option of the Oracle Server. With release 7.3, this is available with the base product. When data is brought in from external sources and is made up of text data, Oracle's SQL*Loader product is used to place the data in the DSS repository.

In the "Parallelism" section of Chapter 7, we discussed processing done by multiple server processes; hence, the term *parallel*. Using SQL*Loader in parallel, and with direct path data loading, improves the throughput of the product manyfold.

SQL*Loader normally reads input data and passes it to the Oracle SQL engine, which places it into the database using the SQL **insert** statement. You may be familiar with creating rows in the database using the following syntax:

```
insert into account_summ values(129,'12-DEC-99',1929100,249,'VRP');
```

When working with an end-user tool such as Oracle Forms, the tool simply passes SQL statements off to Oracle for processing. If a user has a screen where new rows are created and there is a Save button, when this button is pressed the data on the screen is formatted and passed to Oracle as an insert statement. By parallelizing SQL*Loader in conjunction with the direct path load option, the load process runs faster than using the conventional load mechanisms. Say there are three sets of data to load into a data warehouse; each set is destined for the same table. When the load is complete, the target table will contain the merged contents of the three input datafiles. The next listing shows how to accomplish this:

```
sqlldr userid=/ control=acct1.ctl direct=true parallel=true
sqlldr userid=/ control=acct2.ctl direct=true parallel=true
sqlldr userid=/ control=acct3.ctl direct=true parallel=true
```

Multiple sessions perform the load, with two profound differences from the conventional load; these two differences (direct and parallel) make SQL*Loader a worthwhile part of the DSS data loading process:

1. The processes performing the load do so concurrently and the workload is partitioned among the processes. By balancing the work and distributing it between more than one process, the work is done faster and consumes fewer resources. The parallelization also allows the processes to load data into the same table at the same time.

2. With the direct option, SQL*Loader assembles and then formats the data in memory in the same structure as it will be stored in the database table. The conventional load (using the SQL insert statement for each row) is more time consuming and requires more resources.

Before moving on to export and import, let's have a look at some features that can drastically affect the speed with which SQL*Loader can move information into Oracle when using the direct load approach.

Put Another Log on the Fire

Actually, with Oracle8, that familiar adage is totally opposite—don't bother! As we all know, loading data into Oracle using SQL*Loader (as discussed in this main section) or any other mechanism generates redo. Redo is written by Oracle every time a **commit** or **rollback** command is received by the database. The redo contains a copy of transactions against the database, and the end result of that activity is one of the following:

■ **commit**   The act of making the work performed by one or more SQL statements permanent. Data created or updated becomes available to other users of the database; data deleted is no longer available to any users of the database.

■ **rollback**   The act of reversing any changes to data that may have been made by one or more SQL statements.

To illustrate the concepts of these two statements, the next listing follows two sessions against an Oracle8 database when a **commit;** is issued to terminate one transaction while a **rollback;** is issued for another. At the start of the two sessions, a row in PERSON has a PIN value off "199881" and a SURNAME value of "Richer."

```
SQL> -- This is session #1       | SQL> -- This is session #2
SQL> select surname from person  | SQL> select surname from person
  2    where pin = 199881;        |   2    where pin = 199881;
SURNAME                          | SURNAME
-------------------------------- | ------------------------------------
Richer                           | Richer
SQL> update person set surname = | SQL> -- Session 2 does not yet know about
  2    'Baggs' where             | SQL> -- the change since it has not
  3   where pin = 199881;        | SQL> -- been committed (or rolled back).
1 record updated.                | SQL> -- It still looks at the old value.
```

```
SQL> select surname from person   | SQL> select surname from person
  2    where pin = 199881;         |   2    where pin = 199881;
SURNAME                           | SURNAME
------------------------------    | ------------------------------
Baggs                             | Richer
SQL> commit;                      | SQL>
SQL> Commit complete.             | SQL>
SQL> -- Change made permanent.    | SQL> -- Now has access to change.
SQL> select surname from person   | SQL> select surname from person
  2    where pin = 199881;         |   2    where pin = 199881;
SURNAME                           | SURNAME
------------------------------    | ------------------------------
Baggs                             | Baggs
SQL> -- Pretend the data is like  | SQL>
SQL> -- it was at the start       | SQL>
SQL> -- of this listing.          | SQL>
SQL> update person set surname =  | SQL> -- Session 2 does not yet know about
  2    'Baggs' where              | SQL> -- the change since it has not
  3   where pin = 199881;          | SQL> -- been committed or rolled back.
1 record updated.                 | SQL> -- It still looks at the old value.
SQL> select surname from person   | SQL> select surname from person
  2    where pin = 199881;         |   2    where pin = 199881;
SURNAME                           | SURNAME
------------------------------    | ------------------------------
Baggs                             | Richer
SQL> rollback;                    | SQL>
Rollback complete.                | SQL>
SQL> -- Change undone.            | SQL> -- Oblivious to change.
SQL> select surname from person   | SQL> select surname from person
  2    where pin = 199881;         |   2    where pin = 199881;
SURNAME                           | SURNAME
------------------------------    | ------------------------------
Richer                            | Richer
SQL>                              | SQL>
```

Disabling Redo with SQL*Loader

Simply put, *redo* can be defined as the tracking of changes to the database
so these changes can be reapplied for whatever reason, the most common
being media failure. The **nologging** keyword can be used in conjunction
with the **alter table** command to ensure no redo is generated using
the SQL*Loader direct path. The format of the command is shown in the
next listing:

```
-- Disable generation of redo
SQL> alter table sales nologging;
Table altered.
-- Re-enable generation of undo
SQL> alter table sales logging;
Table altered.
```

Disabling Undo with SQL*Loader

In Chapter 9, we discuss ways of disabling generation of undo using the **unrecoverable** keyword as part of a **create table as select** or **create index** SQL statement. When using the SQL*Loader direct path, the same keyword can be used as shown in the next extract from a loader control file:

```
unrecoverable
load data
infile 'account.dat' …
```

The most common error with this feature in the control file is when you do not specify the **direct** option and SQL*Loader finds the **unrecoverable** keyword in the control file. This is shown in the next listing:

```
SQL*Loader: Release 8.0.4.0.0 - Production on Mon Dec 26 21:58:46 1999
(c) Copyright 1998 Oracle Corporation.  All rights reserved.
SQL*Loader-268: UNRECOVERABLE keyword may be used only in direct path.
```

The time saved when using the features to disable redo and undo generation as discussed in the last two sections can be quite remarkable. To get the best performance out of SQL*Loader, we recommend the following:

- Place the table(s) being loaded in **nologging** mode using the **alter table** construct.

- Include the **unrecoverable** keyword in the control file.

- Invoke SQL*Loader with the **direct=true** option.

Now we spend a bit of time on export and import, two workhorses in the Oracle8 toolset that are used to move data into and out of the Oracle repository.

Import and Export

These two sister products allow copying Oracle data (export) to a compressed binary file readable only by Oracle and copying data from that file back into one or more Oracle tables (import). Export and import have been around since day one; they are continually part of the backup strategy used by most Oracle installations. Export and import can be used as part of the migration strategy when moving data from operational systems into the Oracle data warehouse. First, look at the three modes of operation for export and import, then at three methods within which they operate.

Modes of Operation

Export and import operate in one of three modes. Each mode is used in different situations, depending on what must be accomplished. These modes are outlined in Table 8-4; they apply to both export and import.

The User and Table modes are used most when extracting data from one or more operational repositories for insertion into the data warehouse. A few points are important about using the three modes listed in Table 8-4:

1. The owner of the tables in the source database need not be the same owner as in the target. Using two parameters detailed in the section on import, the data can be moved from one user to another.

2. Tables belonging to more than one user can be specified when running import, using the **fromuser** and **touser** parameters used in the "Import Example #2" section later in this chapter.

3. When importing tables, if they do not already exist, there is code in the export file to create them before their data is brought in.

Mode	Details
Full database	Exports/imports the complete database, including all the data and the definitions of the structures and files that support the database as it operates
User	Exports/imports the data and corresponding data definitions for one or more users
Table	Exports/imports the data and corresponding data definitions for one or more tables belonging to one or more users

TABLE 8-4. *Export and Import Modes*

Methods of Operation

Three ways exist to invoke export, summarized in Table 8-5. Now look at the export and import and the methods with which they are run.

Export

The command to invoke export in most environments is

```
exp80 {parameter1=value1,parameter2=value2,…parametern=valuen}
```

where the parameters and their values are entered one after the other, with commas separating them. Online help is obtained by entering the following command and by receiving the screen of help listing the export parameters:

```
C:\> exp80 help=y
Export: Release 8.0.4.0.0 - Production on Thu Nov 8 9:18:40 1999
(c) Copyright 1998 Oracle Corporation.  All rights reserved.
You can let Export prompt you for parameters by entering the EXP
command followed by your username/password:
     Example: EXP SCOTT/TIGER
Or, you can control how Export runs by entering the EXP command followed
by various arguments. To specify parameters, you use keywords:
     Format:  EXP KEYWORD=value or KEYWORD=(value1,value2,...,valueN)
     Example: EXP SCOTT/TIGER GRANTS=Y TABLES=(EMP,DEPT,MGR)
              or TABLES=(T1:P1,T1:P2), if T1 is partitioned table
Keyword   Description (Default)          Keyword        Description (Default)
--------------------------------------------------------------------------
USERID    username/password              FULL           export entire file (N)
BUFFER    size of data buffer            OWNER          list of owner usernames
FILE      output file (EXPDAT.DMP)       TABLES         list of table names
COMPRESS  import into one extent (Y)     RECORDLENGTH   length of IO record
GRANTS    export grants (Y)              INCTYPE        incremental export type
INDEXES   export indexes (Y)             RECORD         track incr. export (Y)
ROWS      export data rows (Y)           PARFILE        parameter filename
CONSTRAINTS export constraints (Y)       CONSISTENT     cross-table consistency
LOG       log file of screen output      STATISTICS     analyze objects (ESTIMATE)
DIRECT    direct path (N)
FEEDBACK  display progress every x rows (0)
POINT_IN_TIME_RECOVER    Tablespace Point-in-time Recovery (N)
RECOVERY_TABLESPACES     List of tablespace names to recover
```

Mode	Details
1. Interactive dialog	Causes export to enter into a dialog with the operator by asking a number of questions and receiving answers
2. Command-line parameter	Invokes export supplying parameters and values on the command line
3. Parameter file	Invokes export and supplies a value for the keyword **parfile=** that names a file within which keywords and their values should be read

TABLE 8-5. *Export and Import Methods*

Parameters Fed to Export

Table 8-6 shows the parameters that will be used time and time again when extracting data bound for the warehouse. The only mandatory keyword is **userid**, which must be followed by a value that relates to a valid Oracle account.

A Word on Exporting Partitions

The text placed after the keyword **tables=** on the call to export can also refer to one or more partitions in one or more partitioned tables. The extended table partition syntax used for SQL*Loader is a bit different for export, as shown in the next listing, with the table name and partition name separated by a colon:

```
exp80 userid=dw_holder/dwp
tables=(account:east_dat,account:west_dat,sale)
```

Note how partitions and whole tables can be mentioned alongside one another on the call to export. All three examples in the next few sections export data from a partitioned table—the first and third from all partitions at once, the second from only one partition in the ACCOUNT table.

Parameter	Details	Default
Userid	The Oracle username and password of the account running the utility. If you supply only the username, Oracle will prompt for the password.	None
Buffer	The data buffer size in bytes. If you request too large a size, Oracle will carry on with whatever it can obtain.	4096
File	The name of the file being written to. If you do not specify a file name extension, Oracle assumes the .dmp extension.	expdat.dmp
Compress	Writes storage parameters to the export file that would place all table data in one extent when the data is imported.	Y
Grants	Writes SQL **grant** statements to the export file.	Y
Indexes	Writes SQL **create index** statements to the export file.	Y
Rows	Exports the data in the tables' rows, as well as the definitions of the underlying objects.	Y
Constraints	Writes SQL statements to the export file needed to re-create declarative integrity when the objects are imported (for example, primary key and reference statements).	Y
Log	Instructs Oracle to write the screen I/O from the export file to a disk file.	None
Full	Controls whether or not Oracle writes SQL statements to the export file to re-create all the system-associated datafiles, tablespaces, rollback segments, etc.	N
Owner	Provides a list of Oracle accounts whose objects must be written to the export file.	None

TABLE 8-6. *Export Parameters*

Parameter	Details	Default
Tables	Provides a list of tables whose definitions or data must be written to the export file.	None
Parfile	The name of a file containing parameters to feed to export.	None
Consistent	Instructs Oracle to maintain cross-table consistency. This ensures export will make copies of table data as of the time the export began, even if tables being exported are being used while the export runs.	N
Statistics	Writes SQL **analyze** statements to the export file.	Estimate
Feedback	Instructs Oracle to display the # character on the screen for every number of rows exported per table.	None

TABLE 8-6. *Export Parameters (continued)*

Export Example #1

The requirements for this example are shown in Table 8-7. This example is started by issuing the command **exp80** alone.

Mode	:	interactive
Method	:	user
Object owner	:	account
File name	:	account.dmp

TABLE 8-7. *Specifications for Export Example #1*

Oracle enters into a dialog. The text of this dialog is shown in the following listing in normal print; explanatory notes are shown in **bold** with each question and answer:

```
Export: Release 8.0.4.0.0 - Production on Thu Nov 8 14:48:16 1999
(c) Copyright 1998 Oracle Corporation.  All rights reserved.
Username: account
Password:
```
The password can be entered on the same line as the username by separating the two with the forward slash "/".
```
Connected to: Oracle8 Enterprise Edition Release 8.0.4.0.0 - Production
With the Partitioning and Objects options
PL/SQL Release 8.0.4.0.0 - Production
Enter array fetch buffer size: 4096 >
```
Oracle wants a figure entered in bytes that will be allocated for moving data out of Oracle and writing it to the export file.

```
Export file: EXPDAT.DMP > account
```
You enter the name of the export file here. If you simply press RETURN here, the name defaults to "expdat.dmp". Notice the file name shown here is "account". Oracle tacks the file extension ".dmp" onto the name entered here.

```
(2)U(sers), or (3)T(ables): (2)U > u
```
Here you are being asked the mode of operation of the export. These modes are discussed earlier in the "Export" section of this chapter.
```
Export grants (yes/no): yes >

Export table data (yes/no): yes >
```
Answering yes to this question causes export to extract the data from the specified tables. Answering no here causes the definition of the data, but not the data itself, to be written to the export file.

```
Compress extents (yes/no): yes >
```
This question deals with a concept discussed on its own after this listing.

```
Export done in WE8ISO8859P1 character set and WE8ISO8859P1 NCHAR character set
About to export ACCOUNT's objects ...
. exporting foreign function library names for user ACCOUNT
```

```
. exporting object type definitions for user ACCOUNT
About to export ACCOUNT's objects ...
. exporting database links
. exporting sequence numbers
. exporting cluster definitions
. about to export ACCOUNT's tables via Conventional Path ....
. . exporting table             ACCOUNT
. . exporting partition                ACCOUNT_P1      11331 rows exported
. . exporting partition                ACCOUNT_P2      13554 rows exported
. . exporting partition                ACCOUNT_P3      12361 rows exported
. . exporting table            ACCOUNT_TRANS          67331 rows exported
. exporting synonyms
. exporting views
. exporting stored procedures
. exporting referential integrity constraints
. exporting triggers
. exporting posttables actions
. exporting snapshots
. exporting snapshot logs
. exporting job queues
. exporting refresh groups and children
Export terminated successfully without warnings.
C:\orant\exports>
```

Compress Extents Parameter

Oracle stores its data in datafiles and, as further space is required for more data, additional space is allocated in extents. An *extent* is a predetermined amount of space made available to tables that need more space than is currently allocated. Figure 8-1 shows the space allocated to the ACCOUNT table in its database file.

When export is asked to compress extents, the request is for all the space allocated currently in the table (using Figure 8-1 as an example, this would be 5MB or 5,242,880 bytes) to be acquired in one chunk of space called "extent 0". Figure 8-2 shows what this entails for the ACCOUNT table.

Here's what would happen: The export of the table would detect 5MB of space (that is, extent0+extent1+extent2+extent3=5MB) used by the ACCOUNT table. When the table is brought back in using import, Oracle would reserve the full 5MB as the initial allocation.

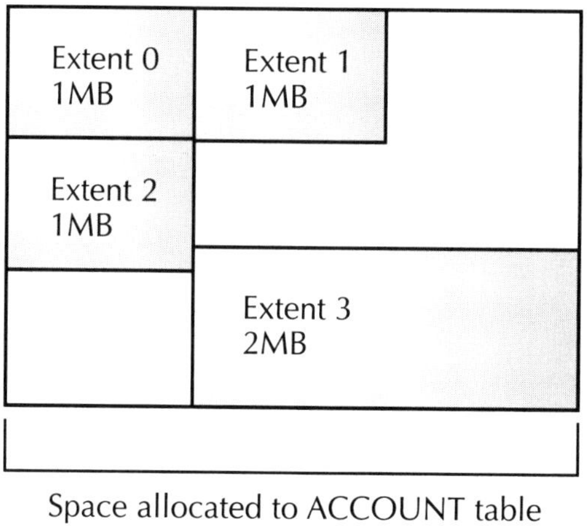

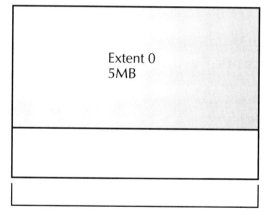

Space allocated to ACCOUNT table

FIGURE 8-1. *ACCOUNT table spread over four extents*

Space allocated to ACCOUNT table

FIGURE 8-2. *ACCOUNT table spread over one extent*

Export Example #2

The requirements for this example are shown in Table 8-8. The command used to start export using these requirements is

```
exp userid=account/account file=accreg grants=n buffer=1048576
tables=(account.account:east_dat,account.account_trans,region.state,region.geo)
```

The command is split across two lines in the listing, but it must be entered on one line when passed to Oracle for execution. Once export is invoked, the next listing shows the output produced. The text placed on the screen by export is shown in normal print and explanatory notes are shown in **bold**.

```
Export: Release 8.0.4.0.0 - Production on Thu Nov 8 14:48:16 1998
(c) Copyright 1998 Oracle Corporation.  All rights reserved.
Connected to: Oracle8 Enterprise Edition Release 8.0.4.0.0 - Production
With the Partitioning and Objects options
PL/SQL Release 8.0.4.0.0 - Production
Export done in WE8ISO8859P1 character set and WE8ISO8859P1 NCHAR character set
Note: grants on tables/views/sequences/roles will not be exported
```
This warning is caused by asking not to export the grants. Because this
is required, no problem.
```

About to export specified tables via Conventional Path ...
. . exporting table              ACCOUNT
. . exporting partition                   EAST_DAT      11331 rows exported
. . exporting table               ACCOUNT_TRANS   67331 rows exported
Current user changed to REGION
```
This indicates the export routine has now changed to export tables
belonging to the other user.
```

. . exporting table                         STATE        50 rows exported
. . exporting table                           GEO      8712 rows exported
Export terminated successfully without warnings.
```

Mode	:	command-line parameter
Method	:	table (for two different users)
Grants	:	do not export
Buffer	:	1MB (1,048,576 bytes)
User	:	account
File name	:	accreg.dmp

TABLE 8-8. *Specifications for Export Example #2*

Export Example #3

The requirements for this example are shown in Table 8-9. The command used to accomplish this is

```
exp parfile=acc.parfile
```

and the parameter file (acc.parfile) would contain the following text:

```
userid=account/account
file=account
buffer=8192
```

Mode	:	parameter file (name is acc.parfile)
Buffer	:	8,192 bytes
User	:	account
File name	:	account.dmp

TABLE 8-9. *Specifications for Export Example #3*

The output from this export example is shown in the following listing:

```
Export: Release 8.0.4.0.0 - Production on Thu Nov 8 14:48:16 1998
(c) Copyright 1998 Oracle Corporation.  All rights reserved.
Connected to: Oracle8 Enterprise Edition Release 8.0.4.0.0 - Production
With the Partitioning and Objects options
PL/SQL Release 8.0.4.0.0 - Production
Export done in WE8ISO8859P1 character set and WE8ISO8859P1 NCHAR character set
About to export specified users ...
About to export ACCOUNT's objects ...
. exporting database links
. exporting sequence numbers
. exporting cluster definitions
. about to export ACCOUNT's tables via Conventional Path ...
. . exporting table               ACCOUNT
. . exporting partition                   ACCOUNT_P1        11331 rows exported
. . exporting partition                   ACCOUNT_P2        13554 rows exported
. . exporting partition                   ACCOUNT_P3        12361 rows exported
. . exporting table               ACCOUNT_TRANS            67331 rows exported
. exporting synonyms
. exporting views
. exporting stored procedures
. exporting referential integrity constraints
. exporting triggers
. exporting posttables actions
. exporting snapshots
. exporting snapshot logs
. exporting job queues
. exporting refresh groups and children
Export terminated successfully without warnings.
```

Import

The command to invoke import is

```
imp80 {parameter1=value1,parameter2=value2,…parametern=valuen}
```

where the parameters and their values are entered one after the other, with commas separating them. Online help is obtained by entering the following command and receiving the screen of help listing the import parameters:

```
Import: Release 8.0.4.0.0 - Production on Thu Nov 8 15:10:47 1999
(c) Copyright 1998 Oracle Corporation.  All rights reserved.
You can let Import prompt you for parameters by entering the IMP
command followed by your username/password:
     Example: IMP SCOTT/TIGER
Or, you can control how Import runs by entering the IMP command followed
by various arguments. To specify parameters, you use keywords:
     Format:  IMP KEYWORD=value or KEYWORD=(value1,value2,...,valueN)
     Example: IMP SCOTT/TIGER IGNORE=Y TABLES=(EMP,DEPT) FULL=N
             or TABLES=(T1:P1,T1:P2), if T1 is partitioned table
Keyword  Description (Default)        Keyword      Description (Default)
--------------------------------------------------------------------------
USERID   username/password           FULL         import entire file (N)
BUFFER   size of data buffer         FROMUSER     list of owner usernames
FILE     output file (EXPDAT.DMP)    TOUSER       list of usernames
SHOW     just list file contents (N) TABLES       list of table names
IGNORE   ignore create errors (N)    RECORDLENGTH length of IO record
GRANTS   import grants (Y)           INCTYPE      incremental import type
INDEXES  import indexes (Y)          COMMIT       commit array insert (N)
ROWS     import data rows (Y)        PARFILE      parameter filename
LOG      log file of screen output
DESTROY  overwrite tablespace datafile (N)
INDEXFILE write table/index info to specified file
CHARSET  character set of export file (NLS_LANG)
POINT_IN_TIME_RECOVER  Tablespace Point-in-time Recovery (N)
SKIP_UNUSABLE_INDEXES  skip maintenance of unusable indexes (N)
ANALYZE  execute ANALYZE statements in dump file (Y)
FEEDBACK display progress every x rows(0)
Import terminated successfully without warnings.
```

Parameters Fed to Import

Table 8-10 shows the parameters that will be used frequently when moving data into the Oracle data warehouse repository.

Five of these parameters—the **ignore** parameter, the **commit** parameter, and the **fromuser**, **touser**, and **full** parameters—require an explanation.

Parameter	Details	Default
Userid	The Oracle username and password of the account running the utility. If you supply just the username, Oracle will prompt for the password.	None
Buffer	The data buffer size in bytes. If you request too large a size, Oracle will carry on with whatever it can obtain.	30720
File	The name of the file being read. If you do not specify a file name extension, Oracle assumes the .dmp extension.	expdat.dmp
Ignore	Instructs Oracle on how to deal with SQL **create** statements in the export file.	N
Grants	Executes the SQL **grant** statements in the export file.	Y
Indexes	Executes the SQL **create index** statements in the export file.	Y
Rows	Imports the data in the tables' rows, as well as the definitions of the underlying objects.	Y
Log	Instructs Oracle to write the screen I/O from the import to a disk file.	None
Fromuser	The owner(s) of the data written to the export file.	None
Touser	The user(s) into which the data should be imported.	None
Tables	A list of table names to be imported.	None

TABLE 8-10.   *Import Parameters*

Parameter	Details	Default
Commit	Controls the frequency with which Oracle commits data as it is imported. This is useful when importing large amounts of data.	N
Parfile	The name of a file containing parameters to feed to import.	None
Feedback	Instructs Oracle to display the # character on the screen for every number of rows imported per table.	None

TABLE 8-10. *Import Parameters (continued)*

The ignore Parameter

When tables are read from an export file into Oracle, if the table exists before the data is brought in, the **ignore** parameter must be set to **y**; otherwise, the Oracle error shown in the following listing is encountered:

```
Import: Release 8.0.4.0.0 - Production on Thu Nov 8 15:10:47 1999
(c) Copyright 1998 Oracle Corporation.  All rights reserved.
Connected to: Oracle8 Enterprise Edition Release 8.0.4.0.0 - Production
With the Partitioning and Objects options
PL/SQL Release 8.0.4.0.0 - Production
Export file created by EXPORT:V08.00.04 via conventional path
. importing ACCOUNT's objects into ACCOUNT
IMP-00015: following statement failed because the object already exists:
 "CREATE TABLE "ACCOUNT_TRANS" ("ACCOUNT_NBR" NUMBER(10, 0), "ACCOUNT_TYPE"
  VARCHAR2(2), """OWNER" VARCHAR2(30), "LAST_ACTIVITY" DATE, "STATUS"
  VARCHAR2(2))  PCTFREE ""10 PCTUSED 40 INITRANS 1 MAXTRANS 255
  STORAGE(INITIAL 10240 NEXT 10240 MINE"
  "XTENTS 1 MAXEXTENTS 121 PCTINCREASE 50 FREELISTS 1 FREELIST GROUPS
  1) TABLESPACE "ACCOUNT""
Import terminated successfully with warnings.
```

Bringing data from the operational environment into tables that already exist in the data warehouse is a common occurrence. The error is avoided by invoking import with the following command:

```
imp80 userid=account/account full=y file=account ignore=y
```

At this point, the output that generated the previous Oracle error becomes

```
Import: Release 8.0.4.0.0 - Production on Thu Nov 8 15:10:47 1999
(c) Copyright 1998 Oracle Corporation.  All rights reserved.
Connected to: Oracle8 Enterprise Edition Release 8.0.4.0.0 - Production
With the Partitioning and Objects options
PL/SQL Release 8.0.4.0.0 - Production
Export file created by EXPORT:V08.00.04 via conventional path
. importing ACCOUNT's objects into ACCOUNT
. . importing table               "ACCOUNT_TRANS"      67331 rows imported
Import terminated successfully without warnings.
```

The commit Parameter

Oracle uses the **commit** keyword the same as some other software uses the word *save*. When a commit is issued running import, the data inserted into the target Oracle table is saved in the appropriate datafile, and the resources—such as memory allocated for data insertion—are freed up. Large data loads using import use large amounts of memory for sort and other operations. Thus, setting the **commit** parameter to **y** helps the import run to completion without running out of resources.

NOTE
*If you omit the **commit** parameter, the frequency of commit is determined by the size of the insert array, controlled using the **buffer** parameter. Too small a buffer can have the effect of slowing down import, and we recommend coding a value around 1,000,000 to start.*

The following listing is similar to the one in the previous section, but it uses the **commit** parameter:

```
imp80 userid=account/account full=y file=account ignore=y commit=y
```

The fromuser, touser, and full Parameters

After writing an export file, using data from the operational system as input, the **fromuser/touser** or **full** parameters must be coded on the call to import or the following error will be generated:

```
Export file created by EXPORT:V08.00.04 via conventional path
IMP-00031: Must specify FULL=Y or provide FROMUSER/TOUSER or TABLES
          arguments
IMP-00021: operating system error - error code (dec 2, hex 0x2)
IMP-00000: Import terminated unsuccessfully
```

Likewise, attempting to run import when specifying values for **fromuser**, **touser**, and **full** will create the following error text:

```
Export file created by EXPORT:V08.00.04 via conventional path
IMP-00024: Full Import mode, cannot specify FROMUSER or TABLES parameter
IMP-00021: operating system error - error code (dec 2, hex 0x2)
IMP-00000: Import terminated unsuccessfully
```

A Word on Importing into Partitions

Importing into partitioned tables works pretty much the same as when nonpartitioned objects are the target of the exercise. The next listing illustrates the table name, colon, and partition name convention when importing into a partitioned object.

```
C:\> imp80 userid=part/part ignore=y tables=account:p2
Import: Release 8.0.4.0.0 - Production on Fri Dec 16 19:13:6 1999
(c) Copyright 1998 Oracle Corporation.  All rights reserved.
Connected to: Oracle8 Enterprise Edition Release 8.0.3.0.0 - Production
With the Partitioning and Objects options
PL/SQL Release 8.0.4.0.0 - Production
Export file created by EXPORT:V08.00.04 via conventional path
. importing PART's objects into PART
. . importing table          "ACCOUNT"      67331 rows imported
Import terminated successfully without warnings.
```

The only gotcha with using partitions with import is when you specify a partition as the target and there is no data in the export file that qualifies for placement in the desired partition. The errors and text displayed are shown in the next listing:

IMP-00057: Warning: Dump file may not contain data of all partitions
                    of this table
IMP-00055: Warning: partition "ACCOUNT":"P2" not found in export file
Import terminated successfully with warnings.

Import Example #1

The requirements for Example #1 are shown in Table 8-11.

    The command used to accomplish the desired results would simply be

imp80

at which point Oracle would take over by initiating the dialog shown in the following listing. Text put on the screen by Oracle is in normal print; our comments are shown in **bold**:

Import: Release 8.0.4.0.0 - Production on Thu Nov 8 15:10:47 1999
(c) Copyright 1998 Oracle Corporation. All rights reserved.
Username: account
Password:
***The password can be entered on the same line as the username by
separating the two with the forward slash "/"***

Connected to: Oracle8 Enterprise Edition Release 8.0.4.0.0 - Production
With the Partitioning and Objects options
PL/SQL Release 8.0.4.0.0 - Production
Import file: ./expdat.dmp > account
***You enter the name of the export file here. If you simply press RETURN
here, the name defaults to "expdat.dmp". Notice the file name shown
here is "account". Oracle tacks the file extension ".dmp" onto the
name entered here.***

Enter insert buffer size (minimum is 4096) 30720>
Export file created by EXPORT:V08.00.04 via conventional path
***Oracle wants a figure entered in bytes that will be allocated for
the insert array size.***

List contents of import file only (yes/no): no >
Ignore create error due to object existence (yes/no): no > yes
Import grants (yes/no): yes >
Import table data (yes/no): yes >
Import entire export file (yes/no): no > yes
. importing ACCOUNT's objects into ACCOUNT
. . importing table   "ACCOUNT_TRANS"   67331 rows imported
Import terminated successfully without warnings.

Mode	:	interactive
Method	:	user
Object owner	:	account
File name	:	account.dmp

TABLE 8-11. *Specifications for Import Example #1*

Import Example #2

The requirements for Example #2 are shown in Table 8-12. This is a common example of how data is moved from one database to another, especially into a data warehouse.

The command used to accomplish the desired results would be

```
imp80 parfile=arb.parfile
```

and that parameter file would contain the text:

```
userid=account/account
file=arb_data
fromuser=(account,region,branch)
touser=dw_holder
```

Because only one user is listed as a target, all the data will be deposited into that user's account. According to the preceding parameter file entries, if any of the tables already exist in DW_HOLDER's account, they will not be brought in because no entry **ignore=y** exists in the parameter file.

```
Export file created by EXPORT:V08.00.04 via conventional path
. importing ACCOUNT's objects into DW_HOLDER
. . exporting table               ACCOUNT
. . exporting partition                     ACCOUNT_P1      11331 rows exported
. . exporting partition                     ACCOUNT_P2      13554 rows exported
. . exporting partition                     ACCOUNT_P3      12361 rows exported
```

```
. importing REGION's objects into DW_HOLDER
. . importing table                    "CITY"       11219 rows imported
. . importing table                    "CNTY"         129 rows imported
. importing BRANCH's objects into DW_HOLDER
. . importing table                    "COMM"        3440 rows imported
. . importing table                    "SELF"        2129 rows imported
. . importing table                    "STOR"        7562 rows imported
. . importing table                    "BUSI"        3481 rows imported
Import terminated successfully without warnings.
```

Import Example #3

Example #3 shows an error and how it can be fixed. The requirements for this example are shown in Table 8-13. Sometimes, as data is moved into the data warehouse, due to lack of existing space available to the target user, the database administrator must intervene and allocate more space to receive the data.

The command to fulfill this requirement would be

```
imp80 userid=account/account file=account tables=account_trans ignore=y
```

Suppose the ACCOUNT_TRANS table now has over 120,000 rows and it has been allocated a total of 95MB of space (the equivalent of 99,614,720 bytes). The data being added needs another 16MB of space (or 16,777,216

Mode	:	parameter file
Method	:	user
Object owners	:	SOURCE - account, region, branch TARGET - dw_holder
Parameter file	:	arb.parfile
File name	:	arb_data.dmp

TABLE 8-12. *Specifications for Import Example #2*

Mode	:	command line
Method	:	table
Table name	:	account_trans
Existing data	:	table exists and contains data
Object owners	:	account
File name	:	account.exp

TABLE 8-13. *Specifications for Import Example #3*

bytes) and, currently, 120KB (or 122,880 bytes) of the 95MB allocated are not yet used. The following listing shows the output from running this import session:

```
Connected to: Oracle8 Enterprise Edition Release 8.0.4.0.0 - Production
With the Partitioning and Objects options
PL/SQL Release 8.0.4.0.0 - Production
Export file created by EXPORT:V08.00.04 via conventional path
. importing ACCOUNT's objects into DW_HOLDER
. . importing table                      "ACCOUNT_TRANS"
IMP-00003: ORACLE error 1653 encountered
ORA-01653: unable to extend table DW_HOLDER.ACCOUNT_TRANS by 8208 in
          tablespace DW_DATA1
Import terminated successfully with warnings.
```

Figure 8-3 shows what is happening with this import session. Because 16MB is obviously larger than the available 120K, it raises the Oracle error 1653.

The database administrator must allocate more space to the ACCOUNT_TRANS table and reissue the same import command. Suppose an additional 20MB (20,971,520 bytes) have been added to the tablespace that holds the ACCOUNT table. The output of the same import command is shown in the next listing:

```
Export file created by EXPORT:V08.00.04 via conventional path
. importing ACCOUNT's objects into DW_HOLDER
. . importing table            "ACCOUNT_TRANS"      21893 rows imported
Import terminated successfully without warnings.
```

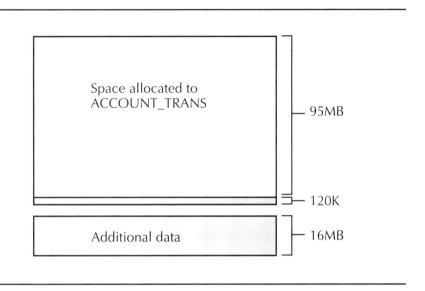

FIGURE 8-3. *Space allocated and required for ACCOUNT_TRANS*

To close this section on import and export, here is a suggestion, a fact, and a caveat of export and import. First, the data warehouse Oracle specialist must become fluent in the use of export and import and make it a solid component in her or his skillset with the Oracle8 Server. Second, as data warehouse data are assembled from a number of source hardware platforms—for example, Oracle running on a Sequent UNIX machine, as well as a corporate Digital Alpha—export and import can be used to move data between different hardware platforms. The mechanisms used by Sequent that differ from those used by Digital are known to Oracle (export and import) and allow their use as a translation vehicle. Third, regardless of how well you have followed this discussion, coupled with your previous experience, export and import can sometimes be a challenge. Inordinate amounts of time can be spent ensuring they run properly and move data efficiently into the data warehouse.

But I Want to Use Oracle Enterprise Manager (OEM)

The Data Manager is the piece from OEM where you run import, export, and SQL*Loader. The OEM console must be running to successfully invoke the Data Manager. All three are invoked after starting the OEM main console. The Data Manager button shown next highlights the Export, Import and Load buttons.

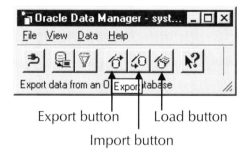

OEM uses wizards to accomplish many tasks in the Data Manager. Let's use one of the examples from the SQL*Loader section and walk through the most common Loader Wizard screens; this will give you a flavor of using the Data Manager to accomplish what was done from a DOS window. Figure 8-4 shows where the SQL*Loader control file can be found. By default, Oracle expects the file extension on the control file to be ".ctl"; you can change to other characters if you desire.

After selecting the name and location of the control file, you move a screen shown where we specify the input datafile, log file, bad file, and discard file. The dialog box shown in Figure 8-5 is where advanced options are specified; we have left Conventional Path highlighted and left the number **64** for Rows per Commit as well as **50** for the number of errors to allow before terminating the load. The load is initiated by clicking Finish from this screen. After the load completes, it is your responsibility to browse the log file.

There are similar wizards for export and import, with a series of dialog boxes where you specify values for all the parameters you code when using a DOS window to perform the exercise. The wizards present screens where you specify the objects and schemas for the export or import activity. We

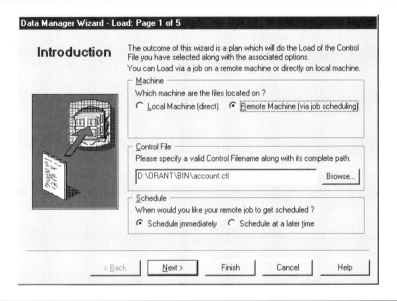

FIGURE 8-4.   *Control File specification dialog*

found the Import Wizard Object Selection screen the best example to illustrate the flexibility of the Data Manager operator interface. This is shown in Figure 8-6.

NOTE
The assortment of Oracle errors that may be raised when using export, import, or SQL*Loader in a DOS window will come up as well when using the Data Manager. It is your responsibility to ensure the correct privileges are in place to permit any of these tools' activities to run successfully to completion.

Enough said on OEM—we now move on to having a look at Oracle's offering called Data Mart Suite for NT and how it can become part of your data warehouse loading mechanisms.

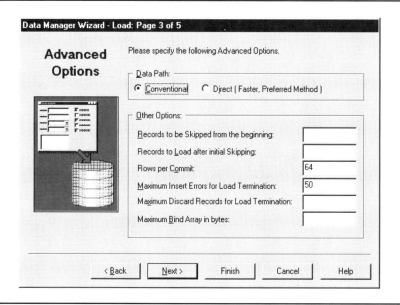

FIGURE 8-5. *Optional files specification*

Oracle Data Mart Suite

The Oracle Data Mart Suite is portrayed as the most complete, integrated solution for building data marts. The suite is a bundling of the database, tools, documentation, and training designed to be a one-stop shopping experience. The suite has the following components:

■ Data Mart Builder is where you design and implement the data mart. After the design exercise is complete, the tool allows the Oracle Data Mart Builder to perform the extraction, transformation, and migration of source data into the mart via one common, familiar user interface. There are three components to the Data Mart Builder:

1. The Transformation Designer is a graphic environment to describe the process of populating the data mart from operational systems and corporate data warehouses. Sources like Oracle, Sybase, and Microsoft SQL Server are directly supported, and many other sources are accessible using ODBC (Open DataBase Connectivity).

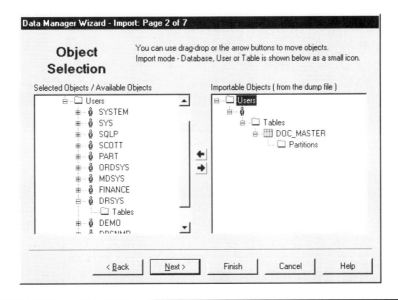

FIGURE 8-6.   *Import Wizard Object Selection*

2. The Administration Tool is where you manage and administer the Oracle Data Mart Builder. The Administration Tool provides extensive facilities to manage all the components; the administrator implements security from here using a flexible, familiar environment.

3. The Data Mart Builder Service provides the server activities necessary to glue the components of the Data Mart Builder together. The Data Flow Editor, imbedded in the service, is used to develop comprehensive data flows required to populate the target data mart. Routines native to the Data Flow Editor can be used to convert operational data schemas into star schemas that reside in the data mart. Custom transforms can be created and stored using development environments such as Visual Basic and C++.

■ Data Mart Designer supports the mapping of the structure of the source databases to a repository that is read by the Data Mart Builder, and is comprised of the following components:

1. Reverse engineering mechanisms perform the familiar activity of reading existing repositories and making their object definitions available to the builder component.

2. Schema design is performed here using common data modeling drag-and-drop functionality without the need to do manual SQL coding to create the data mart objects and relationships.

3. Web publishing is easily performed here by generating Oracle Webserver applications. This allows quick and painless creation of Web documents by creation of HTML documents using the data within the mart.

■ Oracle Server Enterprise Edition database engine provides a robust, rich storage and query processing environment for the data mart information. The Server's enhanced parallel processing capabilities are especially well suited to the complex query and high-volume data requirements of the data mart.

We now move on to having a look at a breed of tools designed to assist the movement of data bound for the data warehouse.

NOTE
Most of the material in the "Engine-based Tools" section is courtesy of Andrew Flower, a data warehouse specialist and manager for the Kansas City, MO USA office of Dataspace Inc. Andrew is a colleague who has been kind enough to perform half of the technical editing for Oracle8 Data Warehousing. He can be reached via email at aflower@dspace.com and welcomes your interest in the following material.

Engine-based Tools

There are a number of engine-based data migration/extraction, transformation, and load tools (*ETLs*) for use in data warehouse projects. The two main characteristics we are looking for in these tools are robustness and completeness of functionality. ETL tools are software products that provide a method for transferring data from a source system to a target system. Traditionally, this function is handled by programmers who write data extraction and load programs that are specific to each data warehouse's data transfers. With ETL tools, a developer can access various data sources and graphically build transformation loads into data warehouses. By using an ETL tool, the amount of effort needed to develop data transfers is significantly reduced. Some estimates show a 70 to 80 percent reduction. A lot of vendors are starting to integrate mainframe connectivity into their tools to compete with the code generator loading tools such as ETI*EXTRACT.

Much of the criteria for evaluating ETL tools, and ultimately making a choice, are generic and independent of the organization evaluating the tool. However, some criteria can only come from individuals who will be affected by the implementation of such a tool.

NOTE
This is along the lines of something we say throughout this book—make sure the end user (the consumer) is involved and listened to during all phases of warehouse development.

The market for engine-based ETL tools is fairly immature. As a result, we are seeing a relatively fast release cycle from the major vendors. We suggest you keep an eye on who are the current leaders in sales as well as those vendors that are introducing new products that may catapult them above the market leaders. Let's move on to having a look at characteristics that are fundamental to ETL tools.

Tool Characteristics

This section looks at characteristics in ETL tools that are mandatory and desirable.

NOTE
The definition of "mandatory" and "desirable" may change from warehouse to warehouse or customer to customer. Again, involve the user in determining what these two terms mean in your implementation.

Vendors strive to deliver as many of the features as possible along the lines of those we discuss in the next list of points. After each point, we will list a number of details about what we look for during an evaluation process.

- **Price** Including all components such as licenses for servers, users, etc.

- **Updates** The ability to insert data into a target table and update the data after record creation.

    1. Insert data into an empty table.

    2. Insert data into a table that has data in it.

    3. Update existing records with revised data.

    4. Update existing records with revised data and insert new records that do not currently exist.

- **Track dimensions** The ability to track changes in dimensions and to retain historical relationships (slowly changing dimensions). The tool must be able to track slowly changing dimensions. Slowly changing dimensions are used when the history of a dimension needs to be retained.

    1. Update current dimension record to make it inactive (either with a flag or an end date).

    2. Insert the new dimension record that is marked as active.

- **Surrogate keys** Support and manage these keys. *Surrogate keys* serve as unique identifiers for rows in relational database tables and are generated during processes such as the data warehouse load. Surrogate keys are meaningless and outside the fact they uniquely identify each row in a table, they serve no purpose.

    1. Generate surrogate values.

    2. Supply surrogate key values to the records being processed.

- **Conditional reads and change data capture** Support conditional logic when reading source data. For example, conditional reads need to show a tool can select data from the source repository based on

   1. Time stamps or log files.

   2. Record types.

   3. Other conditional values.

■ **Intelligent query**   Intelligently structures queries from source databases with minimal user effort.

   1. Process foreign key information and join conditions for selects.

   2. Choose the best available query execution when joining multiple tables (letting the source DBMS determine query execution is an acceptable choice).

■ **Multisource joins**   The act of joining two tables from multiple data sources, including flat files and relational data sources.

   1. Joining tables from different instances of an RDBMS (i.e., two different Oracle databases).

   2. Joining tables from different relational sources (i.e., an Oracle database and an Informix database).

   3. Joining a relational table with a VSAM or flat file. A *VSAM* stands for virtual storage access method—a file format found on IBM mainframe computers, a proprietary storage mechanism allowing random access to the information within the file.

   4. Joining two flat files and/or VSAM files.

■ **Aggregates**   The ability to build aggregates and efficiently populate the aggregate tables.

   1. Aids in creation of aggregates.

   2. Can build and load aggregates in parallel with load of base fact table.

   3. Allows third-party aggregate tools (e.g., Syncsort)

■ **Data warehouse tool integration**   Easy integration with other data warehouse tools.

   1. Design/CASE (Computer Assisted Software Engineering) tools.

   2. Query tools.

   3. OLAP tools.

■ **Metadata**   Propagation of metadata and descriptions of transformations to the users. *Metadata* details the makeup of the information stored in the data warehouse, mapping the data types, sources, and relationships between the warehouse tables.

1. What types of metadata are to be collected (both design and operational metadata).

2. Metadata reporting, while ensuring that the repository is based on an open architecture such as a relational database management system.

■ **Customization**   Writing customizations into the tool using a native language or a third party.

1. Native language programs can be written to customize processing.

2. Third-party languages can be used to customize processing.

3. Pre- and postprocessing can be done on a transformation.

■ **Logging**   Sophisticated error and status reporting.

1. Generate an execution log for each plan/job/session/batch (or whatever the vendor chooses to call the compiled load process).

2. Generate an error log for each warning or error that occurs during an execution of a plan/job/session/batch.

■ **Tool architecture**   The ability to load multiple tables in parallel, use of system resources, staging grounds, etc.

1. Multiprocess, multithread capabilities.

2. Staging area.

3. Database.

4. Use of system resources.

■ **Schedule**   The ability to schedule batch jobs to run either once or on a periodic basis without user intervention.

1. Automatic startup of plans/jobs/sessions/batches.

2. Scheduling recurring plans/jobs/sessions/batches.

3. Grouping of plans/jobs/sessions into batches.

4. Scheduling plans/jobs/sessions/batches for both parallel and sequential execution.

5. Use with UNIX- or NT-based scheduling tools.

■ **Quality Management**   This tool provides the ability to review the data quality on an initial and repetitive basis.

Now that we have looked at these characteristics, let's spend a few minutes inspecting two types of tests that we recommend you perform in the midst of an ETL tool selection exercise.

Complex Functionality

A functionality test extracts data from a source database and populates a dimension in the target database while checking for changes to existing records in the dimension. Some transformations are deliberately performed on the data along the way. We recommend trying this test first by using a single source table and multiple tables on the target database. Develop logic to be followed prior to running the test. Run the test, then inspect the results. Try the same test with multiple source tables, or files from disparate sources if this best approximates how your actual transformations will occur (and if you have the time). The logic shown next is an example of a complex functionality algorithm used at one of our sites during a tool evaluation. For this test, rows were moved from a source table, paying specific attention to the value in the source and target tables' STATUS columns. Both source and target tables are keyed the same; the comparison of the keys can be used to decide whether a record in the target table exists that matches one coming in from the source.

```
if no matching record exists in the target table then
    create a new record in the target table
elsif a matching record exists then
        if the status code in source is the same as status code in target then
            update the existing record with the changed information
        else
            update the expiration date on the existing record
            create a new record into the target table
        endif
endif
```

Volume

A volume test consists of moving a large VSAM or flat file—while joining with a relational source—into a relational target, and producing a flat file that matches the relational target. Figure 8-7 shows a simple example of this operation.

Code Generator Tools

Another approach to getting the data out of the source operational systems is to generate compiled code to perform the extraction. Many readers have

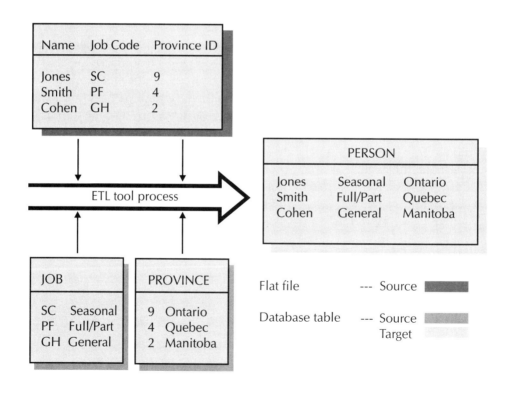

FIGURE 8-7. *Using flat file and relational objects together*

been doing this exercise for nondata warehouse requirements for large portions of their information technology careers already. We have seen data warehouse products that generate COBOL and C code (and are now coming out with Java) that is sent to the source data store for extraction of warehouse-bound information.

The code generators are best suited to getting data from mainframe sources, whereas the engine-based products are better when source data resides in nonmainframe repositories. We believe the main issue here is node independence and speed. Engine-based tools still can't reach the speed of code generators (even if they allow multiple engines). Also, in a global project, the engine-based tool would be very network intensive and not allow processing at decentralized locations easily. Expansion is limited, and all processing is usually done on a single node, which is now a single point of failure.

It used to be that the code generators were very difficult to manage and didn't have a common user interface. This is no longer the case, and, in fact, some of them now adhere to emerging cooperative processing standards. Some large client sites could not even begin to solve their warehousing problems with engine-based tools. Engine-based products use their own engine to get source data and populate the Oracle database. Sagent Technologies' engine-based tool, bundled with the Oracle Data Mart Suite discussed in this chapter, actually sends a steady stream of data directly into Oracle's SQL*Loader engine for placement in Oracle tables. Some believe the engine-based solutions are more comprehensive than the code generators since they theoretically require less intervention. The Oracle Data Mart Suite section looked at the load portion of warehouse data management from an engine-based approach. Let's look at ETI*EXTRACT from Evolutionary Technologies International for an example of a code generator. Figure 8-8 shows how ETI sees their data extraction, transformation, migration, and load (ETML) family of products.

ETI*EXTRACT

This suite of tools, designed to assist and automate the movement of data into the warehouse, is made up of the following components as shown in Figure 8-8.

■ The Master toolset is where superusers configure, customize, and administer the processes carried out by the tool. This is where the hardware and software platforms for conversion projects are specified, as well as source and target databases, file structures, programming languages used by platform, and security requirements.

■ The Conversion Specialists toolset is where conversion specialists specify data mappings and the custom business rules used for a conversion process. The preliminary setup and definitions work done in the Master User piece of the Master toolset is inherited by the Conversion toolset as specialists set out doing their customization. The Conversion Specialists toolset interface is used to map data from one or more sources to one or more targets, as well as the definition and creation of summary or aggregation fields in the target tables.

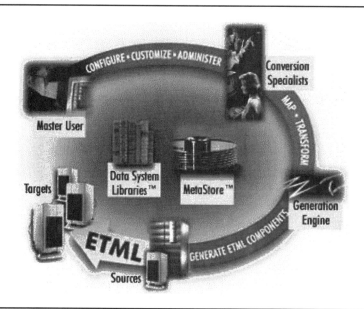

FIGURE 8-8. *ETI family of ETML tools*

■ The Generation Engine is actually three pieces in one:

1. The Parser/Translator translates natural language statements into statements meaningful to the programming language used for the extract. For example, the natural language statement "all records in the Eastern region" is translated to **where reg_code = 'E'**.

2. The Analyzer is where ETI's knowledge of databases, file structures, and programming languages pays off big time by accelerating the extraction and load process. The Analyzer determines the steps required to perform an extract and load, the order of steps to bring the exercise to completion, and optimizes activities along the way.

3. The Executive monitors the work submitted by the Analyzer, ensuring it is done according to the specifications detailed by the Analyzer. It can monitor the piece that moves code to where it will be executed all the way to the component that completes the transformation process before the extraction terminates and the data is made available in the target location.

ETI provides a handful of Data System Libraries (DSL) for the generation of code to go against the databases shown in Table 8-14.

Code Generated	Database Accessed
C	file system
	Oracle
	Sybase
	Informix
	Teradata
COBOL	file system
	DB/2
	IMS
SAP	R3

TABLE 8-14. *DSL Languages and Databases*

Hardware platforms supported include the likes of IBM's MVS, VSE, AS/400, SP/2, and RS/6000 AIX as well as popular UNIX platforms such as HP-UX, Sun Solaris, and DEC UNIX. The ETI DSL architecture is unique in the industry in providing access to any databases and file structures, relational or nonrelational. The DSLs allow you to quickly develop efficient data conversions by providing the following (source: *www.eti.com/products/dsl.html*):

- Direct access to data using native calls for the database or file system
- Data transformations using the programming language of choice
- Support for bulk load, insert, update, or delete operations
- Customizability to meet site-specific standards
- Extensibility for adding functionality to meet your specific needs
- The ability to create new DSLs to address homegrown or proprietary storage systems

We are now going to have a look at the data loading solution provided by Prism Solutions, an example of another code generator.

NOTE
The following material on Prism Solutions was prepared by Kevin Downey, a partner in Newport Technologies Group Inc., based in Ottawa, Canada. Mr. Downey, an expert in the management of data warehouse projects, can be reached via email as kdowney@newport-tech-group.com 30 hours a day, 8 days a week.

Prism Solutions Data Warehouse Software

Prism Solutions Inc., a warehouse software and consulting company based in Sunnyvale, CA, USA produces leading-edge warehouse construction software that is an excellent example of warehouse code generation software. Code generators have the advantage of execution on the platform of choice (either source or target) as well as the speed of fully complied code. This class of tool has traditionally struggled from difficult to use interfaces and nonintegrated toolsets. However, leading-edge vendors like Prism Solutions are changing this perception and, in fact, are changing reality.

Prism's Warehouse Executive (PWE) and Prism Warehouse Directory (PWD) are next-generation software with integrated capabilities for design, construction, and maintenance of warehouses and marts. Together, these products address several key issues warehouse administrators are facing today, including the following:

- Scalability to meet changing business needs and demands

- Graphical design and construction for simplified and consistent development

- Open relational metadata repository to manage data warehouse or mart contents

The Prism solution focuses on a complete product set throughout the warehouse life cycle. This includes tools from the data acquisition phase through to the data quality and verification phase. This differs from many other specialty vendors who focus on only one phase of the warehouse construction cycle. Prism believes the complete approach will result in complete metadata and simplified construction. Figure 8-9 is a roadmap to the Prism solutions, showing how the pieces fit together and integrate.

PWE

The PWE software automates the data warehouse analysis, design, construction, and maintenance processes. PWE provides an intuitive, graphical user interface for designing and documenting warehouse requirements. It allows developers and analysts to combine their knowledge to specify the source files, output tables, data mappings, and data transformations needed for warehouse development. These specifications serve as the basis for generating programs to integrate, transform, and map source data to the target warehouse database. Programs are generated using COBOL, and soon users will be able to generate the transformation code in Java. Figure 8-10 shows where the relationships between some warehouse objects are set up using PDW.

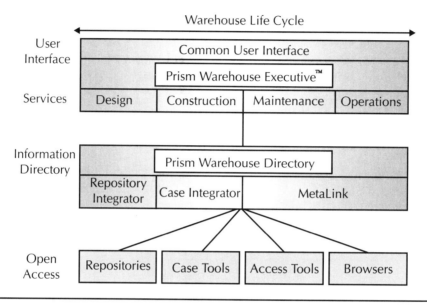

Prism's Scalable Solution: *The Foundation for Next Generation Warehousing*

FIGURE 8-9. *Prism Solutions roadmap*

One of the distinguishing characteristics of the Prism suite of tools is the number of source and target database types supported. The source databases supported are shown in Table 8-15 and the target databases in Table 8-16. The PWE software will run on Windows 95 and NT 4.0.

PWD

PWD is a product that provides a single source of consistent and accurate metadata throughout the data mart or data warehouse. This makes it easier for users to manage, intelligently navigate, and access business information. PWD tells users where to find specific information across different levels of the warehouse, how that information is defined, where it originated, the quality of the data, and when it was last updated.

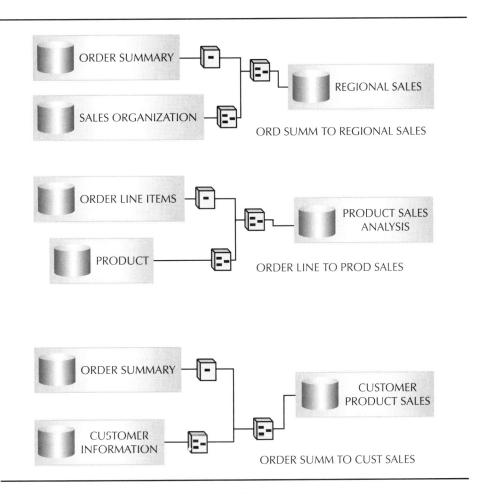

FIGURE 8-10. *The PDW designer interface*

PWD provides a graphical user interface, extendable/open repository, and the ability to add a Web access component through another Prism offering called Prism Web Access (PWA). PWD physically stores its information in a relational database; Oracle is fully supported. PWD's open architecture allows the exchange of metadata with the industry's leading warehousing tools and repositories, including repositories from Platinum, R&O, and HP's Intelligent Warehouse. As well as the exchange of

Oracle	DBS/400	Enscribe
IDMS	IMS	Informix
NonStop SQL	MVS sequential	DB2/MVS
Rdb	RMS	SQP R/3
Sybase	Teradata	VSAM
UNIX sequential		

TABLE 8-15. *Source Databases Supported by Prism*

information, PWD also allows access to the metadata from any query tool that can access a relational database.

We have concentrated on the mainstream Prism warehousing products. It's also important to note that they offer other products such as data quality software, change data capture software, data fast load and update software, warehouse process scheduling software, warehouse methodologies, consulting, and more. This chapter will conclude by covering some of

Oracle	DB2/MVS	DB2/MVS
Informix	NonStop SQL	Rdb
Sybase	Microsoft SQL Server/NT	Teradata
Red Brick Warehouse		

TABLE 8-16. *Target Databases Supported by Prism*

Oracle's Transparent Gateway technology and how it can be used to read data warehouse data from other vendors' repositories.

Oracle Transparent Gateways

One of the secrets of building a useful information repository to support data warehousing is the ability to access data in non-Oracle databases. Using Oracle's Net8 product, Figure 8-11 illustrates how easily this can be accomplished.

This section looks at some advantages of the gateway technologies and how they can assist the transfer and load of data into the warehouse.

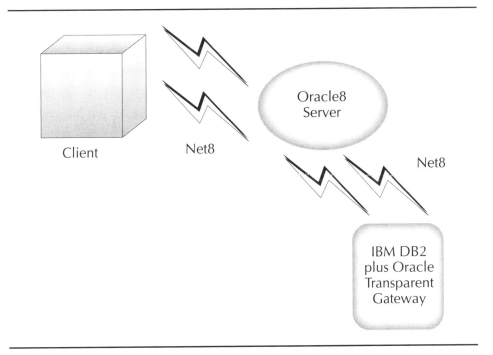

FIGURE 8-11. *Gateway to IBM DB2 using Oracle Server and Net8*

Advantages of Gateway Technology

A must for the implementation of a data warehouse is to enable the gathering of information from external sources. The following are features of gateway technology:

- Allows for integration of different environments by setting up seamless access to data throughout corporate systems.

- Programmers, analysts, and end users leverage Oracle's standard SQL to access non-Oracle data sources. Even with an end-user query tool, users end up passing predefined SQL statements to the Oracle8 Server and, with the cooperation of the gateway, data is retrieved from external databases.

- The "lock, stock, and barrel" rush toward retirement of legacy systems need not exist because state-of-the-art products can access data that still resides on their native hardware platform.

- Easy-to-use GUIs can be used on the client to access data virtually anywhere operational systems reside. GUI tools are more familiar to the end user and are intuitive, considering the point and click interface end users have come to love.

- No preparatory programming must be done. From the time the gateway is successfully installed, Oracle and other third-party tools can be used to access data as though it all resided in the Oracle8 Server.

- The gateway transparently maps the data types on the non-Oracle platform to Oracle's native data types.

The gateway runs on the same machine where the non-Oracle database resides, and it comes with SQL*Net for that machine to enable the transparent data access.

Gateways as the Seed to Data Transformation

While the gateway permits transparent access to non-Oracle data, it also allows data transformation, such as summarization, building derived columns, and changing display and data type of the non-Oracle data as it is moved into Oracle. A common requirement is to change date formats from legacy system representation to the Oracle standard DD-MON-YY. This is accomplished by passing a SQL statement as shown in the following listing:

```
select to_date (ext_date_field,'YYYYMMDD'). . .
```

where the non-Oracle database date field has a format that represents December 8, 1999 as 19991208. If you need to perform more complex data transformations, the data can be brought from the non-Oracle source, put in some sort of intermediate holding table, then massaged with a more sophisticated mechanism such as Oracle's procedural implementation of standard SQL (PL/SQL), based on a popular programming language used by many locations (including the Department of Defense (DOD) in the United States). PL/SQL is often used to build specialized functions within the warehouse to extend those present in most query tools.

Gather your thoughts as we move on to the next item in our long list of data warehousing ideas and issues. Chapter 9 deals with the Partitioning Option with the Oracle8 Server. In the database arena, we feel that range-based partitioning is the second most important invention after the wheel. Oracle's implementation of partitioning is flexible, easy to use, and will become part of your information repository management skillset from day one.

CHAPTER
9

Partitioning

n this chapter, we are going to look at partitioning—in the purest sense (a technique used by Oracle administrators for decades) and the Partitioning Option with Oracle8. Partitioning is nothing new with many database administrators; however, the way Oracle delivers this functionality starting with release 8.0.3 is new. We believe the Oracle8 Partitioning Option is nothing short of a dream come true. In the Oracle world, the deployment of a partitioning approach is nothing short of the reinvention of the wheel!

What Is the Partitioning Option?

Partitioning involves the deliberate splitting of table and index data into smaller, more manageable chunks. The Partitioning Option is an add-on to the Oracle8 Server base product and, in our opinion, is money well spent. With the proliferation of multiterabyte information repositories, management of the structures that contain your data becomes more cumbersome. Unless indicated, the balance of the discussions in this chapter use the term "partitioned table" to refer to both tables and indexes. Partitioning is a big deal for the following reasons:

- Each partition in a partitioned table can be treated logically as its own object when placed in its own tablespace. Thus, a partition can be taken offline by taking the tablespace within which it resides offline.

- Rows in each partition can be deleted or updated separately from the contents of other partitions. Oracle offers an extended partition syntax as illustrated in the next listing and discussed further later in the chapter:

  ```
  select count(*) from sale partition (fy1995);
  ```

- Partitions can be dropped without affecting the data resident in the table's other partitions.

- As volume increases in one partition, it can be split into two partitions without affecting other partition contents.

- Maintenance operations can be performed on one or more partitions in a table without affecting other partitions. Oracle refers to this as *partition independence*.

Differences

Partitioned tables and indexes are different from their nonpartitioned counterparts for the following reasons:

- Storage parameters (e.g., **initial** and **next**) can differ between partitions in the same partitioned table or index. This is shown in the next listing—first for a nonpartitioned table, then for the same table partitioned:

```
-- Non-partitioned version of SALE
create table sale (sale_id       number,
                   fy            number
                                       ..)
          storage (initial 14m next 2m) tablespace trans_mn);
-- Partitioned version of SALE
create table sale (sale_id       number,
                   fy            number
                                       ..)
partition by range (fy)
(partition sale_p1 values less than ('92')
          storage (initial 4m next 1m) tablespace trans_b1,
 partition sale_p2 values less than ('94')
          storage (initial 8m next 1m) tablespace trans_b2,
 partition sale_p3 values less than (maxvalue)
          storage (initial 2m next 1m) tablespace trans_b3);
```

- Transaction environment parameters (e.g., **initrans** and **maxtrans**) can differ between partitions.

- Each partition is stored in the data dictionary as a separate segment. This is evidenced by the listing of the columns from the USER_SEGMENTS dictionary view shown in the next listing. Notice the column name in bold that uniquely identifies each partition as a separate segment.

```
SQL> desc sys.user_segments
 Name                    Null?    Type
 ------------------- -------- ----
 SEGMENT_NAME                    VARCHAR2(81)
 PARTITION_NAME                  VARCHAR2(30)
 SEGMENT_TYPE                    VARCHAR2(17)
 TABLESPACE_NAME                 VARCHAR2(30)
```

```
BYTES                    NUMBER
BLOCKS                   NUMBER
EXTENTS                  NUMBER
INITIAL_EXTENT           NUMBER
NEXT_EXTENT              NUMBER
MIN_EXTENTS              NUMBER
MAX_EXTENTS              NUMBER
PCT_INCREASE             NUMBER
FREELISTS                NUMBER
FREELIST_GROUPS          NUMBER
BUFFER_POOL              VARCHAR2(7)
```

■ Partitioned tables cannot contain some of the new datatypes supported with Oracle8, specifically columns with LONG or LONG RAW datatypes, or the large object datatypes BLOB, CLOB, NCLOB, or BFILE. Attempts to include one of these datatypes in the creation of a partitioned table raise error ORA-00902: invalid datatype.

■ Statistics gathered for the cost-based optimizer are stored in the USER_TAB_PARTITIONS, USER_IND_PARTITIONS, and USER_PART_COL_STATISTIC data dictionary views rather than USER_TABLES, USER_INDEXES, and USER_TAB_COLUMNS.

■ Partitions can be loaded and unloaded independently without affecting other partitions in the same table. For example, to delete the rows from one partition in a table, you would use code similar to the following:

```
delete sale partition (sale_p1);
```

Building Partitioned Objects

The following listing illustrates the creation of a partitioned table (with lines 4 to 16 cut since they contain information irrelevant to this discussion):

```
SQL> create table sale (sale_id      number,
  2                     cust_id      number,
  3                     init_date    date,
                       ..
                       ..
 17                    desc_f       varchar2(90))
 18  partition by range (sale_id)
 19    (partition sale_p1 values less than (33333333)
```

```
20                        tablespace sale_ts1,
21     partition sale_p2 values less than (55555555)
22                        tablespace sale_ts2,
23     partition sale_p3 values less than (88888888)
24                        tablespace sale_ts3,
25     partition sale_p4 values less than (maxvalue)
26                        tablespace sale_ts4);
Table created.
```

Partitioning introduces the concept of *partition key*. A partition key is made up of from 1 to 16 columns and is specified as a partitioned table that is created. Line 18 in the previous listing is where the partition key is defined for the SALE partitioned table. As well, the numbers in parentheses in lines 19, 21, 23, and 25 are where the range boundaries for the table are defined. In Chapter 10, we look at creating partitioned indexes and cover some terminology specific to working with indexes on partitioned tables.

Before moving on, let's look at a few lines in a portion of code that would create a partitioned table with a multicolumn partition key:

```
create table order (
…
partition by range (fy, po_num, region)
…
    partition order_p1 values less than (1997,'A9999','E')
…
```

The code established a three-column partition key FY, PO_NUM, and REGION and places rows in the table's first partition based on the partition key values bolded in the listing.

Choosing the Partition Key

This activity is synonymous with one that some call "Deciding How to Partition." Making the decision of how to partition your data is more than half of the exercise. The secret to partitioning is deciding whether to split a section of partitioned table data by distribution of key data, row counts, nature of your data (i.e., static or refreshed frequently), or for I/O balancing. Let's look at what is involved in each approach, then make some recommendations about which way to proceed. The next few sections refer to the table shown in Figure 9-1. The TST_SURP table is not partitioned but, with a recent purchase of the Partitioning Option for Oracle8, you are

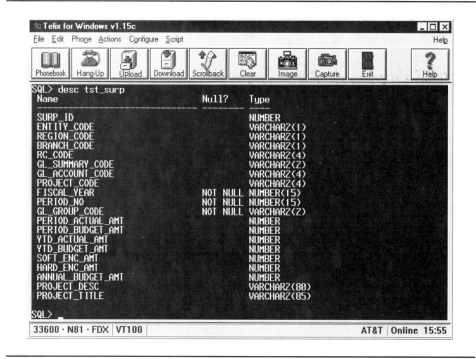

FIGURE 9-1. *Description of a partitioned table*

looking at breaking up the table. Based on the success of the exercise, you are going to look at partitioning the large, frequently accessed tables throughout the warehouse.

The TST_SURP table has over 400,000 rows, with distinct column values as shown in Table 9-1.

NOTE
The steps we lead you through to select the partitioning approach may appear too simplistic for the real world; they indeed may be, but we are more concerned with process than content for this portion of the chapter.

Column	Distinct Values
entity_code	1
region_code	11
branch_code	13
rc_code	718
gl_summary_code	91
gl_account_code	518
project_code	500
gl_group_code	5

TABLE 9-1. *Candidate Partition Key Distinct Column Values*

The numbers in Table 9-1 were gleaned from the owner's USER_TAB_COLUMNS data dictionary view by doing the following:

■ Gathering statistics on the table using the SQL*Plus command **analyze table tst_surp estimate statistics sample 20 percent;**.

■ Issuing the query **select column_name,num_distinct from user_tab_columns where column_name like '%CODE';** against the dictionary.

TIP
When investigating partitioning options, the best way to start is by gathering statistics on the nonpartitioned source table, then using the num_distinct column values.

Based on Column Values

The next step in the analysis is to figure out the optimal number of partitions. Suppose we have 18 disk packs at our disposal. One has been used for the Oracle software and one other is being used for backups, leaving us 16 packs across with which to spread the database. By looking at the information in Table 9-1, we decide to spread the table into as many as six partitions. It is now our job to go look at the distribution of data over the candidate partition key columns. To keep the discussion from getting too unwieldy, let's suppose we are going to consider partitioning on REGION_CODE alone, or a combination of GL_GROUP_CODE and BRANCH_CODE, in that order. Thus, we will first look at a single-column partition key, then at a multicolumn approach. The following listing looks at output that needs to be assembled for the decision to be made:

```
SQL> select region_code,count(*)
  2      from tst_surp
  3    group by region_code;
R    COUNT(*)
-    ----------
A        1720
B       62650
C       59120
D       57900
E       51590
F       67450
G       52860
H       93760
I       10800
J        8360
K        1730
11 rows selected.
SQL> select branch_code,count(*)
  2      from tst_surp
  3    group by branch_code;
B    COUNT(*)
-    ----------
X      200710
Y       29360
Z      237870
3 rows selected.
SQL> select gl_group_code,count(*)
  2      from tst_surp
  3    group by gl_group_code;
GL   COUNT(*)
--   ----------
0A       4390
1B     150740
```

```
2C      207300
3D       64610
4E       40900
5 rows selected.
SQL>
```

BY REGION_CODE   Using the REGION_CODE column value counts
from the previous listing, we now try to arrive at the correct number of
buckets (partitions) within which the data will reside. After crunching the
numbers in a few different ways, we arrive at two possible scenarios.
Column names and attributes not relevant to the exercise are cut from the
next few listings.

1. Four partitions with roughly 110,000 rows in each, creating the table
   with the code shown below:

```
create table tst_surp_p (
    surp_id         number,
    ..
    region_code     varchar2(1),
    branch_code     varchar2(1),
    ..
    ..
    gl_group_code    varchar2(2) not null,
    ..
    ..
    project_title    varchar2(85))
 storage (initial 50m next 50m pctincrease 0)
 partition by range (region_code)
(partition tst_surp_p1 values less than ('D')
        tablespace tsurp_1,
 partition tst_surp_p2 values less than ('F')
        tablespace tsurp_2,
 partition tst_surp_p3 values less than ('H')
        tablespace tsurp_3,
 partition tst_surp_p4 values less than (maxvalue)
        tablespace tsurp_4);
```

2. Two partitions with roughly 230,000 rows each, using the
   following code:

```
create table tst_surp_p (
    surp_id         number,
    ..
    region_code     varchar2(1),
    branch_code     varchar2(1),
    ..
    ..
    gl_group_code   varchar2(2) not null,
    ..
    ..
    project_title   varchar2(85))
storage (initial 100m next 100m pctincrease 0)
partition by range (region_code)
(partition tst_surp_p1 values less than ('F')
         tablespace tsurp_1,
partition tst_surp_p2 values less than (maxvalue)
         tablespace tsurp_2);
```

Let's flip a coin—heads use four partitions, tails use two partitions. Naturally, in real life it's not a flip of the coin that decides. Further on in this chapter we will look at issues that will assist in making this decision. The coin's in the air...tails! Let's load the TST_SURP_P table from the TST_SURP nonpartitioned table with the simple statement shown first in the next listing, then issue the next few queries shown to verify the data is placed as we expected:

```
SQL> insert into tst_surp_p
  2    select * from tst_surp;
467940 rows created.
SQL> select count(*)
  2    from tst_surp_p partition (tst_surp_p1);
  COUNT(*)
------------
    232980
SQL> select count(*)
  2    from tst_surp_p partition (tst_surp_p2);
  COUNT(*)
------------
    234960
SQL> -- We know there are 467940 rows in the partitioned table since we
SQL> -- just inserted the contents of TST_SURP in the first SQL
SQL> -- statement but, being overly cautious as one tends to be, let's
```

```
SQL> -- verify!
SQL> select count(*)
  2    from tst_surp_p;
    COUNT(*)
------------
      467940
SQL> -- Surprise, surprise!
```

Now that the partitioned table exists, let's create a primary key constraint, a few foreign key constraints, and an index on the foreign keys. This is shown in the next listing.

NOTE

*The keywords **initrans** and **unrecoverable** are discussed in Chapter 10 in the "Transaction Entry Parameters" and "Disabling Undo for Index Creation" sections, respectively.*

```
SQL> alter table tst_surp_p add constraint tst_surp_p_pk
  2          primary key (sale_id) using index
  3          storage (initial 60m next 40m pctincrease 0)
  4          initrans 8 maxtrans 8 tablespace tst_surp_idx1
  5          unrecoverable;
Index created.
SQL> alter table tst_surp_p add constraint tst_surp_p_fk1
  2          foreign key (region_code) references region;
Table altered.
SQL> alter table tst_surp_p add constraint tst_surp_p_fk2
  2          foreign key (branch_code) references branch;
Table altered.
SQL> alter table tst_surp_p add constraint tst_surp_p_fk3
  2          foreign key (gl_group_code) references gl_group;
Table altered.
SQL> create index tst_surp_1 on tst_surp_p (region_code)
  2          storage (initial 60m next 40m pctincrease 0)
  3          initrans 8 maxtrans 8 tablespace tst_surp_idx1
  4          unrecoverable;
Index created.
SQL> create index tst_surp_2 on tst_surp_p (branch_code)
  2          storage (initial 60m next 40m pctincrease 0)
  3          initrans 8 maxtrans 8 tablespace tst_surp_idx1
  4          unrecoverable;
Index created.
```

```
SQL> create index tst_surp_3 on tst_surp_p (gl_group_code)
  2         storage (initial 60m next 40m pctincrease 0)
  3         initrans 8 maxtrans 8 tablespace tst_surp_idx1
  4         unrecoverable;
Index created.
```

BY GL_GROUP_CODE AND BRANCH_CODE   When deciding to look at partitioning with a multicolumn partition key, the distribution of the data based on both parts of the key needs inspection. Based on the distribution of the data among the five GL_GROUP_CODE values (4390, 150740, 207300, 64610, and 40900 rows for each value), using this column alone would not yield a good balance by row count. The following query illustrates how to analyze the skew of data values for BRANCH_CODE within GL_GROUP_CODE:

```
SQL> select gl_group_code,branch_code,count(*)
  2     from tst_surp
  3     group by gl_group_code,branch_code;
GL B      COUNT(*)
-- - -----------
01 X         1900
   Y          690
   Z         1800
02 X        77930
   Y         6950
   Z        65860
03 X        92580
   Y        16960
   Z        97760
04 X         7100
   Y         1710
   Z        55800
05 X        21200
   Y         3050
   Z        16650
15 rows selected.
```

Now you're talking! We can analyze the row counts and, after deciding how many partitions, zero in on the partition keys and code the **create table** statement. First, we are going to try and separate the data into three partitions, therefore trying to place as close to one-third of the data in each piece. Let's march through the last listing, adding up the row counts until we get a piece of about 156,000 rows, then build a partition key and carry on.

```
1900+690+1800+77930+6950+65860  =  155130
92580+16960+97760+7100          =  214400
1710+55800+21200+3050+16650     =   98410
```

Obviously, the fit into three partitions is not going to work as we had hoped. Partition 2 is heavy whereas partition 3 is light. Let's use the same numbers trying for four partitions of roughly 117,000 rows each.

```
1900+690+1800+77930+6950                 =   89270
65860+92580                              =  158440
16960+97760                              =  114720
7100+1710+55800+21200+3050+16650         =  105510
```

Stubborn as we may be, let's look at trying five partitions, targeting 81,400 rows each.

```
1900+690+1800+77930                       =   82320
6950+65860                                =   72810
92580+16960                               =  109540
97760                                     =   97760
7100+1710+55800+21200+3050+16650          =  105510
```

This is probably the best balance we are going to get. If we were to drop down to six partitions, the partition holding GL_GROUP_CODE=03 and REGION_CODE=X will have 92,580 rows and GL_GROUP_CODE=03 with REGION_CODE=Z will have 97,760, which cannot be broken down more. Let's run with five buckets and define the TST_SURP_P, then put rows in from TST_SURP.

```
create table tst_surp_p (
     surp_id           number,
     ..
     region_code       varchar2(1),
     branch_code       varchar2(1),
     ..
     ..
     gl_group_code     varchar2(2) not null,
     ..
     ..
     project_title     varchar2(85))
 storage (initial 40m next 40m pctincrease 0)
 partition by range (gl_group_code,branch_code)
(partition tst_surp_p1 values less than ('02', 'X')
         tablespace tsurp_1,
```

```
partition tst_surp_p2 values less than ('03', 'X')
        tablespace tsurp_2,
partition tst_surp_p3 values less than ('03', 'Z')
        tablespace tsurp_3,
partition tst_surp_p4 values less than ('04', 'X')
        tablespace tsurp_4,
partition tst_surp_p5 values less than (maxvalue,maxvalue)
        tablespace tsurp_5);
```

After adding the same primary key index, three foreign key constraints, and three indexes on the foreign keys, we stuff data into the table, then look at the row count in each partition.

```
SQL> select count(*)
  2    from tst_surp_p partition (tst_surp1);
  COUNT(*)
-----------
     82320
SQL> select count(*)
  2    from tst_surp_p partition (tst_surp2);
  COUNT(*)
-----------
     72810
SQL> select count(*)
  2    from tst_surp_p partition (tst_surp3);
  COUNT(*)
-----------
    109540
SQL> select count(*)
  2    from tst_surp_p partition (tst_surp4);
  COUNT(*)
-----------
     97760
SQL> select count(*)
  2    from tst_surp_p partition (tst_surp5);
  COUNT(*)
-----------
    105510
```

Voilà! We have our partitioned table built, and we have the rest of the infrastructure in place (i.e., indexes and constraint). The TST_SURP_P table is ready for a hungry data warehouse user community. We now move on to looking at partitioning a table based on the nature of the data it contains—be it historical or "likely to expand" each time the table is refreshed.

Based on the Nature of Data

There are basically two types of data stored in the warehouse—static and dynamic. *Static* data is usually, but not always, historic in nature or some kind of DIMENSION table in a star schema. *Dynamic* data is refreshed regularly in the data warehouse repository to reflect changes made to its underlying operational counterparts. The interesting part about what we call static data is the word "static" itself. In Chapter 11, where we talk about backup and recovery, we speak fondly of our wording of Murphy's law—if anything can possibly go wrong, it will! It reminds us of the familiar adage, "Never say never." The point is that so many times we brand data as truly static and, guess what?? Something has to be changed (fixed).

This is a very common occurrence. Recently, while on a client site, we were asked to promote an updated version of a script that built a warehouse object that served as a rollup of costing information by product (the outfit is involved in the business of regulating air traffic control, among other things). We were told there had to be a base table containing year-to-date information, broken out by branch and responsibility center. The data had been inspected by senior management, and the program was moved into production. It ran successfully, as it always had in development and testing, creating $4\frac{1}{2}$ million rows and occupying close to 1.6 gigabytes of disk space. Being resource-efficient-minded data warehouse/database administrators, we placed the data in tables spread across more than one datafile in the same tablespace, and marked the tablespace read-only. (The *read-only tablespace* feature of Oracle8 is discussed in Chapter 20 alongside other data warehouse tuning ideas.) The read-only tablespace was backed up during the next backup cycle, then deliberately excluded from backups (as intended). A mere 36 hours later, there was an obscure bug identified in the refresh program, and one column in 10–15 percent of the rows had to be updated. Read-only? Uh huh! Uh huh!

Based on Frequency of Access

The personnel accessing a data warehouse usually know their business inside and out. They know what pockets of information in the warehouse are going to be the heaviest hit. They have spent $7\frac{1}{2}$ hours per day working with the suite of operational systems they have come to love (and hate??). Speak with them, find out what is the most frequently used data, and partition the information based on how busy portions of that data are during warehouse activity.

Perhaps the users are unable (though they would like to) help with the assessment of just what is the most "popular" data. Oracle8 permits access audits of the information in the database; armed with audit information that's been collected, the architect can decide what is truly accessed the most. This exercise can translate the feeling, "Here is a list of the most heavily accessed tables" into a fact. Let's briefly look at auditing, and then look at a few issues involved after suggesting you might want to be led down that path (i.e., a feeling of what is most used rather than fact).

TURNING AUDIT ON AND OFF   While logged onto the database as SYS or SYSTEM, run the following script to turn auditing on for the objects in the schemas owning the data warehouse data:

```
set echo off feed off ver off pages 0
spool audon.sql
select 'audit select on '||owner||'.'||object_name||
       ' by access;'  -- The default is by SESSION, so this keyword
  from dba_objects    -- is IMPORTANT for this scenario.
 where object_type in ('VIEW','TABLE')
   and owner in ('FINANCE','HR','PURCHASE','CABLE');
spool off
set echo on feed on ver on
```

This produces output called "audon.sql," which contains statements of the format shown in the next listing:

```
audit select on cable.subscriber by access;
audit select on hr.posn by access;
audit select on finance.accpay by access;
audit select on purchase.po by access;
```

Invoke the code to turn auditing on using the command **@audon**; the output will resemble the following:

```
SQL> audit select on cable.subscriber by access;
Audit succeeded.
```

```
SQL> audit select on hr.posn by access;
Audit succeeded.
SQL> audit select on finance.accpay by access;
Audit succeeded.
SQL> audit select on purchase.po by access;
Audit succeeded.
```

NOTE
The schema owners shown in the code are examples; edit and change to the appropriate schema names for your warehouse.

The following script will build code to turn auditing off for these same objects:

```
set echo off feed off ver off pages 0
spool audoff.sql
select 'noaudit select on '||owner||'.'||object_name||';'
  from dba_objects
 where object_type in ('VIEW','TABLE')
    and owner in ('FINANCE','HR','PURCHASE','CABLE');
spool off
set echo on feed on ver on
```

The "audoff.sql" output resembles the following:

```
noaudit select on cable.subscriber;
noaudit select on hr.posn;
noaudit select on finance.accpay;
noaudit select on purchase.po;
```

The command **@audoff** displays the following output:

```
SQL> noaudit select on cable.subscriber;
Noaudit succeeded.
SQL> noaudit select on hr.posn;
Noaudit succeeded.
SQL> noaudit select on finance.accpay;
Noaudit succeeded.
SQL> noaudit select on purchase.po;
Noaudit succeeded.
```

CLEANING UP AUDIT INFORMATION   The audit information is stored in the data dictionary view DBA_AUDIT_OBJECT, whose OBJ_NAME and OWNER columns are of interest.

NOTE
Sometimes when auditing operational systems, we pay attention to the date the access was audited; not so in the data warehouse being audited here.

Cleanup is important since the data collected by auditing can be significant. We would be remiss in this discussion were we not to look at keeping the audit information to a minimum. This is a three-step process:

I. Set up a table to hold summary information using the following SQL statement (this is only done at the start, and is not a repetitive step like the next two).

```
create table aud_summary (
    obj_name            varchar2(30),
    owner               varchar2(30),
    hits                number)
storage (initial 5m next 5m pctincrease 0);
```

2. Move atomic audit information out of DBA_AUDIT_OBJECT into a summary table using a statement similar to the following:

```
insert into aud_summary
select obj_name,owner,count(*)
  from dba_audit_object
 group by obj_name,owner;
```

3. Wipe records from DBA_AUDIT_OBJECT, as they are no longer required, using the statement **delete sys.aud$;**. Notice the table used for the deletion is actually AUD$, not DBA_AUDIT_OBJECT. The following error is raised if you try the delete against the DBA_ view rather than AUD$:

```
delete dba_audit_object
       *
ERROR at line 1:
ORA-01752: cannot delete from view without exactly one
key-preserved table
```

ANALYZING AUDIT INFORMATION   The audit information can be displayed with the few lines of code shown in the next listing:

```
col obj_name form a30
col owner form a20
col hits form 99,990
select obj_name,owner,hits
  from aud_summary;
```

Let's present some output from the previous code segment, then discuss its impact on the decision of how and what to partition.

```
OBJ_NAME                        OWNER                    HITS
------------------------------  --------------------  --------
REGION                          FINANCE                  1,929
RESPONSIBILITY                  HR                      17,992
BR_ROLL_UP                      FINANCE                110,982
RC_ROLL_UP                      FINANCE                 80,887
PROJECT                         PURCHASE                71,278
SUBSCRIBER                      CABLE                   21,766
```

HOW THIS AFFECTS PARTITIONING CHOICES   It appears from first inspection that BR_ROLL_UP, RC_ROLL_UP, and PROJECT are candidates for partitioning. Before going down that road, you need to look at the row counts in these tables. For example, the PROJECT table belonging to PURCHASE has only 1,722 rows; it is not a suitable table for partitioning even though it was hit more than 70,000 times during the auditing period. Table 9-2 shows hit rate, row count, and partitioning recommendation.

Table	Row Count	Hit Rate	Partition
Region	12	1,929	N
Responsibility	1,109	17,922	N
br_roll_up	91,887	110,982	Y
rc_roll_up	112,821	80,887	Y
Project	1,722	71,278	N
Subscriber	11,887	21,766	N

TABLE 9-2.   *Partitioning Suggestions*

NOTE
As unrealistic as these figures may appear, they are designed to handhold you through a partitioning experimentation and decision exercise. They are used to illustrate the methodology to follow when deciding what to partition and how.

Row Placement

As records are created in a partitioned table, their partition is decided by their column values in the table's partition key. Let's summarize in Table 9-3 the partitioning approach from the SALE table mentioned a few listings back, using a single-column partition key.

Now let's look at placement of some rows in the SALE partitioned table based on their column values in the SALE_ID column. Table 9-4 shows where each row will be placed and the reason why.

It gets a little more complicated with a multicolumn partition key. Table 9-5 shows the range boundaries for the SALE partitioned object that we will use for this discussion.

The algorithm used to place rows in a table with a multicolumn partition key is as follows:

I. For a row to qualify for placement in a partition, all the row's column values must be less than or equal to their corresponding partition key column values in a partition. The only exception to this rule is when all the column values in a row match all the partition key values, in which case a partition is ruled out.

Partition	Key
1	33333333
2	55555555
3	88888888
4	Maxvalue

TABLE 9-3. *SALE Table Partition Keys*

SALE_ID	Partition	Reason
22832822	1	Value is less than the range boundary defined for partition #1
33333333	2	Value is greater than boundary defined for partition #1 and therefore is placed in the next highest partition whose range boundary value it does not exceed
90000001	4	Value is greater than that defined for the second to last partition, and goes into the highest number partition with **maxvalue** as the partition range boundary

TABLE 9-4. *Placement of Rows in SALE Table Partitions*

2. Oracle moves from the left to the right, comparing column values against partition keys.

3. A partition is ruled out if any column value is greater than its corresponding partition key.

Partition #	FY	CUSTOMER
1	1995	DZZ999
2	1995	ZZZ999
3	1996	ZZZ999
4	1997	MZZ999
5	1997	ZZZ999
6	1999	ZZZ999
7	maxvalue	maxvalue

TABLE 9-5. *Two-column Partition Key Example*

Table 9-6 shows the placement of a handful of rows in the same partitioned table by applying these three rules.

Traditional Partitioning

Ever since the dawn of Oracleization, DBAs have used a number of techniques to partition the information they have been tasked to manage. Many tuning works, including *Oracle8 Tuning* (Corey, Abbey, Dechichio, Abramson: Osborne/McGraw-Hill and Oracle Press, 1998), look at performance issues in the light of deliberate separation of data and indexes based on usage patterns, available disk drives, and nature of applications. Let's look at the more traditional partitioning tricks, starting with splitting.

FY	CUSTOMER	Partition	Reason
1995	AER676	1	Rules 1&2: The FY column value (1995) matches the partition key, but the row's CUSTOMER value (AER676) is less than the partition key value (DZZ999).
1998	CFT213	6	Rule 1: The FY column value (1998) is less than the partition key for partition #6 (1999).
1997	XXX000	5	Rules 1&2: The FY column value matches partition #4's range boundary, but XXX000 is greater than the boundary for #4 for CUSTOMER (MZZ999). The range boundary for the next FY key matches, and that partition's other key value is greater than the row's CUSTOMER value.

TABLE 9-6. *Row Placement in Multicolumn Partitioned Table*

Splitting

Splitting involves the storage of table and index data in different tablespaces. Since tablespace is a logical grouping of one or more datafiles, this is the same as saying that table and index information should be stored in different files as well. Let's look at the Schema Manager and the Storage Manager in the Oracle Enterprise Manager (also called *OEM*), and the pointing of table and index information at different tablespaces.

Figure 9-2 shows the Storage Manager startup screen, where the list of tablespaces is displayed.

After right-mouse clicking on Tablespaces, then selecting Create from the drop-down menu presented, you arrive at a screen where you create tablespaces, as shown in Figure 9-3. Superimposed on top of the Create Tablespace screen shown in Figure 9-3 is the Create Datafile dialog box.

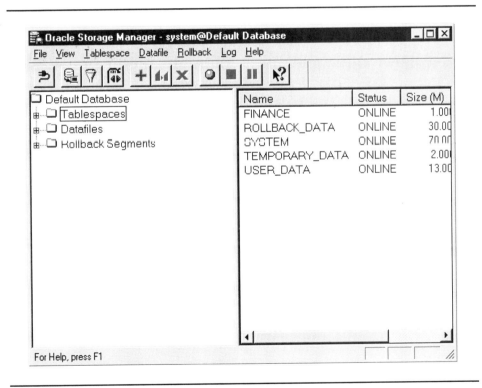

FIGURE 9-2. *Storage Manager main console*

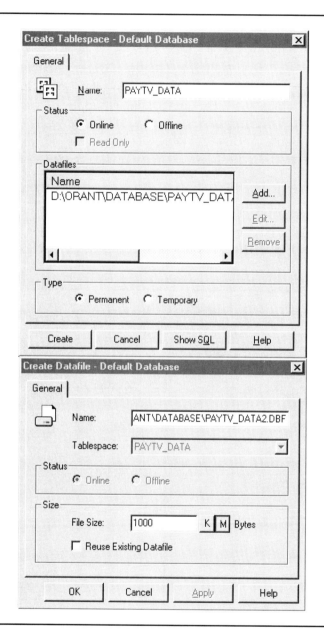

FIGURE 9-3. *Create Tablespace and Create Datafile dialog boxes*

Let's have a brief look at the highlights of these two screens and the effect they have on traditional partitioning:

- **Name (paytv_data)**   We have chosen a name that is meaningful from a double standpoint. First of all, the name indicates the nature of the data within the tablespace, in this case pay TV order information. Secondly, the text "DATA" as part of the name indicates it is the holder of the data portion for the pay TV order data mart.

- **Type**   The Permanent button in the Type area is highlighted as the dialog box appears. Ensure the Temporary option is not selected by mistake or you will not be able to create any tables in the tablespace at any time after creation, or until the type is reset.

- **Name (d:\orant\database\paytv_data.dbf)**   This is the operating system file name again, containing text indicative of the nature of the data in the mart and the fact that it contains data rather than index.

- **File Size (1000 M)**   We selected a size to be measured in megabytes (1,048,576 bytes). Be careful when working on this screen, as once the datafile has been created with the tablespace to which it belongs, it can be difficult to resize the datafile.

When ready to proceed, the tablespace is created by clicking Create to pass the SQL to Oracle for processing. Let's look at creating the corresponding index tablespace for the pay TV order data mart data tablespace just created. The next listing shows the SQL commands used to set up the index tablespace. They could be run from Server Manager, SQL*Plus, or the SQL*Worksheet.

```
create tablespace paytv_index
    datafile 'c:\orant\database\paytv_index.dbf' size 500m,
             'g:\orant\database\paytv_index2.dbf' size 500m;
```

To inspect the results of the work just performed, let's issue a query against the data dictionary view DBA_DATA_FILES. This is shown in the next listing:

```
SQL> select tablespace_name,file_name,bytes
  2    from dba_data_files;
TABLESPACE_NAME      FILE_NAME                                    BYTES
----------------     ----------------------------------     ----------
PAYTV_DATA           D:\ORANT\DATABASE\PAYTV_DATA.DBF       1048576000
PAYTV_DATA           E:\ORANT\DATABASE\PAYTV_DATA2.DBF      1048576000
PAYTV_INDEX          C:\ORANT\DATABASE\PAYTV_INDEX.DBF       524288000
PAYTV_INDEX          G:\ORANT\DATABASE\PAYTV_INDEX2.DBF      524288000
3 rows selected.
```

NOTE

These examples are Windows NT 4.0, which supports long file names. Some administrators prefer sticking to the eight-character name with three-character extension for Windows-based database file names.

Striping

The technique ensures that data and index portions for the same table are spread across more than one datafile belonging to the same tablespace. This is a four-step process, regardless of how many datafiles make up the same tablespace.

1. Create a data tablespace made up of more than one data datafile, deliberately placing each file that makes up the tablespace on different drives.

2. Do the same for the index portion of the tables to be striped.

3. Load the data into the data tablespace and create the index. The easiest way to force table data into more than one datafile in the same tablespace involves the following:

   - Figuring out the amount of space required to hold the data in the database (let's pick the figure 2Gb for this discussion).

   - Deciding how many datafiles will be set up to hold table data (using the number 2 for now).

- Dividing the space allocation evenly across the number of datafiles chosen. In this example, we would make each datafile 1Gb (i.e., 2Gb / 2 datafiles).

4. Creating the indexes.

Voilà! Table data and index entries are striped across four datafiles each. Let's have a look at the DBA_FREE_SPACE data dictionary view to ensure the information resides where it is supposed to.

NOTE
For the sake of this discussion, we are pretending the tablespaces were created just before the data was loaded and indexes created. Thus, all the free space in the next listing is in one chunk.

```
SQL> select tablespace_name, file_id, bytes
  2    from dba_free_space
  3    where tablespace_name like 'PAYTV%';
TABLESPACE_NAME                 FILE_ID            BYTES
------------------------------  ---------  ---------------
PAYTV_DATA                           23        629145600
PAYTV_DATA                           24        419430400
PAYTV_INDEX                          25        367001600
PAYTV_INDEX                          26        157286400
```

This listing confirms that 60 percent of the free space in PAYTV_DATA is in one datafile, and 40 percent in the other. The PAYTV_INDEX free space is 70 percent in one datafile and 30 percent in the other. Mission accomplished.

This concludes our brief journey through partitioning land. So many clichés come to mind when thinking of the concept of partitioning—the whole is the sum of its parts; six of one, half-dozen of the other; the team is as strong as its weakest member. Naturally, with or without the Oracle8 Partitioning Option, partitioning alone is the single most effective means to manage very large information repositories that hold data for a large percentage of data warehouses. In a recent presentation we gave at a user conference, we did a spin-off on the famous $e=mc^2$ equation. We used the equation $e=cp^2$ that stood for "efficiency=clever partitioning and parallelism," hence the $\mathbf{p}^2$. We spoke of parallelism in Chapter 7, and will spend more time on it in Chapter 20.

The next chapter deals with indexing the warehouse. With such large volumes of data, getting at that information in a quick and accurate manner is fundamental to warehouse user satisfaction. The indexing approach you use for your warehouse can affect the happiness of the end user; therefore, indexing is the most important aspect of data warehouse setup after the data has been selected, migrated, transformed, and loaded to its desired location.

CHAPTER
10

Indexing the Warehouse

his chapter of *Oracle8 Data Warehousing* discusses indexing the warehouse. Data warehouse administrators (we call them DWAs) are responsible for ensuring the warehouse is set up in a way that supports optimal access to the information using the least amount of CPU, disk access, and other precious computer resources. This chapter is aimed at these administrators, and is one of the few chapters in this book that contains some material specifically for the technical readership. We will look at different approaches to indexing data in the Oracle8 database, then discuss the ways they are created and maintained, the benefits of each approach, and some caveats we have experienced with their implementation and usage.

NOTE
Chapter 9 discusses range-based partitioning with Oracle8, part of the Partitioning Option. All the discussions in this chapter pertain to building indexes on partitioned and nonpartitioned tables and indexes except where indicated.

An *index* is, in most cases, a structure separate from the table data it refers to, storing the location of rows in the database based on the column values specified when the index is created. Indexes are like mini copies of the table data they refer to. Examine the following query and its results, showing the first few and last few rows:

```
SQL> select emp_id, last_name,first_name
  2    from emp_mast;
  EMP_ID LAST_NAME                FIRST_NAME
  -------- ----------------------- -----------
   10000 ANDREWS                  LAWRENCE
   10002 SMITH                    KEN
   10005 DEFWAYNO                 FRANCIS
   10006 ABBEFLANTRO              BORIS
   10091 PRENDIN                  ROBERTO
...
...
...
   11881 BESDESMITH               NANCY
   11901 NADROJIAN                NORMAN
7850 rows selected.
SQL>
```

Suppose a query were to restrict the LAST_NAME, looking for names that started with the text "SM" (called the *lookup string*). Without an index on LAST_NAME, Oracle would read from the first row to the last row, looking for the rows with the desired lookup string. With an index, Oracle would proceed to the index, obtain an address of the qualifying row, then present the data in the qualifying row to the process that issued the query. In a nutshell, that is what indexes are all about.

TIP
Index lookups are the secret to optimizing the response time to most queries, and are used systematically in a data warehouse to improve warehouse throughput.

Enhanced throughput contributes to three words so crucial to the success of a data warehousing project—*enhanced customer satisfaction.* Let's get started by having a look at the types of indexing available with Oracle8.

What Columns to Index

Two main rules or guidelines exist about what columns to index in the Oracle8 database. First, some terminology. *Selectivity* is a measurement of the number of distinct values in a table column compared to the number of rows in the whole table. The *predicate* of a SQL statement is that part where the selection criteria are specified. These *selection criteria* specify which rows of information are to be included in the query result set. The first criterion starts with the **where** keyword; all subsequent criteria start with the keyword **and**. The *result set* is a set of one or more rows that qualify for inclusion in a specific query.

Selectivity Consideration

Using the NUM_ROWS column value from USER_TABLES, coupled with the NUM_DISTINCT column value from USER_TAB_COLUMNS, you can assess the selectivity of a column. Suppose there were 79,000 rows in a table in a finance data mart, and the ACC_TYPE column had eight distinct values. The selectivity of any row in a table is calculated according to the following formula:

```
                    rows in table              1
selectivity =  --------------    *  -------------
                  distinct values      rows in table
```

which is the same as saying the selectivity is the inverse of the value found in NUM_DISTINCT for that column. In this example, the selectivity equals the inverse of 8, which is .125, or 12.5 expressed as a percent. This leads to the following guideline:

TIP
When a column value is found in less than 5 percent of all the rows in a table, that column is a good candidate for an index.

Mentioned in Predicate Consideration

Say a purchases data mart continually processed queries using the PURCHASE_DATE and CUST_NUM as part of the predicate. These two columns should be considered for indexes.

Columns displayed as part of the query results but not used as part of a predicate are not good index candidates. In other words, the italicized column in the following listing may not be considered for an index, whereas the one in boldface may be a candidate:

```
select sum(aggr_day),region, …
   from day_summary,region
 where trans_date between '01-JAN-1999' and '31-JAN-1999' …;
```

TIP
Columns that are commonly parts of query selection criteria are candidates for indexes.

Naturally, because this is a rule (actually a guideline), exceptions exist. Columns continually mentioned in a predicate, but upon which a function or operation is performed, are not candidates for indexes. If a function is to be performed on a column, the column's index is not used. We call this *index suppression*. The following listing shows two examples of how the TRANS_DATE column from the previous listing may be used that do not warrant an index:

```
select sum(aggr_day),region, …
   from day_summary,region
 where to_char(trans_date,'Dy') in ('Mon','Tue') …;
select sum(aggr_day),region, …
   from day_summary,region
 where months_between(trans_date,sysdate) > 6 …;
```

There is one more guideline about columns mentioned in predicates with and without a function. Suppose the TRANS_DATE column from DAY_SUMMARY is used in the SQL statement:

```
select …
   from day_summary …
 where to_char(trans_date) …
```

as well as in the SQL statement:

```
select …
   from day_summary …
 where trans_date between (…
```

TIP
A column that is used in a predicate with and without a function performed on it may still be a candidate for an index. Analyze the number of SQL statements using a function, and implement an index if it optimizes the statements without a function.

Data Warehouse Uniqueness

In a way, we have found that indexing a data warehouse or data mart is a dream come true. A common occurrence when designing operational systems is that the database the programmers use during development contains only a small subset of production data. The tables used during program development are a fraction of the size they are in production. Some of our clients have very large tables with 30 or 40 million rows in production and a 30 or 40 thousand row subset in development. In the data warehouse or data mart, enough data exists throughout development that tough indexing decisions can be made against realistic volumes of data. With this volume of data, it is easier to assess the efficiency of indexes, and run tests to zero in on additional indexes that could aid performance. Tables can be analyzed and calculations about selectivity can be made to decide appropriate columns for indexing. A word of warning will serve as the next guideline before a discussion of init.ora parameters.

TIP
Columns that are indexed in operational systems are not necessarily good candidates for indexing in the DSS.

A well thought out and meticulously implemented indexing scheme for an operational system needs careful review and ongoing scrutiny as the data is moved into the decision support arena.

Single-Column and Composite Indexes

There are two types of indexes that can be built using the traditional Oracle B-tree index mechanism—single-column and composite. *Single-column* indexes are built on one column of a database table using code similar to that shown in the next listing:

```
create index purchase_1
    on purchase (purchase_id)
    storage (initial 2m next 2m pctincrease 0)
tablespace purch_ind1;
```

A *composite index*, or concatenated index, is built on two or more columns in the same table, as shown in the following listing:

```
create index purchase_2
    on purchase (cust_id,purchase_date,total_amt)
    storage (initial 4m next 2m pctincrease 0)
tablespace purch_ind1;
```

The same activity is accomplished using the Schema Manager bundled with the Oracle Enterprise Manager (affectionately called *OEM*) using the dialog box shown in Figure 10-1. Notice how this component of the

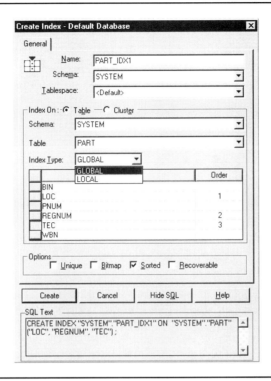

FIGURE 10-1. *Creating an index in the Schema Manager*

Schema Manager is Oracle8 ready; the PART table is a partitioned table, and the picklist beside Index Type allows you to pick **global** or **local**.

We have entered a name for the index and selected the following for the index creation:

■ The index will be owned by the SQLP user in the database.

■ The table upon which the index is being created is owned by SYSTEM.

■ This will be a three-column index built on LOC, REGNUM, and TEC, in that order.

The Show SQL button has been pressed in the dialog box, causing the SQL text to be displayed at the bottom of the screen.

Oracle8 Indexing Approaches

In the not too distant past, there was only one method used by the Oracle Server to build indexes and make their functionality available to applications. Oracle calls this traditional indexing technique a *B-tree approach.*

B-tree Indexes

By default, this is the type of index Oracle sets up with the familiar **create index**, **create unique index** or **alter table … add constraint … primary key … using index** syntax. This indexing approach has been used by Oracle for a number of versions. Think of a B-tree index as containing a hierarchy of highest-level and succeeding lower-level index blocks. There are two types of blocks in the B-tree index:

- Branch blocks, or upper-level blocks, simply point to the corresponding lower-level blocks.

- Leaf blocks, where the actual meat of the indexing method lies, contain the Oracle ROWID that points at the location of the actual row the leaf refers to.

Oracle has stuck to the B-tree organization for so long mainly due to its simplicity, ease of maintenance, and retrieval speed of highly selective column values (high cardinality). This organization is especially suited to queries looking for index column values in equality (i.e., **where colA = 'ABC123'**) and range searches (i.e., **where colA between 'A12' and 'R45'**). The size of a table, be it a few hundred or a few million rows, has little or no impact on the speed with which B-tree indexed data can be fetched from its corresponding tables. When working with one or more large objects, the B-tree index is not the culprit when queries take long times to return the result sets. The culprit is the massive amounts of information that make up that set. Oracle presents formulae in the *Oracle8 Server Administrator's Guide* for calculation of the space required for indexes using this B-tree model.

Bitmap Indexes

Until release 7.3, Oracle's indexing mechanism consisted of B-tree indexes, in a tree fashion. With this new bitmap index feature, query processing and index access can improve manyfold. The following section looks at what bitmap indexing involves, then discusses how to set them up and when they should be used. Bitmap indexes are built on one column at a time.

What Is a Bitmap Index?

This alternative indexing mechanism has become part of the industry standard for query-intensive applications, such as DSS/EIS OLAP for columns with very few unique values (low cardinality). *Bitmap indexing* involves building a stream of bits: each bit relates to a column value in a single row of a table. Suppose you built a bitmap index on the PERSON table shown in Table 10-1.

Using bitmap indexes, the SQL statement to create the index would be

```
create bitmap index person_region on person (region);
```

Suppose the region could have the values "north", "east", "west", or "south". Oracle goes through a two-step process in building the index:

1. It scans the table, sorts the column values for region, and decides how many bitmaps will be required for the index, based on the number of distinct values found in the column. In this case, four unique values exist.

Column	Data Contained
PIN	Number
Region	Varchar2(10)
hire_year	Varchar2(4)
pensioned	Varchar2(2)

TABLE 10-1. *PERSON Table*

2. It then builds the number of bit streams to populate the index decided in step 1. The REGION column bitmap index is shown in Table 10-2. The PENSIONED column bitmap index is shown in Table 10-3. This index is created with the following statement:

```
create bitmap index person_pensioned on person (pensioned);
```

Storage parameters and a tablespace name can be explicitly defined when you create a bitmap index. The statement that created the REGION index would become

```
create bitmap index person_region on
    person (region) tablespace indexes_prd
    pctfree 20 pctused 80 initrans 4 maxtrans 16
storage (initial 1m next 1m pctincrease 0 initrans 4);
```

Row	Region	North Bitmap	East Bitmap	West Bitmap	South Bitmap
1	North	1	0	0	0
2	East	0	1	0	0
3	West	0	0	1	0
4	West	0	0	1	0
5	East	0	1	0	0
6	West	0	0	1	0
7	South	0	0	0	1
8	North	1	0	0	0
9	East	0	1	0	0
10	South	0	0	0	1

TABLE 10-2. *REGION Bitmap Index Entries*

Row	Pensioned	Bitmap
1	Y	1
2	Y	1
3	N	0
4	N	0
5	Y	1
6	Y	1
7	Y	1
8	Y	1
9	N	0
10	Y	1

TABLE 10-3. *PENSIONED Bitmap Index Entries*

When Bitmap Indexes Should Be Used

Guidelines exist for you to follow before you decide where and when to use
bitmap indexes.

NOTE
*Tables that undergo little or no insert/update
activity are good candidates.*

Transaction tables in the operational system usually undergo constant
record creation and update activities. The overhead involved in updating a
bitmap index is higher than for Oracle's traditional indexing mechanisms. In
the data warehouse environment, where data is normally static, however,
this is acceptable.

TIP
*Columns in this type of table that have low
cardinality are good candidates for having
bitmap indexes.*

Cardinality is a measurement of the number of unique values in a
column in the table, compared to the total number of rows in that table. We
also use the term *selectivity*, as mentioned in the "Selectivity Consideration"
section earlier in this chapter. In some circumstances, low cardinality means
the number of unique column values is less than 5 percent of the rows in the
table. In the DSS environment and Oracle's bitmap index implementation,
the rule of thumb to follow is as follows:

TIP
*If the degree of cardinality of a column is <= .1
percent (yes, 1/10th of 1 percent), it is an ideal
candidate for a bitmap index.*

This does not mean that any column whose cardinality is greater than .1
percent cannot be a candidate for a bitmap index. Oracle believes this
figure could go as high as 1 percent and still be a candidate for a bitmap
index. Are columns with cardinality between .2 percent and 1 percent
candidates? Perhaps they should be considered. That's your decision to
make, based on response time using the bitmap approach as compared to
Oracle's traditional indexing scheme.

For example, a table that records cities and ZIP codes in the United
States may have 123,000 rows. Because there are 50 states in the union, the
degree of cardinality for the STATE column in the table is less than 1 percent
(.0406 percent is a closer figure). The STATE column in a data warehouse,
therefore, is a good candidate for a bitmap index. Picture a table with
2,500,000 rows; there are 56,213 distinct values in a specific column in that
table. That column's degree of cardinality is roughly 2.24 percent, so it is
not a candidate for a bitmap index.

If you are used to studying reasons for creating indexes in online
transaction processing (*OLTP*), in Oracle systems, you may remember that
the high-cardinality columns are usually candidates for indexes. OLTP is the
overriding characteristic of operational systems, and these systems support

many **insert**, **update**, and **delete** activities. Their data is dynamic and undergoes high activity, which is in direct opposition to the static data commonly stored in the data warehouse.

TIP
Bitmaps are inappropriate for heavy OLTP (transaction-oriented) systems.

As with the B-tree indexing approach, columns commonly referenced in SQL queries in the **where** or **and** parts of the statements (coupled with low cardinality) are the best upon which to use this new indexing approach. Suppose ad hoc queries in a data warehouse against the PERSON table shown in Table 10-1 never use the HIRE_YEAR column in this part of the query. A common query resembling

```
select count(*)
  from person
 where pensioned = 'Y'
   and region = 'NORTH';
```

uses the PENSIONED column as part of the selection criteria, which makes it a good candidate for either indexing approach.

Space Trade-offs Using Bitmap Indexes

Because bitmap indexes are highly compressed when they are set up for columns with low cardinality, they can offer a double gain to the data warehouse system—marked performance gains over their traditional counterparts, coupled with what can be significant space savings. In some situations, using a bitmap index instead of the traditional approach could use 1/100 of the space of the B-tree index, Oracle's other indexing mechanism. Table 10-4 shows how radically different storage requirements can be for bitmap and B-tree indexes on a table with 1,000,000 rows.

TIP
These figures are used only as an example to show the relative size of each type of index. They can be related to a real-life situation.

Unique Column Values	Cardinality (%)	B-tree Space	Bitmap Space
500,000	50.00	15.29	12.35
100,000	10.00	15.21	5.25
10,000	1.00	14.34	2.99
100	0.01	13.40	1.38
5	<0.01	13.40	0.78

TABLE 10-4. *Space Comparison Traditional Vs. Bitmap Index*

Saving space is neither a primary reason nor part of any reason for using bitmap indexes. Low cardinality coupled with the static nature of a table's data makes one or more of its columns candidates for bitmap indexing.

Indexes on Partitioned Tables

This section deals specifically with indexes built on partitioned tables. Let's cover some terminology first that will assist in understanding the discussions, and expand the partition definitions we presented in Chapter 9.

■ A *local index* is one built on a partitioned table when the partition keys of the index match those of its underlying table.

■ A *global index* is one built on a partitioned table with a different set of partition keys than the corresponding data segment.

■ A *prefixed index* is one whose leftmost column in a partitioned index matches the leftmost column in that index's partition key.

■ A *nonprefixed index* is one whose leftmost column in a partitioned index differs from the leftmost column in that index's partition key.

To summarize the material in the previous four definitions, let's look at the SALE table partitioned based on the information in Table 10-5 using a two-column partition key on the FY and REGION columns.

Partition #	Values Less Than
1	95,D
2	96,A
3	96,T
4	97,F
5	97,Z
6	Maxvalue,maxvalue

TABLE 10-5. *Two-Column Partition Key*

Using this partitioning approach, let's now look at code that builds a few indexes, then discuss each index's type. The code **create index sale_u1 on sale (sale_id)...** creates a global nonprefixed index since the indexing column (SALE_ID) is not the same as the leftmost column in the partition key. Even though the keyword **global** is not mentioned in the creation statement, the index assumes this property as the default. The code **create index sale_fy on sale (fy,region)... local;** creates a local prefixed index since the FY column is the first mentioned in the index creation statement and the first in the partition key. Getting a little more complicated, inspect the code presented next:

```
create index sale_spec on sale (fy,region)
partition by range (fy,region)
    (partition ss_ip1 values less than ('96','G')
            tablespace sales_idx1,
    partition ss_ip2 values less than (maxvalue,maxvalue)
            tablespace sales_idx2);
```

This index is local prefixed even though it does not include the **local** keyword; by explicitly mentioning the partitioning method in the SQL **create** statement, the index becomes **local**. As well, notice that the table is broken into six partitions, whereas the index is split between only two. In Chapter 20, where we discuss issues related to tuning the warehouse, we will offer some recommendations on which type of index to use for what situation.

TIP
Use local indexes (the default) as much as possible to make your indexes on partitioned tables and the underlying data partitions easier to manage.

Index-organized Tables

Oracle8 delivered a new type of structure that can prove beneficial for some requirements in a data warehouse. Traditional database tables have a data segment (the area set aside for storage of the column values for all columns defined for a table) and an index segment (where quick reference information is stored by column value). Index-organized tables (table type *IOT*) with Oracle8, on the other hand, merge the two traditional segments into one. Thus, the data is the index and the index is the data.

Defining Index-organized Tables

After saying that, the rows in some index-organized tables are stored partially in a regular area and, when required, partially in an overflow area. To illustrate this phenomenon, let's look at creating an index-organized table in the following listing:

```
SQL> create table country (
  2      country_code    varchar2(3),
  3      name            varchar2(30),
  4      capital         varchar2(30),
  5      free_form1      varchar2(1200),
  6    free_form2        varchar2(1200),
  7  constraint country_pk primary key (country_code))
  8  organization index tablespace misc_look
  9  pctthreshold 20 overflow tablespace misc_look_overflow;
Table created.
```

Let's pick apart three important lines in the SQL statement:

- **Line 7** Definition of a primary key is mandatory as the table is created. With IOT, you cannot create the table without the primary key definition and **alter** the table to add this constraint.

■ **Line 8**   Sets the table to type index-organized, specifying the misc_look tablespace for the primary key column data.

■ **Line 9**   Specifies that when the cumulative length of all nonkey column data is more than 20 percent of the Oracle block size, the nonkey columns are stored in the misc_look_overflow tablespace. Suppose your Oracle block size were 8,192 bytes. A row whose NAME, CAPITAL, FREE_FORM1, and FREE_FORM2 column values were 1,801 bytes would find these four nonkey columns stored in the overflow tablespace (since 1,801 > overflow percent of block size), whereas one whose four column values were 709 bytes would find all its column values stored in the regular area.

As well, when you specify an **overflow** tablespace name and percentage, Oracle8 creates a table to hold the overflow data transparent to the SQL statement that creates the index-organized table itself. This is illustrated in the following query results:

```
SQL> select table_name,iot_type
  2    from user_tables
  3    where iot_type = 'IOT_OVERFLOW';
TABLE_NAME                      IOT_TYPE
------------------------------- ------------
SYS_IOT_OVER_3327               IOT_OVERFLOW
```

Benefits of Index-organized Tables

The major benefit when using index-organized tables is the retrieval time to get at the data. In the traditional table with one of the normal index approaches, retrieval can involve two reads. The first is to scan the index segment looking for column values matching the desired selection criteria. The second gets the rows from the data segment to which the qualifying index entries refer by using a ROWID fetch. The first operation is referred to as an *index range scan* and, in most but not all cases, is the way Oracle processes a query. There is only one segment with the index-organized tables; in other words, the index is the data.

Using the traditional table/index method, Oracle stores the ROWID of each row in the index segment. The rowid prior to Oracle8 was a 17-character hexadecimal number. The rowid could be picked apart to reveal the block address, the row number within that block, and the file number of the database file where that row resides. There is no rowid stored with index-organized tables, which is a double gain—it conserves database space and provides for primary key access to the values in the index-organized table. Queries involving exact match or range searches will run faster using index-organized tables. With a separate data and index segment and traditional tables, the index duplicates column values from the data segment, thereby consuming double the space for those indexed columns.

TIP
The data warehouse is an ideal location for index-organized tables, but don't rush out and implement them everywhere without testing their performance in your Oracle8 databases.

Where to Use Index-organized Tables

Code tables are ideal candidates for index-organized tables. Retrieval is done using the primary key columns; most of the time, the description field populates a drop-down picklist. Applications that support text searches on document collections may also benefit from using index-organized tables. Spatial applications should consider using index-organized tables since they provide for efficient retrieval alongside minimum space allocations as compared to a more traditional indexing approach. OLAP applications, being multidimensional in nature, benefit from an index-organized methodology because it speeds up access to portions of the multidimensional blocks.

NOTE
Not all tables seeming to meet the requirements for the index-organized approach should be set up using this Oracle8 feature. Experience and familiarity with your data warehouse data will assist with deciding whether or not to use this method.

Optimizer Histograms

Since the release of Oracle7 (circa February 1993), Oracle has had two optimization approaches. The *rule-based optimizer* uses an intelligent set of rules and, based on examining available ways to access data to satisfy a query, selects an access path based on the application of those rules. The *cost-based optimizer* inspects the data and, armed with statistics in the data dictionary, selects an access path that costs the least. Cost is measured using a number of factors, two of which are anticipated degree of resource consumption and length of time expected to produce results.

To use the cost-based approach, you need to collect statistics on table data. This can be done manually using the following SQL statement:

```
analyze table {table_name} compute statistics;
```

A number of variations in options exist that can be used in this statement. In this discussion, the simplest statement format—analyzing a table and computing statistics—is being used. The cost-based optimizer allows Oracle to select access paths that may change with the data as it changes; for example, a week ago, 120 column values satisfied a query selection criterion but, for some reason, there are now 972. A *histogram* is a graphic representation of the distribution of data. The **analyze** statement was expanded in release 7.3 to incorporate histograms. They track data distribution in Oracle tables. The syntax for their creation is

```
analyze table {table_name} compute statistics for table for all
indexed columns size {num_buckets};
```

Recall the PERSON table shown in Table 10-1. Suppose an index exists on the HIRE_YEAR column called PERSON_HY. The values and count of rows for each unique HIRE_YEAR column value are shown in Table 10-6. You can build a histogram on PERSON_HY with the following command:

```
analyze table person compute statistics for table for all indexed
columns size 6;
```

HIRE_YEAR	# Rows	Running Total
1962	4	4
1970	33	37
1971	93	130
1983	1,918	2,048
1991	5,120	7,168
1994	448	7,616

TABLE 10-6. *Distribution of Column Values in HIRE_YEAR*

This would put six rows (commonly referred to as buckets) in the USER_TAB_HISTOGRAMS table. Look at what is stored in that histogram using the command shown in the next listing:

```
SQL> select endpoint_number
  2    from user_tab_histograms
  3  where table_name = 'PERSON';
            4
           37
          130
         2048
         7168
         7616
6 rows selected.
```

Using a number equal to or greater than the number of distinct column values is best. The number of distinct column values in the HIRE_YEAR column of the PERSON table can be found; then, the histogram is set up using the following SQL code:

```
SQL> col a new_value b
SQL> select count(distinct hire_year) a from person;
         7
SQL> analyze table person compute statistics for table for all
  2    indexed columns size &b;
```

```
old   2: indexed columns size &b
new   2: indexed columns size          7
Table analyzed.
```

Histograms provide the benefit of optimal query performance because they provide for accurate selectivity estimates based on knowledge of actual data; they can reveal actual column data distribution.

NOTE
You can build optimizer histograms on partitioned tables, the details of which are available in the data dictionary by looking at USER_PART_HISTOGRAMS.

Primary Key Indexes

The data warehouse is chock full of *referential integrity*, designed through a network of primary and foreign keys, to ensure parent-child relationships are maintained and enforced. We call referential integrity by its initials—*RI*. There are a few ways to define primary keys in the Oracle8 data warehouse, but there is really only one way to do it properly. Inspect the following listing, commented to illustrate the points we are making:

```
-- The table already exists, so must be altered to set a primary key.
alter table sale add constraint  -- We name the constraint rather than
  sale_pk primary key (sale_id)   -- let Oracle build a default name that
  using index storage (initial    -- is unnecessarily cryptic. Notice how we
  410m next 410m pctincrease 0)   -- place the primary key index in our own
tablespace dw_idx21               -- tablespace with appropriate storage
unrecoverable;                    -- parameters and the unrecoverable
                                  -- word.
```

TIP:
*Use the **alter table add constraint** convention
to build all primary key constraints with the
unrecoverable keyword, naming the constraint
as it is built. Make the name meaningful.*

We recommend using primary key constraints to enforce uniqueness for
tables in your data warehouse repository rather than unique indexes. This is
a double win since many query tools are sensitive to the primary key/foreign
key relationships defined in the data dictionary as well as Oracle's star
schema optimization technique. This optimization technique in particular is
discussed in Chapter 20. Inspect the following SQL statements that these
tools pick up automatically:

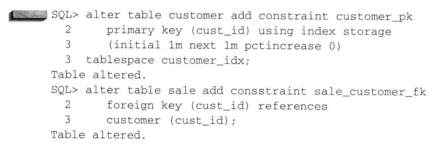

```
SQL> alter table customer add constraint customer_pk
  2      primary key (cust_id) using index storage
  3      (initial 1m next 1m pctincrease 0)
  3  tablespace customer_idx;
Table altered.
SQL> alter table sale add consstraint sale_customer_fk
  2      foreign key (cust_id) references
  3      customer (cust_id);
Table altered.
```

We have defined the primary key for the CUSTOMER table using the
appropriate **alter table** command. We then reference that primary key using
the next **alter table** command against the SALE table whose CUST_ID
column values are related to the primary key in CUSTOMER.

NOTE
*When designing the layout and location of
tables in the data warehouse, pay attention to
the relationships between columns in different
tables as the network of objects is mapped.*

Optimizing the Index Creation Process

Regardless of the approach taken to index your warehouse with Oracle, there is a way to decrease the time and resources required to build indexes and re-create existing indexes. Oracle keeps track of all activities in the database using its redo logs and saves information with which transactions can be undone in the rollback segments. As an index is being written, Oracle keeps information in its rollback segments to allow it to undo the changes in the index segments of the affected table or partition. The first trick we highlight is instructing Oracle not to write transaction information to the rollback segments while creating an index.

Disabling Undo for Index Creation

This is not rocket science—one simple keyword makes this happen. Simply put the word **unrecoverable** last in the SQL statement used to create the index. This is illustrated in the following listing:

```
create index person_1 on person (hire_year)
   storage (initial 1m next 1m pctincrease 0)
tablespace dw_idx9 unrecoverable;
```

It is quite remarkable the time saving this can achieve, and the end results are exactly the same except there is no time taken to generate undo information. We created an index on the first two columns in the PERSON table containing 16,384 rows using both methods. The results are shown in the following listing:

```
SQL> create index person_1 on person (pin,region);
Index created.
 real: 11126
SQL> drop index person_1;
Index dropped.
 real: 1021
```

```
SQL> create index person_1 on person (pin,region) unrecoverable;
Index created.
 real: 6429
```

The statement with the **unrecoverable** option completed in 57 percent of the time taken to create the index and generate undo at the same time. When building large information repositories to support decision support, suppose it takes about 3h44m, on average, to build indexes. Using this feature, the time could be reduced to 2h7m—tell that to your users! Table 10-7 summarizes the results of building indexes on a number of data warehouse objects.

TIP
*Always use the **unrecoverable** option when building indexes to speed up the creation process.*

As you can see in Figure 10-2, the Schema Manager wants you to use this option when creating indexes. The Recoverable checkbox is not selected when the dialog box appears.

Fast Index Rebuild

Since release 7.3 of Oracle7, this feature allows quick index rebuild. Oracle8 reads the information in an existing index, rewriting the index from start to finish in a new area in the tablespace where the index currently

| | | unrecoverable Keyword | |
Rows in Table	Indexes	With	Without
46,340	13	57s	3m57s
1,094,814	6	10m5s	24m36s
4,013,309	4	27m54s	60m48s

TABLE 10-7. *Index Builds with and without **unrecoverable** Option*

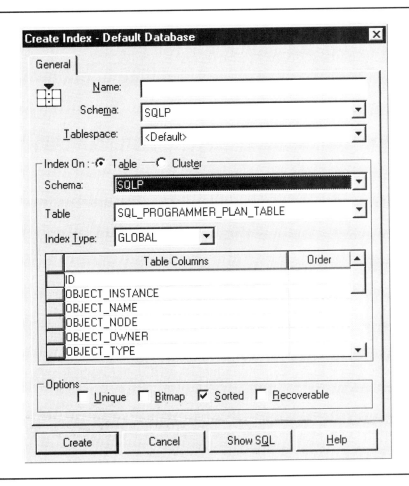

FIGURE 10-2. *Specifying **unrecoverable** using the OEM Schema Manager*

resides. This is a double whammy! Not only can you use the **unrecoverable** option as the index is re-created, but by using the existing index as input (rather than reading the table data as it does with the **create index** statement), the operation runs to completion in far less time than the traditional approach of dropping and then creating the index. The following listing illustrates fast index rebuild:

```
SQL> alter index finance_1 rebuild;
Index altered.
```

NOTE
The table upon which the index is built must be quiet when the index is rebuilt since the rebuild writes the new index based on the makeup of the old.

Index Creation and Maintenance Guidelines

Before moving on to the next episode in the Oracle8 data warehousing opera, let's close this chapter with some guidelines that will ensure your successful implementation of an indexing approach and help you deliver a decision support solution that leads to a satisfied user community.

Load Data, then Create Indexes

It is best to load the data into your warehouse objects, then create the indexes manually. As we illustrated in the "Disabling Undo for Index Creation" section, using the **unrecoverable** feature alone is probably the best way to speed up index creation. If indexes exist on tables as they are populated, the indexes must be updated as the data is inserted.

Allocate Large Sort Space for Index Creation

Since the index creation process is resource intensive, a great deal of sorting and re-sorting can request large amounts of workspace. The workspace used by Oracle is best set aside in memory. The SORT_AREA_SIZE in the warehouse initialization parameter file controls the sort area put aside in memory. When setting up primary key constraints, thereby writing the constraint equivalent of unique indexes, the sorting activity can be many times more than the indexing using a **nonunique** index approach.

Temporary Workspace

As well as memory, Oracle uses a great deal of temporary workspace when creating indexes, especially unique indexes or those built to define primary keys. This workspace is used in a tablespace specifically set aside for temporary objects. These objects may be created during the life of a **create index** statement, then be dropped after the activity completes. There is so much index creation work to be done that many administrators end up allocating many gigabytes of disk to the tablespace dedicated to this activity.

Shared Pool and Index Creation

The *shared pool* is a location in Oracle's shared memory structures we spoke about in Chapter 7. We spoke there of the three parameters in the initialization parameter file related to the size of the pool. When looking at creating large indexes on many tables, the reserved space parameters come into effect and can play a significant role when working with large indexes. As we mentioned in Chapter 7, index creation operations can be so pool intensive that they inevitably look for large space allocations in the shared pool. We like to set the reserved parameters and the major pool-sizing parameter as shown in the next listing:

```
shared_pool_size = 100000000
shared_pool_reserved_size = 30000000
shared_pool_reserved_min_alloc = 30000000
```

NOTE
As always, when setting the size of the shared pool via SHARED_POOL_SIZE, be sensitive to the amount of memory on the computer(s) supporting your warehouse. Coupled with the initialization parameter DB_BLOCK_BUFFERS, this entry is a large determinant on the size of Oracle8's SGA.

For most transaction processing applications running against the Oracle Server, we recommend setting the reserved size to approximately 20 percent of the total pool size; here, we use 30 percent. Also, in OLTP databases, we usually set the minimum allocation for the reserved area to 50 percent of the reserved size. Here, we set it equal to the reserved size.

Number of Indexes per Table

Since tables in the data warehouse are primarily read-only by the user community, you should not worry about the number of indexes like you may remember from operational system indexing. In the operational system, we caution creating indexes for applications light on reporting and heavy on transaction processing. With a large number of indexes in place, each time rows are added or deleted and the indexed column values change, index maintenance can be costly. It's a balancing act as well as a trade-off—there is work involved in keeping the index up to date, however the index may be required for reporting requirements.

TIP

In the data warehouse, you may find yourself "overindexing" tables if you come from a transaction processing background. Minimizing retrieval time for query processing is the primary concern in the data warehouse at almost all cost.

The gist of the previous tip is not to worry about placing more indexes on your DSS tables than you may be accustomed to doing in the operational systems environment. It is the nature of the beast, and something you will have to get used to in the data warehouse. In OLTP environments, most of the time the following three queries will return the displayed results:

```
SQL> select count(*) from user_constraints
  2    where table_name = 'FINANCE';
    COUNT(*)
------------
           1
SQL> select count(*) from user_indexes
  2    where table_name = 'FINANCE';
    COUNT(*)
------------
           2
SQL> select count(*) from user_ind_columns
  2    where table_name = 'FINANCE';
    COUNT(*)
------------
           5
```

This indicates there is one constraint (usually the primary key index), two indexes, and five columns indexed in total on FINANCE. In the data warehouse, it is not uncommon to return the following results on some heavily accessed tables:

```
SQL> select count(*) from user_constraints
  2   where table_name = 'SALE';
     COUNT(*)
------------
            1
SQL> select count(*) from user_indexes
  2   where table_name = 'SALE';
     COUNT(*)
------------
           19
SQL> select count(*) from user_ind_columns
  2   where table_name = 'FINANCE';
     COUNT(*)
------------
           28
```

It gets even more interesting looking at the results of the space allocation to the SALE table indexes and data itself, as shown next:

```
SQL> select segment_name, bytes, extent_id
  2     from user_extents
  3   where segment_name = 'SALE'
  4     and segment_type = 'TABLE';
SEGMENT_NAME                  BYTES    EXTENT_ID
-------------------- ------------- ----------
SALE                      440401920            0
SQL> select segment_name, bytes, extent_id
  2     from user_extents
  3   where segment_name like 'SALE%'
  4     and segment_type = 'INDEX';
SEGMENT_NAME                  BYTES   EXTENT_ID
-------------------- ------------- ----------
SALE_PK                    41943040            0
SALE_1                     41943040            0
SALE_2                     41943040            0
SALE_3                     41943040            0
SALE_4                     41943040            0
SALE_5                     41943040            0
SALE_6                     41943040            0
```

```
SALE_7                        41943040              0
SALE_8                        41943040              0
SALE_9                        41943040              0
SALE_10                       41943040              0
SALE_11                       41943040              0
SALE_12                       41943040              0
SALE_13                       41943040              0
SALE_14                       41943040              0
SALE_15                       41943040              0
SALE_16                       41943040              0
SALE_17                       41943040              0
SALE_18                       41943040              0
SALE_19                       41943040              0
20 rows selected.
```

If we looked at the total space consumed by the table of 400MB and the index allocation of 800MB, we identify a characteristic of the data warehouse repository built on Oracle—often the index space requests will be significantly larger than the allocation requested for the data segment.

Set Storage Parameters Explicitly

When data is stored in the database or indexes are created on that data, administrators specify storage characteristics under which the information is packed into Oracle blocks. In the data warehouse, there is no user-initiated **insert**, **update**, or **delete** activity as they use the database. For that reason, especially crucial to minimize space requests, set the storage parameters for your indexes separately from those in place for the data itself. What works for the data blocks may or may not work for the index blocks.

Transaction Entry Parameters

This is one of the most effective ways to tweak the environment within which insert transactions generate index entries. When an index entry is created (as is the case 99.9 percent of the time in the warehouse), multiple entries can be created concurrently by setting the **initrans** storage parameter to a value higher than the default.

TIP

*Set the **initrans** transaction entry parameter to 8
for indexes created in the warehouse. The
default of 2 may not be appropriate for
warehouse databases.*

As you no doubt have seen from the preceding pages, indexing the
warehouse is a job that requires decision making. Those decisions will
contribute down the road to the success or failure of your warehouse built
on the Oracle8 technology. Follow the suggestions and tips presented in this
chapter and devour any recommendations you run across elsewhere. The
choice of indexing approach need not be all consuming. The next chapter
discusses backing up the data warehouse, and will sweep you off your feet
with the sheer complexity of the task at hand. We trust the material we
present will help re-anchor those feet to the ground. The theme of the next
chapter is, "Back up and take a good look at backup; the secret is getting the
warehouse backup and the warehouse back up."

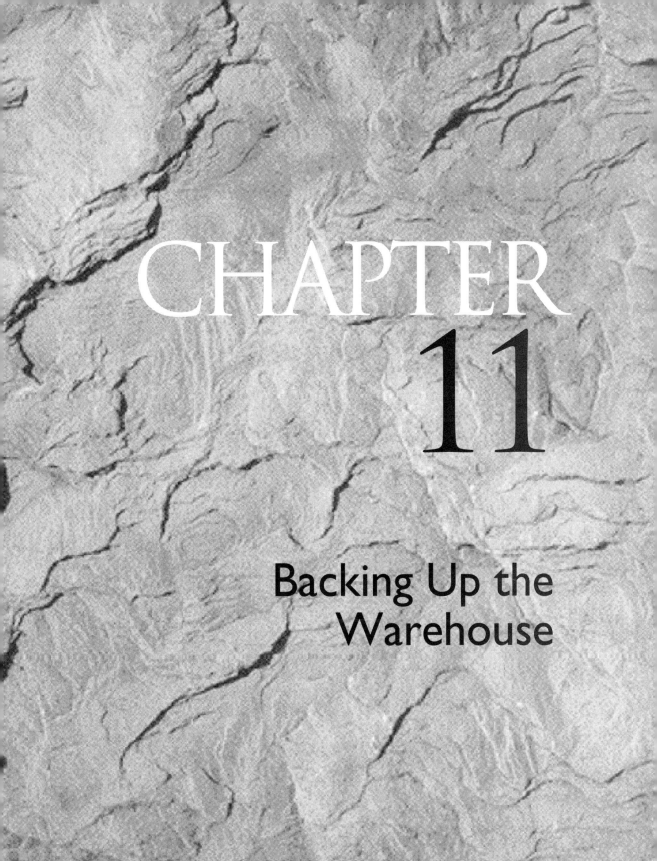

CHAPTER
11

Backing Up the Warehouse

his chapter discusses backing up the data warehouse. Interestingly enough, the word "backup" is actually two, yes two, yes two words in one —"backup" and "recovery." We are going to look at some issues related to writing successful backup scripts or performing successful backups, cover many Oracle8 specifics, look at recovery, and do an overview of tape hardware backup technology.

The data warehouse administrator must be fluent with Oracle8 backup and recovery scenarios based on the technology constraints dictated by the software. Oracle (the company), is not operating in a black hole. They are jumping through hoops to keep pace with the requirements of their install base as their customers move to large decision support repositories in excess of many hundreds of gigabytes. Think of it—with Oracle8, you could conceivably manage a database of up to 512 petabytes in size, where a petabyte is 1,024 exabytes, which in turn is 1,024 terabytes. This means that a 10-petabyte data warehouse would check in at a mere $1.1259E+16$ bytes!

Backup

Back to basics—*backup* involves making a copy of your information to protect yourself against data loss due to human error, machine error, or programming error. In this section, we are going to look at the complete backup spectrum and consider why one dedicates so much time to this component in the data warehouse decision support world, as well as any other types of applications that use Oracle8 or any other software. First, we are going to have a look at the reasons to perform backups, coupled with the types of situations that come up that make backup a player in all system design.

The funny thing about backup is how much more you miss it when you don't do it. This reminds us of a Wayne and Shuster skit in the 1960s that contained a story about the first totally automated, electronic flight from Malton to Idlewild and, as the passengers were strapping themselves in, a recording was played, "Welcome to the first completely automated flight of TCA. Everything on this plane is recorded, and there is very little or no involvement of real people on the crew or making these announcements from the cockpit. Nothing can possibly go wrong, go wrong, go wrong..." Our point? When something can go wrong, it will. This reminds us of

Murphy's Law. Backup will come to be one of your favorite words as the result of your roles in the data warehouse, which includes everything from technical keeper to end user.

Providing Protection Against Errors

Most computer systems, large or small, are made up of a wide assortment of datafiles, system setup files, initialization files, and libraries. Though we all do our best, hardware problems and unfortunate human errors warrant protection that allows recovery from error situations as quickly as possible. Let's start by looking at the three most common kinds of errors we've run across in our travels.

Human Error—Operating System Level

Face it! We are all human, and we do make errors. From our experience, the majority of the trouble we get ourselves into is a result of typographical errors. To illustrate this, suppose you wanted to remove a set of files from a directory that contained many Oracle8 database files, starting with the text FY95, and issued the set of commands shown in the next listing, where the space between the "fy" and the asterisk was entered by mistake. The datafiles belonged to a tablespace that has been dropped, and, being a smart DBA, you are cleaning up the leftovers at the operating system as well.

```
/oradata3/rep01> ll
total 1475728
-rw-r-----   1 oracle     dba      154624 Nov 24 05:53 ctl2rep01.ctl
-rw-r-----   1 oracle     dba    524296192 Nov 24 09:08 fy95find.dbf
-rw-r-----   1 oracle     dba    524296192 Nov 24 05:53 fy95peri.dbf
-rw-r-----   1 oracle     dba    524296192 Nov 24 06:03 repdata2.dbf
-rw-r-----   1 oracle     dba    209723392 Nov 24 05:53 rollback3.dbf
/oradata3/rep01> rm fy *.dbf
rm: fy non-existent
/oradata3/rep01>
```

The command completes as expected, but returns the message saying there is no file called "fy" to be erased. Since there is a space between "fy" and the asterisk, you have just wiped the directory of all files that end with the extension ".dbf". The next time a user attempts to read data from a file that has been inadvertently erased, the following message is returned by Oracle:

```
ORA-00376: file 24 cannot be read at this time
ORA-01110: datafile 24: '/oradata3/rep01/repdata2.dbf'
```

Likewise, if the command had been issued when the Oracle8 database was not running, the following would occur as you tried to restart the instance:

```
/oracle/home> svrmgrl
Oracle Server Manager Release 3.0.4.0.0 - Production
(c) Copyright 1998, Oracle Corporation.  All Rights Reserved.
Oracle8 Enterprise Edition Release 8.0.4.0.0 - Production
With the Partitioning and Objects options
PL/SQL Release 8.0.4.0.0 - Production
SVRMGR> connect internal
Password:
Connected to an idle instance.
SVRMGR> startup
ORACLE instance started.
Total System Global Area       7505584 bytes
Fixed Size                       35748 bytes
Variable Size                  7052044 bytes
Database Buffers                409600 bytes
Redo Buffers                      8192 bytes
Database mounted.
ORA-01157: cannot identify datafile 24 - file not found
ORA-01110: datafile 24: '/oradata3/rep01/repdata2.dbf'
SVRMGR>
```

Human Error—Oracle Level

Heaven forbid, yes, database administrators make errors as well. Suppose the DBA is doing tablespace or schema maintenance, and as the result of a typo deletes the rows in a central warehouse table. Picture the following series of SQL*Plus commands, commented to illustrate how this happens:

```
SQL> -- Wipe the contents of the FIN9596 transaction table.
SQL> truncate table fin9697;
Table truncated.
SQL> -- Realizing my error (i.e., I wiped FIN9697 by mistake),
SQL> -- let's roll back the truncate
SQL> rollback;
Rollback complete.
SQL> -- Make sure the contents have been restored
SQL> select count(*) from fin9697;
      COUNT(*)
  -------------
            0
SQL> -- Oh oh! Should I find another line of work??
```

The point here is that the SQL*Plus **truncate** verb generates no undo, and cannot be rolled back. The backup that was written in the wee hours of this morning can be used to recover the contents of FIN9697 that was just wiped by mistake.

Machine Error

This type of error is the result of a hardware problem with the gamut of pieces that make up the input/output or control chain of a computer's operations. Many problems manifest themselves with an Oracle error 600, shown in the next listing:

```
00600, 00000, "internal error code, arguments: [%s], [%s], [%s], [%s],
                                          [%s], [%s], [%s], [%s]"
// *Cause:  This is the generic internal error number for Oracle program
//          exceptions.  This indicates that a process has encountered an
//          exceptional condition.
// *Action: Report as a bug - the first argument is the internal error number
```

Suppose a disk controller or disk fails. This will interrupt the smooth operation of the Oracle database and, in some cases, cause the instance to terminate. If the instance shuts itself down, Oracle8 will write a message to one of its trace files showing the following error:

```
01092, 00000, "ORACLE instance terminated. Disconnection forced"
// *Cause:  The instance this process was connected to was terminated
//          abnormally, probably via a shutdown abort. This process
//          was forced to disconnect from the instance.
// *Action: When instance has been restarted, retry action.
```

What Backup Can Provide

Basically, backup protection is available at different levels. Customers speak of hot spots within their database applications, and how data resident in those high-activity areas is mission critical. Implementing a mature backup scenario can protect against data loss in these and, indeed, all other areas of your applications. Think of the last time you were told by one system manager that minimal downtime must be attained at almost all costs. Another conceded that system availability 24 by 7 is crucial to business operations, and how *OLTP* (online transaction-processing system) must be available to the user community or business grinds to a halt.

In a perfect world, the wishes of both those managers would be granted without question. We are dealing with a machine — the machine: some think it is defined as an apparatus that works most of the time, except those when it is needed most—at those times it's broken. Read on and find out what backup can provide.

Object Level

Backup at the object level is done using export, invoked using the command **exp80** in Windows NT or simply **exp** with UNIX. Export is a parameter-driven utility that creates a compressed binary copy of data in the Oracle database. The following listing is the output of the command **exp80 help=y**:

```
Export: Release 8.0.4.0.0 - Production on Mon Nov 24 18:15:21 1998
(c) Copyright 1998 Oracle Corporation.  All rights reserved.
You can let Export prompt you for parameters by entering the EXP
command followed by your username/password:
     Example: EXP SCOTT/TIGER
Or, you can control how Export runs by entering the EXP command followed
by various arguments. To specify parameters, you use keywords:
     Format:  EXP KEYWORD=value or KEYWORD=(value1,value2,...,valueN)
     Example: EXP SCOTT/TIGER GRANTS=Y TABLES=(EMP,DEPT,MGR)
               or TABLES=(T1:P1,T1:P2), if T1 is partitioned table
Keyword  Description (Default)          Keyword        Description (Default)
-----------------------------------------------------------------------
USERID   username/password             FULL           export entire file (N)
BUFFER   size of data buffer           OWNER          list of owner usernames
FILE     output file (EXPDAT.DMP)      TABLES         list of table names
COMPRESS import into one extent (Y)    RECORDLENGTH   length of IO record
GRANTS   export grants (Y)             INCTYPE        incremental export type
INDEXES  export indexes (Y)            RECORD         track incr. export (Y)
ROWS     export data rows (Y)          PARFILE        parameter filename
CONSTRAINTS export constraints (Y)     CONSISTENT     cross-table consistency
LOG      log file of screen output     STATISTICS     analyze objects (ESTIMATE)
DIRECT   direct path (N)
FEEDBACK display progress every x rows (0)
POINT_IN_TIME_RECOVER    Tablespace Point-in-time Recovery (N)
RECOVERY_TABLESPACES     List of tablespace names to recover
```

There is no need to delve into the ins and outs of export, since it is covered in detail in many works in the Oracle Press and other series' works. Chapter 15 in *Oracle8: A Beginner's Guide* (Abbey and Corey, Oracle Press,

1997) is one of many good places to start for an overview of the export utility. The following list outlines the types of objects that can be backed up using export; when we think of objects in the Oracle8 repository, we first think of tables. Export can do a great deal more to preserve things and record their details for recovery purposes.

- **Tables**   Definitions of the actual database entities that store the warehouse data, with the assortment of column names and attributes as well as the data itself.

- **Indexes**   An organized record of values in columns specified by the DBA by table, used to speed up retrieval of the data painstakingly loaded into the warehouse. An export file contains the SQL statements required to create indexes, not images of the index structures themselves.

- **Constraints**   Rules that constrain data values inter (i.e., between different) tables and intra (i.e., within the same table) tables. The familiar parent-child and primary-foreign key relationships the data modeler defines are brought to life based on SQL statements stored in an export file.

- **Grants**   Privileges given out on the objects that reside in any information repository. These privileges allow users or logical groups of users to access warehouse information to satisfy their analytical requirements.

- **Views**   A predefined query that retrieves a subset of data that resides in one or more tables in the warehouse. In Chapter 12, we look at views and how they can be used to define who can look at what in the warehouse.

- **Stored objects** (procedures, packages, and functions)   Code created and stored in the data dictionary and invoked as queries and data loading activities are carried out.

Instance Level

On all platforms where Oracle8 operates, the files that come together to make up the instance are backed up all at once or in a set of predefined groups. Instance-level backups use an operating system command such as

UNIX **cpio** or Windows NT **ntbackup** to make copies of database files on a secondary storage medium.

In the "What Needs to Be Backed Up?" section later in this chapter, we look at deciding what files need to be backed up based on how dynamic and volatile the data they contain may be. The answer when looking at what to back up at this level is driven by factors such as how long the information would take to reconstruct were it not backed up, coupled with the volume of information. It may be easy to reconstruct a summary table containing 123,000 rows of information, but the atomic level of information that resides in three four-million-row tables may need to be backed up at the instance level.

NOTE
Careful analysis must be done during the backup design process to see what objects can be rebuilt. In some cases, careful planning is especially needed in areas where objects can not be rebuilt—rare, but it can happen.

Factors that Affect Backup Strategy

The size of the DSS repository has an effect on how the information is configured and, therefore, backed up. Here are a few configuration issues that would be addressed by the warehouse analysis team early in the project.

Amount of Data in the Warehouse

The size of a data warehouse or mart is usually measured in gigabytes or terabytes. Peripherals exist for example, tape drives, which permit copying gigabytes of data—but how about multiterabyte systems? High-speed tape drives commonly move upwards of one half a megabyte per second. The technology in this area is moving rapidly; it is simply a matter of time before vendors start producing hardware that exceeds our wildest expectations. The section on "Unattended 24 by 7 Backups" in this chapter highlights where the industry is going and how it fits so nicely into the large data warehouse industry.

Configuration to Permit Backup

Experience shows partitioning alone is the single most important concept that enables data warehouse administrators to plan an optimal backup strategy. *Partitioning* is a process of deliberately storing data warehouse information in multiple database files. It may be tempting to look at a table in a data warehouse with millions of rows and to place it in a file along with a number of other multimillion-row tables because they are functionally related. An example of functionally related tables is a table that does a rollup by district and one that does the rollup by department.

TIP

Split the data warehouse data into manageable chunks to allow for optimal backup protection.

Chapter 10 discusses the Oracle8 Partitioning Option and how range-based partitioning of data in the warehouse enhances performance and makes the warehouse easier to back up. When looking at multiterabyte DSS repositories, this feature alone is more than worth its weight in gold when looking at the Oracle8 database solution to support your warehouse. When you think of manageable chunks, think of files that fit on one and only one tape, or files that can be copied to multiple tapes during the quiet hours in the middle of the night. Figure 11-1 shows a partitioned network of database files in a warehouse.

Following the partitioning ideas we presented in Chapter 10, Figure 11-1 shows an ORDER, SALE, and PART table broken into four, two, and two partitions, respectively. Not only does this make the backup of this portion of the warehouse easier, but also the likelihood of writing useable backups is enhanced because it can be done in smaller chunks. Suppose the FY95 and FY96 partitions in the ORDER table were static and not refreshed during warehouse rebuild. They would be backed up once without the need to back them up again. With the Oracle8 Partitioning Option mechanism in place, this scenario is easily realized in the midst of planning what to back up and when.

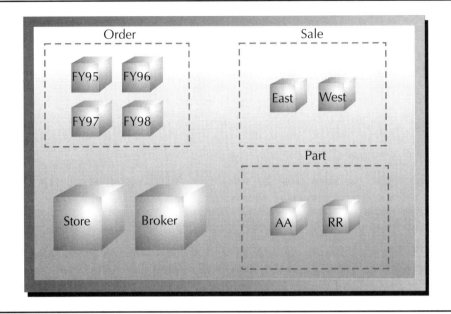

FIGURE 11-1. *Partitioned file structure used in a data warehouse*

TIP
A good way to partition data into manageable chunks with Oracle is to spread your warehouse data across many partitions in one or more tablespaces, and to build each tablespace from more than one datafile.

This suggestion blends nicely with a deliberate plan to back up portions of the data warehouse at a time. Table 11-1 gives an example of how this could be implemented, with the size measurement in megabytes (1,048,576 bytes). A good backup strategy may be to copy the first two datafiles of each tablespace to tape during one portion of a backup plan, and then copy the other files during another step.

Tablespace	Size	Datafile	Size
ORDER	4,096	d:\orant\database\order95_dwp.dbf	1,024
		g:\orant\database\order96_dwp.dbf	1,024
		h:\orant\database\order97_dwp.dbf	1,024
		k:\orant\database\order98_dwp.dbf	1,024
PART	1,024	d:\orant\database\partaa_dwp.dbf	512
		g:\orant\database\partrr_dwp.dbf	512
SALE	2,048	d:\orant\database\salee_dwp.dbf	1,024
		d:\orant\database\salew_dwp.dbf	1,024
BROKER	1,024	d:\orant\database\broker_dwp.dbf	1,024
STORE	512	d:\orant\database\store_dwp.dbf	512

TABLE 11-1. *Tablespace and Database File Layout*

NOTE
In Chapter 9, where we discuss partitioning, we cover some material related to how to partition (e.g., by activity date or fiscal year) that has an impact on what gets backed up when.

What Needs to Be Backed Up?

In a data warehouse configuration, the contents of various tables change all the way from daily to never. "Never say never"—a familiar saying—is so applicable in the data warehouse. In the operational system, most data is classified as either tombstone or transaction. *Tombstone* data resides in tables also referred to as code or lookup tables. The names and abbreviations of the 50 states in the U.S. are tombstone, as is a reference table that maps the first three characters of the Canadian postal code to a geographical area in the country. *Transaction* data is the heart of operational systems and is created, modified, and deleted on an ongoing basis. The level of transactions in the data warehouse is extremely low. Some may insist no transactions whatsoever occur in the DSS repository. We realize this is not true across the board.

In several places throughout this book, you have read of the need to propagate changes from operational systems to the data warehouse. This propagation is done either by completely replacing warehouse information by refreshing contents of tables or by applying a mechanism manually to effect the desired changes. Some data warehouse software providers have invented solutions to help ensure changes are migrated to the data warehouse from their source applications. Whatever decision you make in how to refresh your warehouse has an impact on how the warehouse is backed up. A decision must be made in the midst of working with the warehouse user community, and commitments would have been made to deal with the following issues, which affect what is backed up and when:

- **Time-to-warehouse**   The length of time (usually measured in days) between which operational data changes and the affected tables in the warehouse will reflect the changes.

- **Downtime**   The amount of time the users can be without the warehouse for full or partial refreshes and backups. Finding the overnight backup time is more evasive if you are working with a distributed warehouse with servers in drastically different time zones!

- **Data what?**   Whether the exercise is backing up a series of independent data marts or a full-blown enterprise data warehouse. Each data mart may be from 500 megabytes to 1 or 2 gigabytes, whereas a corporate warehouse may stretch the size to well over 100 gigabytes.

The method used to back up the warehouse has a direct relationship with the following points:

1. The components of the warehouse that are refreshed.

2. The amount of truly static data.

3. The amount of data that is refreshed.

4. The status of the warehouse as it is backed up; that is, is it backed up while Oracle is running or is Oracle shut down to do backups?

5. The mechanisms that are used to do the refreshes.

6. The length of the window of opportunity to do the backups.

Although this list is not exhaustive, it brings attention to the most common issues we have come across during our tenure with large databases like the data warehouse. Now, let's delve into some of these issues, and then cover when to do your backups.

THE COMPONENTS OF THE WAREHOUSE THAT ARE REFRESHED The structure of your warehouse should lend itself to easy recognition of what components need to be backed up. The cycle of refreshes—whether you use export/import or SQL*Loader as discussed in Chapter 8, or some commercial off-the-shelf software to implement operational to warehouse changes—determines when components should be backed up.

THE AMOUNT OF TRULY STATIC DATA Read-only tablespaces are discussed in Chapter 20. Mechanisms such as this feature should be applied to data that is truly read-only. Historical information that has not changed from the operational systems environment and will not be changing in the future is an ideal candidate for running read-only. Again, the saying, "Never say never" applies. As soon as a collection of warehouse data is flagged as "read-only" and the tablespace in which the data resides is marked accordingly, you will inevitably need to make some changes to that information. A *tablespace* is simply a collection of one or more datafiles grouped together to hold data in the Oracle database. When this occurs, you mark the tablespace as read-write and change the "static" data; then reset its status to read-only. When that status is registered with Oracle, the data within that tablespace need only be backed up once, and the data is not included in regular system backups.

THE STATUS OF THE WAREHOUSE AS IT IS BACKED UP After appropriate preparation, you are able to back up the Oracle database when it is running and in use by the users. Thus, what is backed up has a direct correlation to whether Oracle is active or dormant when backups are written.

NOTE
If the warehouse is closed and Oracle is unavailable, export is not suitable as a tool for backup. Oracle must be running to make use of export. Oracle is running when the database is accessible to the users and they can connect and go about their business without interruption.

HOW THE WAREHOUSE IS REFRESHED   After a specified period of time, portions of the data warehouse are refreshed. Refreshes either wipe out existing data and build a complete new set of tables, or they use a mechanism to propagate changes from operational systems to the data warehouse database and layer new information on top of that already existing. Significant portions of the warehouse are static and are refreshed infrequently. Historical summary data, which cannot change because it is no longer active in the operational environment, is the primary type of data that undergoes no refresh.

Optimal Backup Schedule

Deciding when to back up your data is anything from a question to an absolute nightmare. Two main factors drive the decision. The first factor has to do with the nature and power of your hardware; the second factor is fueled by the answer to a question you and your colleagues ask yourselves during development of any system: "How long can the user community be without their data if we need to perform some sort of recovery?" *Recovery* is a process initiated because of the loss of some data, whereby data is copied from a backup and placed back in the hands of the user community.

Determining the schedule for backing up your warehouse is driven by a number of issues, which will be discussed in the next section.

When to Back Up

The time to perform backups of your warehouse depends on the method you select to do the backups. The next section of this chapter discusses two methods for backing up your warehouse. If you enable the feature that permits backups to be taken when the database is open and in use by your user community, you may back up portions of your warehouse during normal business hours. If you shut down the warehouse to perform your backups, normally they are done in the quiet evening hours. If you are running a distributed data warehouse in widely separated geographic areas of the globe, quiet hours in one time zone may be the middle of the business day on the other side of the international date line.

The decisions you have made about when to back up your operational systems, for the most part, apply to those you will make with regard to your data warehouse.

Image Backups

Oracle permits two types of image backups. An *image backup* copies database files to a secondary storage device, usually tape, or to an alternate area on the set of disks attached to the machine where Oracle is running. The *offline* or *cold* backup is done when the database is closed. The Oracle database is put in the closed state by the database administrator issuing the **shutdown** command. When this command is passed to Oracle, the processes running that enable access to the database are terminated, all the files that have been opened to permit access are closed, and memory allocated to support access is released. The *online* or *hot* backup is performed when the database is open. An open database is available to users, with support processes running and memory structures in place to facilitate user access.

Offline Backups

Performing offline backups is a three-step process. Offline backups are carried out in the middle of the night or any other time that user access to the database can be taken away. All the files associated with running the Oracle database are copied to tape. Three types of files exist that become part of the Oracle offline backup:

- **Datafiles**   The files that make up the tablespaces that hold the data itself

- **Redo log files**   The files that record all the transactions against the database

- **Control files**   One or more files that contain information about the structure of the database files, including their location and size, as well as any other important information required to run the Oracle database

Online Backups

Backing up the data warehouse while it is open is possible once some groundwork has been laid by the database administrator. Most DBAs have experience with enabling online backups by placing the database in archivelog mode. When running in archivelog mode, Oracle copies each redo log to a location on the disk you have specified before it overwrites each log. This copying process is called *archiving*, hence the term *archivelog*.

Let's look at placing an Oracle8 database in archivelog mode using the SQL*Worksheet from the Oracle Enterprise Manager folder in Windows NT:

1. Invoke the worksheet by clicking the shortcut in the folder. Enter the connect information as shown in Figure 11-2, selecting SYSDBA from the Connect As picklist.

2. Once positioned on the worksheet main console, shut down the database by entering **shutdown** and pressing F5 or clicking the Execute button (fourth from the top on the lower pane) as shown in Figure 11-3. Oracle responds with the message, "ORACLE instance shut down."

3. Enter the command **startup mount**, then press F5 to receive the readout of the size of the SGA terminated with the message "Database mounted."

4. Enter the command **alter database archivelog;**, and receive the "Statement processed." message from Oracle.

5. Enter the command **alter database open;** to make the warehouse available to the user community.

Login Information   ☒

Username: internal

Password: ××××××

Service:

Connect As: Normal   ▼

Normal
SYSOPER
SYSDBA

OK

FIGURE 11-2.   *SQL*Worksheet Connect As dialog*

A number of issues now come into play, coupled with a few other tasks you must do now that the database is in archivelog mode. In the book, *Oracle8 Tuning* (Corey, Abbey, Dechichio, and Abramson, Oracle Press, 1998), Chapter 10's section on "Tuning Online Backups" covers some of these issues and explains what must be entered in the initialization parameter file ("init.ora") to facilitate the archiving process. This init.ora file is read when an Oracle database is started. The *Oracle8 Server Administrator's Guide* spends considerable time discussing online backups and explains the steps you must follow to ensure your backups are useable.

TIP
Simply putting your warehouse in archivelog mode alone is not enough to allow backing it up when it is open. As suggested, you MUST consult other sources for advice on how this backup can become part of your DSS backup and recovery strategy.

FIGURE 11-3. *Interaction placing database in archivelog mode*

We have gone to client sites numerous times and discovered they have been meticulously backing up their databases while they are open. We inform them the backups are useless without implementing additional features alongside archivelogging. More than one client has looked knowingly at us and said, "We had a problem with restoring from one of our backups a while ago, but we attributed this to some unknown reasons we didn't have time to investigate."

Unattended 24 by 7 Backups

Given the multigigabyte, if not terabyte, nature of many enterprise data warehouses, technology exists that permits you to run backups continually to hardware that supports volumes of data of this magnitude. The hardware supports QIC cartridges (also common on desktop personal computers), DDS DAT technology-based media, and an assortment of autochange/management products. Quarter-inch cartridge (QIC) and digital data storage/digital audio tape (DDS DAT) are supported by most vendors of tape backup hardware and software.

Designers and implementers of large databases and data warehouses are guided by a recurring theme with respect to backups. This theme reminds us of a rhetorical question similar to one Kevin Costner asked in the film, *Field of Dreams:* "If we build it, will the backup technology come?" The technology is here now. It gets more flexible and stronger every time we browse manufacturer collateral material or see demos of the latest and greatest solutions. Data compression plays a big role in tape backup. One of the machines used to write this book has a Conner minicartridge tape drive that copies upwards of 800MB of data to QIC-type media. This volume of data can be copied to tape and compared in a mere 11 hours (sarcasm intended!). This is a Pentium-166 processor running Windows NT, which supports a backup configuration suitable for the personal computer. The *compare* phase of a tape backup inspects the data copied to tape and verifies that it is an exact copy of what resides on the disk from where it came. Data compression of 2:1 is common. When deciding on your data warehouse backup strategy, the following points need consideration before a selection is made:

1. **The data transfer rate**   This affects how much media will be required and will affect the size and location of your tape backup archive. A *tape backup archive* is simply a place where many generations of backup are stored. Wise technologists store tapes off-site, and many commercial providers exist who will organize and manage off-site storage.

2. **The types of files being backed up**   In the Oracle data warehouse arena, the Oracle software as well as the database (tablespace datafiles, control files, redo logs) support files are binary. They are not readable by a text editor, and they are already somewhat compressed as they sit on the disk drives.

3. **The type of hardware on which the warehouse runs**   Manufacturers of data-warehouse-suitable computers support the industry-standard tape media. Some offer their own proprietary solutions for optimal and secure backup routines.

4. **The volume of data that requires backup**   This impacts on the type of drive that will be acquired and, when options are available, even the nature of the backup media. Some backup solutions hardware includes a single drive with 20 cartridges. The Spectra 9000 from SpectraLogic, for example, comes equipped as a single-drive, 20-cartridge library, which can be upgraded to 40 cartridges and allows for up to four separate drives.

5. **The frequency of the backup** Given the size of many data warehouse repositories, most installations are looking for a solution offering hardware that runs virtually all the time, backing up sensitive warehouse data based on a scale of frequency decided by the warehouse administration personnel. The warehouse data volatility affects how often segments of data are backed up. Static data residing in read-only tablespaces is an example of information whose backup frequency is less than the data in parts, if not all, of your data marts.

6. **The level of automation desired** Automated management systems exist to match your backup needs. Data warehouse sites are looking for automation of full backups, incremental backups, backup aging, media aging, and media management. Organizations want to leave the backup hardware on its own, be notified if and when problems arise, and be able to manage backup across a widespread network. Some schedulers handle from one to many background tasks, which support repeated backups of all or part of the data warehouse information. In addition to software-provided scheduling, some vendors offer a robotic-like solution that manages multiple streams of tapes written simultaneously by multiple tape drives. The robotics change the tapes, barcode the tapes after they have been written, and read the bar codes of tapes on the way into the tape carousel.

Other Issues Affecting Backup

The planning and implementation of a data warehouse backup strategy almost leads the architect and analyst through unfamiliar territory. Here are two other issues affecting backup in the DSS.

INDEXES Indexes form an integral portion of your data warehouse repository. Because data warehouses have more indexes than operational systems, these indexes take up a much larger percentage of your total database size. If the primary object of your backup is to recover from a failure, then you probably don't want to waste time or tape space in backing up the indexes.

BACKING UP HISTORICAL DATA One huge headache in warehouses is changes to historical data; for example, through a programming error, $14 million of sales get attributed to the wrong branch. This is an even bigger problem if you have created summary tables that used this incorrect data as input. Data warehouse administrators must design and adopt an approach to what historical data should be backed up and when.

Trends in Backup Technology

The hardware vendors are providing mature backup solutions at a blistering pace. It seems that the technology is moving so fast that what was state of the art a few months ago is like old technology today. This is good for the installations enabling themselves with this technology, but the road can be riddled with pitfalls if a solution cannot be upgraded as the technology progresses. As an example, we are going to look at the solutions offered by Legato Systems, Inc. of Palo Alto, CA, USA, which develops, markets, and supports network storage management software products. Their product will give you a flavor of what is out there. Following that, we will look at the Alexandria solution by SpectraLogic Corp. of Boulder, CO, USA.

The Gartner Group reports that the average database will grow 1,000 percent in size by the turn of the century. The volume of database information is growing at an exponential rate, far faster than the technology available to back up the repositories as they swell to a few hundred gigabytes and more. Common backup solutions are labor-intensive for hardware and database administrators. Installations crave solutions that are easy to manage, can handle many gigabytes per hour, and require little human intervention for tape swapping and catalog management. High application availability requirements dictate that data warehouse systems need to be up all the time. Gone are the days when one could afford the luxury of having a wide window of opportunity for backups while the database was shut down. The quiet hours in eastern North America are the middle of the afternoon in Southeast Asia. The multinationals cannot for a minute think of shutting down mission-critical operations at a time of day convenient to one part of the world but not another.

So many advances have been made in peripherals that support the machines upon which your warehouse resides. Installations are looking for ways to increase the productivity of their administrators. With the trends in database size and complexity, the precious time of these highly skilled (not to mention highly priced) people should not be wasted minding database backups and manually tracking existence, identification, and cataloging of media.

Before we get started on sample product specifics, let's have a look at what we believe are the fundamental qualities to look for when selecting backup software and hardware.

Factors Affecting Product Selection

You name it—it's out there. Talk about a jungle. With the proliferation of corporate sites on the Internet, try entering the words "tape backup" into your favorite Web search engine, and find yourself treated to a list of over 700 hits. Vendors believe their solution is the dream come true. Perhaps it is. Here's our list:

- The solution must be highly configurable, with the ability to specify the location and names of files to be backed up coupled with a flexible scheduling ability. The software must permit the administrator to select different schedules for a large network of information that is accessed, refreshed, and updated according to a wide range of frequencies.

- The administrative overhead must be as low as possible, such that the administrator spends as little time as possible on configuration management.

- The solution must be able to manage backup on a wide range of platforms including, but not limited to, servers running Sun Solaris, HP-UX, and Windows NT.

- The solution must be able to implement cataloguing and backup scheduling from one server. The system administrator should be able to work anywhere on the corporate network from a central server console. The catalog maintained by the software should allow individual users to extract and retrieve their own lost or missing files at their convenience, without administrator involvement where possible.

- The solution must be able to copy very large volumes of data in short time periods. The company should boast speeds in excess of one terabyte per hour and keep current with speed enhancements as the industry progresses into the next chapter of tape backup hardware.

- The solution must offer sophisticated library management for backups to be written to multiple volumes without the need for costly and time-consuming human intervention. The robotics must label and track active members of the tape library to protect the client against accidental erasure using barcode technology or other appropriate management approaches. On the other side, the library management module must release volumes for overwriting when they are no longer active.

- The solution must offer mature alert mechanisms to notify operators via email, paging, and cell phone messaging when specified events complete or problems are encountered that compromise the operator-specified parameters within which the backups are written.

- The solution must be tightly integrated with Oracle to minimize DWA (data warehouse administrator) time spent scripting and maintaining custom code to perform backup and recovery.

Now we will have a brief look at the Legato solution.

The Legato Solution

In this section, we will look at NetWorker® BusinesSuite™ Module for Oracle on Windows NT. Beginning with Oracle8 release 8.0.4, Oracle has integrated NetWorker technology from Legato Systems, providing Oracle customers with a complete base-level backup and recovery solution. The Legato Systems home page is shown in Figure 11-4.

The BusinesSuite Module for Oracle (Network Edition and Power Edition) offers additional functionality such as remote management and distributed filesystem backup, support for autochange of media, and high-speed tape device support with up to 64 concurrent data streams and 32 tape devices. Let's spend a bit of time on the architectural baseline that Legato believes fundamental to its offering.

DATA ZONES AND CONTROL ZONES   A *data zone* bounds a set of data servers and desktop clients managed by a single NetWorker Server. The data concerned takes the form of application information as well as the metadata that defines the makeup and location of that business-specific information. A *control zone* contains many data zones, being more of a logical rather than physical entity.

FIGURE 11-4. *Legato Systems home page*

One chooses server locations to group together in a data zone based on activity on each candidate node and the version of the server operating systems coupled with the database versions. In this heterogeneous computing world, clients running data warehouses on Oracle use every possible variant of Oracle7 alongside 8.0.3 and 8.0.4. The choice of members for each data zone is driven by a desire for simplicity; Legato believes this enables reliability and allows for optimal performance. The control zone groups data zones together for the purpose of centralized administration and policy management. The number of data zones in each control zone can vary.

Their Global Enterprise Management of Storage (GEMS) product manages the environment using an intranet Java-based Web user interface. The initial release offered mechanisms to distribute Legato software across data zones as well as management and tracking of all tape media within each control zone. Subsequent offerings monitor library status, diagnose problems, and initiate corrective actions from a single location.

Deployment of the Legato solution is based on the definition of data and control zones. As Legato customizes a client installation based on its unique requirements, this definition phase is done up front before selection of software components to manage the backup task at hand.

THE NETWORKER BUSINESSUITE MODULE FOR ORACLE   The NetWorker BusinesSuite Module for Oracle performs fast online backup for Oracle8 databases on UNIX and Windows NT servers. As a member of the NetWorker BusinesSuite product family, it works alongside the NetWorker Backup Server product to provide reliable backup and restore for the following:

■ Entire databases located anywhere in a distributed corporate server network

■ Tablespaces anywhere in that network, whether they contain data in partitioned or nonpartitioned tables

■ Datafiles making up those tablespaces without the need to synchronize the backup of all datafiles that make up a tablespace during the same backup run

■ Archived redo logs, so precious for the recovery of the warehouse data in the event of some media failure

From a centralized backup server, installations can perform backups either locally or over a distributed set of servers. Through autochanger support and media handling, the Power Edition allows for unattended 24-hour backups. Clients looking for protection of their data can enable Legato data encryption as backups are written to tape. Legato and Oracle together can leverage the power of parallelism, writing to tape systems during the backup phase and reading from tape during a recovery exercise.

A press release, dated October 29, 1997, outlines an alliance between Oracle Corporation and Legato Systems, Inc. The press release mentions, "This agreement will allow Oracle's existing Windows NT customers to leverage the benefits of the NetWorker technology to create a more robust data management solution. Now Oracle universal data server customers will receive out-of-the-box backup and recovery capability for protection of their Oracle databases." It then goes on to suggest, "Legato will provide a smooth upgrade path to the company's BusinesSuite Module for Oracle, Network Edition, as well as higher performance products such as Power Edition. These products combine additional functionality (network backup/restore, filesystem backup); automation (autochanger support); and performance (high-speed tape device support, up to 64 concurrent data streams and 32 tape devices). This provides Oracle customers with a clear migration path for Oracle backup and recovery as their data grows."

NETWORKER BUSINESSUITE BENEFITS SUMMARY   Legato outlines the following benefits for clientele using their BusinesSuite solution (source: *www.legato.com*):

- Increase database application availability by reducing the time needed to perform database backup and restore

- Improve DBA productivity by automating much of the backup and restore process, and by providing a consistent set of backup solutions for multiple databases and applications

- Manage multiple RDBMS systems on multiple operating systems with the same look and feel

- Insured quality of backup from Legato's strong alliances with major DBMS and application vendors such as Informix, Oracle, SAP, and Microsoft

- Centralized management of distributed databases and applications

- Uniform solution for managing all application data, database files, and filesystem data

- Common interface for managing backup and restore for multiple DBMS systems and applications

RECORDED BENCHMARKS   Several benchmarks have been performed in cooperation between Legato Systems, Ampex Corporation, and Oracle Corporation. Most were performed using a midsize hardware configuration such as the Sun Ultra ES 4000 server with four Ampex DST tape devices attached. Ampex Corporation, based in the Bay Area around San Francisco, CA, USA, is one of the biggest players in the high-speed data storage industry, boasting speed and cost efficiency so attractive to deployers of very large databases on Oracle. Their DST412, DST712, and

DST812 lines of data storage machinery toot Ampex's horn to the tune of transfer rates up to 15 megabytes per second coupled with media search capabilities of up to 1.6 gigabytes (so crucial to the restore phase).

LEGATO, ORACLE8, AND THE RECOVERY MANAGER Before moving on, let's have a look at Legato's interaction with the Oracle8 Recovery Manager (affectionately called RMAN). The Legato Storage Manager (LSM) is the heart of this interface, with the splash screen shown in Figure 11-5.

LSM is bundled with Oracle Enterprise Manager, and the hooks into RMAN allow RMAN and LSM to interact with the Oracle Enterprise Manager (also called OEM) as if one product; the integration is very tight, but LSM is designed to be able to move with OEM technology as it evolves. RMAN is the successor to Oracle7's Enterprise Backup Utility (EBU), offering:

FIGURE 11-5. *Legato Storage Manager startup*

- Incremental backup and partition support

- Direct connect capability to a wide variety of 4m, 8mm, and DLT tape devices

- Use of up to four backup devices for concurrent read or write

- Media management, including tape labeling, media tracking, and retention policy management

Legato's BusinesSuite, a superset to LSM for Oracle8, permits remote backup and recovery, supports tape libraries, works with tape autochangers, and supports enhanced disaster recovery including tape cloning. Figure 11-6 shows the channel creation screen in LSM where you enter the device type (e.g., SBT_TAPE as shown in the screen shot) that ties a backup to the NetWorker.

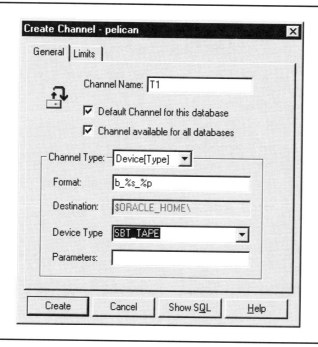

FIGURE 11-6. *Channel creation dialog*

The SpectraLogic Solution

Alexandria, the flagship of SpectraLogic's tape solution, is an enterprise-class backup/restore. The SpectraLogic home page is shown in Figure 11-7.

It is used in the industry to back up and restore databases, Internet servers, and data warehouses on the gamut of vendors' UNIX offerings. Alexandria's comprehensive features, coupled with automated tape storage libraries, provide a complete backup/recovery environment.

SpectraLogic (source: *www.spectralogic.com*) believes the strength of their solution lies in the following:

■ The industry's high-performance/low-CPU overhead leader

■ Proven scalability to meet gigabytes- to terabytes-per-hour requirements

■ Most comprehensive UNIX platform support (over 20 server platforms)

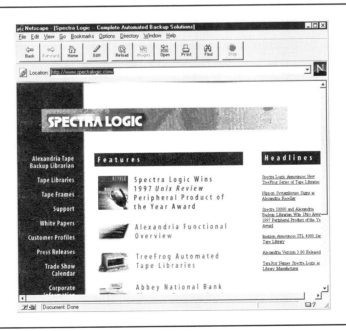

FIGURE 11-7.   *SpectraLogic home page*

- Extensive tape library support—over 60 tape library systems

- Three-tiered disaster recovery (DR) feature

- High availability through fault-tolerant architecture

- Support for high-end clustered SMP and MPP systems

- Superior support for Oracle, Informix, Sybase, SAP, and others

- Industry's most extensive media management

- Integration with systems management products, like Tivoli TME

- Customizable through user exit points

- Microsoft Windows NT and Windows 95 client support

- Java-based HTML, X11/Motif, and command-line interfaces

SpectraLogic has designed and built Alexandria with hardware platform independence, so crucial in an organization's network of distributed servers communicating with the likes of the popular TCP/IP protocol. Media management capabilities all the way from 8mm to Ampex DST and optical changers enhance this mature backup software solution. SpectraLogic boasts access to databases via a Java-based HTML interface using common desktop browsers such as Netscape Navigator and Internet Explorer. Alexandria provides an easy-to-use administrator interface alongside robust problem determination capabilities.

Alexandria is supported on a wide range of platforms including Sun (Solaris and SunOS), HP9000 (Series 700 and 800) HP-UX, DEC Alpha UNIX, DG AViiON (DG-UX), and Siemens Nixdorf to name a few. Common configurations leverage Windows 95 and Windows NT clients. Tape library support includes SpectraLogic's own STL series, TapeFrame, and the Spectra 4000 through 10000 line of product.

COBRA SpectraLogic's *COBRA* (Comprehensive Online Backup and Recovery Agent) works reliably and easily to perform hot or cold backups of Oracle databases. Working with the range of Oracle Server versions used in the field, Alexandria is tightly integrated with Oracle's backup/recovery technology to provide fail-safe protection for the customer's corporate information. COBRA has been around for a number of years, first appearing alongside early releases of Oracle 7.0. Installations support SpectraLogic's claim that it operates in a widely disparate set of Oracle Server configurations over different operating systems using a minimum of precious CPU and other system resources.

RECORDED BENCHMARKS   In cooperation with Silicon Graphics Incorporated (*SGI*), Oracle Corporation, and IBM, SpectraLogic has achieved lightning fast results writing information to 35 tape drives simultaneously. Some of the most recent benchmark exercises were run using SGI's Origin 2000 S2MP server running IRIX 6.4 and IBM's Magstar 3590 tape subsystem.

Using Alexandria's Oracle Backup Agent, SpectraLogic reports backup speeds upwards of 1.5Tb per hour for an online backup, the most common type in the large database world. They report a CPU utilization figure of 6 percent (source: *www.spectralogic.com*). This leaves 94 percent of the processor power available for other user activities running concurrently to system backups. The benchmark also reported an average transfer rate of 1.1Tb per hour running alongside a simulated transaction load of 4,500 transactions per minute.

SPECTRALOGIC DIRECTIONS WITH ORACLE8   SpectraLogic offers an Oracle RecMan Agent (ORMA) that integrates and exploits the capabilities of RMAN. ORMA is in addition to their COBRA product which supports Oracle 7.0.16-8.0x; both products retain their high-performance/low-CPU overhead characteristics of SpectraLogic's previous offerings in the Oracle7 arena.

Where the Technology Is Headed

Based on the results discussed in the previous two sections, it is perfectly clear to us that the sky is the limit. In the CPU/memory chapter in *Oracle8 Tuning*, we mentioned how we believe the advances in CPU technology have far outstripped those accomplished with peripherals such as disk drives and printers. Perhaps the backup solutions are becoming more sophisticated at a blistering pace as well. We have noticed in our travels around the very large database world over the past number of years that the backup/recovery technology (hardware and software) has done a nice job of keeping pace with the increasing volume of many corporate databases. Rest assured, the price of that technology has risen in parallel; however, the cost of storage per kilobyte (1,024 bytes) or megabyte (1,048,576 bytes) has been dropping with every new generation of solutions.

Recovery

This close relative to backup involves fetching copies of data from a backup medium, usually (though not always) tape, and rebuilding portions of your Oracle8 database. We commonly use the term "disaster recovery" when looking at protecting information; this becomes even more critical in a data warehouse environment since it can be a mix of data from a hodgepodge of operational systems.

Types of Recovery

In the Oracle world, there are primarily two types of recovery—file-based and object-based. The former involves recovering one or more database files, the latter recovering one or more objects that reside in the repository. Let's have a closer look at these two types.

Database File Recovery

There are three types of files that come together to support a data warehouse running on the Oracle8 Server—control files, log files, and tablespaces comprised of one or more datafiles. The control files contain information about the datafiles that make up the tablespaces such as name, size, location, and most recent change information contained in the tablespace. With all other support files in place (i.e., all tablespace files and log files), recovering a control file is done by doing the following:

I. Starting Server Manager with the command **svrmgr30** and receiving the following feedback from Oracle:

```
Oracle Server Manager Release 3.0.4.0.0 - Production
(c) Copyright 1998, Oracle Corporation.  All Rights Reserved.
Oracle8 Enterprise Edition Release 8.0.4.0.0 - Production
With the Partitioning and Objects options
PL/SQL Release 8.0.4.0.0 - Production
SVRMGR>
```

2. Entering the command **connect internal** followed by the appropriate password if running on Windows NT, and receiving the message "Connected" from Oracle.

3. Entering the command **startup mount** and receiving the feedback "ORACLE instance started" from Oracle.

```
Total System Global Area        12071016 bytes
Fixed Size                         46136 bytes
Variable Size                   11090992 bytes
Database Buffers                  409600 bytes
Redo Buffers                      524288 bytes
Database mounted.
SVRMGR>
```

4. Entering the command **alter database backup controlfile to trace;** and receiving the message "Statement processed" from Oracle.

5. Editing the text file produced by the previous command, cutting out the portion up to and including the text "*** SESSION ID:(9.6) 1999.11.24.17.48.23.062" shown in the next listing:

```
Dump file D:\ORANT\RDBMS80\trace\ORA00191.TRC
Mon Nov 24 17:48:23 1999
ORACLE V8.0.4.0.0 - Production vsnsta=0
vsnsql=c vsnxtr=3
Windows NT V4.0, OS V5.101, CPU type 586
Oracle8 Enterprise Edition Release 8.0.4.0.0 - Production
With the Partitioning and Objects options
PL/SQL Release 8.0.4.0.0 - Production
Windows NT V4.0, OS V5.101, CPU type 586
Instance name: orcl
Redo thread mounted by this instance: 1
Oracle process number: 10
pid: bf
Mon Nov 24 17:48:23 1999
Mon Nov 24 17:48:23 1999
*** SESSION ID:(9.6) 1999.11.24.17.48.23.062
# The following commands will create a new control file and use it
# to open the database.
# Data used by the recovery manager will be lost. Additional logs may
# be required for media recovery of offline datafiles. Use this
# only if the current version of all online logs are available.
```

```
STARTUP NOMOUNT
CREATE CONTROLFILE REUSE DATABASE "ORACLE" NORESETLOGS NOARCHIVELOG
    MAXLOGFILES 32
    MAXLOGMEMBERS 2
    MAXDATAFILES 32
    MAXINSTANCES 16
    MAXLOGHISTORY 1630
LOGFILE
  GROUP 1 'D:\ORANT\DATABASE\LOG2ORCL.ORA'  SIZE 200K,
  GROUP 2 'D:\ORANT\DATABASE\LOG1ORCL.ORA'  SIZE 200K
DATAFILE
  'D:\ORANT\DATABASE\SYS1ORCL.ORA',
  'D:\ORANT\DATABASE\USR1ORCL.ORA',
  'D:\ORANT\DATABASE\RBS1ORCL.ORA',
  'D:\ORANT\DATABASE\TMP1ORCL.ORA',
  'FINANCE.DBF'
;
# Recovery is required if any of the datafiles are restored backups,
# or if the last shutdown was not normal or immediate.
RECOVER DATABASE
# Database can now be opened normally.
ALTER DATABASE OPEN;
```

When this command completes, Oracle responds with the message "Statement processed." and, with the control file rebuilt, the database is open and available to the user community.

Object Recovery

Object recovery is done in one of two ways:

1. Using Oracle import to reinstantiate a table from an export file.

2. Rebuilding the object by running the portion of the data warehouse refresh that populated the table in the first place.

There are a few factors that need to be considered when deciding which is the best and quickest way to go when you need to rebuild an object in the warehouse.

TIP
When rebuilding a table, the secret is to get the right data back and accessible to the users with the least amount of downtime.

Let's look at the basics of each method, and suggest the things to consider when deciding which way to proceed. When deciding to go the import way, one looks at the volatility of the information in the table—static data can be restored using an export file from the previous day, the previous week, or even further back. When performing exports of warehouse data, the smart administrator logs the extraction of the data. The **log** parameter fed to export accomplishes this easily and efficiently. Suppose an export is run weekly on supposedly static data and, after searching a few weeks' worth of log files, you notice that the row count of the ACCOUNT table is always 23,990,988. I'd bet the data in ACCOUNT is static. When we speak of "stale data" in the next note, we are referring to information that would best not be used for OLAP or query processing as opposed to static data, which is something entirely different. Stale data contains out-of-date information, drawn from time periods that should no longer be direct input into the OLAP exercise. Suppose a company has grown in the past five years from a three-hundred-million to a two-billion-dollar organization; it is possible that some of the data from the beginning of the five-year period may have been good input to decision making two years ago, but not anymore.

NOTE
Err on the side of caution when deciding what export file to use for object recovery. It's better to take longer to get a table back than run the risk of bringing back stale data. Business decisions made on stale data are not sound!

When leaning towards the rebuild path, you need to weigh the time to availability using this approach. Object recovery via import can be as time-consuming as, if not longer than, building the table again from scratch.

NOTE
This is only a guideline, and we realize very intensive data scrubbing and transformation can be more time-consuming than import.

When looking at which way to go, keep in mind that bringing a large table back from an export is at least a two-step process. The first step is bringing in the data itself, the second rebuilding any indexes manually with the **create index** SQL*Plus command (or a primary key or unique constraint via the **alter table … add constraint** command). Situations outlined in Table 11-2 are not uncommon. The first value in the Indexes column is the number of indexes on each table. The data in Table 11-2 was gathered by:

1. Importing the table, letting import create the object and build necessary indexes.

2. Dropping the table, and importing just the data (parameter **indexes=n**), letting import create the table.

3. Running the index creation statement(s) in SQL*Plus. Since this was a four-CPU machine, the degree of parallelism for all creation statements was set to 4, and the **unrecoverable** keyword was used.

Let's summarize our findings based on the data in Table 11-2. The first object took 5m9s to import by allowing the data, indexes, and constraints to come in together. The same activity partitioned up between data and indexes took only 3m45s. The second table was 49m22s all together, and 41m25s broken into data then indexed. The last checked in at 1h22m24s when letting import do all the work, and 1h2m46s when the work was broken into smaller chunks. These results are indicative of how object recovery using import alone can be more time-consuming than using import to recover the data, and SQL*Plus for the indexes and constraints.

TIP
*When performing object recovery with Oracle, bring the data in with import and do the index and constraint creation in SQL*Plus.*

	Import			SQL*Plus
Rows in table	**All Together**	**Data**		**Indexes**
123220	5:09	2:04	5	1:41
3212304	49:22	19:02	16	22:23
8009122	1:22:24	29:14	7	33:32

TABLE 11-2.   *Times for Import of Three Tables—All at Once, Then Piece by Piece*

After saying that, let's consider another test that will illustrate another interesting phenomenon (big word, eh!!) about object recovery. This is what we did for this example:

1. Export a table with data, index, and constraint definition statements imbedded in the export file.

2. Drop the table and re-create the object using the day-to-day portion of the warehouse refresh program responsible for object creation.

3. Drop the table and do an import from the export created in step 1.

Now, let's have a look at the information in Table 11-3. The R column shows the time required to rebuild the table in SQL*Plus; the I column is the time for import to do the same job. The 1 to 6 columns show the row counts of the tables joined to make the data in the table being re-created.

Let's summarize the three rows of information in Table 11-3:

■ The 26,039-row table has no indexes and is built from a single table with just over one million rows. It took 24 seconds to import and 2m59s to rebuild in SQL*Plus.

■ The 153,262-row table has two indexes and is built from a join of six other tables—ranging from a low of 12,084 rows and a high of 330,594. It took 4m8s to import and 6m35s to rebuild.

■ The 1,059,457-row table has six indexes and is built from a join of four other tables—two small ones, one with over 94,000, and one with almost four million rows. It took 59m57s to import and 23m8s to rebuild.

Before moving on to looking at recovery from image backups, we would like to leave you with one more tip based on the findings displayed in Tables 11-2 and 11-3. We might be tempted to call this a rule, but, with the experience we have in computers, as soon as one says something is a rule rather than a tip, it springs a leak (i.e., someone finds evidence to the contrary!).

TIP

Regardless of the size of the tables in your DSS, index creation is time-consuming and resource-intensive; do not allow import to create indexes during an object recovery exercise. It is quicker in most cases to do them in SQL*Plus.

Restoring from Image Backups

Restoring and using backups of the warehouse is an entirely different issue. Recovery is one mechanism that requires skilled technical personnel, completely familiar with the recovery process using Oracle. *Recovery* is a process whereby an image backup from a previous time is copied back from

Rows	R	I	I	2	3	4	5	6
26039	2:59	0:24	1059457					
153262	6:35	4:08	330594	109242	104904	94276	14940	12084
1059457	23:08	59:57	3942520	94276	1	390		

TABLE 11-3. *Times to Rebuild and Import Three Tables*

tape and synched with the current copy of the warehouse. Recovering an Oracle database is a fairly straightforward process. A number of issues come up during the process, and some tough decisions must be made. These issues and their resolutions are beyond the scope of this book but, in an overview, Figure 11-8 shows the recovery process components.

Let's discuss these components, using the letters A through D, as indicated in Figure 11-8.

- Component A is an image backup of part of the Oracle data warehouse written at 3 A.M. While the database files were being backed up, the warehouse was open.

- Component B is the series of redo log files that were written between the time the image backup was written and the data warehouse as it sits at 4 P.M.

- Component C is the data warehouse at 4 P.M.

- Component D is the segment of the data warehouse whose contents were written to tape at 3 A.M.

The recovery process is three steps:

1. Copy the data back from tape and place on the disk, overwriting the file that sits there at 4 P.M.

2. Reapply the transactions in the redo logs (component B) using Server Manager. The process applies transactions residing in the redo logs that affect the database file just copied back from tape.

3. Inform Oracle the recovery process is complete.

When the recovery completes, the affected datafile will be consistent with the rest of the warehouse and the users can carry on with their business.

We've bitten off a lot in this chapter. Backup and recovery are two of our favorite topics; we can bore each other in a matter of minutes when we talk techie among ourselves and our colleagues. Unless, of course, the topic is backup/recovery or the topic of the next chapter, "Securing the Warehouse."

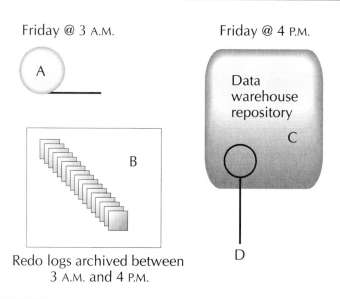

Friday @ 3 A.M.

Friday @ 4 P.M.

A

Data warehouse repository

C

B

D

Redo logs archived between
3 A.M. and 4 P.M.

FIGURE 11-8. *Recovery process components*

Security is such an important issue in the warehouse. Of all other issues we are going to cover in Chapter 12, the biggest is ensuring users are not allowed to stumble into data in the warehouse that they are not able to see in the operational system environment.

CHAPTER
12

Securing the Warehouse

ecuring the warehouse—three words that conjure up visions of the warehouse police ensuring people only see what they are allowed. This is not too far from the main security mechanisms placed in the warehouse. These mechanisms enforce a flavor of business rules native to the decision support system arena.

Operational systems implement a network of security that protects confidential information and ensures data integrity while ensuring users have access to the information needed to go about their daily business. Let's get started by looking at security policies.

A Security Policy

There are many different ways to slice and dice a security policy. When deploying the data mart solution (special interest pockets of data in isolated sections of the corporate infrastructure), security and access to data can prove less cumbersome than when dealing with the enterprise data warehouse. There are a number of issues related to plain common sense. As we walk you through the items, keep in mind your habits as you interact with all the electronic information you come in contact with during a normal business day.

Workstation Security

This is the simplest, and the bottom line of a security policy. Whether you are using Windows 3.x, Windows 95, or Windows NT, something as simple as a screen saver password is a good place to start. As new personnel are brought into companies, they are usually briefed on the general security measures that are in place—why not ask personnel to lock their workstations when they leave their office or cubicle? The Windows NT security dialog, invoked by pressing CTRL-ALT-DEL, is the easiest of the three Windows platforms to lock the workstation. There are many inexpensive third-party products out there that engage the screen saver when the user moves the mouse cursor to a predefined spot on the screen, presses a hot key combination, or clicks on a desktop or button bar icon. Figure 12-1 shows

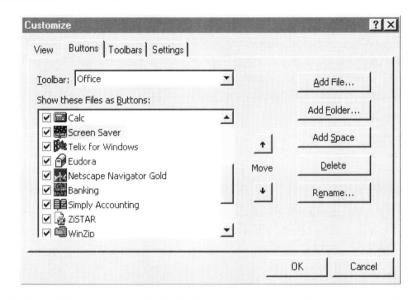

FIGURE 12-1. *MS Office Screen Saver icon selector*

where the Microsoft Office Shortcut button bar can provide an icon to turn on the password protected screen saver.

Speaking of Windows NT, many organizations are deliberately not giving users access to administrator accounts on their own personal computers.

Snooping

Snooping involves browsing or capturing of information on someone else's computer that you have no access to on your own. This can take the form of inspecting (and in some of the worst cases, responding to) another person's email and viewing results of analysis of information to which, using your own means, you do not normally have access. There are two main ways to promote behavior that lessens the likelihood of snooping. The first is outlined in the previous section on workstation security, the other involves training users to exit their applications when they leave their work area and log off the network at the end of the business day.

Security

All businesses go through a series of exercises during operational system development. These exercises define who should be able to do what with what data. Some users, based on predefined security profiles, are allowed to **select**, **create**, **update**, and **delete** information in the database, while other users have a handful of these privileges suited to their needs. No matter how you access your data, two levels of security exist:

1. Privileges granted via the Oracle **grant** mechanism where users or groups of users are explicitly given permission to access the data

2. Rights to perform certain operations on the data, based on who they are and where they sit in the company's administrative structure

As these two mechanisms are discussed, the word "user" will be used to refer both to each separate user who may access the warehouse and to a class or group of users. The first level of security for most users of the warehouse will suffice for them to go about their business. The second level only comes into play for those Oracle users who own the data sitting in the DSS repository. Let's look at these issues and highlight some suggestions specific to the warehouse environment.

Viewing the Warehouse Data

This is the heart of the security system with most, if not all, relational databases. Because the data in a warehouse is read-only by nature, the Oracle **select** privilege is given out to warehouse users. This privilege allows specified users to view data once a universal name for the data has been established. *Universal name* means a handle of sorts for the database object within which data is stored. Figure 12-2 illustrates the progression of setting up these names.

Oracle calls this universal name a *public synonym,* which can then be used by all users who connect to the database to refer to, for example, the PERSON table.

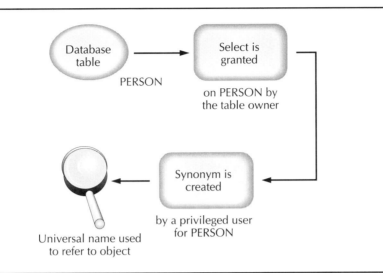

FIGURE 12-2. *Setting up the universal name*

TIP
Both setting up the synonym and granting privileges to users must be done before users can reference objects in the warehouse.

Regardless of what tool is used to access the data—Express Objects, Discoverer/2000, or any other choice—this first level of security must be in place.

How to Manage Privileges in the Warehouse

Oracle8 contains a rich feature called role-based security that is ideal for operational as well as DSS environments. Let's briefly discuss role-based security, and then views.

Role-based Security

A *role* is a logical grouping of one or more users of the Oracle database to which privileges can be given, based on the functional responsibilities of the persons registered in that role. A role is created using the following syntax:

```
create role dss_finance;
```

Enroll describes the process of giving membership in a role to one or more users. People need an Oracle account before they can connect to the database. This is facilitated by issuing the familiar statement shown in the next listing:

```
create user {user_name} identified by {password};
```

The username component of the preceding listing is usually hooked up to a user's name. For example, suppose user Sandra Swanson gets the Oracle name "sswanson" and the password "nosnaws." The username should contain only letters or the digits 0-9, begin with a letter, and contain no embedded spaces. Once this person has the ability to connect to Oracle, she is enrolled in the appropriate database role by the command

```
grant {role_name} to sswanson;
```

Armed with the basics, let's set up a few users and roles, then grant privileges:

```
create user showard identified by drawoh;
create user warnock identified by kconraw;
create user babramson identified by nosmarba;
create role finance_mgr;
create role finance_sen;
create role finance_user;
grant finance_mgr to showard;
grant finance_sen to fwarnock;
grant finance_user to babramson;
```

Once the users are set up in their appropriate roles, the owner of the database objects in the warehouse grants privileges to roles, using code similar to the following:

```
grant select on fin_plan to finance_mgr;
grant select on fin_hist to finance_user,finance_mgr,finance_sen;
```

The power of role-based security is that once roles have been created and they have received the appropriate database privileges, new users are simply enrolled in one or more roles, which they need to interact with the data warehouse. Even better, when a new user is given membership in a role, this new user automatically inherits the privileges that go along with the role. Membership in a role is taken away using the following code:

```
revoke finance_mgr from showard;
```

and, when necessary, access to the database is taken away using the code:

```
drop user {username};
```

Before discussing more issues related to keeping the warehouse safe, one of the most important things to remember can be summed up in the following tip.

TIP
Do not allow data warehouse users to see information in the warehouse that they are not allowed to view in the operational systems.

Suppose managers have decided their senior directors can interact with departmental information in their region, but not in regions that belong to other directors. In the warehouse, this same rule must be enforced. This could affect how the data is modeled in the warehouse and, after that modeling activity, how the data is moved into the DSS repository. This could mean an additional network of rollups may need to be created and stored in the mart or warehouse. A *rollup* is a level of summary containing data created by the manipulation of information at a lower level. Reporting a figure of $128,000 as the gross profit of four divisions, whose individual numbers range from $34,000 to $51,000, is an example of a rollup.

Views

Views are the heart of many security mechanisms, not only in the data warehouse but also in many operational systems. A *view* is a logical table built as a subset of the data in one or more physical tables. *Logical* means the view itself contains no data; the data in a view is assembled from the underlying table(s) when a view is mentioned in a SQL statement. Here is a simple view definition; the criteria are in bold:

```
create or replace view dept_south as
select *
  from dept_rllup
 where reg_cd = 'S';
```

Using this view, queries only have access to the rows in the DEPT_RLLUP table whose REG_CD column value is "S." Suppose you wanted to restrict viewing of rollup information for users in each region to data in their own region. The secret is to grant these users (or a role of which these users are members) the **select** privilege on the view built from their region alone. The next listing shows how this would be accomplished using a combination of role-based security and views:

```
-- Create a role for each region
create role southern;
create role northern;
create role eastern;
create role western;

-- Create a view of DEPT_RLLUP for each region
create or replace view dept_north as
      select * from dept_rllup where reg_cd = 'N';
create or replace view dept_west as
      select * from dept_rllup where reg_cd = 'W';
create or replace view dept_east as
      select * from dept_rllup where reg_cd = 'E';
create or replace view dept_south as
      select * from dept_rllup where reg_cd = 'S';
-- Grant select on each region's view to the proper role
grant select on dept_south to southern;
grant select on dept_north to northern;
grant select on dept_east to eastern;
grant select on dept_west to western;
```

Where to Implement Security

Stories exist of data warehouses where the security is implemented at the tool level rather than in Oracle. *Tool level* means situations where warehouse implementers use features in query and analysis tools to control the data the users are allowed to view. Even though these security mechanisms may solve a short-term problem, you are probably wiser using Oracle database security. The problem with tool-based security is twofold:

1. Security features embedded in certain tool vendors' products only work for that tool. If you were tempted to implement tool-based security, you would have to do so manually for each tool. It would be too easy to inadvertently allow users to view data in one area of the warehouse using tool A, whereas tool B's security restricts them from seeing the same data.

2. Each vendor's proprietary security features must be learned by all warehouse security personnel. As personnel changes (and it always does), the learning curve can get in the way of the transfer of responsibility process.

Tool-based Security

In this section, we will look at implementing security using Oracle Discoverer as an example. Tool-based security, though not as fluid and portable as database engine-based security, is a matter of fact. With many tools, Oracle Discoverer included, you have no choice. The tool cannot be turned over to the user community before its security features have been implemented. Oracle Discoverer uses *business areas* to collect a set of related information with a common business purpose, organized into *folders*; folders contain *items,* which are a particular category of information within a folder. Access to business areas is where baseline security is implemented in Discoverer. Let's briefly look at the activity of giving users access to one or more of these areas.

There are two versions of the Discoverer 3 product—the Administrator Edition and the User Edition. The separation of the product into these two versions controls who has access to the power of setting up and changing business areas and who can simply work with areas to which they have been granted access. When the administrator starts Oracle Discoverer, the Administration Tasklist menu appears, as shown in Figure 12-3. Notice how the "Grant business area access" task is flagged as mandatory.

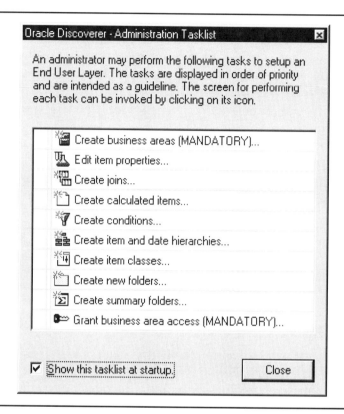

FIGURE 12-3. *Discoverer Administration Tasklist menu*

Access to Tables

After setting up a new business area, using a set of wizard dialog boxes as shown in Figure 12-4, the administrator picks and chooses the schemas and the objects within those schemas that the user will view using the business area. By selecting FND_FLEX_VALUES, FND_FLEX_VALUE_HIERARCHIES, and GL_BALANCES, only those tables' data will be brought together in the business area being set up.

Access to Business Areas

After defining the business area and choosing the objects for inclusion, the administrator then proceeds to the Security dialog box. There are two folders to this screen:

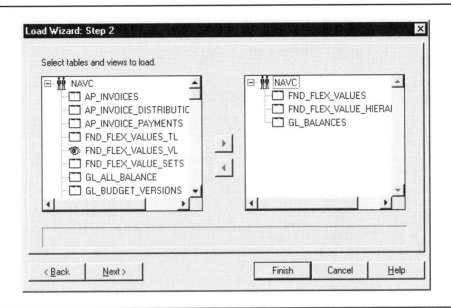

FIGURE 12-4. *Load Wizard dialog box*

1. The first is where you pick a business area from the picklist shown in Figure 12-5, then transfer user or role names from the Available to the Selected portion of the screen.

2. The second is where you pick a user or role from the picklist shown in Figure 12-6, then transfer business area names from Available to Selected.

Password Security with Oracle8

Oracle8 delivers password aging and a sophisticated set of password control features. Most people, other than those tasked with database security, find password management a nuisance. Nuisance shmuisance! Nobody wants any unauthorized access to their sensitive data (yes, you too!). Let's look at password selection and control features with Oracle8. The facility is based on Oracle profiles, discussed in more detail in the "Governors" section of Chapter 20. In a nutshell, profiles are used to handle password management

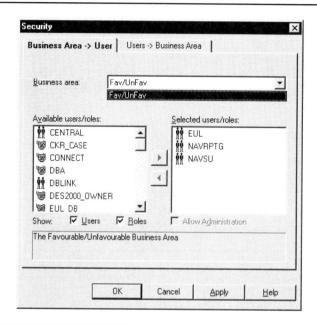

FIGURE 12-5. *Access by business area*

with Oracle8—a *profile* being a set of resource limits that can be given out to users of the database. These limits are in areas such as CPU consumption per session or allowable terminal idle time before being disconnected from the database. Without worrying about the nitty-gritty details about syntax, let's look at two areas provided in the password management facility in Oracle8—account locking and password aging.

Account Locking

This is where the DBA specifies the number of failed login attempts after which an account is locked. The **failed_login_attempts** parameter is specified as an integer. Suppose a profile is limited to four failed login attempts; upon a fifth login, the following Oracle error is returned:

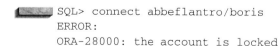

```
SQL> connect abbeflantro/boris
ERROR:
ORA-28000: the account is locked
```

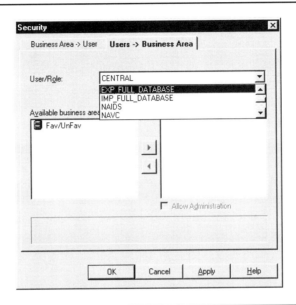

FIGURE 12-6. *Access by user/role*

A locked account is unlocked using the **alter user abbeflantro account unlock;** SQL statement. Account locking can serve two purposes. It assists in prevention of deliberate or undeliberate hacking into a database by an unauthorized person, plus it detects when someone is trying to break into an account.

Password Aging and Expiration

Password aging limits the life of a user's password. The **password_life_time** is the parameter Oracle8 uses to control this time to expiration, and accepts an integer argument. Suppose a user is assigned a profile with this parameter set to **60**. This means that a password can be used for authentication for a period of 60 days before it has to be changed.

Management of Database Users

There are a number of schools of thought in this area. Some feel user management should be the responsibility of the database administrator

(DBA); others feel the management should be given out to a handful of trusted users. We prescribe, most of the time, to the second approach. We are not, however, suggesting that you should give the keys to the car to people without implementing a security infrastructure. Let's look at that infrastructure in the next few sections.

System Privileges

Oracle8 allows the deployment of over 80 system privileges. *System privileges* allow users to perform activities previously only available to DBA accounts. This feature addresses the desire to partition activities out to non-DBA accounts without compromising the overall security of the database. Let's look at a handful of system privileges and what they permit the recipient to perform, using username "floydp" as an example.

Create User

This privilege allows someone to create accounts in the Oracle8 Server. The syntax is shown in the next listing:

```
grant create user to floydp with admin option;
```

A few points are worth noting in this statement:

- The recipient of the **grant** must already have an account.

- The **with admin option** allows user floydp to give the privilege out to others. If these three words are inadvertently omitted, the error "ORA-01031: insufficient privileges" is raised.

Armed with the privilege, user floydp can now do activities as shown in the next listing:

```
SQL> connect floydp/wall
Connected.
SQL> create user waters identified by roger;
User created.
SQL> create user barret identified by syd;
User created.
```

```
SQL> create user gilmour identified by david;
User created.
```

At the same time, it is wise to give a user receiving the **create user** privilege the ability to remove a user account using the **drop user** system privilege. This is done using the next SQL statement.

```
grant drop user to floydp with admin option;
```

Create Session
This privilege allows a user to connect to the database. Creating an account as shown in the previous section does not yet allow a session to be initiated until commands similar to those in the next listing are run:

```
SQL> connect floydp/wall
Connected.
SQL> grant create session to waters;
Grant succeeded.
SQL> grant create session to barret;
Grant succeeded.
SQL> grant create session to gilmour;
Grant succeeded.
```

Alter User
This allows a user to change the password for other database users, as illustrated in the next listing:

```
SQL> grant alter user to floydp;
Grant succeeded.
SQL> connect floydp/wall
Connected.
SQL> alter user waters identified by fender;
User altered.
```

We'll now wrap up this chapter on securing the warehouse by looking at using Oracle Enterprise Manager (OEM) to manage security in the Oracle8 data warehouse.

Oracle Enterprise Manager and Security

Many prefer using the GUI interface in OEM to perform security-related tasks with the Oracle8 warehouse. The SQL commands built while working with OEM are exactly the same as those built manually using the line-mode Server Manager interface or even SQL*Plus. The Security Manager in OEM is where roles, users, and system privileges are handled. The main console is shown in Figure 12-7.

Let's look briefly at working with the three folders shown in Figure 12-7—Users, Roles, and Profiles.

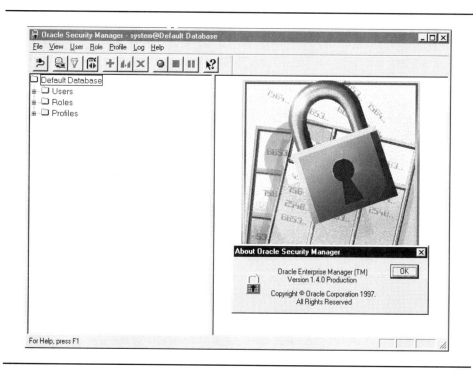

FIGURE 12-7. *Security Manager main console*

Users

A mouse click on the "+" sign beside Users expands the user list, which can be further expanded to list the following:

- **Roles Granted**   The roles defined in the database of which the user has been made a member.

- **System Privileges Granted**   The privileges given out to the user. Some of these privileges are discussed in the "Management of Database Users" in the previous section of this chapter.

- **Object Privileges Granted**   The privileges the user has received on objects owned by other users in the database.

Figure 12-8 shows the expanded lists for user SCOTT; note that a right-mouse click over one of the branches on the user tree brings up a menu containing Revoke and Add Privileges to Users options, as shown in Figure 12-8, as well.

Roles

Roles—a logical grouping of one or more users. The Roles folder is used to create roles and add privileges to existing roles. A right-mouse click on the folder brings up a drop-down menu with those two options.

1. Add Role brings up a dialog box where the role is named and the authentication method is specified. By far the most common method is None, meaning there is no password required for users when enabling a role using the **alter session set role** SQL command. Another folder in the Add Role dialog is where other roles and system privileges are given to the role being created. After picking the privilege type, a list of available roles and system privileges is presented where the work is done using the standard Windows point-and-click interface.

2. Add Privileges to Roles is a shortcut to the second folder in the Add Role dialog box, as shown in Figure 12-9.

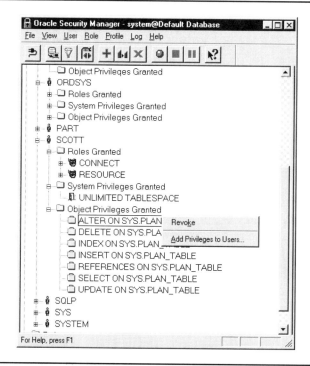

FIGURE 12-8. *Expanded Object Privileges with drop-down menu options*

When giving a role or a system privilege to a user or role, the With Admin Option checkbox should be selected if you wish to allow the recipient to pass the role or privilege on to other users or roles.

Profiles

When sitting over the Profiles folder, a right-mouse click brings up a menu where profiles can be created and assigned to existing users. We discuss profiles in this chapter in the "Password Security with Oracle8" section as well as the "Governors" section of Chapter 20. There are two folders to the Create Profile feature—General, where some limits can be set for the likes of terminal idle time and maximum connect time; and Password, where

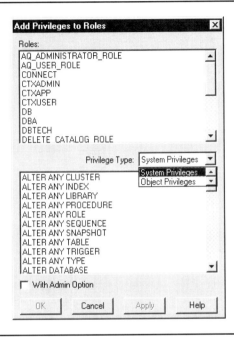

FIGURE 12-9. *Add Privileges to Roles dialog*

password complexity, aging, expiration, and details on password history are maintained. Figure 12-10 shows the General folder as a new profile is being created.

The Show SQL button has been clicked in the dialog box, causing OEM to display the SQL statement that will be passed to Oracle when the Create button is pressed. Most of the limits have a picklist that contains the special limit of **default**. This means that the profile should assume the limit for that item to match that defined for the profile called "default".

NOTE
The "default" profile is delivered with the Oracle database and need not be defined manually.

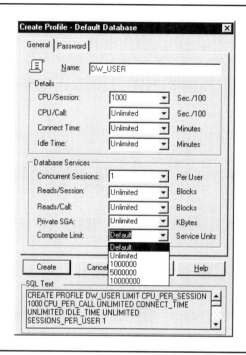

FIGURE 12-10. *Creating a new profile*

The Assign Profile to Users screen, shown in Figure 12-11, is where existing profiles are given out to database users.

A Word on the Power of OEM

To close this chapter, a word from our lawyers (so to speak). The SQL commands that can be built and passed out to users in OEM are very powerful and can sink the efforts of the warehouse team if abused. For example, in a client/server environment, when doing user maintenance, selecting External for Authentication in the Quick Edit User dialog box can keep a warehouse person from connecting to the database until the option is reset to Password.

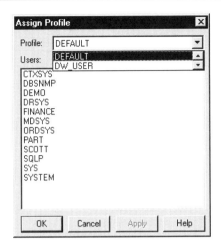

FIGURE 12-11. *Assigning profiles to users*

NOTE
Be very conservative when giving access to OEM to power users in the user community; there is a great deal of damage that can be done inadvertently to the warehouse in the hands of the inexperienced. These people would not do anything deliberately—the power can be misused, not abused.

Enough said on securing the warehouse. As we alluded to earlier, security is seldom an issue until an incident comes up that compromises the data in the warehouse. The bottom line, as we state in a few spots in *Oracle8 Data Warehousing*, is to ensure the data is safe and users are not allowed to see something in the warehouse they do not have access to in the operational system environment. The next stop on the warehousing journey looks at RAID technology for storage of your precious data warehouse information. The RAID phenomenon has been around for quite some time, and it gets even more sophisticated as we speak.

CHAPTER
13

RAID

very year, newer and faster microprocessor chips are developed. This trend of increased microprocessor speeds continues to be a constant within the high-technology industry. Based on this recurring trend, the consumers of technology now expect CPU speeds to at least double each year. In one of our books, *Oracle8 Tuning* (Osborne/McGraw-Hill, 1998), this fact was used as a basis for favoring a computer's CPU power in the tuning process. This means that whenever your system is upgraded with a new CPU (a likely case), the newly tuned applications will only improve. This trend of faster microprocessor CPU chips was so consistent, even the chip name became predictable. For example, first it was the 8086, next the 80286, then the 80386 and, finally, the 80486. Just as everyone became used to the standard name for the latest and greatest chip, Intel Corporation announced the Pentium chip. Whatever happened to the 80586?

What happened was Intel Corporation realized the name could not be trademarked, so they decided to change the game to a name that could be trademarked: Pentium. A *Pentium* is what would have been called an 80586 chip. What is clear from all these announcements is that chips are making the CPU faster by a substantial factor every year. CPU speed is not considered a major barrier to machine performance today.

The problem, to quote a familiar saying, is "a chain is only as strong as its weakest link." In this case, the "weakest" chain link represents your I/O throughput. The disk drives can be a major source of performance problems in a data warehouse environment or even in a typical computing environment. Even though the I/O capabilities of disk drives have improved over the past few years, they have not kept pace with the dramatic improvements of CPU speeds. Accessing your data through disk drives is, and continues to be, one of the slowest operations a computer does, compared to accessing data stored in memory. This issue is further intensified in a data warehouse environment due to the large volumes of data. When we are asked to tune a database, many times we learn a major source of performance problems has to do with the configuration of the disks attached to the computer upon which the database operates.

What makes this issue of choosing the "right" disk configuration even more critical is that it has one of the greatest probabilities of failure. Any point of failure within a computer system is critical, but when a disk drive fails, you not only risk the availability of the data but also the reliability of the data stored on the disk. Any system failure always puts you at risk of the user community losing trust in your ability to deliver the end-user systems that can meet their demands. They will seek out other solutions. Once lost, trust is difficult to regain. This may be your greatest risk when a system fails. Can you afford to lose face?

In a data warehouse environment, preventing failure becomes even more critical. You are probably storing historical information that if lost or destroyed will be difficult to recover. Another key problem is that a typical data warehouse has a large dataset associated with it. The larger the dataset, the longer the time to recover the data in the event of a disaster. This can quickly become a critical issue, which should be addressed early in the process. The key question here should be "If I create a backup, do I have the time it takes to recover the data?"

With large datasets, speed of retrieval also becomes a critical issue. Retrieving a hundred records is always faster than retrieving a million records. For a particular warehouse initiative to be successful, you must turn your users' "what if?" questions around in a timely manner. You must provide the end users with the capability to sift through vast amounts of information quickly.

History has taught us that whenever a vacuum is created in the marketplace, a movement will occur within the marketplace to fill that vacuum and, over time, a movement will occur to improve upon the solution. As business needs for information and the ability to ask "what if?" questions have become more acute, we have seen the trend toward building enterprise data warehouses grow. As these data warehouses grow in size and complexity, the need for disk storage solutions that improve retrieval speeds and minimize the likelihood of failure have become critical. This vacuum for improved disk I/O throughput and reliability has been a major catalyst for the development of redundant array of independent disks (RAID) technology, although the vendors often like to say "redundant array of inexpensive disks."

If you are reading this book, you and your organization must be thinking about building a data warehouse. A data warehouse will be the most complex and data-intensive system you will ever encounter. The impact on poor performance from your disk farm or a high failure rate would mean disaster.

In this chapter, RAID technology and some of its key evolution points will be explained. Then you can make a determination if RAID is appropriate for your data warehouse, given your needs and resources. Experience has taught us that RAID is often a necessity for data warehouses.

NOTE
Understanding RAID technology is imperative; then, and only then, can you determine if you can live without its fault-tolerance and performance characteristics.

What Led Us to RAID?

In the beginning, you had a disk. Over time, numerous improvements have been made to this disk. A disk has become much faster at retrieving data. Many remember the "seek time" wars in favorite trade journals. *Seek time* is a measurement of the amount of time required to position a read/write head over a predetermined spot on a disk platter. Imagine yourself trying to play your favorite song on a record player. Seek time would be the amount of time it takes you to move the arm on a record player to your favorite song on the record.

The size and density each drive can contain has also steadily increased. A great example of this is the old 5 1/4-inch floppy drive compared to the 3 1/2-inch high-density drives that are standard with all personal computers sold today. The original 5 1/4-inch drive could only hold 360Kb worth of information compared to the 3 1/2-inch drive, which can hold over 1MB worth of information. Another major trend has been the movement toward physically much smaller disk drives, which require much reduced floor space and power needs. Figure 13-1 is a quick illustration of this discussion. Just the comparison of the floppy disk to the current 3 1/2-inch disk provides an excellent framework for the overall industry trends in the storage industry. Remember, even though great movement has been made in the size, capacity, and speed of disks, they are a poor shadow of their cousin, the CPU.

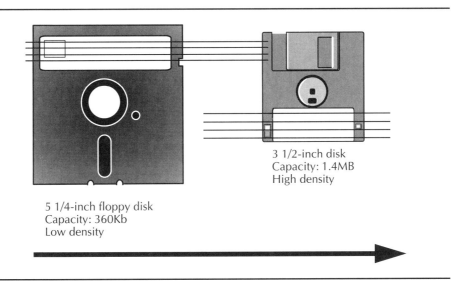

3 1/2-inch disk
Capacity: 1.4MB
High density

5 1/4-inch floppy disk
Capacity: 360Kb
Low density

FIGURE 13-1.   *Trends toward smaller, faster, more fault-tolerant disks*

Over time, hardware vendors have created numerous improvements to disk drive technology to meet customers' needs for faster, more reliable disk drives that are more fault tolerant. *Fault tolerant* is a computer architecture that has mechanisms in place to compensate for one or more components' failures. In the IBM world, these improvements were known as direct access storage devices (DASD); in the world of Digital Computers, they were known as VMS shadowing. Even though these technologies work quite well, they are still proprietary. What has been clear is the move toward open systems. *Open systems* provide a commodity-like computer system, which, in turn, brings down price points while maintaining quality. In fact, this trend toward open systems is just a reflection of the marketplace and how all products and services move through it. Figure 13-2 highlights the standard life cycle for all products and services.

The Product/Service Life Cycle

- **Innovation:** A unique product or service is created. Once it gains market acceptance, it enjoys no competition and very lucrative pricing and profits.

- **Imitation:** As a unique product gains acceptance, a number of copycat products appear. They mimic the core functionality of the original, and, in addition, they boast the inclusion of many features that should not have been forgotten by the originator. The imitators initially come in underpriced and yet overvalued compared to their functionality list.

- **Maturation:** At maturation a number of brand-name products or services have established themselves. They are constantly adding features, hoping to encourage brand loyalty and achieve improved pricing. At this time, the RDBMS marketplace is between maturation and consolidation. The key vendors are constantly looking for new functionality that will encourage brand loyalty. For example, the move towards Oracle 7.3 is an example of making the RDBMS data warehouse-savvy, which demands a premium in the marketplace.

- **Consolidation:** As the marketplace becomes saturated, there is no longer a need for so many different product or service providers. Typically during this period, vendors package multiple products together hoping to show value. The net result is that there will be fewer players in the field. The consumer will have fewer choices.

- **Commodity:** Eventually, all products or services become a commodity. There is no major difference between vendors, so the consumer will go for the best price. The keys to survival here are efficiencies and economies of scale. For example, when a consumer buys a laser printer today, it does not matter whose name is on the outside; there are only two or three key vendors who make the parts.

FIGURE 13-2. *Product/service life cycle*

If you understand the product life cycle, you can understand a major trend that affects the product and services each vendor is offering you. Through this understanding, you can better judge where the marketplace is going and when it makes sense to buy the brand name.

Innovation Phase

All products/services begin at the innovation phase. The birth of the innovation phase is due to a failure or a need of a current product or service within the marketplace. Once this vacuum in the marketplace is identified, some entity builds a product or service to fill this need. In the innovation phase, a new, unique product/service is born. Because it is first, no competition exists and one of two situations occurs:

1. The marketplace quickly embraces the product/service offering, which generates immediate high demand. The problem then becomes how you meet the high demand in the marketplace. The high demand also quickly begins to raise price points due to the limited supply. This is the supply and demand curve at work.

2. The marketplace does not understand the need for new products/ services. So a market strategy must be developed to teach the marketplace the need. If this is not done, the product/service will fail. A basic strategy is developed to help the marketplace understand the need for the product/service. Pricing is a major factor for any customer and, in this scenario, it will initially be lowered to help induce the marketplace to try the new product/service. After the marketplace understands and embraces the new product/service, the need for steep discounting no longer exists and higher pricing follows.

Imitation Phase

As the product/service gains market acceptance, it quickly enters the imitation phase. This is where a number of copycat products/services arise. If a short supply of the original product/service occurs, then these imitators quickly gain market acceptance based on the need the original product/ service created. If, on the other hand, the original product/service is meeting the demand, then the imitations begin to develop strategies to show what features they have, which will cause you, the consumer, to choose them over the original product/service.

Maturation Phase

As the imitators begin to gain market acceptance, the product/service makes the transition into the maturation phase. From all the imitators that appear, a few key brand names emerge. In addition to the brand-name products that evolve, quite a few generic products evolve. Let's review the word processor marketplace. Some key brand-name products exist: Microsoft Word, WordPerfect, AmiPro, and a series of second-tier products such as Claris Works and QuickWrite. If you choose WordPerfect over Microsoft Word, will your effort fail? No, both are excellent choices. The key is to look beyond the product/service and evaluate all other factors that affect your effectiveness with the product/service. For example, what materials and education are available to help you better use the service? The Oracle Press series is an advantage when you buy Oracle: you now have a set of materials written by well-known experts to help supplement the Oracle documentation set.

Consolidation Phase

As these brand names become more entrenched, they move into the consolidation phase. As differences between the brand names become less apparent to the consumer, a common trend is to package many different products into one. This is done to help show added value. For example, Microsoft Office incorporates a spreadsheet (Microsoft Excel), a word processor (Microsoft Word), and some presentation software (Microsoft PowerPoint). Because each of these products is tightly integrated, each hopes to show it has a unique added value. Any time vendors can show unique added value, they can move back toward the innovation phase. Vendors can get the greatest return in the innovation phase. Yet, as one vendor announces an office suite, another brand name announces a competing product. Once again, this is the consolidation phase, where the weaker vendors will not survive or the stronger vendors will absorb them.

Commodity Phase

Eventually, all the differences between product/service begin to fade away; then it makes no difference which service you purchase. This is where the commodity phase is entered. For example, when you look at the hamburger industry, does a major difference exist between a cheeseburger at McDonald's and a cheeseburger at Burger King? Once a business enters this stage, the name of the game is price. For example, when you buy a Sun Microsystems computer, it might contain a Seagate disk drive when you purchase it in May and a Micron disk drive when you buy it in June. This is because key vendors have the ability to maintain a consistent level of quality but to use different disk drive vendors. This has given Sun Microsystems the ability to meet its supply and demand for disk drives at the best price points. You, the consumer, benefit.

In the computer industry today, consolidation is being experienced in many areas. We are reaching the point of fewer hardware vendors. In addition, many areas in this industry are already approaching commodity status. This is most evident in peripheral business. In fact, many customers are demanding commodity-like ability. Customers want to purchase a printer that will work on any computer system in-house. We are moving toward a trend where your computer peripherals will work like the electrical appliances in your home, where you have a standard electrical plug and all devices simply plug into it. Can you imagine a world where each appliance you bought required a different type plug? That kind of world would reflect many of the situations that currently exist in the computer hardware world. This is a key frustration for businesses purchasing proprietary systems, and it has begun to move us closer to open systems.

Why RAID?

As we move toward open systems, this need to plug and play is becoming critical, which is most apparent in the disk storage arena. For example, a customer might need to make a substantial purchase of disk storage for a legacy system, and that legacy system may be slated for replacement by an open system within a year. Business needs dictate you improve the storage capability of the disk farm on the legacy system today. To purchase a proprietary solution, which will make this investment obsolete when you migrate into open systems, would be foolish.

This is a common occurrence in today's world. Now consumers are looking for an open system solution; they are looking for a disk farm that will work on both the legacy system and the new open system. They want disk drives to be a commodity. The disks are serving the same business purpose on both the legacy system and open system: they are storing information. This need for one solution to meet all needs has helped to fuel the need for open system solutions; hence, a RAID disk farm. The following section looks more closely at RAID and how it has evolved. This discussion of RAID and its various levels/incarnations will help you understand how to use it to your advantage in a data warehouse.

RAID Level 1—Disk Mirroring

RAID level 1 is perhaps the simplest form for many to understand because its roots are found in DASD and VMS (a popular Digital Equipment operating system) shadowing, which contain functionality with which many readers are familiar. In RAID level 1, there are two disks and each disk contains an exact copy of the data. As the computer makes a request to write or record a block of information, the data is recorded twice, once on disk A and simultaneously on disk B.

As you can see from looking at Figure 13-3, as the data that needs to be recorded (represented by the letters and numbers going into the funnel) is passed along, it is recorded on two disks at once. RAID level 1 does provide for data redundancy because you always have a constant backup occurring on the second disk.

Other common terms for this practice of having two disks record the same information simultaneously are *mirroring* or *shadowing*. This is a more expensive system to build because it requires twice the normal number of disk drives. Over time, this solution evolved beyond just two disks. A chain

FIGURE 13-3.   *RAID level 1 (disk mirroring)*

is only as strong as its weakest link. So, if the one power supply failed, the failure affected both disks. Over time, RAID level 1 evolved, as shown in Figure 13-4.

When the disk controller and the disk drives are duplicated, this is known as *disk duplexing*. Over time, all components were duplicated; for example, you would commonly see dual power supplies. This was done so no matter which component failed, your disk subsystem would continue to operate unhindered.

As the technology improved over time, you were even able to repair the broken disk while the system was online. This allowed you to do repairs without any downtime. As soon as a new disk was installed to replace the defective one, the RAID system was smart enough to start copying the data present on the good disk to the replacement disk.

FIGURE 13-4. *RAID level 1 improved*

To summarize, RAID level 1 has duplicate disks operating side by side in parallel disk mirroring. The mirroring has created greatly improved system reliability because if both disks failed, downtime would be experienced. This was an unlikely situation. In terms of storage, you got only 50 percent capacity because you needed two disks to do the job normally done by one disk. This approach was considerably more expensive because you needed two disks, two controllers, and two power supplies instead of one. This level of RAID was not as successful as future levels, primarily due to price points. The marketplace sent a clear message: We want the improved retrieval speeds, we want the fault tolerance, we are willing to pay a premium, but we want better price points.

RAID Level 2—Incompatible

RAID level 2 is not currently used due to its incompatibility with current disk drives.

RAID Level 3—Data Striping with Parity

The following information was clear from RAID level 1: having the fault tolerance that mirroring provided was desirable only if a way existed to do it without doubling the costs. Once again, a vacuum was created in the marketplace and the forces at work found ways to improve upon the original solution.

The concept of a parity drive was created. A *parity drive* allowed hardware vendors to have a number of disks share an extra drive. In the event of a device failure, the parity drive would be used with the remaining functional disks to determine the contents of the defective drive. Under RAID level 1, a configuration of five drives would require five additional mirror drives, for a total of ten drives. This same configuration under RAID level 3 requires five data drives and only one parity drive, for a total of six drives. As transactions are recorded, they are striped across all drives and the parity drive. By striping the data across multiple drives and a parity driver, the data can be recovered in the event of a failure. The price points were much lower because all data drives in a set could share a single parity drive. See Figure 13-5 for an illustration of this point.

Now for a closer look at the magic of parity and how it works.

Parity—How It Works

Parity uses basic math to accomplish its task. Each transaction is spread across each of the drives with the parity bit set on the parity drive. In the event of a failure, applying basic math can derive the contents of the missing

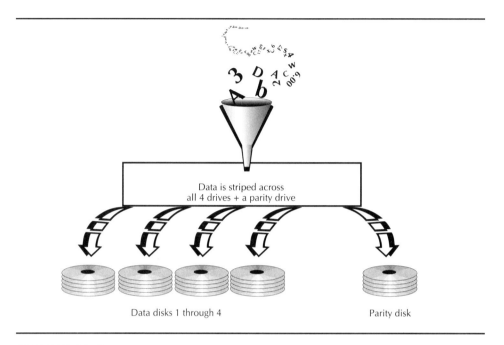

Data is striped across
all 4 drives + a parity drive

Data disks 1 through 4

Parity disk

FIGURE 13-5.   *RAID level 3 data striping and parity*

drive. In Figure 13-6, you will see three examples of parity at work. Because we know the parity is 15, the missing value can be determined by applying basic math. In example one, the missing value is *3*. In example two, no defective drive exists. In example three, by applying basic math, we know the missing value is *1*.

This works because the data is striped across all drives. So, when a transaction happens, the data is written to the disk array. One byte/bit is written to each disk drive, including a parity bit on the parity drive. Think of this as the logical record being interwoven across all drives. This is conceptually how parity works. By having this dedicated parity drive, the ability now exists to recover information on a defective drive. This provides good fault tolerance at a substantially reduced cost. The down side is, during a disk operation, each drive is accessed at the same time. This limits you to one I/O transaction at a time. The up side is you have high data transfer rates. This level of RAID works best for large data requests.

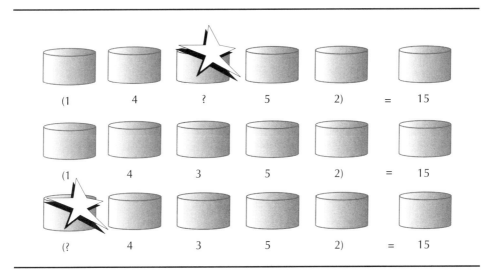

FIGURE 13-6. *Parity examples*

RAID Level 4—Data Striping (Block at a Time) with Parity

In RAID 4, data is still striped across the set of drives all at once, only instead of a byte/bit of information, it is a block of information. This means you have a much higher I/O rate than in level 3.

RAID Level 5—Independent Disk Access, No Parity Disk Bottleneck

In RAID level 3 and 4, during a read/write request, all the drives are accessed at the same time in a set. This is not the case in RAID level 5, which has the ability to access as many drives as it needs at the same time for different individual read/write requests. This gives RAID level 5 the highest I/O transfer rate of all its predecessors.

This ability to have multiple readers and writers is a powerful feature. Figure 13-7 shows two users making requests for information that resides on

FIGURE 13-7. *RAID level 5 (multiple readers/writers)*

two different locations within the set of two disks. One request is being serviced by one disk and disk controller, while the other disk is servicing the other request and disk controller. The configuration of RAID level 5 gives you greatly improved retrieval speeds; in addition, write operations are not done together.

Unlike RAID level 3, where information was striped at a byte/bit level, in RAID level 5, it is done in a block or even record-striping segments. A need no longer exists for a dedicated parity disk, which was a performance bottleneck. In RAID level 5, the parity information is rotated. This means you no longer have the cost associated with the additional parity disk. In the event of a disk failure, you still have the needed parity information.

RAID—The Future and Why Every Data Warehouse Needs It

Future trends in RAID clearly show the I/O barrier will continue to be broken. Getting your data from a RAID stack of many smaller disks is now faster than getting it from a larger traditional disk. As RAID technology further develops, it continues to remove the performance constraints associated with disk retrieval speeds.

Fault tolerance continues to improve. RAID is now at the point where it is *hot swappable*, which means, in the event of a disk failure, you can fix the problem without impacting the availability of the data. RAID vendors are also reaching the point of keeping your RAID box up and running transparent to the customer. Many times when a failure happens, the box can now notify the vendor to send in a repairperson.

Bigger, improved disk caches are in the works. Bottlenecks can occur with high-performance systems due to the slower speeds of physical disk I/O. The RAID vendors are providing for bigger and bigger memory caches to remedy this problem. With these bigger caches, user requests never have to wait for a physical read or write. In the event of a read, the RAID box reads ahead of the users' requests and has the data sitting in memory, which is the fastest way to service a read request. In the event of a write request, the RAID box places the write in memory and signals the waiting process it is ready. Because the box is so fault tolerant, no fear exists that the write request might get lost due to a hardware problem.

On the horizon are numerous improvements to enhance your ability to back up the data warehouse using the RAID configuration. The RAID vendors realize a data warehouse is the most complex system a customer may ever face when working from a disk farm or a backup perspective. They are now building in tools that allow customers numerous backup options. This occurred because many of the vendors had customers who had no way to back up their large data warehouses.

Bottom line—a RAID box is the fastest, safest way to store your data. With the improved price points, increased memory caches, and new options on how to back up your data, you cannot afford to miss looking at RAID as an option for your warehouse endeavor.

Time to move on. In Chapter 14, we are going to have a look at getting the data to the users. Is that not what this whole effort focuses on in the first place? Get it out of the operational systems, scrub it, load it, make it available, and turn the user community loose.

CHAPTER
14

Getting Data
to the Users

The data warehouse is a powerful repository of information, but it is not the total solution. As we have already discussed, the data warehouse is an integrated database that serves as a one-stop shopping center for the organization's information. The data in the warehouse can be used to better understand the business, but without access to this data, the power is meaningless. We are very aware that in organizations that do not have data warehouses, getting the information is half the battle for performing analysis on our business. How often do we find that we spend an exorbitant amount of energy going from department to department collecting information? This information can be in hardcopy reports or spreadsheets, or if we are lucky, it is contained in a well-organized operational system. Next, we become concerned with collating the data into a report, which may or may not be time based, or we have a number of reports that have numbers contained within them that do not match or correspond. The problems with getting the data together and then putting it into a meaningful report can be a challenge in the best of times.

The data warehouse provides us with a great vehicle for business analysis. It has organized our business into manageable parts that are simple for end users to navigate. The overall success of your data warehouse depends upon providing simple and fast access to data. Yes, in fact, we often like to point out that to most end users the data warehouse is the access tool—they have no idea of the work and effort that went into the beautiful database behind the scenes. The selection and use of your query tools will therefore directly impact your data warehouse's success. Users must be able to easily answer the business questions that are supported by data in the warehouse. Many query tools exist today that help us gain reporting and ad hoc access to our data. These tools range from the simplest, such as SQL*Plus, to the complex, such as Oracle's Discoverer product. Which tools you would use depend on the type of access your end users require. If you have power users who are comfortable using a tool such as SQL*Plus, this may suffice for certain requirements. Others will require more "hand holding," and will need tools that have data prepared for them, like Cognos' Impromptu. The tool that is used to access the data by the users will then allow them to become empowered and perform business analysis that previously was difficult or impossible to achieve from the operational database. The goals of getting data from the data warehouse must achieve the following criteria:

■ It must allow users to view and print regular reports.

■ It must provide the ability to drill-down and investigate the "numbers" generated by the report.

■ It must allow users to easily develop their own reports and reproduce these reports as required.

■ It must move costly personnel hours from data gathering to data analysis.

We can separate data access into three specific areas:

■ Standard reports

■ Ad hoc queries

■ Multidimensional analysis

Standard reports are our old friend. These are specific reports that can be distributed to users as a stand-alone entity. Reports such as a listing of the current financial position would meet these criteria. The distribution of these reports can be handled by many different methods. Reports can be created and the resulting output can either be printed (but, how many trees need to die?), distributed electronically (email or Internet), or made available for viewing on a LAN (*local area network* in a confined area of one's business). Almost any tool can perform the creation of these reports. The factors that will help you decide what tools will be used and how these reports will be created is dependent upon the flexibility required by these reports. If a report does not require a high degree of customization and formatting is not a big concern, then a simple query tool like SQL*Plus will meet this requirement. In cases where you need more customization of a report, then the more complete tools will be required.

Ad hoc data access presents a completely different set of output requirements. The method of extracting data from the data warehouse depends upon the expertise of the user community as well as formatting needs. If the end users are a confident group who have a relatively good grasp of SQL, then SQL*Plus can meet their needs. Many end users do not have this level of expertise in SQL and would like to be insulated from the database as much as possible. Who can blame them? Today's generation of end-user data query tools meet this requirement head-on. These tools have been evolving at such a quick pace that it seems that every day another tool provides more functionality and better ease of use. For our discussion in this chapter, we will illustrate this with two of these tools: Oracle Discoverer and Cognos Impromptu. Both these tools are considered to be among the best of the breed and provide a significant amount of power to the end user, balancing ease of use and customization.

The last type of data access we need to discuss is multidimensional analysis. This is the online analytical processing (OLAP), which you have heard so much about. OLAP provides users with the ability to view their data from many different perspectives while maintaining a sound and efficient data structure. OLAP will be more extensively discussed in Chapter 16.

Whichever method you decide upon to extract data from your warehouse, just remember to evaluate each solution based upon your needs. The success of your data warehouse depends on it. Your solution will be a combination of tools. One product will rarely meet all data warehouse reporting needs, so you will probably require a multiproduct solution to meet all your needs. Salespeople are very convincing, and many can sell an electric lamp to someone during a blackout. However, by following some simple guidelines, you can decide on the tool best suited for your data reporting requirements. When evaluating the various products, you will need to reconcile the following questions:

- What type of reports do you plan to create?

- Is there a requirement for ad hoc data query?

- Do your users have SQL knowledge?

- Will you be performing multidimensional analysis?

- How will you be distributing the report output?

- Will the Internet be used for distribution?

- How will you maintain these reports?

- How will you define your metadata, the layer that describes your data in the warehouse?

The choice of the right query tool will be one that will allow users to exploit the power of your data warehouse in the long term. Therefore, you must make this choice intelligently. Let's now move into some of the important characteristics of data warehouse query tools so that you can better understand the tools and utilize them to their fullest potential.

Query Tool Characteristics

The evaluation and selection of query tools is one of the most important decisions that you will make in the development and deployment of your data warehouse. This product will form the window through which your users will access their data. You could choose the cheapest option, that being SQL*Plus, but the long-term cost to this option is one that will become apparent. So, you then need to decide on a query tool. Will it be Oracle Discoverer, Cognos Impromptu, Business Objects, or some other query tool? Why is it that every question when it comes to product selection is critical? Just because! Select the wrong tool and you can handicap the success of the data warehouse mission. It's just like putting the wrong di-lithium crystals into the warp drive. This discussion does not apply to using SQL*Plus as a reporting tool for your data warehouse. If you do decide to use SQL*Plus as your only reporting tool, then you may want to think about a new career. It is, however, a robust product that can produce many of the reports that you may require, but it does not meet the needs of many of today's analysts. SQL*Plus should form one part of the solution, but it does not provide all the functionality needed to leverage the work that we have done in creating the data warehouse, and usually will not provide an interface that the CEO will be willing to consider an acceptable solution.

When evaluating the various tools, what should you look for? It is just as important to evaluate your reporting requirements as it is to determine the cost to roll it out to your organization. The following are some criteria that you should evaluate during your product selection process:

- Ease of use
- Performance
- Multiple data sources
- Centralized administration
- Data security
- Web-enabled
- Integrated analysis

This chapter will not make the decision for you of which tool is the best, but it will help you towards making the appropriate decision for your business. Experience has shown us that many products will meet all the criteria at some level, but the final selection must be based on your own business requirements. Let's now look at each of the criteria we have defined and how each one impacts the data warehouse and the query use of our end users.

Ease of Use

First, and probably most important, is ease of use. This factor is probably the most important to your users, and if you can make your users happy, you are halfway to a successful data warehouse. The ease of use is centered in two areas: building reports and presentation flexibility. The product must make it easy for your users to draw information from the database. Many tools provide this through a simple and intuitive graphical user interface (GUI). These tools often provide seamless installation and setup. They also possess the ability to insulate the users from the complexities that are inherent in many databases. Through ideas such as a "Catalog" or "End-User Layer," query tool administrators can prepare an environment that allows users to access the database without needing to understand how the data is linked together. By providing this simple administration and end-user layer, analysts can now focus on collecting the data they need instead of becoming intimidated by a complex data structure that requires a road map and a sextant to navigate. Figure 14-1 illustrates how the user is insulated from the data warehouse via the user interface catalog.

The architecture depicted in Figure 14-1 provides users with a simple interface that they can use to access the database. This layer is created and maintained by the tool administrator, and is used and accessed by the end users via the end-user product.

The users must also have the ability to easily manipulate and change their reports to meet their needs. Whether this simply means that they can move data and change the presentation of the data or the deeper investigation of the information, this functionality needs to be present within the tool that you select.

Ease of use is a very personal matter. What may seem to be easy to one person may be cumbersome to another. During your evaluation of the tools,

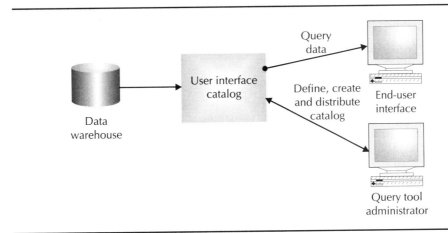

FIGURE 14-1. *Query tool architecture*

you should put together a cross-section of users, and together with this team determine what best suits your business' goals and user expertise.

Performance

Performance is one item that can be the difference between users analyzing their data and users sitting around talking about what the Ottawa Senators need to do to win another Stanley Cup. The level of performance is related to the whole data warehouse environment—the database, the query tool, and the SQL that is used to access your data. Together, all these items influence performance. Each of these influences affects performance. Together, they can conspire to doom your warehouse project, which will allow for some serious discussions on sports.

Multiple Data Sources

Your data warehouse has been constructed and you need to answer numerous questions that your business requires. You start to write a new report and then discover that you need some information that is not contained in the warehouse. What should you do? Your options include the alteration of the warehouse to include this data, but this will take too long.

So, you decide that you will include data from a second data source. This data source could be a flat file containing the data, or it may be another database. For example, your warehouse may contain the sales that have been completed but not contain the budget numbers—these are contained in your budgeting system. The query tool that you select must have the ability to combine data from these two sources so that report you produce reflects the business requirement. Most query and reporting tools allow you to include data from multiple data sources, but ensure that the types of sources supported by the product will integrate well into your data warehouse and information systems.

Centralized Administration

During your evaluation, it is important to consider centralized administration of the data that you present to your users. This is the feature that separates the men from the boys (women from the girls) in query and reporting tools. A centralized administration of the tool allows knowledgeable individuals within your organization to present a simple and efficient user interface to the end users. Each query tool calls it something different. If you are using Oracle Discoverer, it is called the User Interface Layer and in Cognos Impromptu it is known as the Catalog. Whatever you call it, the purpose of this layer is to allow users to view their data in their own terms and to eliminate the need to understand data structures and join strategies. Figure 14-2 illustrates how Oracle Discoverer has insulated the user by allowing the administrator to define the data to which the user will have access.

The end user does not need to be concerned with this aspect of the warehouse. The user is required to simply select the data to include in the query, and the program will format the data according to the rules and formats defined during the creation of the layer.

During your appraisal of the tools, you must decide how simple and effective the administration of the tool appears, and how it will impact your reporting strategy. The administration of the end-user layer must be simple enough to use while still allowing for quick changes. These changes will be required, as the data available to the users may need to be altered to meet their quickly changing information requirements.

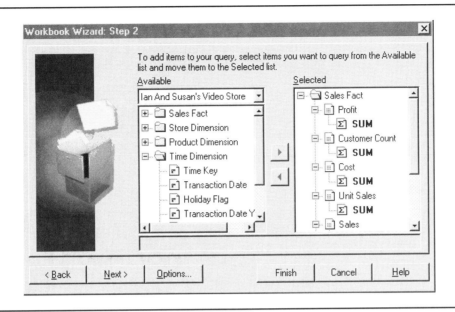

FIGURE 14-2. *Oracle Discoverer end-user layer*

Data Security

Security is an issue that could be ignored or dealt with, depending on how important you consider your data. Today, in most organizations, data security is always a concern, and we understand that completely. Any query tool that does not incorporate some additional security features is a tool that may not be one that you should consider in a data-sensitive environment. It is for this reason alone that the wide use of SQL*Plus concerns us in any data warehouse environment. Although we can define a certain degree of data security within the database, we are exposing our users to data that must be carefully managed. When it comes to SQL*Plus, we prefer to limit the use and access to the tool to only selected data warehouse users. Query tools are much more powerful in that we have the ability to define the data dictionary that the users will access by predefining what the user can see. We also can define different business views for the various groups within our organization. You can have a catalog for your human resource department that may include the salary data for all employees, whereas in the corporate directory you may have details on all employees, without any financial information. The following represents how Oracle Discoverer manages security:

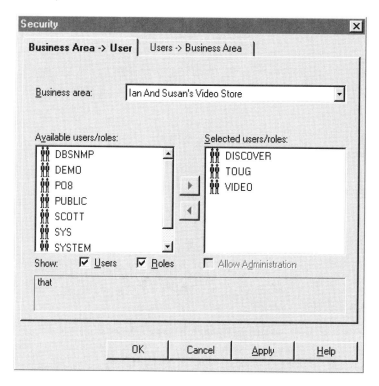

This shows us just how simple security is within Oracle Discoverer. When creating your end-user layer, you define the users and roles that will have access to the model.

NOTE

Security within the product is performed in addition to database-level security and should not be used to replace it.

Security should always be a concern to every organization, as the data warehouse will usually contain a plethora of information—some of which may be confidential. The security of your data from a query tool should be considered during your evaluation so that you can best protect your information. Chapter 12 addresses some security issues in the warehouse and data mart environment.

Web-enabled

The impact of the Internet is in turn having a profound impact on the way that we gather and distribute information. It has allowed us to make information available to many people who previously had not been able to see it. The Internet is quickly becoming our window into the world, and data warehouse information can now be distributed via the Web. Most query tools will allow you to publish your results to a page, and even to allow for drill-down capabilities provided through this interface. Figure 14-3 illustrates how your Internet or intranet users may see their reports when viewing them in their Web browsers.

As you can see from Figure 14-3, the results can be formatted to meet just about any requirements. Although query tool integration with the Web is in its infancy, it is quickly developing into a required element for any tool that you may choose for your organization.

Integrated Analysis

The power of any reporting tool is its ability to offer users the flexibility to investigate the numbers that are displayed to them. For example, if you have a summary report that displays the sales figures for your organization by region—providing the sales and profit values—you may want to "drill" into data within a specific region to see how its numbers are broken down. Therefore, you should select a product that has the ability to allow you to "slice and dice" your data. This ability to investigate your data includes the following functions:

- Drill-down into data

- Transpose columns and rows (also known as pivoting)

- Conditional filtering of data

- Format your data

- Exclusion of columns from your display

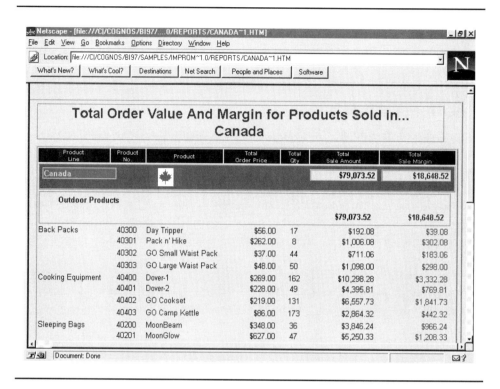

FIGURE 14-3. *Sample query results viewed via the Internet*

These features that we have previously listed will be just as important when we discuss online analytical processing (OLAP) in Chapter 16. It is also advantageous for your OLAP tool to integrate with your query tool. For example, when viewing summaries within a tool like Cognos' PowerPlay, you may decide that you would like to view the detailed information that generated the summary. Cognos' Impromptu would then be invoked and a query executed that would display the detailed records. This integration can provide an extra level of functionality that will improve the flexibility of your end-user data warehouse access. Let's now look at some tools that can be used to access your data warehouse. Figure 14-4 shows a simple database. This data mart focuses on sales at a video store. We will use this model to look at SQL*Plus and Oracle Discoverer.

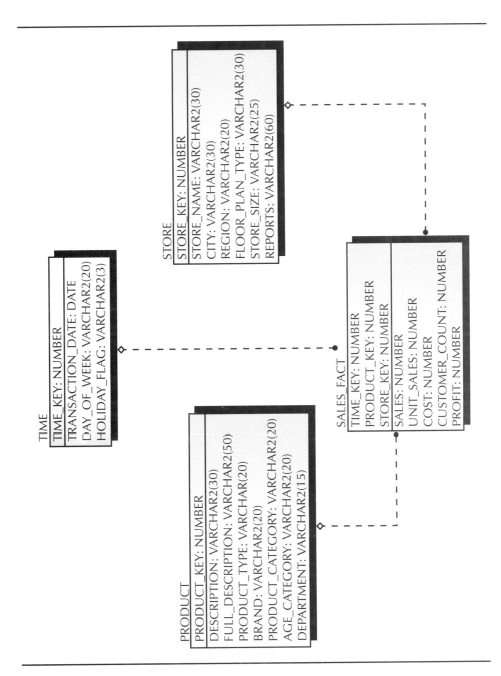

FIGURE 14-4. *A simple database model*

Using SQL*Plus for Reporting

SQL*Plus is one of those underappreciated tools available to end users. It can produce predefined reports with the greatest of ease, but it can also be used to create ad hoc reports. What it does not provide is the ability to investigate the numbers, since a report must be rerun to change the format and data that is being displayed. Figure 14-5 shows you a sample SQL*Plus report.

Although it is not highly formatted (all right, the data is not formatted at all), we have generated a simple report that provides the user with a total of sales by store and product type. This report, which is simple to construct, does provide users with a great deal of information. These are the types of reports that you will create using SQL*Plus. These will be static reports, which will be displayed or printed.

The downside to a tool such as SQL*Plus is its limited functionality. It will only produce static reports, and this product does not address the need

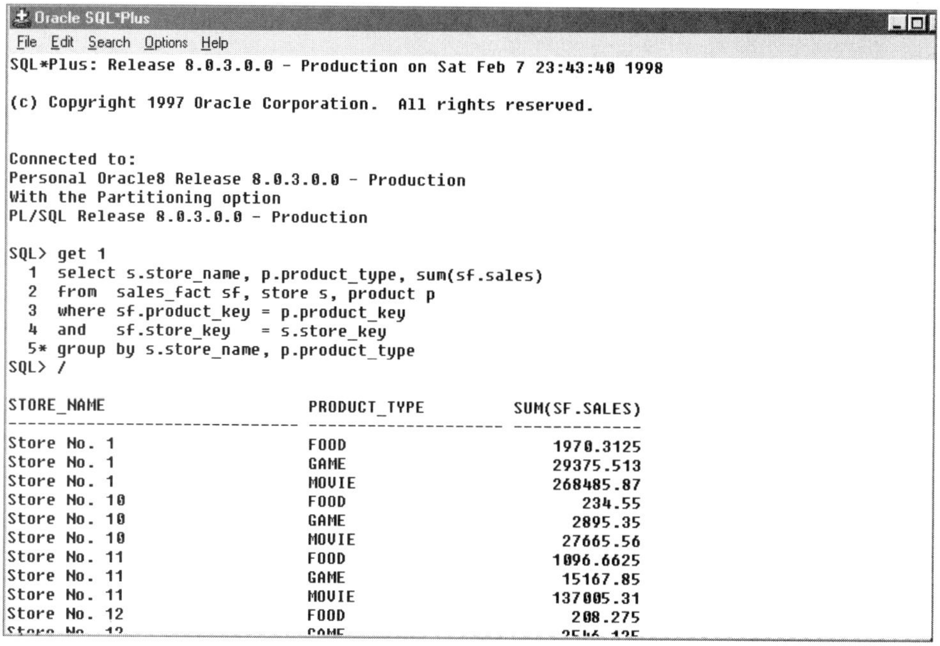

FIGURE 14-5. *SQL*Plus selection of data*

for integrated analysis. The other area that should concern any data warehouse administrator is runaway SQL. So often we have heard of a user waiting two to three days for a query to return results, while at the same time the other users are complaining that the system performance is "SLOW"! This danger always exists if you include SQL*Plus in the reporting toolset in your organization. You must train your personnel to optimize their SQL and help them to understand the data warehouse database schema in order to build their efficient reports.

Oracle Discoverer

Oracle talks about Discoverer as a part of their decision support system. It provides users with an ad hoc query tool, which allows them to perform reporting, data exploration, and Web publishing capabilities. Sounds just like what we want, so let's look at how Discoverer performs this task. Oracle Discoverer is comprised of two components—the administrator and user tools.

The Administrator prepares the data structures that the user will use to access the data warehouse. It also manages security for each business area that is created. Let's now look at how we run each component and see if we can create a simple end-user layer, and use this to create a report for our users.

Oracle Discoverer Administrator

The Discoverer administration component is installed so that we can create the end-user layer required by the Discoverer end-user tool. It separates the more difficult database administration tasks from the simpler querying and reporting tasks so that analysts, managers, and other information workers can easily get their work done without having to know about either databases or SQL. The administrator is able to create a metadata dictionary, called the end-user layer, that hides the complexity of the database from users, and that reflects the particular business areas of your company.

Before we can begin, we must first look at the concept of the business area, which is a logical grouping of tables and/or views that apply to a user's specific data requirements. For example, the accounting department wants data about budgets and finance, while project leaders want data specifically about their projects as well as about budgets. Although some of the data that these professionals need may be the same, the exact combination of tables and views for each department is usually unique. Using the Discoverer Administrator Edition, you tailor the grouping of data to provide users with the proper access to the precise data they need for ad hoc query, decision support, and presentation of results.

NOTE
Your username must be granted with the privilege to perform the Administrator task. To grant the 'Administration' privilege use the Privileges command in the Tools menu of the Discoverer Administrator Edition.

We will begin by using the Administrator to create a business area for sales at our video store. Discoverer has a number of wizards that we use to simplify the construction of our data layer without imposing assumptions that will just have to be "fixed" later. To create or manage a business area, the Load Wizard will aid you in the process. The Load Wizard is pictured here:

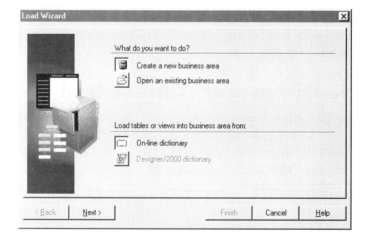

Now you have the option to select a new business area or to open an existing one. If you select a new business area, the source can either be the online dictionary or from Oracle's Designer/2000. When you open an existing business area, you can select from the list of existing business areas. You can open either a single business area or multiple areas. You then can change and alter the characteristics of these business areas.

The creation of a new business area is facilitated by the second step of the Load Wizard. It is here that you select the users who will have access to this business area that you are creating. You then define the source of the raw data tables that you would like to include in your end-user layer. Step 2 of the Load Wizard is shown in here:

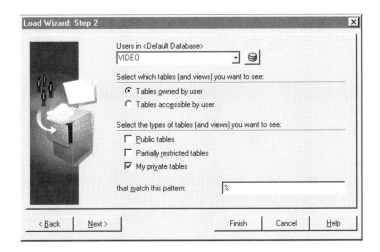

From this screen, you can select tables that are owned by the Administrator or all tables to which you simply have access. You then define the type of tables to which you have access. Once you have defined the criteria for selecting the tables that may be included in the model, you will then be presented with a listing of the tables that met your criteria. This list is then available to create the business area. You then can select complete tables or individual columns; it is from this list that you will build the infrastructure for your business analysis.

NOTE
Create models that focus on single areas of business analysis. Think of each business unit and end-user layer as a focused data mart.

The selection of the tables or columns is merely a matter of pointing and clicking. By moving the selected tables and columns into the selected window, you are making the information contained in these tables available for use in this business area. In the following illustration, you can see that we have selected the TIME, STORE, SALES_FACT, and PRODUCT tables for inclusion in this model:

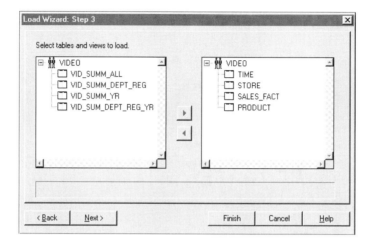

After you have selected the data that you should include in your end-user layer, you are required to name the model that you are creating. This name should be meaningful, and descriptive enough for all users. These options include naming standards and conventions that should be made to standardize the names and headers within the model. As well, it will generate the default joins required by the model. The joins are based upon either primary key to foreign key relationships or common column names. We recommend that you always implement your data warehouse with referential integrity in place, as you can see the advantages when using tools such as Discoverer.

The resulting model definition is then displayed in the Discoverer Administration window, shown in Figure 14-6.

Figure 14-6 shows us an Explorer type view of our business area. It includes a list of dimensions that are included, along with the attributes of each of these dimensions. It is from this window that you can manage and customize the business area model. You also should note the Administrator tasklist. The tasklist is useful to remind you of the activities that you will need to follow to complete the model. All the tasks to complete your model will be performed here and the model then saved to the database. Since we now have centralized administration, we need only to install the Discoverer user product on your analysts' workstations. Now

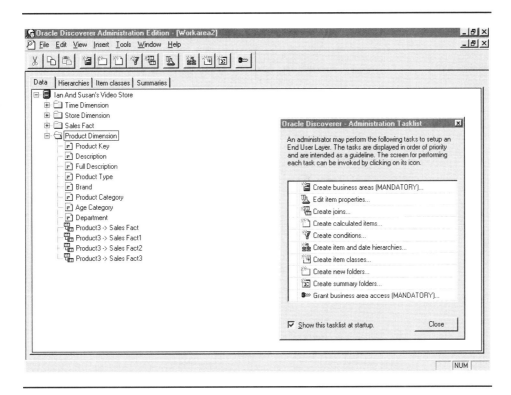

FIGURE 14-6. *Basic Discoverer model*

that you have completed the initial business area model, we can move to the Discoverer end-user tool.

Discoverer End-User Tool

The end-user version of Discoverer is provided to allow users to define, create, and customize reports based upon data defined in a business area model. This section will not go into depth on how to use the end-user tool, but it will provide you with an introduction to the product. It is the Discoverer End-User version that allows you to present queries and reports to your organization using a simple and intuitive interface.

Upon opening the end-user tool, you will select the business area or predefined query. When you wish to create a new report, you open a business area that has been previously defined by the Discoverer Administrator. If you wish to run a query, you will select Open a file and then retrieve the query definition from the file system. The following illustration shows opening a business area that will form the basis of the report you require:

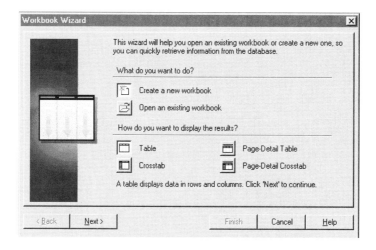

NOTE
You must be granted access to the business area to be able to create reports based on the model definition.

Discoverer will create a default layout for your report. As with many tool defaults, you can customize the final report format and content. Discoverer provides default table and crosstab formats, each of which can then be formatted in a master-detail relationship. After you define the type of report you require, you then need to define the source of the information in your report. Figure 14-7 shows that Discoverer provides a drop-down list of business areas to which you have access—where it says "Ian And Susan's Video Store" in the Available area.

You can then select data from one or more business areas. You can select entire business areas or only required elements for use in your report. The figure shows you that we have selected the Sales Fact and Time

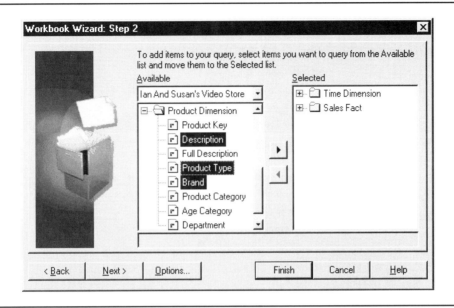

FIGURE 14-7. *Discoverer data source selection*

Dimension, and we are about to select the Description, Product Type, and Brand attributes from the Product Dimension. This information will then be collated and formatted into a default report format. While the query is running, you will see a projected execution time to perform the query.

NOTE
If your query will require an excessive amount of time, Discoverer will warn you about the projected execution time. You then have the option to continue or return to adjust your source data.

As you can see next, the expected time to completion is displayed, and every once in a while it is close, but this is not an exact science.

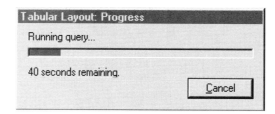

Upon the completion of your query, you will have a default report based on your selected data. This report can then be further formatted. The following is just a small list of the types of formatting that you can perform:

- Format columns and rows

- Change order of displayed columns

- Define titles, add images, and set background appearance

- Define exceptions, which can highlight data such as low profits or high sales

The result of this customization will allow you to create a report, as has been done in Figure 14-8.

To illustrate how simple it is for you to modify the look of your report, we will define an exception that will highlight all profits above $7,000. The new exception that we will create will change the background color and font of the Profit SUM field. The exceptions definition is shown in Figure 14-9, followed by the same report with the exception enlivened in Figure 14-10. Notice the amounts greater than 7,000 are italicized, as specified when the exception was defined.

You can observe that we have done more than just change the format of the profit column. We have also drilled down to the city level. Placing the cursor over the region column displays a list of additional refinements for you query. You can then select the desired drill-down category. We selected the City column for a drill-down. The report now displays the various cities contained in our database. The exception has added additional formatting on the profits above $7,000. As well as the added italics, notice that the background color is different.

We are merely touching the surface of Oracle's Discoverer product. Discoverer is a product with great depth. It can provide your organization

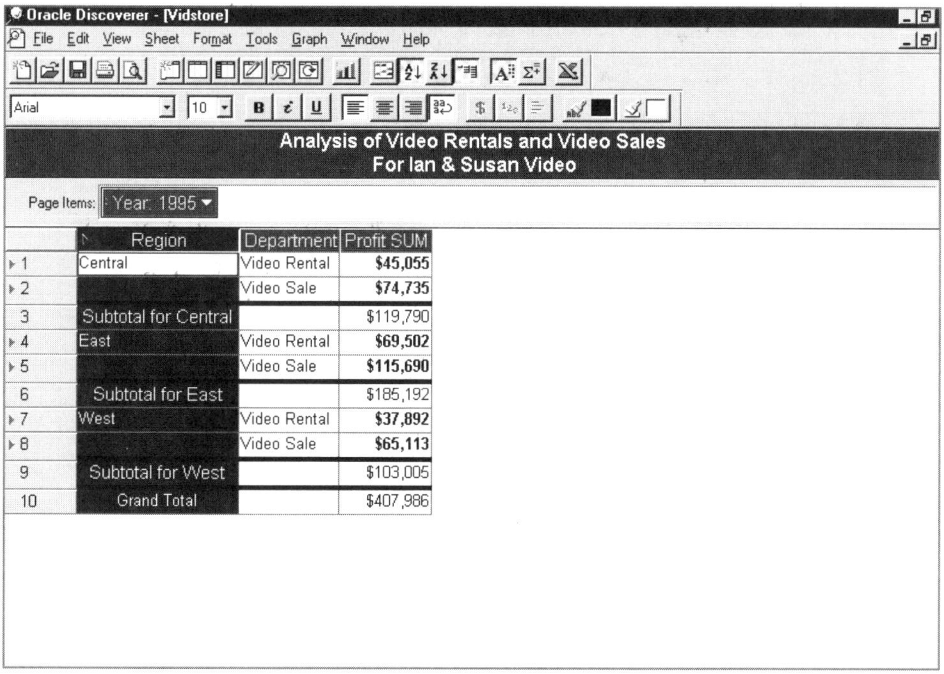

FIGURE 14-8. *Discoverer report output*

with a product that is both simple to implement and easily customizable while still providing you with the results that your organization will require to make sound decisions.

Cognos Impromptu

The purpose of this section is to take an in-depth look at Impromptu. Impromptu will be discussed from both the Administrator and the end-user perspectives. Impromptu is available in a number of different flavors: Impromptu Server (UNIX), Impromptu Web Server, and Impromptu Desktop. This book deals with Impromptu Desktop.

The heart of Impromptu is its catalog. A *catalog* contains information on how to connect to a database and acts as the end-users' interface into that

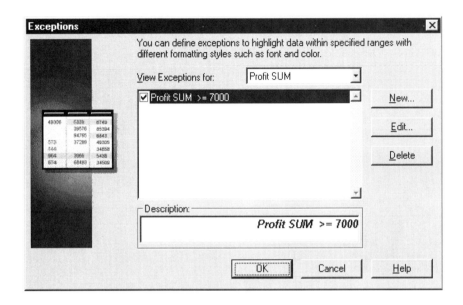

FIGURE 14-9. *Exceptions definition window*

	Region	City	Department	Profit SUM
▸1	Central	St. Louis	Video Sale	*$13,755*
▸2		St. Louis	Video Rental	*$7,420*
▸3		Nashville	Video Sale	$4,107
▸4		Nashville	Video Rental	$3,681
▸5		Minneapolis	Video Sale	$5,251
▸6		Minneapolis	Video Rental	$3,192
▸7		Louisville	Video Sale	*$19,264*
▸8		Louisville	Video Rental	*$12,194*
▸9		Dallas	Video Sale	$4,524
▸10		Dallas	Video Rental	$3,363
▸11		Cincinnati	Video Sale	*$22,036*
▸12		Cincinnati	Video Rental	*$12,087*
▸13		Chicago	Video Sale	$5,798
▸14		Chicago	Video Rental	$3,118

Analysis of Video Rentals and Video Sales For Ian & Susan Video — Page Items: Year: 1995 — Font

FIGURE 14-10. *Query results with new exception*

database. The catalog should be designed to provide a business view of the database. Building folders, columns, calculations, and filters creates this business view. As an administrator, you will be required to perform the following tasks:

1. Define the connection to the database.

2. Create the Catalog.

3. Add the required tables.

4. Define the required joins.

5. Create a folder structure.

6. Add profiles.

The following subsections will guide you through the tasks that you must complete to generate reports from Impromptu.

Define the Connection to the Database

The first step in creating an Impromptu application is to connect to the database. This is accomplished through the database definition section. It is a good idea to have your technical support people work with you through this step. Problems at this stage are often related to infrastructure and not to the product. Impromptu supports Oracle through a native driver via Net8. Under the "Database Details" tab, you simply supply the Net8 connection string.

TIP
Ping the database using the Net8 Ping utility to ensure Net8 has been installed properly. Generally, if this works, you are home free.

Create the Catalog

Now that you have defined your database definition, you are ready to create your catalog. Remember, a catalog is simply a file with a ".cat" extension. The Catalog definition screen is where you name your catalog, choose your catalog type and then tell Impromptu which database to connect to (using the definition that you created in the previous step). As well, a "Select tables" and an "Include all tables" radio button is clicked after you decide if all tables or a subset of all tables should be made available as the catalog is set up. By default, you are choosing which tables are to be included in the database. It is a good idea to leave this option set.

NOTE

If you choose "Include all tables," then unnecessary tables may enter into your catalog, such as system tables.

Impromptu supports four types of catalogs. The different catalog types support different needs and rollout strategies. Catalog types can be changed—for instance, you may start with a personal catalog for development purposes and then switch it to either a shared or distributed catalog. Listed next are the four catalog types and their suggested uses.

Personal

This is a catalog that is not to be shared by any other users. This type of catalog can be used to support local applications. A good example is connecting to a local Microsoft Access application that resides on a single-user workstation.

Shared

Designating a catalog as "shared" allows many people to connect simultaneously to the catalog. The deployment of this catalog is simple. Create the catalog and put it on a common networked drive where all users can see it.

Distributed

A distributed catalog is in many ways similar to a shared catalog. In the case of a distributed catalog, the first time the user opens the catalog, a copy of it is made onto their local PC. Subsequently, each time the catalog is opened locally, it synchronizes with the master catalog. Distributed catalogs can be used to allow users to make changes to their local catalog (add their own folders, local administration, etc.) while staying in synch with the master catalog.

Secure

This type of catalog is used if you want a user to just be able to run reports created on their behalf. By defining the catalog's properties, we can now move into selecting the data that we will require based on our reporting requirements.

Add Tables

Impromptu allows you to include some or all tables from a database into your catalog. If a table is not included in the Catalog, then there is no way for the end user to access that table. You also have the choice of including a table but not including all the columns from that table.

Consider the purpose of your catalog carefully. Only tables that are necessary to support this purpose should be included. Many organizations struggle with the question of whether to create one multipurpose catalog or to create many purpose-driven catalogs. Do I create a sales catalog and a separate accounting catalog? Do I create one catalog for both departments and administer it with user profiles (see "Add Profiles" section)? These questions need to be answered before embarking on catalog creation.

We are seeing more organizations lean towards the purpose-driven catalogs. The rationale is that the joins are easier to administer. Based upon your catalog definition, you then select the required tables that you need for this purpose. Figure 14-11 illustrates how your tables will be selected.

As you can see in Figure 14-11, Impromptu allows you to include Oracle tables and/or views into your catalog. Additionally, you can add a table as an alias. This feature allows you to resolve many complex join issues.

Once you have selected the tables and views to include in your catalog, you must decide how you would like Impromptu to handle the joins. Impromptu can define your joins for you automatically or you can elect to define the joins yourself. We recommend that you define your joins manually. Impromptu's automatic join generation capabilities may result in a less than perfect join strategy. In particular, an automatic join strategy can create unwanted loops.

Define the Required Joins

Impromptu allows you to put in place a join strategy for the end users. How the tables are joined is the responsibility of the administrator. The end user is shielded from the joins, and must only be concerned with the creation of

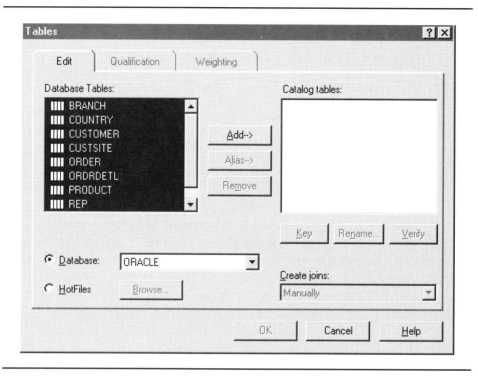

FIGURE 14-11. *Tables selection window*

reports. The end user should be able to select any columns from within a folder and Impromptu should return a correct result set. We will touch on this again when we discuss folders in the next section. Let us now look at how we define the required joins in Figure 14-12.

To create a join between two tables, you must first select the tables to be involved. Once the tables have been selected, you must then select the columns which are to form the join. Impromptu supports a wide array of joins, including equijoins, outer joins, complex joins, and compound joins. Remember that how tables are joined affects performance.

To assist you with your join strategy, Impromptu provides two helpful features. The "Analyze tab" feature checks your join strategy for possible problems such as loops and isolated tables. The "Test" feature allows you to choose tables to see how Impromptu resolves the join.

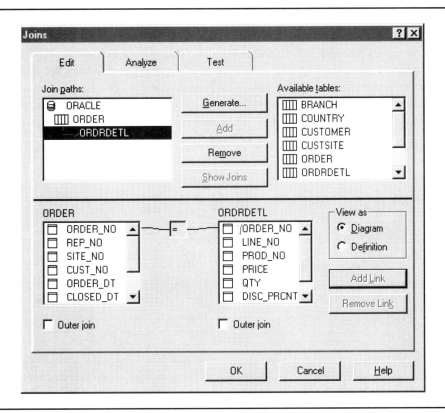

FIGURE 14-12. *Joins definition window*

Create a Folder Structure

Creating a folder is critical to the implementation of a successful catalog. The folder structure is what the end user views. This structure should reflect the business processes of an organization. It should be easy to navigate and contain English names (Discount Percentage, not Disc Prcnt).

Impromptu, by default, creates a folder for each table that has been added to the Catalog. It is a good convention to move all these tables into a folder named Admin. This folder is for administration purposes only and can be hidden from the common user. Organizations that do not modify the default strategy are often unsuccessful with their Impromptu rollout. I have seen implementations that have 50 root folders. These implementations offer little value to the end user.

We suggest renaming the subfolders and columns from within the Admin folder. These names should be proper English names that reflect terminology used within the business. This provides consistency as you create further folders. Next, organize the folder in a fashion that makes sense to the business. Folders can contain columns from any number of different tables. The key is to have columns grouped together in a manner that the user would expect. The following illustrates how to manage your folders:

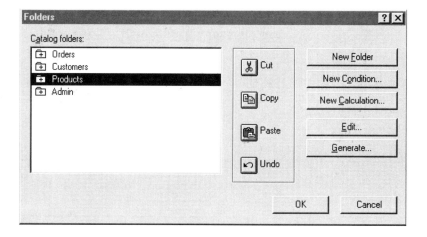

Furthermore, you can add value to the catalog by including calculations and conditions. The inclusion of calculations and conditions in the catalog ensures standard definitions are being employed throughout the organization.

We try to create major folder groups that contain all relevant subfolders underneath. This strategy causes duplication of folders but makes navigation simple for the user. Within a major folder, any combination of columns should result in a valid join. Again, this is why the ability to alias tables is so important—it permits you to use the same table in different join combinations. At the completion of the folder definition, you then move into defining profiles for your model.

Add Profiles

Impromptu has a variety of useful administrative functions that control access and use. Impromptu allows you to add user classes, which define what a user can see and do. It is this functionality that allows you to roll out one multipurpose catalog to many users.

It is not necessary to use profiles, and some organizations don't, but it can be useful. Consider the following—you can hide certain folders, tables, or columns from an end user. Your security may require that salespeople obtain information about their sales but restrict them from seeing what margin they are achieving.

Filters can be applied based on selected values from the database. As an example, you could restrict a user from viewing a certain product type. The key is that the catalog is the central point of administration. A variety of different users can be supported through the same catalog. In Figure 14-13, the folder access area is particularly useful in ensuring the database is used in a secure manner. This area allows you to grant users access to folders that would be of interest to them. The Governor tab will allow you to place restrictions on a number of different areas, which can ensure optimum performance. Consider sorting restrictions, protection against cross-product queries, limits on data retrieval, etc.

Congratulations! You have completed your catalog and are now ready to deploy it to your end users.

Impromptu from the End-user Perspective

The purpose of this section is to discuss the functionality that Impromptu delivers to end users. Impromptu offers the same interface regardless of the database platform. The end users are not aware if they are connected to a local Dbase database or a remote Oracle database.

Getting Started

Remember that in its simplest form, a catalog is just a file. The first step in working with Impromptu is to open the catalog. Depending on how the catalog has been set up, you will have to select a user class, enter a password,

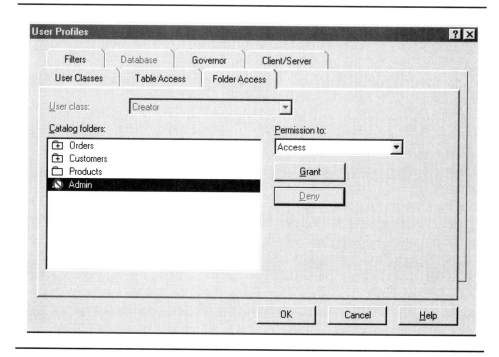

FIGURE 14-13. *Folder Access Control*

and enter a database user ID and password (the Oracle user ID and password can be embedded in the catalog). This login window is shown here:

You will then connect to the required database and catalog while Impromptu handles all the administration.

Creating a report in Impromptu is a very simple process. The process is quite similar to creating a report in Word. First of all, you choose a template. The template predetermines how your data will be displayed. As an example, if you want to create a professional memorandum, Word has a template to assist you with the design. A screen listing the types of templates that you have available after an initial Impromptu installation is shown here:

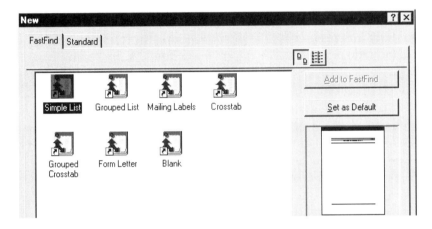

Similarly, Impromptu has templates that support most of the popular report styles. The most common template is the Simple List. The Simple List report displays each record as a row. Once you have selected a template, you will be presented with the Query dialog box where you specify items such as what data to retrieve, how to sort the output, what type of summarizing (grouping) to perform, and the conditions for data selection (referred to as filtering).

The Query dialog box is where you choose which columns you want displayed on the report. You are presented with the same folder structure that you designed in the Administration section. Simply navigate the folder structure to locate the columns you require for the report and then double-click it or highlight it and then press the Add-> button, or drag and drop it to the Query section. If it is easy to navigate through this section and locate the columns you require, then you probably have a good folder design in place. Remember, all the end users care about is how easy it is to create their reports.

Impromptu allows you to apply sorting, grouping, and filtering prior to displaying the report. This method is the most efficient manner of creating a report. However, these options can also be applied afterwards, which is what we will do. In many cases, to get started, users begin using the Simple List template, which presents their report in a familiar columnar and tabular format.

Impromptu now displays the report using the first 100 records, based on the selection criteria. At this stage, Impromptu allows you to apply formats, rename columns, and move columns, all without requerying the database. Next, you may want to apply a filter, group your data, and add headers. Each of these functions can be applied by simply highlighting a cell and then clicking the accompanying icon. If you don't like the result, you can simply press Undo (Impromptu allows you to apply 10 Undo's by default).

To add column totals, simply highlight the column containing the values you want to sum and then click on the Total icon. Impromptu adds a footer and a total for every level of grouping that has been defined. Figure 14-14 shows you how the report might look after applying these functions.

This report can now be saved and be made available to other users. Impromptu saves all reports with an ".imr" extension. Remember that all Impromptu saves is the query (the formatting and the SQL), and not the data. The following listing contains the SQL that is used to create the report:

```
select c19 as c1,
       c18 as c2,
       c22 as c3,
       c21 as c4,
       rsum(c21 for c19,c18) as c5,
       rsum(c21 for c19,c18) as c6,
       rsum(c21) as c7,
       c20 as c8,
       rsum(c20 for c19,c18) as c9,
       rsum(c20 for c19,c18) as c10,
       rsum(c20) as c11
from
(select t1."PROD_LINE" as c18,
       t1."PROD_TYPE" as c19,
       (t1."PROD_PRICE" - t1."PROD_COST") as c20,
       t1."PROD_COST" as c21,
       t1."PRODUCT" as c22
```

```
from "PRODUCT" t1
where (t1."prod_line" in ('TENTS                   ',
                          'BACK PACKS               '))
order by c19 asc,c18 asc
) d1
```

The SQL generated can always be viewed from under the "Report Profile" tab. This is very useful in determining how Impromptu produced your result set. In particular, you can see which tables have been used in intermediate joins. Impromptu provides solutions for exporting the data to other programs. You can save your reports as HTML, Excel, Word, ASCII, and a host of other popular formats.

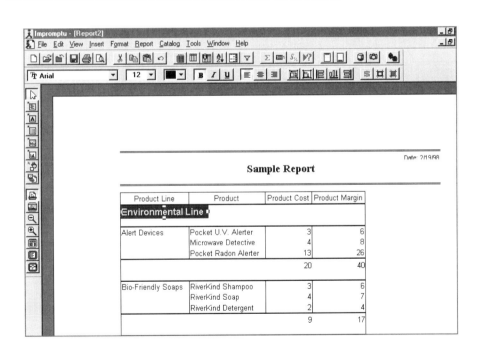

FIGURE 14-14. *Formatted report*

Summary

Query tools allow you to extract data from your warehouse on a defined or ad hoc basis. They form an important component of your data warehousing strategy. Just as you must decide on a database for your warehouse, you must complement it with the proper tools. By following our approach to selecting a product for your reporting requirements, with additional criteria based on your organization's requirements, you will select a tool that is right for you and your organization.

Chapter 15 discusses relational OLAP—online analytical processing—and aggregate navigators. Analysis is the key feature provided to the manager through participation in the design, delivery, and deployment of the data warehouse solution. When we speak of OLAP, that familiar adage "turning data into information" springs to the forefront of our minds. It almost reminds us of Old McDonald—here an OLAP, there an OLAP, everywhere an OLAP—Old McDonald sold his mainframe EIEIO....

CHAPTER
15

Relational OLAP and Aggregate Navigators

nline analytical processing (OLAP) is one of the technologies for querying the warehouse—but not the only technology. OLAP is particularly suited for rapidly analyzing large quantities of data. It is also frequently misunderstood. In this chapter, we will discuss OLAP—what it is and what it isn't. If you manage to complete this particularly grueling chapter, you should understand the following:

- What constitutes OLAP...and what doesn't

- What the two most popular approaches to storing data for OLAP are and what you need to know to evaluate these technologies in light of your business requirements

- How to cut through some of the vendor noise in the relational OLAP (ROLAP) field

- How to improve your ROLAP performance by optimizing storage of data in your relational OLAP environment

OLAP: A Four-letter Word?

Well, OK, perhaps OLAP is an acronym, not a word—but, hey, *you* try to sit in a moderately priced hotel room in Chicago at midnight and write entertaining stuff on the topic of data warehousing. Now that I've gotten that little poke at my employer off my chest, what is OLAP?

OLAP stands for *online analytical processing.* OLAP constitutes a set of technologies that are great for summarizing and analyzing huge quantities of data. E. F. Codd, one of the fathers of the relational database, developed a set of 12 rules to which OLAP systems must adhere. However, these rules are somewhat controversial, in part because they were developed in conjunction with Arbor Software, a vendor of OLAP technologies.

In lieu of a clear, independent definition, we need some way to describe OLAP. Most data warehousing professionals would agree that OLAP systems must support the following functions: multidimensionality, drill-down, rotation, and multiple modes of view. Let's look at these functions in more detail.

Multidimensionality

The concept of multidimensionality is discussed in many chapters in this book—especially Chapters 5 and 17, which describe star schema design. In an OLAP context, this means that online analytical systems allow users to view measures of organizational performance broken down by the dimensions of those measures.

Let's review the concept of multidimensionality to refresh your memory and put you into the frame of mind of a user rather than a data architect. If you think about it, of all things, bloodthirsty business people are most interested in how well they, and their organizations, are performing. For example, have you ever dealt with software sales people? We have a standing rule that salespeople, even those with whom we are friendly, are barred from calling us during the months of March, June, September, and December. Why? Because these are the last months in most software companies' fiscal quarters. During these months, salespeople undergo a metamorphosis—trying to make sure that they push enough product to meet their sales quotas for that quarter. As a friendly hint, if you can stomach these people during those months, they are great times to buy software. This is because salespeople are frequently willing to discount heavily, and stretch expense accounts on lavish meals, to increase their total sales for the quarter. Please keep this between you and us. Our point here is that the salespeople and the managers above them are obsessed with total sales and how that total will compare to their quotas. Thus, if you think about it, sales, quota, and the difference between sales and quota are the measures by which these people's performances are judged. Your friendly salesperson will either make the next boat payment or be looking for a fast food job, depending on how these figures end up. Note that a synonym for performance measure is *performance metric*.

Now, suppose you are the vice president of sales, responsible for the performance of 50 salespeople. At the end of December, you have a stack of 40 bonus checks and ten pink slips on your desk. How will you distribute these? Well, by performance, of course. And how will you see how well each of your salespeople performed? By using your OLAP system, of course. So, you turn on the system and you see that sales were 50 billion yen and quota was 46 billion yen. This helps you because—hey, wait a minute, this doesn't help at all! Unless you can break those sales and quota numbers down by salesperson name, this information is useless! And, in fact, since all you see is a total figure, you don't even know if these sales were for the fourth quarter, the whole year, or for the past five years.

You quickly realize that for your OLAP system to have any value, it has to break down performance by salesperson, quarter, and date. And then you start to fantasize, "Wow, wouldn't it be great if the system also let me break down sales by product? Then I could quickly tell which products are selling well and which are weak."

Clearly, you need more information in your OLAP system than just performance measures. You need to see that performance information inside a useful framework. You need to see those measures broken down by their dimensions. For example, you would like to see sales broken down by things like:

- Order date

- Ship date

- Salesperson

- Product sold

- Customer

Dimensions thus combine to describe, to frame, measures. The exact measures and dimensions tracked by your system will vary according to your industry, your strategy, and sometimes, sadly, even by the kinds of information that your systems capture. After all, while McDonald's might want to know the address of every one of their customers, have you ever had your address typed into a McDonald's cash register?

It's also interesting to note that two companies in the same industry might measure themselves differently depending on their strategies and management philosophies. While a company that specializes in sit-down pizza restaurants might follow a measure called *average number of patrons per table*, this is meaningless to a pizza delivery chain—but that chain might have a measure called *average delivery time*. This, in turn, likely has little meaning to the sit-down chain.

OLAP queries are multidimensional. A multidimensional query provides data about performance measures, broken down by one or more dimensions of those measures. These queries can also be filtered by dimension and/or measure value. The next listing details a typical OLAP query for a music (record, tape and CD) wholesaler:

```
QUERY              :  Show me the monthly trend in sales of pop
                      music for 1997 broken down by media.
MEASURE / METRIC :  Sales
BREAK DOWN         :  Month and media
FILTERS            :  Year = 1997 and Category = Pop
```

Figure 15-1 shows how the filtering is addressed as a query is translated into electronic format for delivery to a hungry user community. The X-axis presents periods and the Y-axis three popular media types.

Drill-down

Drill-down, drill-down, drill-down. One of the first data warehousing benefits sold to user management is a concept called *drill-down*. The term then permeates organizations to the point that when project teams are

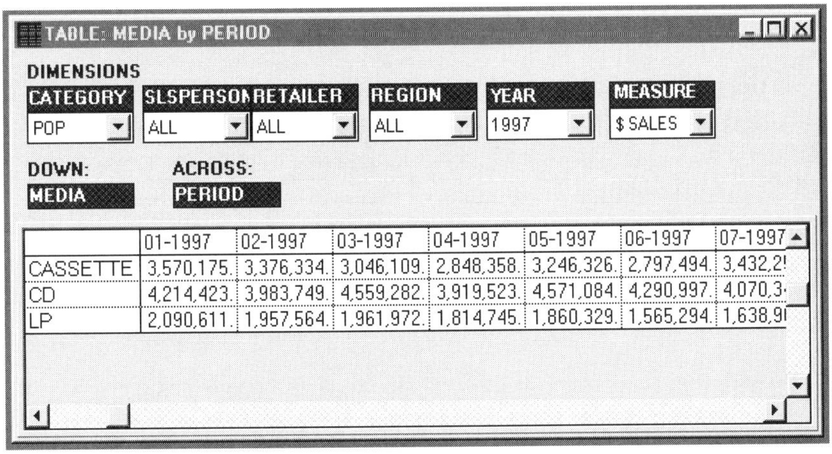

FIGURE 15-1. *OLAP electronic representation for music wholesaler*

assembled, upper management knows the warehouse simply as, "that drill-down computer thing." Then people like us are brought in to build that "drill-down thing." So, what is that drill-down thing? The brief answer is that to drill-down is to break a summary item into its detailed components. Let's look at an easy example to define this familiar concept.

To understand drill-down, think a bit about dimensions. As we've already said, OLAP systems show data in terms of measures and dimensions. While we didn't mention it before, most dimensions are hierarchical—they have clear levels or hierarchies. For example, let's consider the date dimension. It really consists of a series of levels as shown next:

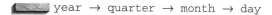 year → quarter → month → day

The quarters start on January 1, April 1, July 1, and October 1. The months, as you would expect, use the pattern January 1, February 1, March 1, and so on through December 1. Days are normal days, with 365 per year. Thus, an OLAP system that adheres to this date dimension would allow users to show information broken down by any level in this hierarchy.

NOTE

Not all dimensions are as simple as the date dimension. In fact, the date dimension might not be as simple as it seems upon first examination!

Let's spend a bit of time on this note before getting on with it. A common complication is multiple parallel hierarchies. For example, perhaps your company also views data using the concept of seasons. Seasons start on March 21, June 21, September 21, and December 21. Just like a standard month, each of these seasons can be tracked down to a day. The Season hierarchy of the date dimension might look like:

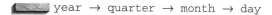 seasonal year → season → day

While it doesn't start on January 1, the seasonal year is simply a way of grouping four seasons together. In analyzing data, you might want to compare the seasonal year starting 21 March, 1998 with that starting 21 March, 1999. Note that year and seasonal year both share a common atomic data element: day. These are just different ways of viewing the date dimension. They are multiple parallel hierarchies of that dimension, as illustrated here:

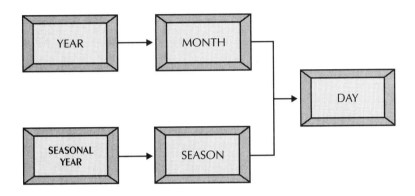

When you think about it, just about every query in an OLAP system is a summary or aggregate query. Users ask questions like, "What are total sales broken down by month and state for 1998 and 1999?" or "Can you show me the trend of employee count by month for the past two years for each facility we have in Europe?" These aren't asking for detailed information about one transaction but, rather, for summary information about large groups of records. However, users frequently want to view highly summarized data and then navigate down to less summarized data.

Imagine you're a manager again, this time for a large Canadian company. Now you're trying to figure out where potential problems might lie. You start by asking the following question, "What were total sales for 1997?" The result is a table that looks something like this:

Sum of SALES	YEAR	
	1997	Grand Total
Total	568	568

You then start to think, "That's great," but the following questions (which are pretty much just different ways of asking the same question) immediately leap to mind:

- Well, $568 is a pretty nice number. But, what exactly does it mean?

- How does that break down by month?

- What are the monthly components that make up the $568?

- Can we break this figure down by the date dimension?

- Can we drill-down from the total for 1997 into the total by month?

You click your mouse to drill-down into the 1997 total to break it down by month. Your result appears:

Sum of SALES	YEAR MONTH												1997 Total	Grand Total
	1997												1997 Total	Grand Total
	Jan	Feb	Mar	Apr	May	Jun	Jul	Aug	Sep	Oct	Nov	Dec		
Total	45	48	43	43	44	45	52	51	53	48	47	49	568	568

Thus, drilling down is simply breaking a figure into its component parts. People generally drill-down into the hierarchies of a dimension—from year to month in the date dimension, for example. A related concept is called *drilling across.* Drilling across is a powerful variation on the drilling-down concept. Drilling across allows you to drill-down into a completely different dimension rather than simply within the hierarchy of one dimension.

For example, suppose you thought that rather than drilling from the 1997 total to the months in 1997, it would be more interesting to drill from 1997 total sales to that total broken down by product line. Instead of the table just shown, you would drill across into the product dimension and have a result similar to this:

Sum of SALES	YEAR PROD LINE		1997 Total	Grand Total
	1997		1997 Total	Grand Total
	Beer	Hockey		
Total	394	174		568

Now you see total sales for 1997 broken down by your two product lines: Hockey supplies and beer (we did mention that this is a Canadian company, didn't we?). After this, you are free to drill-down and across to your heart's delight. By the way, one more interesting point—you can also drill from a detail figure back up to a total. Many OLAP tools will allow this. While this is frequently called *drilling up*, we believe the correct term is actually *rolling up*.

Rotation or Slicing and Dicing

Another function that OLAP systems support is rotation. Rotation is also sometimes called *slicing and dicing*. Rotation allows you to change your view perspective. OLAP systems can display data broken down on both the X- and Y-axis of a report. For example, the next illustration shows a report broken down by month on the Y-axis and product line on the X-axis.

YEAR	1997 ▼		
Sum of Sales	PROD LINE		
MONTH	Beer	Hockey	Grand Total
Jan	25	20	45
Feb	25	23	48
Mar	25	18	43
Apr	28	15	43
May	32	12	44
Jun	35	10	45
July	45	7	52
Aug	46	5	51
Sep	44	9	53
Oct	33	15	48
Nov	30	17	47
Dec	26	23	49
Grand Total	394	174	568

But, suddenly you realize that you would rather see the data with month on the X-axis and product line on the Y-axis. What do you do? Rotate, of course! With one or two mouse drags you can rotate your data to look like this:

Sum of SALES	MONTH												
PROD LINE	Jan	Feb	Mar	Apr	May	Jun	Jul	Aug	Sep	Oct	Nov	Dec	Grand Total
Beer	25	25	25	28	32	35	45	46	44	33	30	26	394
Hockey	20	23	18	15	12	10	7	5	9	15	17	23	174
Grand Total	45	48	43	43	44	45	52	51	53	48	47	49	568

From here, you can drill and rotate further. For example, the next illustration takes the report as just shown and drills down into the product line dimension to the actual products within the hockey line. The whole point is that between drill-down and rotation, the OLAP user should be able to rapidly cut through the data, looking for important nuggets of information.

Year	(All) ▼												
PROD LINE	Hockey ▼												
Sum of SALES	MONTH												
PROD	Jan	Feb	Mar	Apr	May	Jun	Jul	Aug	Sep	Oct	Nov	Dec	Grand Total
Mask	6	7	6	5	4	3	2	1	2	4	5	6	51
Puck	4	5	3	2	1	1	0	0	1	3	3	5	28
Stick	10	11	9	8	7	6	5	4	6	8	9	12	95
Grand Total	20	23	18	15	12	10	7	5	9	15	17	23	174

Multiple View Modes

Before starting this section, find a stopwatch. Take your time, we'll wait. Okay, on the word 'go', start the stopwatch, look at the previous illustration, and find the months with the lowest sales level for any hockey product. Once you find it, stop the watch. Ready, set...go! What was the month? What was the product? How long did it take you to get these answers? Now, do the same thing while looking at the illustration shown in Figure 15-2. Ready, set...go!

How long did it take to get the same information? If you are a normal human being, and if this example has any merit whatsoever, you probably found the answers much quicker with the chart in Figure 15-2. Our point here is that sometimes graphs provide insight into data that might not be available with simple tables. Thus, most OLAP systems provide ways to view data in a variety of formats, not just simple tables. In addition to charts, some OLAP tools allow you to display your data in maps, with each section color coded to reflect sales in that region.

NOTE
We generally expect to see a variety of query technologies used against a single data warehouse.

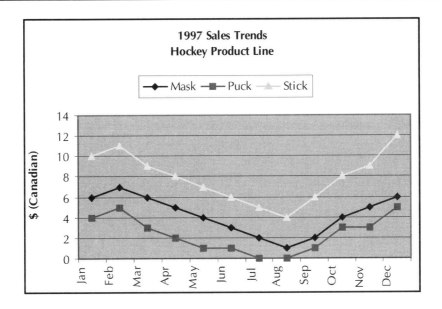

FIGURE 15-2.   *Sales by product line chart*

To expand on that note, it is very possible that the warehouse is accessed with both report writers and OLAP tools. It might, in addition, be accessed with geographic information system, or GIS, tools. GIS tools excel at reflecting the geographic components of data. While each tool we've mentioned is intended for a specific type of analysis or reporting, they do have a certain amount of overlapping functionality.

Closure on OLAP

So, given these qualities: multidimensionality, drill-down, rotation, and multiple view modes, we must ask a quick question. Where did we refer to a method for storing data? Unless our publisher has taken great liberties when editing our materials, you will find this reference nowhere.

NOTE
OLAP is a user interface concept—not a data storage technology.

As we'll see later, there are various database technologies for storing data to be accessed by OLAP applications. In fact, certain vendors would have you believe that unless you use their technology, you're not doing real OLAP. Don't believe it! OLAP is a type of application for querying and viewing data—it exists regardless of how that data is stored. The data can be stored in a relational database, a multidimensional database, a flat file, punched cards, or Crayola-based drawing. So long as the user interface does what an OLAP interface must do, OLAP lives.

Another interesting point: Whenever the user changes the filter, drills down, or rotates her data, she is really issuing a new query. Now, an OLAP user will do a lot of filtering, drilling down, and rotating. Remember also that the vast majority of these queries return summaries of thousands or millions of rows of data. Thus, whatever data structures you use to support your OLAP system, they must provide rapid response to summary-level queries.

Because such a rapid response time is required, it is not unheard of for OLAP to be performed against data marts tuned for specific subject areas rather than against enterprise data warehouses. To handle their broad, diverse nature, enterprise-wide data warehouses are frequently more normalized than simple star schema. Thus, data is often extracted from the warehouse into targeted data marts to achieve the performance necessary for OLAP use. As discussed in the "ROLAP and MOLAP" section, these data marts might be contained in either relational or multidimensional databases.

One more point, those who frequently use pivot tables in Microsoft Excel might guess that many of the examples in this chapter were created with that tool. That guess would be correct. While they don't easily support drill-down, Excel pivot tables are close to being an OLAP environment. The data store for this OLAP environment is usually a spreadsheet containing data, although it can also be a query from an external database. In fact, Arbor Software, a vendor of multidimensional databases (see our discussion of MOLAP next) uses Excel as the default user interface for querying its database.

Now that we've reviewed the basic concepts of OLAP, let's look at some of the common technologies underlying OLAP tools. Some call the following discussion OTW—OLAP technology wars. Enjoy.

ROLAP and MOLAP

Technology has a way of spawning fanatics. Fanatics, in turn, seem particularly adept at spawning conflict. Anyone who has tried to put a Windows PC on the desk of a Macintosh bigot knows what we mean. Perhaps you've seen other cases. They come in a variety of flavors:

- WordPerfect bigots

- Mainframe bigots

- DB2 bigots

The point is not that Macintoshes, WordPerfect, mainframes, and DB2 are bad technologies. In fact, the point may be exactly the opposite. But something about these technologies seems to make their adherents particularly stubborn.

Data warehousing has its own set of fanatics who fight major battles in their own wars. Perhaps you've heard the terms MOLAP and ROLAP (if you haven't—and you care—then we recommend that you go back and reread the earlier part of this chapter). Well, the choice between ROLAP and MOLAP is the warehousing equivalent of Greece and Troy. We have actually witnessed arguments where professionals with competing points of view have viciously ripped each other's limbs off in efforts to force their points of view.

The funny thing about these arguments is that neither side is right. At the same time, both sides are right. Let's start making sense of this mess by describing ROLAP and MOLAP.

ROLAP and MOLAP are simply terms that refer to common methods for storing data used by OLAP systems. ROLAP stands for *relational online analytical processing* while MOLAP stands for *multidimensional online analytical processing*. In either case, the user interface is still an OLAP interface. The only difference is the database technology used to store the data that feeds the user interface.

One term that you will likely encounter when evaluating OLAP database technologies is *hypercube*. Hypercube is simply another way of referring to the dataset you wish to analyze. In attempting to make the concept of multidimensional analysis easier for novices to understand, the OLAP industry invented this twenty-dollar word. It is intended to imply multidimensionality, and is usually accompanied by a poorly explained picture like that in Figure 15-3.

This picture is intended to show that you can locate the value for a measure based on its dimensional coordinates. For example, each cell in the cube in Figure 15-3 holds information about the measure sales. You can locate any sales figure given its product, time, and geography coordinates.

As an aside (as though we haven't already strayed enough), we've always objected to the term hypercube. Hypercube implies three dimensions; a dimensional database is actually a space comprised of any number of dimensions. We, thus, prefer the term dataspace (sometimes seen with an initial capital letter, as in Dataspace Inc.) to hypercube.

Given the technology trends of the past few years, most of us are well versed in relational database technology; we now have a look at a sometimes scary, sometimes misunderstood, but always cheerful partner to this technology—Mr. multidimensional database.

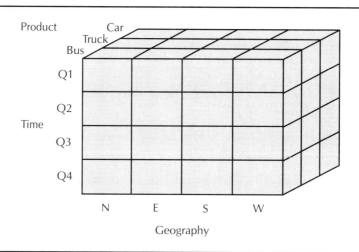

FIGURE 15-3. *Simple hypercube*

Multidimensional Databases (MDDB)

As we noted before, while OLAP is a user interface concept, there are two primary technologies for storing the data used in OLAP applications. These two technologies are multidimensional databases and relational databases. You probably know a bit about relational databases. The following few sections provide some background on multidimensional databases.

Arrays

A multidimensional database is just that—a database, just like the Oracle Server. Data is loaded into, stored in, and queried from that database. A variety of programs can access that data. The major difference between MDDBs and RDBMSs is in how they store data. Relational databases store their data in a series of tables and columns. Multidimensional databases, on the other hand, store their data in large multidimensional arrays. For example, in an MDDB world, you might refer to a sales figure as sales with a date, product, and location component of 12-1-1998, car, and south, respectively.

Multidimensional Database Vendors

Believe it or not, Oracle actually sells two database engines. You are probably familiar with its traditional Server product, currently called Oracle8. But, Oracle also sells a multidimensional database. Acquired with its purchase of IRI a few years ago, Oracle Express Server (OES) is a leading multidimensional database. Chapter 17 contains more information about Express. Much to Larry Ellison's chagrin, there are some other vendors of multidimensional databases. The largest competitor is Essbase, by Arbor Software.

Just like relational databases, there are a variety of tools for accessing multidimensional databases. Many users access these databases using add-ins to spreadsheets, like Excel. Other tools are intended solely as multidimensional query tools/front ends. Tools like Cognos' Powerplay can access multidimensional servers. (Powerplay can, in many ways, be considered the multidimensional equivalent of Microsoft Access. It provides a user interface that not only accesses multidimensional servers but also contains its own desktop multidimensional database.)

Finally, just like relational databases, custom programs can be written to access MDDBs. Many of these databases, Express included, come with their own programming languages. Some can also be queried with other programming languages like Visual Basic.

Is an MDDB a Data Warehouse?

For a while there was some confusion as to whether a data warehouse could be housed in a multidimensional database. Multidimensional databases are wonderful for analyzing narrowly focused sets of data. As such, they can be strong tools for data marts. They are, on the other hand, not capable of supporting the breadth of data required to support an enterprise data warehouse. In a few pages, we will compare multidimensional and relational databases for OLAP data storage. This comparison will further address some of the reasons why multidimensional databases are really data mart tools. Now that we know all there is to know about MDDB, let's back up a bit and look at relational databases.

Relational Databases (RDBMS)

The other primary method for storing data for OLAP is in a relational database. The most common data structure for ROLAP data is the star schema or some variant, like the snowflake schema. In fact, many ROLAP query tools require a particular approach to schema design, such as a star schema. But heed our constant droning: OLAP is a user interface, not a data storage concept. If you encounter tools that provide an OLAP user interface while querying traditional, nonstar schemas, they are still OLAP tools. So…

What Really Defines ROLAP?

A number of query tool vendors profess to offer ROLAP tools. We don't believe that each of these offerings is actually true ROLAP. Tools that don't adhere to the definition of true ROLAP tools can be just as powerful as—in fact, can be more powerful than—true ROLAP tools. These nontrue ROLAP tools are usually some hybrid of other types of query technologies such as combinations of report writers and MOLAP tools. It is important, though, to understand true ROLAP. This understanding will help you determine the best OLAP approach for your application. This should thus help you deliver a successful project. Delivering a successful project could very well save your professional dignity and, perhaps, your job—more proof of a better life through data warehousing. (As a note, if this advice does, indeed, save your job, please recommend this book to your associates, friends, and family—thus returning the favor by saving our jobs.)

The section in this chapter called "The Three Faces of ROLAP" addresses this issue of tools that call themselves ROLAP but don't conform to our definition of true ROLAP tools. To us, a true ROLAP tool adheres to three rules:

- It supports the basic OLAP concepts we've discussed

- It stores its data in some relational database

- It supports some form of aggregate navigation

Let's expand on these three points.

ADHERES TO BASIC OLAP CONCEPTS   True ROLAP is a form of OLAP where the data is stored in a relational database. Thus, like any OLAP application, a true ROLAP application must support multidimensionality, drill-down, rotation, and multiple modes of view.

RELATIONAL DATA STORAGE   This one should be self-explanatory. To have true ROLAP, the application's data must be stored in a relational database. Let's take this a bit further. The data in that relational database must be understandable by any program with access to that database. For example, suppose you stored data in a relational database but before you put the data into the database, you used a programming trick to translate the data into reverse Swahili notation (RSN—OK, yes, we made this one up). Another program reading that database would have to have an RSN interpreter to make your data understandable to users. Suppose, on the other hand, that your program simply stored the data in English. Then, any program that could read your database could use the data it contained.

AGGREGATE NAVIGATION   Aggregate navigation is a bit more complex. One of the things we've mentioned about data warehouses is that they frequently contain summary tables. For example, your warehouse or mart might contain a detailed, atomic-level table of sales information broken down by customer, the products purchased, and the date on which each purchase took place. Let's suppose that this table contains 400 million rows.

As users access the system, you may realize that there are frequent queries looking solely at sales broken down by customer and year, regardless of the products that were purchased or the days on which those purchases took place. As an attentive warehouse manager, you build a summary table to support these queries. The new table, being a high-level summary, contains only about one million rows.

Building the summary is pretty easy (of course in real life, maintaining it is probably a bit harder than in the dream world of books). The query to populate the summary table, in its simplest form, probably looks something like the next listing:

```
create table year_sum_sales as
   select year, customer,sum(sales)
     from atomic_sales
   group by year,customer;
```

Now you have created not only a summary table, but also a problem. How are users going to know that the summary table exists? And even if they know that it exists, how will they know when to use it? And when not to?

Enter the aggregate navigator. Aggregate navigators are software components that automatically select the best table for each query. The best table is usually defined as the smallest available table that can answer the user's request. Remember that all queries could be run against the atomic level table, but we create summary tables to speed query performance.

To perform this function, the aggregate navigator knows which summaries exist and the size of each one. Depending on the query tool, this knowledge is obtained either by the warehouse administrator telling the tool how many rows are in each table or by some automated routine that periodically checks the sizes of each table and records these size values. Imagine that you're the aggregate navigator shown next. Which way should you go? Left or right? Six of one, a half dozen of the other.

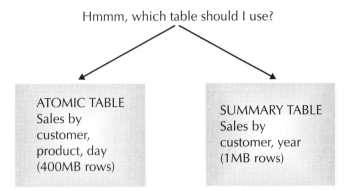

Hmmm, which table should I use?

ATOMIC TABLE
Sales by
customer,
product, day
(400MB rows)

SUMMARY TABLE
Sales by
customer, year
(1MB rows)

Let's see how you might approach three different queries.

- Computicus, a new clerk, just got an angry call from Jones. It seems he thinks we charged him twice for his purchase on March 13 (of course, we couldn't possibly have done this—after all, we use computers. Right?). We need to see what we sold to Jones on 13 March. Which table should we query? Well, given the fact that the summary table contains only annual data for each customer, we couldn't possibly get the answer from the summary table. Thus, we have to query the atomic-level table.

- Spasticus, the company's vice-president of sales, calls with a request, "What were our total sales to the Everding Company in 1997?" What table do we use now? Could we answer the question from the atomic-level table? Well, yes, we could. Could we answer the question with the summary table? Well, yes, we could. Which table is smaller? The summary. Thus, our choice is clear.

- The company's president, Cirrhosis, calls asking for a report showing the trend in total sales for the last three years. Which table to hit here? Well, you could answer this with the atomic-level table. You could also answer it with the summary table. In either case, you will have to aggregate many rows. You therefore choose the summary table. With it, you will have to aggregate far fewer rows than you would if you used the atomic-level table. This should provide much quicker response.

Aggregate tables coupled with aggregate navigation is one tool for improving query performance. Of course, several others exist. These include things like:

- Index creation

- Data restructuring

- Hardware upgrade

Aggregate navigation can occur in a few places. The concept first gained prominence in ROLAP tools such as MicroStrategy's DSS Agent and Information Advantage's Decision Suite. Still, there is a better place for aggregate navigation. That place is directly in the database engine. If your database engine provides aggregate navigation, then you could use this feature regardless of which query tool you use. Sadly, this feature hasn't been baked into Oracle8…yet. But, there are tools that mimic it. For example, Hewlett Packard's Intelligent Warehouse product can intercept your queries and automatically direct them to the best aggregate tables.

Tools that contain aggregate navigators are sometimes referred to as being "aggregate aware." By the way, in marketing its relational OLAP tool, Discoverer 3, Oracle uses the term "automatic summary redirection" rather than aggregate navigation. Clearly, market share has its advantages—the ability to author your own dictionary is only one of them.

In all honesty, Oracle Discoverer breaks some new ground. It is one of the few tools in the marketplace that integrates report writing with true ROLAP functionality. Let's discuss this for a minute.

Differentiating ROLAP from Online Report Writing

It's important to differentiate between ROLAP tools and report writers like Impromptu, Esperant, and IQ. Report writers provide two basic functions:

1. They allow users to point and click to generate and issue SQL calls.

2. They allow users to format the results.

While they access relational data, report writers do not support the other basic concepts of true ROLAP. They do not, for example:

- Support the basic concepts of OLAP (multidimensionality, drill-down, rotation, and multiple view modes)

- Provide aggregate navigation

True ROLAP tools vendors—who are they? Well, the list includes companies and products like:

- Oracle Discoverer 3

- MicroStrategy DSS Agent

- Information Advantage Decision Suite

- Platinum Beacon

Return to Troy: ROLAP Vs. MOLAP

Given that rather wordy description of the relational and multidimensional approaches to OLAP data storage, it's time to enter the fray. Which is better? Well, as is all too often the case, the answer is, it depends. Let's discuss these technologies along a few different dimensions (no pun intended). Please keep in mind that these are generalizations. They may or may not apply to any particular product or application.

Performance

Many people evaluating reporting technologies fail to recognize that there are two key aspects of performance. The first is query time, the amount of time it takes to respond to any user's query. The second is load time, the amount of time required to populate data structures and perform those calculations necessary to prepare the system for use.

QUERY PERFORMANCE   Relational OLAP systems respond just like any other relational database application. Sometimes the answers come back quickly and sometimes not so quickly. Administrators can work to improve response time by building indexes and summary tables, but performance may still be hard to predict and, for certain operations, simply slow.

Multidimensional databases, on the other hand, provide a fairly predictable, and fast, response to virtually every query. This is due, in part, to the fact that multidimensional databases precalculate many, and sometimes all, possible values in their hypercubes. For example, imagine an application that reports monthly employee turnover for the past year. Also, assume that this data has only two dimensions: month and department. Assume that the company has 10 departments. (See Figure 15-4.) Given the traditional limitations of solar-based calendars, you can safely assume that there are 12 months in a year.

As we noted before, multidimensional databases are comprised of multidimensional arrays. Thus, the array holding the atomic-level data in this application would have 120 cells—12 months (JAN to DEC across the top) and 10 departments (1 to 10 along the side).

In addition, the multidimensional database will, when loaded with data, precalculate all combinations and summaries of that data. For example, if we had three dimensions, the database would create

- A three-dimensional atomic-level array

- A two-dimensional array of data for dims 1 and 2

- A two-dimensional array for dims 2 and 3

- A high-level summary array broken down by dim 1

- A high-level summary array broken down by dim 2

- A high-level summary array broken down by dim 3

In this case, because we have just two dimensions, there are no other combinations, but there are summaries. Thus, the database will also store two one-dimensional arrays as appear in Figure 15-5. Notice how we have departmental summaries (DEPT 1 through 10) as well as month summaries (JAN through DEC).

Because of all this precalculation, the response to queries at any level of summarization should be very fast. Of course, such a huge benefit does have its costs, as we shall soon see.

	JAN	FEB	MAR	APR	MAY	JUN	JUL	AUG	SEP	OCT	NOV	DEC
DEPT 1	-5	-10	4	-4	7	0	-6	-9	5	-2	0	-4
DEPT 2	2	-2	4	-2	5	-4	0	6	9	-9	2	7
DEPT 3	4	4	0	4	1	-2	7	1	-4	5	4	4
DEPT 4	6	-8										
DEPT 5	8	-1	0	-4	-5	9	-5	3	1	9	2	-8
DEPT 6	4	-8	6	-6	2	7	-1	-10	-10	-10	5	-7
DEPT 7	0	2	-5	3	4	3	2	-8	9	9	0	5
DEPT 8												-7
DEPT 9	1	1	4	5	-3	-8	-4	-5	8	0	-3	-1
DEPT 10	-6	5	-4	0	2	-9	9	-7	6	-7	-5	5

FIGURE 15-4. *A multidimensional array—120 cells*

LOAD PERFORMANCE   Most multidimensional databases are not refreshed daily. In fact, a recent survey showed that the most common refresh cycle is monthly. Why is this? Wouldn't it be preferable to have more frequent updates and therefore more current data? Sadly, one of the costs of the wonderful performance you can get from a multidimensional database is long database load times.

By Dept:	
DEPT 1	-24
DEPT 2	18
DEPT 3	28
DEPT 4	-2
DEPT 5	9
DEPT 6	-28
DEPT 7	24
DEPT 8	-7
DEPT 9	-5
DEPT 10	-11

By Month:	
JAN	14
FEB	-17
MAR	9
APR	-4
MAY	13
JUN	-4
JUL	2
AUG	-29
SEP	24
OCT	-5
NOV	5
DEC	-6

FIGURE 15-5. *Summary-level arrays*

Assume it takes 24 hours to refresh a database. In such a case, if you tried to do daily refreshes, you would always be refreshing and never reporting. This is one reason why companies have long periods of time between refreshes.

Why does refreshing take so long? Well, precalculating data takes time. In all fairness, MDDB vendors are making progress in shortening load times. One way many are doing this is by not completely precalculating all possible values in their cubes.

Relational reporting structures, on the other hand, can often be loaded more quickly. There are a number of steps to the load process, including loading, indexing, and building summary tables. Still, because you usually don't build all possible summaries, load times are typically shorter than for multidimensional databases. In fact, it is not unusual for relational data warehouses and data marts to be refreshed on a daily basis.

Analytic Capability

Well, what good is an analytic database if you can't analyze the data that it contains? Are there any differences in what you can do with a MOLAP versus a ROLAP approach?

As we've already noted about 44 times, OLAP is a user interface concept, not a data storage concept. Still, given the maturity of query technologies, there are some differences in analytic rigor between MOLAP and ROLAP databases.

MOLAP database applications tend to have better support for time series and statistical analyses. ROLAP database applications, on the other hand, are sometimes hampered by the limitations of SQL.

There are a number of things that can't be easily done with a single SQL statement. For example, suppose you want to calculate the sales of each division as a percentage of your company's total sales. While you may be able to put together a complex SQL statement to answer this question, it is much simpler to run multiple SQL statements and manipulate the results.

ROLAP query tool vendors address SQL's limitations in a number of ways. They may:

- Ignore them, thus limiting their tools' functionality

- Issue multiple SQL statements, putting intermediate results into temporary database tables (the MicroStrategy approach)

■ Utilize three-tier architectures that put computers between client and server machines to manipulate intermediate results (the Information Advantage approach)

As ROLAP technologies mature, look to ROLAP vendors to close the capability gap with MOLAP vendors.

Dataset Sizes

Multidimensional databases tend to grow in size very rapidly, particularly as more dimensions are modeled in the database. Look again at the database in Figure 15-4. Notice that DEPT 4 was dissolved in February. Still, the database stores data for the rest of the year for this department. Even though these values are nulls, they take up space in the database. This is wasteful. If you add dimensions, even more space would be wasted. The term referring to this wasted space is *sparsity*. A sparse database wastes a good deal of space. A dense database wastes little. There are approaches for addressing sparsity, but none is perfect.

For every department that you add, you require 12 cells in the MDDB. Suppose you actually had three dimensions. For example, suppose the database also contains a gender dimension so that they can now analyze turnover by department, month, and gender. Simply by adding this dimension, your database doubles in size. Now, rather than a two-dimensional table containing 120 cells (12 months times 10 departments), the database looks like a three-dimensional cube containing 240 cells (10 departments times 12 months times 2 genders). Thus, as you add dimensions, MDDBs tend to explode in size.

Another reason why MDDBs can rapidly grow large is because of the large number of precalculated summary values that they frequently contain. Put all together, MDDBs can rapidly grow quite large. There are, on the other hand, physical limitations to how large such databases can become.

While it may vary a bit depending on how you model your relational data structures, ROLAP databases typically do not incur sparsity penalties. In addition, they support virtually unlimited growth. While it is not unheard-of to have multiterabyte-sized relational databases, particularly with technologies like Oracle8, the largest multidimensional databases are well under a terabyte.

Dimension Handling

ROLAP databases are usually constructed as star schemas. The dimension tables in a star schema can be quite wide. For example, a customer dimension table may contain columns for things like: customer name, home address, home ZIP, office address, office ZIP, area code, customer type, date of first order, etc., etc., etc. As a user, you can query, summarize, and drill-down on any of these dimension columns. For example, you could ask the database to show total sales broken down by country, then drill into state, then drill into city, then drill into ZIP, then break down by date of the customer's first order.

Multidimensional databases, on the other hand, do not provide such flexibility with dimensions. These systems are limited in the number of different dimension "levels" that they can contain. This limitation is related to the problem of database size explosions as dimensions are added.

Maintenance Effort

MOLAP approaches are very strong in the area of maintenance. Once set up, they are fairly self-maintaining. Load it and go. To load, simply design the database and then feed it a flat file or a SQL select statement (if you think about it, and you really should, the result of a SQL select statement is just a flat file). The engine will accept the rows and build the database.

Relational databases, on the other hand, require more effort to populate and maintain. Population is more complex because not one, but multiple structures must be filled. In addition, indexes may need to be turned on or off during this process. Once loaded, if performance is poor, additional indexes may need to be added or summary tables created. DBAs must regularly analyze the database to keep it in working order.

Lunch Value

In the OLAP technology selection process, it is important to consider what we refer to as *lunch value*. Lunch value is a poorly understood concept, likely because its calculation formula is deceptively complex. Lunch value (LV) is derived by the formula:

$$LV = 2P + S^2 - 4d$$

where:

P = the amount the vendor paid for lunch

S = a factor representing the style of lunch (i.e., French = 7, Italian = 4, Delicatessen = 2, Company cafeteria = .043)

d = the drone factor, a value representing how much mindless sales pitch you had to put up with during the meal

Please note the inverse relationship between total lunch value and drone factor. In our experience, this category is a tie between ROLAP and MOLAP vendors. Still, we strongly recommend that you attempt to maximize total lunch value as you pursue your purchase.

ROLAP and MOLAP Peace and Harmony

So, which technology wins? Well, as you might surmise, the answer is a resounding…"It depends." It depends on a number of factors, but primarily on the scope of your application. If you are building a large, cross-functional, enterprise data warehouse, then you probably want to use a relational database. If you are building a well-defined, highly targeted analysis-focused data mart with limited dimensionality and little need for detailed, atomic-level data, then the multidimensional approach has a lot of merit.

Earlier, we spoke about a corporate data warehousing architecture. In this architecture, a corporate data warehouse feeds smaller, narrowly focused or stand-alone data marts. Ah ha! Think about what this means to the ROLAP-MOLAP debate! It means that these technologies are not competitors but are, in many cases, complementary!

Looming developments in the database industry serve to heighten this symbiosis (yes, we do get more distance out of these big fancy words). In particular, database vendors are starting to integrate ROLAP and MOLAP technologies. The first step was a technology called *drill through*. With drill through, the user can drill-down into an MDDB database. When the lowest level of detail in the database is reached, the user can then request that the system issue a query to a relational database that contains very detailed atomic-level data. Drill through, though, has not been perfect. Most implementations require the system developer to custom code each drill-through query. At run time, what the user is really doing is simply filling in variables of the **where** clause for this relational query. The system then runs it and returns the result.

Depending on the vendor, drill through is not always transparent to the user. He or she must do something different than a normal drill-down to access this relational data.

Coming soon is a more transparent drill through—one in which the user performs a normal drill-down, the MDDB realizes that the data is not stored in the multidimensional database and therefore issues a true ROLAP query to the underlying, detailed, relational database. This ROLAP query will adhere to all the criteria of a true ROLAP query, including aggregate navigation.

In the longer term, we would like to see the industry develop fully integrated query databases. In this fully integrated model, the administrator will lay out a basic definition of the data to be contained in the system and then feed it that data. The database engine will store the data as seems appropriate, in either relational or multidimensional structures. Furthermore, the database will analyze usage patterns. Based on how the database is used, the system will adjust how each data element and summary is stored. And the best part is, this whole process will be transparent to our users. They just keep doing their work and issuing their queries. All we will have to do is feed the system our data and write the vendors our checks!

Let's get our hands a bit dirty in the rich soil of ROLAP land by discussing modeling data for ROLAP performance.

Modeling Your Data for ROLAP Performance

Suppose you are developing a ROLAP application. In no other relational application will you need such rapid access to such large quantities of data. How will you achieve this performance? Well, we've already discussed some techniques. They include things like:

■ Putting your data into a star schema

- Indexing

- Building summary tables

- Partitioning large tables into smaller tables

In fact, there are a lot of things we can do to improve performance. But, in most cases, there are trade-offs. To improve performance, we might pay a price in areas like maintainability and dataset size. For example, each of the steps just noted will have to be administered. And administration is not free. Have you seen the billing rates for DBAs lately?

One often-overlooked area for improving performance is security. For example, if we don't implement row-level security (i.e., security where each user can see only those rows that apply to them), we can probably improve system performance. Is the cost of these performance improvements worthwhile? Only you and your users can judge. But don't worry too much about making the wrong decision—technology jobs are a dime a dozen.

There is one other technique, a technique from the dark side of relational databases. A technique so powerful yet so monstrous that we hesitate to mention it. Use it if you must, but use it with extreme caution. And don't disclose your source for this information (unless, of course, it is to another potential purchaser of this book). Also, keep in mind that this technique will work only if your query tools can recognize this data structure. The name of this dark secret? Denormalization by a dimension.

Imagine a star schema with only two dimensions—customer and month. It contains only one fact: sales. Thus, each record in your fact table represents your sales to one customer during one month. The fact table probably looks something like the one shown next, with an identifier for month (MONTH_ID), one for customer (CUSTOMER_ID), and the sale amount (SALES). The two dimensions are month and customer.

MONTH_ID	CUST_ID	SALES
1	1876	425
2	1876	410
3	1876	430
...		

Now, suppose that the average customer makes at least one purchase per month. How many records will that customer have in this table for a year?

That's right, 12. Very good! So, to figure any customer's total sales for the year (or average monthly sales, for that matter), our program has to access 12 rows.

In the illustration shown here

CUST_ID	JAN_SALES	FEB_SALES	MAR_SALES	...
1876	425	410	430	

we denormalize by the dimension month. Notice how we store separate values in each row for January (JAN_SALES), February (FEB_SALES), March (MAR_SALES), and so on. Now, how many rows must you access to answer the same question? That's right, 1! Thus, you hit the indexes less and the actual data tables less. Which structure will have better performance?

Keep in mind, these structures are very difficult to maintain. For one reason, while in a traditional fact table you would just insert rows for new data, in this denormalized scheme you update existing rows. For another, think about what happens at the end of the year. What do you do for the next year? Add columns to your fact table? Add a new record for each customer? Delete data from existing columns? As you get deeper into data warehousing, you will be faced with opportunities to use unconventional structures such as this. They can be powerful, but they can also be very costly.

As we noted before, true ROLAP is only one of the technologies being marketed as ROLAP. Let's take a look at some of the others.

The Three Faces of ROLAP

One last thing you must understand about ROLAP. There are a number of different data storage approaches that call themselves ROLAP technologies. It is important to understand the difference between these before some vendor tries to convince you that theirs is the best, nay, the only way. Keep in mind, none of these is necessarily "best." Best is defined only by the demands of your particular application.

The first technology is the "true" ROLAP that we described earlier. True ROLAP systems adhere to the basic tenets of OLAP. They store their data in relational databases and every query reaccesses those relational data structures. Finally, these systems utilize aggregate navigators. The process of querying is fairly transparent to the user. She issues queries and the results appear on her screen.

Let's call the next technology "local hypercubing." Local hypercubing is implemented in tools like Business Objects and Cognos' Impromptu/ Powerplay combination. With this technology, the user issues a query against the relational data warehouse. The results of this query are stored in a small, local, multidimensional database. The user can then perform analysis against this local database. If the user needs data not in this database, she must issue another query against the relational database and rebuild, or at least modify, the local MDDB cube.

The last approach is relational storage of multidimensional hypercubes. Think about what a multidimensional (or a relational) database really is. In actuality, these are simply files. Database engines are simply programs that allow users to access and maintain these files. Well, perhaps "simply" is not quite correct, but you get the picture. Right?

Relational storage of multidimensional hypercubes takes the file containing a multidimensional database and stores that file in a relational database. While it's confusing in concept, it works. You can issue queries directly against these data structures. But, you won't be able to decipher the results. To do that, you will need special application programming interfaces (APIs) sold by the vendors of these technologies. Thus, your application, or the vendor's packaged applications, will call the vendor's API. This API will translate the request into a relational query and send it via SQL*Net to the database. The database will return its results to the API, which will translate them and return them to the requesting program.

Storing the cube in a relational database allows administrators to take advantage of typical relational tools like security and replication. Tools that use this type of technology are sold by vendors like IQ Software in their IQ Vision tool and by Cognos in an extension to their multidimensional Powerplay product.

Conclusion

Well, the end of another chapter. And what have we gained? Our key points are

- OLAP is a user interface, not a data storage, concept.

- OLAP systems provide four basic functions: multidimensional view of data, drill-down, rotation, and multiple view modes.

- Relational OLAP (ROLAP) is the access of data for OLAP from a relational database (RDBMS). Multidimensional OLAP (MOLAP) is the access of data for OLAP from a multidimensional database (MDDB).

- There is no always-best approach to OLAP. The best approach will be defined by the requirements of your application.

Ready...set...build! The wheels have just touched down—please stay in your seat with your seatbelts fastened until Air ROLAP is at a full and final stop at the gate. At that time, your data warehouse administrator will extinguish the seatbelt sign; this will be your indication that it is safe to disembark from the warehouse. The next item on the agenda deals with OLAP tools and serves as an overview of what they are all about, what makes them tick, and what they do for the total warehouse analytical solution.

CHAPTER
16

OLAP

his chapter of Oracle8 Data Warehousing deals with a recent phenomenon in the information processing industry—online analytical processing (OLAP). It seems that you can't open a computer magazine without running across these four letters. They're everywhere. *OLAP* is a category of technology that enables users to gain insight into their data in a fast, interactive, easy-to-use manner. The question is then raised: what is OLAP? OLAP provides users with the ability to gain insight into data that they previously could not achieve. This is provided through fast, consistent, and interactive views to a variety of information. It is OLAP that now provides the users with the power to deeply analyze their business. These products allow business users to dig into their data, by approaching it from many new and previously unforeseen angles, providing them with the knowledge to make more informed decisions. You can only hope that these decisions are better than the ones we had been making. But then again, we keep waiting.

TIP

The key to OLAP is that users can express the data in the same way that they think about their data.

A question that often arises about OLAP is that isn't it just data warehousing in a pretty wrapper? They are quite different, but one complements the other. The data warehouse is used to effectively store information, and OLAP is used for the retrieval of information. The two technologies (data warehousing and OLAP) are complementary, so that a good warehouse is designed with reporting in mind. As we discussed in Chapter 5, building the warehouse in isolation is a formula for a warehouse disaster. To fully exploit the warehouse, you need OLAP to draw out the information so the components form a relationship to allow you to fully leverage the information it contains. We must distinguish the capabilities of OLAP from data warehousing. The data warehouse is usually based upon relational technology, utilizing products such as Oracle8, whereas OLAP uses multidimensional views of data for quick access to strategic information. Some OLAP products do allow you to store your data in a database; however, it is usually stored in a proprietary table structure that should only be accessed with the product's user interface. The data in these multidimensional views is often aggregated to maximize its effectiveness. Many of today's OLAP tools also provide you a "drill-down" capability that allows you to investigate the meaning and source of these aggregations. OLAP and data warehouses complement each other. The data warehouse stores data to allow for strategic decision making. OLAP allows user access to this data through such methods as ad hoc querying and browsing, to calculations, time series analysis, and complex modeling. End users, over time, will find that this simple access to their data via OLAP tools will allow them to make more informed decisions.

Rather than think of the data in terms of flat files or spreadsheets, an OLAP application allows you to look at the data in terms of many dimensions. A *flat file* is a collection of text data stored line by line and always read from start to finish. You will remember from the definition in Chapter 5 that *dimensions* describe the components of the study area and are a way to locate the value of a performance measure. This ability to organize the data in the way users think about it is known as *multidimensionality*. This is what distinguishes OLAP capability from a traditional system. The design of an OLAP multidimensional solution is not much different from designing a focused data mart. Then you must ask the following questions, which will then help you formulate your OLAP topology and design:

- When?
- What?
- Where?
- Who?

These questions form the basis for all multidimensional arrays. Although each question may have one answer or many answers, together they will form the dimensional map that will then be translated into your vision of how your information should be viewed. We must remember to separate the qualitative information from the quantitative information. These "numbers" will form the measures that will be used to depict the combinations of the qualitative information.

For example, you could classify a sale by the time a product was purchased, the particular product that was purchased, where the purchase occurred, and the source of the product. Each one of these items could be thought of as a dimension within the database. In this example, you have four dimensions:

- Time (when?)

- Product (what?)

- Geography (where?)

- Salesperson (who?)

The essential unit of an OLAP database is its dimensions. This is where you get the idea of the *multidimensional* data array. If we think of a spreadsheet with its rows and columns as two-dimensional, each being a dimension, and we add an additional dimension, we now create an object that would look like a cube. In terms of geometry, we can say that we have, at minimum, X-, Y-, and Z-axes to our cube. However, when dealing with multidimensional analysis, we are not limited to two or three dimensions in combination. We are limited only by the power of our tools. In our experience, we find that we are usually building cubes no larger than 10 dimensions; the normal sizes of these cubes are comprised of 7-10 dimensions. This makes the cube size manageable while still providing sufficient flexibility for analysis. When you plug in the various dimensions, the intersection of multiple dimensions produces a location called a cell. That cell contains the intersecting values within all the dimensions. A *cell* is a single data point that occurs at the intersection, defined by selecting one value from each dimension in a multidimensional array. In our example, we have time, products, geography, and price as dimensions. This means the dimensional members May 1996 (time), Volvo (product), Boston (geography), and Arlene Kerzner (Salesperson) specify a precise intersection along all the dimensions that uniquely identify a single cell. In this example, the cell contains the value of all Volvo sales in Boston for May 1996 by this salesperson. When you visualize a multidimensional database, you see a Rubik's cube. Rubik's cube was a game that originated in the Soviet Union in which you had a series of blocks in which you moved the various cells of the cube to line up the colors. It was a craze that swept through the world in the early 1980s. This idea of a cube is that it allows you to turn and rotate the various dimensions to provide you with numerous combinations and permutations while existing in a simple form to the casual observer.

Locating the value of sales for Boston is easy. Think of it in terms of its position in the database, as opposed to thinking about which columns you might have to join. Each intersection of all the dimensions creates a cell; but it is possible the cell is empty. If the cell is empty, it is known as *scarcity*. In fact, it's possible, given a large number of dimensions, that many of the cells are empty. The greater the amount of empty cells, the greater the impact on performance. To get around this issue, the vendors have implemented many ingenious techniques. This issue is one of the major reasons why a pure multidimensional database has problems dealing with large datasets. Knowing the position up front will get you to the answer much quicker. Yes, you can make these types of relationships work in a traditional relational database, but SQL is not a natural way of addressing these types of structures.

If you think of OLAP as a stand-alone application that allows you to view your data from many different directions, and allows you to interrogate this information, you start to see the power of OLAP. The data warehouse works in conjunction with OLAP tools, but it is only one method of accessing and investigating "the numbers." Let's move forward and look more deeply at OLAP.

What Is MOLAP? What Is ROLAP? What Is DOLAP?

Terminology—it changes daily in our computer age. Yesterday's OLAP is today's MOLAP, ROLAP, or DOLAP. OLAP is one of those moving targets. Originally, it was a simple concept. It was mandated to provide users with a product used to describe all analysis performed on aggregate data. Just when we become satisfied with the terminology, it changes again.

Originally, OLAP was a simple concept, utilized to describe all analysis performed on aggregated data. Now that we have become satisfied with that concept, we are presented with variations on the theme. From this we get ROLAP, MOLAP, and DOLAP. These three key architectures exist for OLAP systems today—multidimensional OLAP (*MOLAP*), relational OLAP (*ROLAP*), and desktop OLAP (DOLAP). In these three architectures, the interface to the analytic layer is typically the same. How the data is physically stored is quite different.

In MOLAP, the premise is that online analytical processing is best implemented by storing the data multidimensionally; for example, data must be stored multidimensional to be viewed in a multidimensional manner. In contrast, ROLAP architects believe you store the data best in the relational model; for instance, OLAP capabilities are best provided against the relational database. DOLAP, on the other hand, is a variation that exists to provide portability for the OLAP user. It creates multidimensional datasets that can be transferred from server to desktop, requiring only the DOLAP software to exist on the target system. This provides significant advantages to portable computer users, such as salespeople who are frequently on the road and do not have direct access to their office server. The selection of the OLAP technology for your organization will depend upon many factors. However, you still should choose a product based upon user requirements. In the next section, we discuss some of the criteria that you should review during the selection process.

MOLAP or ROLAP?

The next obvious question is "Which is better, MOLAP or ROLAP, and why?" Just as integral in this question is "Does it really matter?" Simply put, we don't think so. Each has its advantages and disadvantages, but each provides you with a solid foundation for analysis. MOLAP databases have a practical limit to the physical size of the dataset they can handle. For example, an Oracle Express database can theoretically handle the equivalent of $2**63$ (i.e., 2 raised to the 63rd power!) cells (Oracle Express equivalent of rows). Storage and performance constraints will limit the Express database size long before the physical capacity is reached. A limit also exists to the number of dimensions it can handle and still provide you with reasonable performance. Before you can access the data, you must first load it into the multidimensional structure. This load process performs a series of calculations to aggregate the data along the orthogonal dimensions and fill the multidimensional database structures. In other words, a mathematical technique is applied, taking in all the dimensions to determine the appropriate values to place in each cell. After this process is finished, a series of mechanisms are invoked to enhance the ability of the search engine against the multidimensional database. Given the complexity of loading the data into a multidimensional format, the process can take some time. This time factor directly correlates between the number of dimensions and physical size of the data being stored. Once this entire compilation process is complete, you can begin to slice and dice the data.

Users then request data through the interface against the multidimensional database (*MDB*). This MOLAP architecture, at least the Express implementation, boasts features that include the following:

- Very robust calculation and aggregation capabilities

- Computation and calculation functionality far above the limits of standard SQL

- Ability to use any kind of derived and calculated measures

The only potential drawback, if it affects the installation, is that you lose broader access to data in your relational database—detail data that has been extracted to form summary data in the MDB or data that has been added or changed since the last MDB update.

MOLAP architecture will shine in a situation where the data can be broken up into smaller pieces. The smaller the sets, the quicker the compilation times. For example, a financial application may be an ideal candidate for MOLAP because each department commonly breaks up the datasets. This lends itself nicely to MOLAP. Because the datasets are small, you can quickly recompile the data into the multidimensional structures if you want to refresh the model.

ROLAP has the advantage of being able to run against large datasets. Once you have established the model identifying where the source data should be located, the OLAP tool is ready to query live data. Because you are running directly against your live datasets, you are always dealing with the most current data. Whether you use ROLAP or MOLAP, you are limited to 32 dimensions (the same as 32 key columns in traditional relational thinking) per variable. This limit is never an issue since most OLAP applications will use five to seven dimensions, and almost all use fewer than ten to twelve. All of this depends upon the business process that you are trying to understand, which defines how many dimensions will be required.

Which should you choose? Neither. You should take the time to develop a robust data warehouse environment before embarking on your OLAP strategy. This is a far more important issue to decide than ROLAP vs. MOLAP. Over time, key vendors will adopt and learn from each other's competitive advantages. We expect vendors to give you the choice of mixing and matching ROLAP with MOLAP (or is that "MOLAP with ROLAP"?).

Oracle's Express offering supports ROLAP mixed with MOLAP. You have the best of both worlds. You can apply the architecture that makes the most sense for your situation. We find Express' flexibility so important in positioning it at the top of the pyramid of OLAP solutions.

NOTE
Some OLAP experts have coined the expression HOLAP to refer to products such as Express— hybrid online analytical processing!

Why Do I Need OLAP?

Organizations first started using relational databases to help them with data production. Oracle and its early toolset were an improved way for companies to run their operational systems. As more and more companies used Oracle's relational engine to run these systems, its OLTP functionality grew.

Today, Oracle is a dominant player in the OLTP arena. With a relational database as the OLTP engine, organizations gain the ability to capture data at the source. This ability to easily capture data at the source never before existed. As the data being captured is analyzed, companies learn valuable information about themselves, their competitors, and their customers. This equates to a competitive advantage. This ability quickly fueled the move toward larger information stores. Over time, these information stores evolved into data warehouses. Companies realized that to take full advantage of the captured data, they required some considerable thought over which data to capture and how to structure it properly within the data warehouse.

As the information available to the user community grew, the complexity of the user requests for information grew. Over time, the types of questions users asked could no longer be served with the standard relational toolset. This need to answer more complex questions fueled the momentum for additional change.

In fact, E. F. Codd, one of the original developers of the relational concept, stated: "As enabling as RDBMSs [relational database management systems] have been for users, they were never intended to provide powerful functions for data synthesis, analysis, and consolidation" (*ComputerWorld*, 1993).

OLAP tools evolved as a way to answer these complex questions. With OLAP's combination of a multidimensional database with easy-to-use analytical tools, it makes data synthesis, analysis, and consolidation easy. By looking at the evolution of relational databases from OLTP systems to data warehouses, we are clearly moving toward environments and toolsets that allow the users to slice and dice the data quicker, smarter, and better. OLAP, with its multidimensional capability, is such an analytical toolset.

Table 16-1 illustrates why we are moving toward OLAP functionality. When you look at the functionality of the OLAP system compared to a data warehouse and OLTP system, you can see that this ability to be able to slice and dice the data is becoming more crucial.

OLAP Tools

Today, there are many OLAP tools available from a multitude of vendors. As with most technology, these products are changing at a very rapid pace.

Characteristics	OLTP	Warehouse Reporting Tools	OLAP
Primary operation	Collect	Report	Analyze
Level of analytical requirements	Low	Medium	High
Data per transaction	Very small	Small to large	Large
Type of data	Detailed	Detail and summary	Summary
Timeliness of data	Must be current	Current and historical	Current and historical

TABLE 16-1. *OLTP Vs. Warehouse Vs. OLAP*

Recently, you would have been happy to be able to generate a multidimensional cube, send it out to each of your users, and have them manipulate the data required by each user's unique data perspective. This may have sufficed in the past, but users have become more demanding as they gain a better understanding of the tools and the advantages provided by data warehousing. OLAP tools must now be able to address all the users' needs. Fundamentally these tools must have the following characteristics:

- Ability to drill-down into your data

- Ability to swap dimensions

- Allow you to alter the appearance of your displayed data

We will show you how each of these fundamental concepts are used within OLAP tools. Other characteristics include distributed cubes that can be viewed and manipulated offline or accessed via internal networks, or access to the information via the Web. If you had asked for access to your data via the Web (Internet or intranet) just a few years ago, your technical staff would have said "It is a great idea, but the tools we have just don't support that functionality." The OLAP vendors have addressed all these needs. Now, with these options for distributing your OLAP information, we have allowed for a variety of information access methods. So, whether you perform your analysis in your office, your home, on an airplane, or even sitting beside the pool on your vacation (although we would not recommend this type of work, as you should not have electrical appliances near water, nor should you upset your spouse by working on vacation), you have ultimate flexibility. Vendors have given us all these features that add significant power to our analysis and provide us with a product that allows us to spend our time making our organizations better, and possibly get a tan at the same time.

The integration of OLAP tools into your overall data warehouse strategy is shown in Figure 16-1.

Notice in Figure 16-1 that we can extract data from numerous data sources, including operational databases and flat files, among other sources. This data is then moved into your data warehouse and then possibly into one or many data marts. This initial topology depends upon your end-user requirements and is defined during your design. The data from your data warehouse, data marts, or flat files can then be used as the

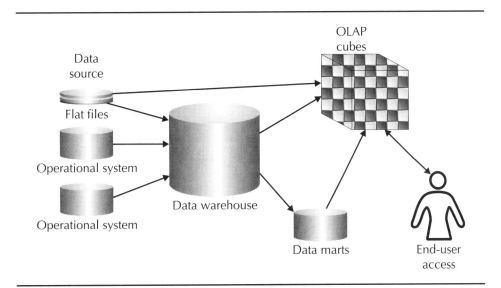

FIGURE 16-1. *Integrating OLAP into your data warehouse environment*

source data for your multidimensional data cubes. Cubes are a way of describing the multidimensional arrays. These cubes are then distributed to your end users for their individual use.

Numerous vendors sell OLAP, ROLAP, and MOLAP tools: Oracle with its Oracle Express suite, Cognos with PowerPlay, Microstrategy DSS Agent, and many others. Since this book is an Oracle Press book, we will focus on the Oracle Express tools in Chapter 17. To introduce you to OLAP tools and the concepts within these tools, and how they can be leveraged within your organization, we will look at the Cognos tools Transformer and PowerPlay as our vehicle for this discussion.

Evaluating OLAP Tools

It is so important to evaluate your OLAP tools before embarking on your OLAP adventure, but what is most important is how it impacts on your business. The following are some questions that you should ask of your vendor before investing in any product. How each vendor fulfills your requirements will help you decide the best product for you. We've attended many vendor presentations in our days, and salespeople are very convincing. How many times have you heard that this is the best product on the market? If you only had a dollar for every best product out there, you could be on a beach instead of reading this book, (then again, reading this book on the beach could be fun). Lets look at some criteria for selecting the OLAP tool for your organization:

- Select the product based on your applications, not the technology.

- Determine if the OLAP product can scale to meet your needs.

- Consider OLAP development the same way you do an application development tool.

- Consider the administrative aspect of the product.

- Compare performance and flexibility.

- Don't worry about ROLAP vs. MOLAP.

- Select the product that suits your organization's analysis requirements.

NOTE
You should not let your OLAP decision design your data warehouse (i.e., don't have "Select OLAP tool" as one of the first tasks on your project plan). Let your data warehouse be a factor in the choice and implementation of an OLAP tool.

Selecting the right product is no simple task, but the success of your data warehouse depends on it. Providing your users with the right tool is extremely important, so understand how you plan to use the product, and then find the best product that meets your needs.

Setting up Your OLAP Model with Cognos Transformer

OLAP tools usually have two components: the administrator and the end-user tool. The administrator component is used to set up and create the data cubes that will be accessed by the users. You can think of data cubes as focused data marts. The first product that we need to look at is Cognos' PowerPlay. Although we refer to it as PowerPlay, it is comprised of two tools: PowerPlay and Transformer. Transformer is the PowerPlay administrator. It is used to transform two-dimensional data into multidimensional cubes. PowerPlay is used to analyze the multidimensional datasets that have been created. Transformer allows you to take your data and build multidimensional models that can then be used to perform OLAP analysis. Transformer is used to design and then build your cubes, as Cognos has named the multidimensional models.

Before we can extract the data, we must decide what data we require. The process of defining the dimensions and measures (facts) follows a process similar to data warehouse design. When collecting your user requirements, you will answer the questions, such as when, what, where, and who, and define your measures. We always create a dimensional map that forms the basis of our data cube. Table 16-2 is a sample dimensional map based upon the example we used earlier in the chapter.

Dimensions

Time	Product	Geography	Salesperson
Year	Product type	Country	
Month	Brand	Region	
Day	Model	State/Province	
Quarter		City	
Fiscal Year			

Measures

Quantity	Sales amount

TABLE 16-2. *Dimensional Mapping Sample*

To get data into the cube, we first have to define where the data will come from. We therefore need to define the source of our data that is to populate our data cube. These sources can include the following:

- Flat ASCII files (delimited with column headings or not)
- Flat ASCII files (fixed format)
- Impromptu queries (required to extract data from Oracle databases)
- Excel and Lotus databases
- PC-based databases such as Dbase, FoxPro, and Clipper

As you can see, these tools are built to allow for maximum flexibility so that your OLAP analysis can be built from numerous data sources within your organization. When we pull data from our data warehouse, we will start with the impromptu query, as discussed in Chapter 14; but for our purposes, we will utilize a flat file.

The flat file will form the basis for the construction of the PowerCube; however, it also allows you to include information from multiple sources. You can perform multiple queries from each source to retrieve additional data for analysis. These sources can either be from flat files or multiple databases. We often use this strategy of multiple extractions to improve performance of the generation of the cube. The advantages include more efficient queries and providing the ability to integrate discrete data sources, such as actuals vs. budgets. In our experience, we have found that it is more efficient to extract the data in the following manner:

1. Initial selection of base information:

- Country code   01
- Product code   G
- Amount sold $100

2. Extract support information for the selected data:

- Country details   Code   01;   Description   Canada
- Product details   Code   G;   Description   Goalie sticks

3. Resulting details in the PowerCube:

■ Country Canada; Product Goalie sticks; Amount sold $100

Since the construction of a multidimensional cube can require a great deal of data to be extracted from the database, it is rare that the data is built directly from the data warehouse. We often are required to build ".csv" files. These are flat files containing data extracted from the data warehouse. These files have new data appended into them, rather then having to be reconstructed each time. The new information is then placed in this file and can be used to build your cubes.

TIP
Use flat files if your datasets are large, instead of direct access to the database to build your multidimensional cubes. This will improve performance of cube construction and will reduce the amount of data transferred from the data warehouse.

We have selected a flat file that will serve as our source data; in this case, it is a sporting goods company's sales information. Sales information can provide us with a great deal of return on investment (ROI) when it comes to OLAP analysis. Figure 16-2 shows you the Cognos Transformer New Model screen; it is from within this screen that you name your model as well as define the data source.

Transformer is an intelligent OLAP tool, since it reviews the file containing the column headings and performs a low-level analysis upon it to determine an initial dimensional map. This is performed by a function called AutoDesign. This feature can save you time by creating the basic model. This is just an initial design that can be customized later based upon increased requirements of your users, or to refine the AutoDesign model. To improve the performance of the AutoDesign feature, you can alter the number of rows that will be sampled to create the default structure. However, as with many features contained in software that are very impressive during demos, AutoDesign is no different. It works extremely well if the data is well organized, but it comes up short if your data is not

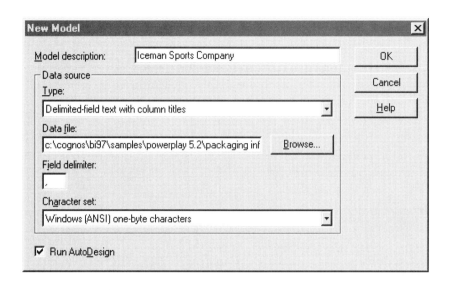

FIGURE 16-2. *New Model screen*

organized as the tool might expect. So, the result may be no time saving at the end of the development, but as with many tools, we expect that you will be able to skip the AutoDesign as you become more familiar with the product. The nature of data in most databases is not always organized so that the software can fully predict the types of analysis that you would like to perform, so Transformer allows you to define dimensions and measures in a very simple manner. As well, it does provide you with automatic help in generating the Time dimension. This is done by dragging and dropping fields from your Queries window into the appropriate dimension or measure. So remember, AutoDesign can be a starting point; however, you will be required to customize the model to meet your users' reporting needs. Figure 16-3 shows dimension definitions.

From a review of Figure 16-3, you will observe that Transformer has defined three dimensions. These dimensions are Order Date, Product Line, and Region. Each of these dimensions is then decomposed into some logical drill-down attributes. The Order Date dimension has been decomposed into the year, quarter, and month. If you remember your star schema theory, you

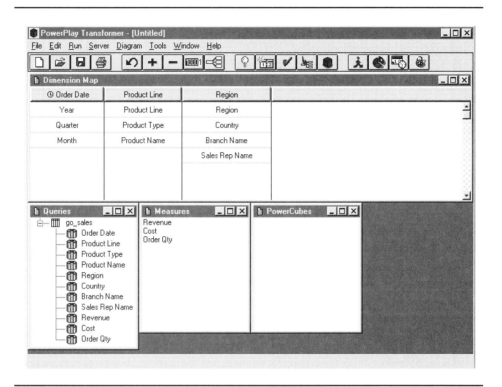

FIGURE 16-3. *Initial model design*

will quickly see that Transformer has created these attributes for the date dimension that will allow for some more detailed analysis, such as quarterly analysis and even year to date. The model has also defined a number of measures. These measures are also known as facts in the star schema topology. So, what the designer has done for us is define our multidimensional model, allowing users to perform some very complex analysis.

The Queries window has a number of fields that were defined based upon the source information, and column headings are based upon the column headers in your flat file or column names from the database. These fields can be viewed as the column headers that are available for use. Each of these can be customized to adopt a standard format and default position in our completed model. Through this customization, Transformer can also form the basis of your metadata dictionary, since you can document the meaning and source of each of the fields. This provides a powerful repository of information for your end users.

As you have seen from the dimensions that Transformer has produced, it has categorized the Order Date, Product Line, and Region dimensions. It also provides you with the ability to customize these categories. In the following diagram, you can see how Transformer has generated the drill-down strategy that can be used in your model. Figure 16-4 illustrates dimensional decomposition.

Figure 16-4 demonstrates the detail available to your users. The breakdown and depth of analysis that a simple dimension such as time can provide is a deep and complex one, and can provide maximum flexibility.

Transformer is the tool that allows you to create and customize the models that you will devise based on your users' needs. Think of Transformer as your programming tool and PowerPlay as your end-user model viewer. The last step after you have completed your model in

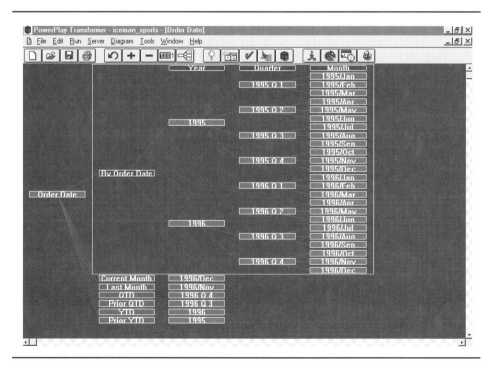

FIGURE 16-4. *Dimension management*

Transformer is to generate the PowerPlay cube. This function is performed from within Transformer by pressing the Generate Cube button. Figure 16-5 shows you what to expect to see while your screen is generating your data cube.

As you observe in Figure 16-5, Transformer is generating the data cube. This process is one that can take several minutes to several hours, depending on the size of the dataset that is being generated by the tool. You have available to you a Cancel key that will halt the processing. By generating the cube, you are creating a dataset that will be accessed by the end-user tool, PowerPlay. This is the fundamental element of OLAP. You are creating the multidimensional array that will provide the foundation of your business analysis. The cube is then saved in a proprietary file format. This

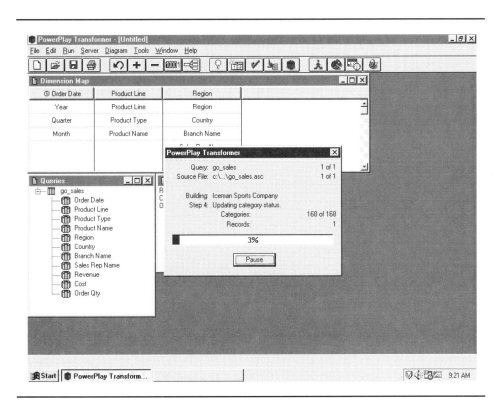

FIGURE 16-5. *Generation of the multidimensional cube within Transformer*

file is then distributed to the user, to be accessed via the PowerPlay analysis product. Let's move on and have a look at PowerPlay.

Cognos PowerPlay

PowerPlay is Cognos' reporting application that allows users to perform analysis on multidimensional data. It lets you explore the data that you previously prepared using Transformer. PowerPlay allows you to analyze your business through the dimensions that have been defined in the model. You can move through your data either up, down, or across the dimensions. Tools like PowerPlay allow you to visualize your data and to examine trends within your information.

PowerCubes are the multidimensional cubes that are used within PowerPlay. These cubes are data that is packaged based on specific processes within your business. With it you can discover and analyze the interactions of the different dimensions in your cubes. The ability to view how your business is doing is provided through measures. These measures are similar to facts in a star schema. They are additive or semiadditive numeric values that can be used as the "hard" numbers on how your business is doing, such as sales amount, quantity sold, percentage of total sales, and so on.

Figure 16-6 is the initial view of the PowerCube that a user will see after opening the cube. Although it may not appear to be all that exciting, the depth that the cube provides shows you that this is just the tip of the iceberg. Figure 16-6 shows the initial cross-tabular display of the first summary report.

Let's look a little more closely at this figure. The PowerPlay multidimensional functionality can be seen at its highest level. The dimensions that can be seen above the data area are Order Date, Product Line, and Region. The Revenue tab defines the measures available in the cube. If you look at these dimensions with your "3-D glasses," you will quickly realize that you are looking at a multidimensional array consisting of four dimensions. Each of the dimensions is broken down further; this allows for drill-down analysis. For example, Order Date can be decomposed in quarters, months, weeks, or even days. The dimensions provide you with the depth of your analysis. The other characteristic of this figure that you should

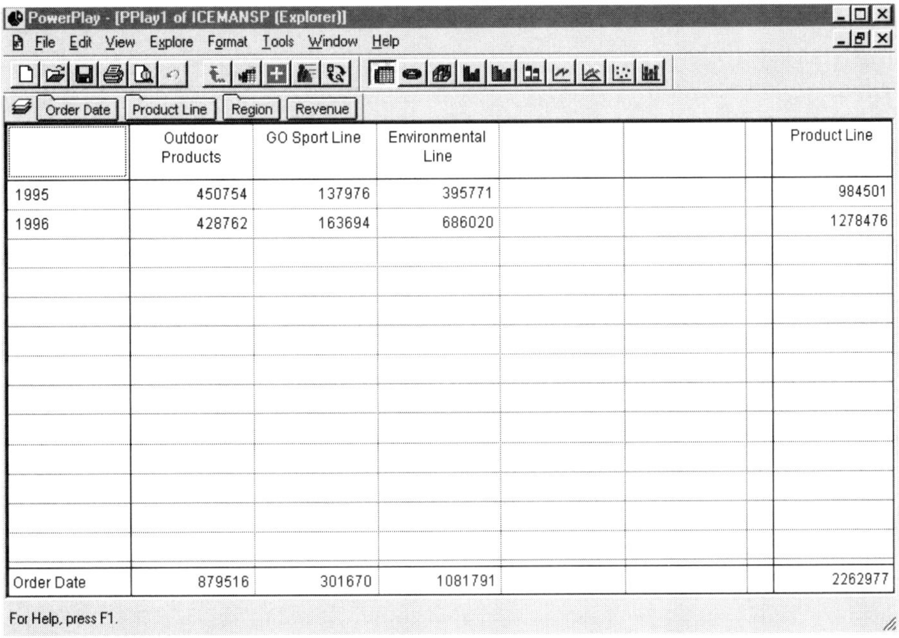

FIGURE 16-6. *Initial view of PowerCube within PowerPlay*

notice is the numbers or measures. In this case, you can see the annual sales (1995 and 1996) for three different product lines (Outdoor Products, GO Sport Line, and Environmental Line). This provides summarized, quantifiable data for you to analyze. This is just one measure that is shown. By placing your cursor over the Revenue tab, other measures can be accessed, such as cost, quantity sold, profit margin, and so on. By having multiple measures defined, you further empower the users by providing additional analysis flexibility. Figure 16-7 shows the decomposition of the Product Line dimension, which has been displayed in the Categories window.

The Categories selection window shown in Figure 16-7 allows you to choose the exact category combination that you would like to display in

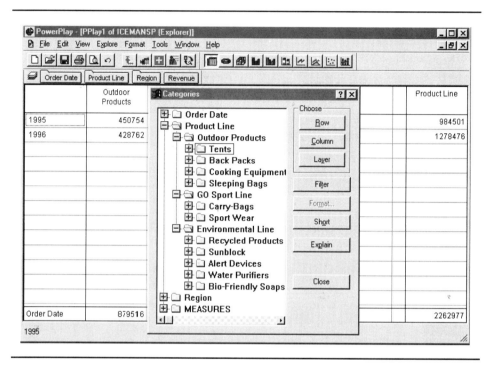

FIGURE 16-7. *Categories selection window*

your report. It is also from this window that you can define any data filters that you can use to exclude data from your result set.

Figure 16-8 shows some of the drill-down capabilities of PowerPlay. As we discussed in Chapter 14, drill-down is an important component in OLAP. Drilling allows you to quickly move from one level to another within a dimension.

Figure 16-8 is similar to the original view of our data cube. What we have done is drill down into the Product Line dimension. We have drilled into the Outdoor Products and then into Tents. As you can see in the figure, this company sells four types of tents. What can we as analysts determine from this data? Let's look at each of the tents that we are selling. We can see that the Star Gazer-3 has been an excellent seller; however, the sales of this

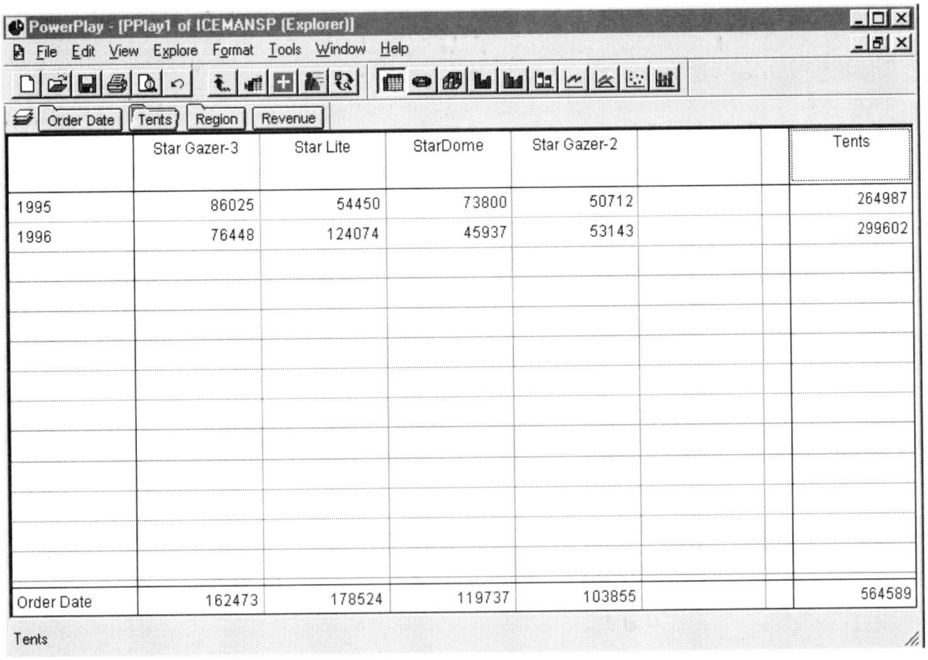

PowerPlay - [PPlay1 of ICEMANSP (Explorer)]						
	Star Gazer-3	Star Lite	StarDome	Star Gazer-2		Tents
1995	86025	54450	73800	50712		264987
1996	76448	124074	45937	53143		299602
Order Date	162473	178524	119737	103855		564589

FIGURE 16-8. *Drill-down on the Product Line dimension*

tent have declined from 1995 to 1996. On the other hand, the Star Lite tent has seen an explosion in sales, with an increase of approximately 125 percent between the two years. This information is useful, but it is only part of the picture. We would need to dig deeper into the data, such as how many units of each we had sold. Figure 16-9 is a different view of a product line, with further drill-down.

Figure 16-9 is similar to Figure 16-8; however, we have slightly changed our perspective. When we noticed a drop in the revenue of the Star Gazer-3, and a great increase in the sales of the Star Lite tents, the question we felt that needed to be asked was, "What impact in the number of units sold corresponded to the increase and decrease of revenue?" As you can easily see, the sales of the Star Gazer-3 were flat the last two years, so we

PowerPlay - [PPlay1 of ICEMANSP (Explorer)]						
File Edit View Explore Format Tools Window Help						
	Star Gazer-3	Star Lite	StarDome	Star Gazer-2		Tents
1995	155	330	120	98		703
1996	154	650	83	113		1000
Order Date	309	980	203	211		1703

Tents

FIGURE 16-9. *A different view of the Product Line dimension by Order Quantity*

can determine that we may have been selling this particular tent at some sort of a discount. The Star Lite tent, which saw the greatest positive change, also had the greatest number of units sold. Are we seeing a trend here?

NOTE
By looking at "the numbers" in different ways, you can gain insight into the reasons for changes within your business.

Another important feature in OLAP tools is the ability to pivot your data. Pivoting is the swapping of your columns and your rows. This allows you to look at your data from a different view. So, instead of comparing Region by Outdoor Products, we can look at Outdoor Products by Region. Figure 16-10 illustrates the resulting row and column swap.

The swapping of the rows and columns allows you to view your results in a new orientation, as well as impacting the graphical reports that are produced in PowerPlay.

Having the ability to look at the hard numbers of your business is a great advantage, but it is only part of the PowerPlay solution. PowerPlay has integrated graphical features. It can present data in pie charts, histograms, 3-D bar charts, and line graphs. So, with only a press of a button, we can

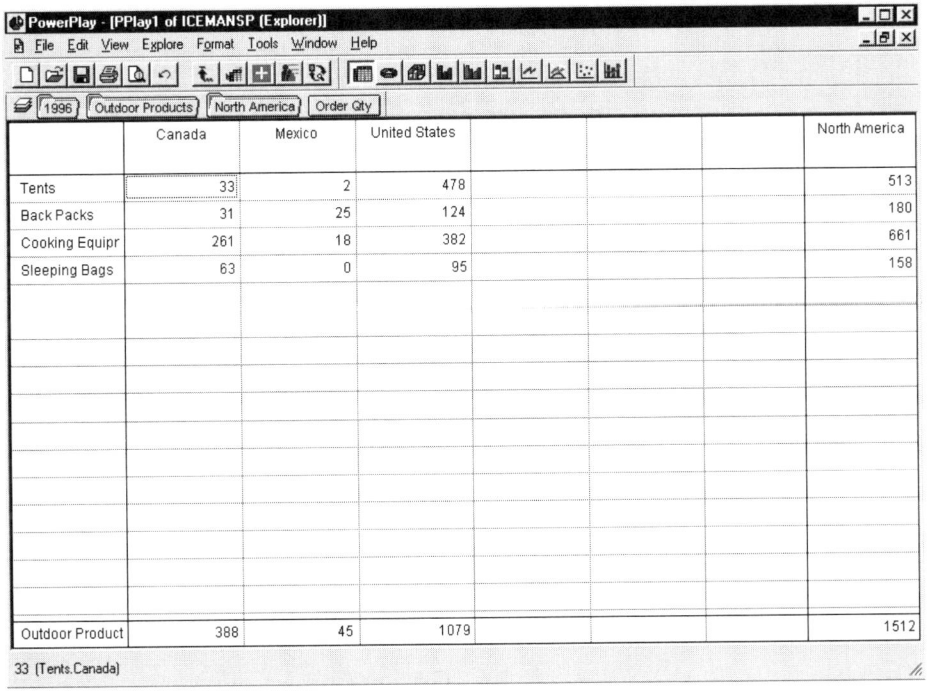

	Canada	Mexico	United States				North America
Tents	33	2	478				513
Back Packs	31	25	124				180
Cooking Equipr	261	18	382				661
Sleeping Bags	63	0	95				158
Outdoor Product	388	45	1079				1512

33 (Tents.Canada)

FIGURE 16-10. *Result of swapping the Region and Product dimensions*

transform our data from just numbers into a really pretty picture. This is shown in Figure 16-11.

Figure 16-11 shows you the results of transforming the sales of Outdoor Products into a histogram. This histogram graphically represents the dollar amount of sales of the individual product groups, as well as a total for the whole product line. As they say, pictures are worth a thousand words...all right, maybe it can stir a discussion amongst friends. Each particular product representation shows us the sales amount of the product for the past two years as well as the total for the product. We also can see that we have a total for the entire product line.

Just as with the spreadsheet view of your data, you have the ability to drill-down while in Graphical mode. By double-clicking on any of the

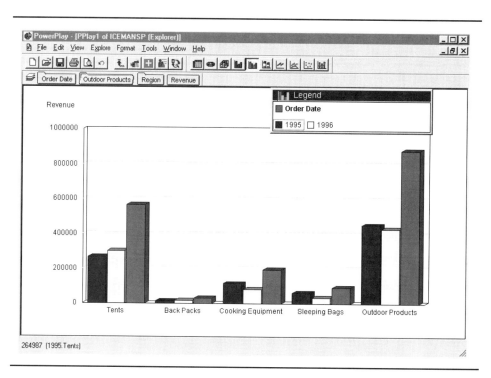

FIGURE 16-11. *Graphical representation of PowerPlay model*

categories, you can drill-down into the product. In Figure 16-12, we have drilled down into the Tents product line, and the resulting graphic is shown.

We have only touched the surface of the power of PowerPlay. There are so many more features in a product like this. You can perform functions such as:

■ Year-to-date analysis

■ Ranking of results

■ Variance reports

■ Exception reports

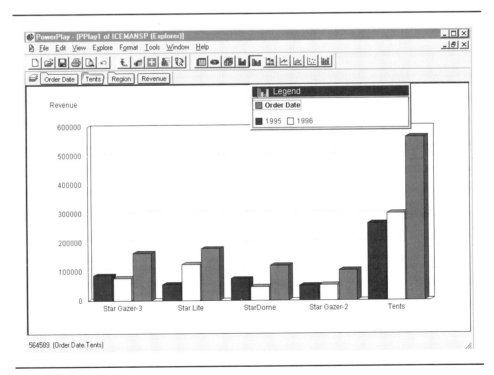

FIGURE 16-12. *Drill-down in Graphical mode*

OLAP tools provide such a rich degree of functionality, and vendors are adding features faster than you can install new product releases. PowerPlay is indicative of the change that we see in product development. Data warehousing is a developing market segment. Just look at the way you design a data warehouse today vs. how we may have been doing it in the past. Let's close this chapter by looking at Oracle's position in the OLAP marketplace.

Oracle and the OLAP Marketplace

In June 1996, Oracle Corporation issued a press release with the banner "Express Technology Acquisition Fuels Oracle's OLAP Success." The press release then went on to state "Oracle Corp. today announced that ten months after acquiring the Express multidimensional online analytical processing (OLAP) technology and business from Information Resources, Inc., the $100 million investment has propelled Oracle into a leadership position in the OLAP market." In a nutshell, this is Oracle's OLAP offering. This is the crown jewel that complements Oracle's data warehouse strategy. In the following sections, you will look at the technology and how Oracle's OLAP offering enhances your data warehouse offering.

TIP

Access to and ability to slice and dice data are critical in today's information world.

Oracle Corporation has shown that it understands this need and that it knows how to stay on the leading edge of technology. Today, Oracle has the premier relational database engine on the market, and it also has the strongest suite of tools compared to all its competitors. It has earned the right to be Number One the old-fashioned way— through hard work. Oracle saw early on that a business needs access to information, and they created a solution. To meet this need, Oracle's relational database engine evolved into an engine that could support large data warehouse implementations. The corporation also realized data warehouses and the information stored within them were fueling a need for robust OLAP environments.

   Oracle did what any responsive industry leader should do—it determined if it could build an OLAP engine better or acquire the technology. Oracle determined it would be best to acquire the technology, and today we have Oracle Express, the leading OLAP choice. Oracle Express not only leads in the OLAP market share, but also in technical functionality. You already know that with Oracle Express you have the choice of ROLAP, MOLAP, or a combination of both. This sends a clear message—Oracle understands the customer's need for, and access to, data. Oracle came to the table with a solution, and that solution is what gives it the leading edge in technology and functionality.

   Speaking of Oracle's solution, let's spend some time on the Express Server-based product set.

CHAPTER 17

The Oracle Express Solution

n Chapter 16, we introduced and discussed OLAP—online analytical processing. It is clear to us that a successful data warehouse must have strong analytical capabilities. Oracle Express may be the answer to this requirement. As you read this chapter, you may get the impression we are high on this product—we are. We believe OLAP is the way to go. By no means does Oracle Express give you the only OLAP solution. It does, however, give you one of the strongest analytical toolsets we have run across.

There is a great deal of meat to this chapter. We will introduce you to the look and feel of three players in the Express solution—Oracle Express Server (OES), Oracle Express Objects (OEO), and Oracle Express Analyzer (OEA). We will also introduce you to the Express Administrator, the administration component of the Oracle Express database, the Relational Access Manager (RAM), Oracle Financial Analyzer (OFA), and Oracle Sales Analyzer (OSA). Acronyms—we love them and we hate them—WNADTTT (we need a database to track them).

Data warehouses that work will incorporate these products from day one, and tools like OEO and OES will become an important part of a user's desktop. Let's start out by looking at why we believe the Express suite of tools is the smartest way to go.

NOTE

Mike Mallia (Spexwest Systems Inc.) was kind enough to provide us with a great deal of the material in the following sections of this chapter. An Oracle7/8 expert in the National Capital region around Ottawa, Mike (and Speedo, his Jack Russell terrier/lapdog) welcomes your communication via email at mmallia@ibm.net—enjoy!

Why Express?

Oracle Corporation decided that it was better to acquire existing technology than to re-create it. Oracle's purchase of Express, in our opinion, is one of the smartest acquisitions in the industry. Take the industry leader in database technology (Oracle) and combine that with the leader in the OLAP industry (Express IRI), and you have a combination that is nearly unbeatable when it comes to the entire data warehouse solution.

Oracle recognized the advantages that the Express database and its tools have over the relational database and existing OLTP tools in solving multidimensional inquiries. *OLTP* stands for online transaction processing, and describes systems familiar to most people—those with multiuser access and high transaction volume. OLTP systems are those we *carry on* business with—data warehouse systems are those we *make business decisions* with. The key is that Express represents its data in a multidimensional model. *Multidimensional*—meaning that information is visualized in grids, like a group of data cells arranged by the dimensions of the data.

NOTE
This model is sometimes called hypercube or cube, which can be a little misleading because only three dimensions can be visualized as a cube—each dimension forming a side—while higher dimensions have no physical representation.

The traditional database view, as displayed in Figure 17-1, is a familiar structure with data organized in tables. Each table consists of a number of columns. This layout helps us in identifying "What is happening?," but is not as useful in determining the queries associated with OLAP—those that answer the "why," "what next," and "what if" questions.

The Express Advantage

The Express database's data storage and access are optimized for multidimensional operations. As for current relational database technologies, the concentration has been mainly on reliability and transaction processing speed, not decision support. If we implemented a multidimensional data model in an Express database versus one in an Oracle relational database, we would find analytical queries written in SQL or PL/SQL usually more complex than the same queries written in Express, as shown in our next listing. *PL/SQL* is Oracle's procedural SQL offering, embedded in almost all the products that interact with the Oracle database.

Record View of Sales

Product	Location	Time	Sales
Pencils	Lawrencetown	Q1 1997	3,039
Pencils	Lawrencetown	Q2 1997	1,783
Pencils	Lawrencetown	Q3 1997	5,000
Pencils	Lawrencetown	Q4 1997	3,105
Pencils	Wolfville	Q1 1997	4,658
Pencils	Wolfville	Q2 1997	2,367
Pencils	Wolfville	Q3 1997	8,907
Pencils	Wolfville	Q4 1997	4,858

Multidimensional View of Sales

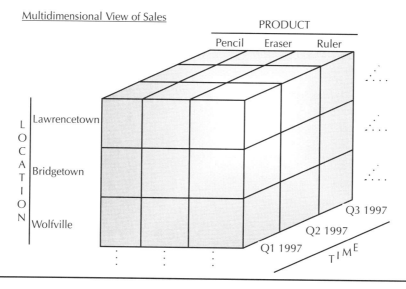

FIGURE 17-1. *Sales variable in Express model and relational table*

The next listing shows how you would report the top 10 clients based on total sales sold in December 1997 in both SQL and Express:

```
PL/SQL version --

declare cursor top10_clients is
  select a.client_name,
         a.sales,
         b.sales
```

```
   from client_summary a,
        client_summary b
  where a.product_group = 'TOTAL'
    and a.month = '1997-12-01'
    and a.product_group = b.product_group
    and a.client_name = b.client_name
    and a.month = months(b.month,1)
  order by a.sales desc;
begin
  open top10_clients;
  for i in 1 .. 10
      fetch top10_clients into :client[i], :sales[i], saleslag[i];
      next;
...
...
Express version --

limit month to dec97
limit client_summary to top 10 based on sales
report down client_summary, sales, lag(sales,1,month)
```

What gives Express database its analytical power and performance is how it organizes its data. Rather than storing information as records, and records in tables, Express (logically) stores data in arrays. Dimension values are used to define the position these data values are in the arrays, somewhat like indices. Referential integrity is secured with the dimension values being stored only once and shared across data values. This type of data storage does not lend itself well for transactional-type processing, but for analytical type queries it is very efficient. Once a particular set of dimension values within a request is resolved, the rest is mathematics (open that old book on discrete mathematics and turn to the chapter on matrix arithmetic)— something your CPU does very rapidly.

How Express Fits in the Data Warehouse

We have determined that the Express database has a definite advantage over existing relational database technology when it comes to analytical processing, but how is this technology used to analyze the volumes of aggregated data within a data warehouse? Data warehouses generally have hierarchies or formula-based relationships of data within each dimension. *Aggregation* involves computing all of these data relationships for one or more dimensions.

As part of the data warehouse solution, Express is generally used as a cache, or staging area where data is accessed directly from the data warehouse and stored in the Express database permanently or temporarily, to take full advantage of the Express analytical tools.

■ **Persistent cache or permanent storage**   Data is extracted from the relational database and permanently stored in the Express database as multidimensional structures. Permanent storage of data in the Express database helps minimize network traffic and increases responsiveness when doing the analytical queries. This strategy is set up generally with a process incrementally extracting data from the relational database when it is updated, and formatting it into a multidimensional structure, updating the data in the Express database.

■ **Transient cache or temporary storage**   Data is extracted from the relational database on an as-needed basis (at time of execution of an analytical query) and stored in the Express database only for the duration of the user's session. Some information that helps identify the data, such as the member lists for each dimension, is stored on a permanent basis to improve performance. Temporary storage requires more processing for each OLAP query, as it has to populate the multidimensional data structures first.

A combination of these two strategies is a common approach, with summary data calculated and stored while detailed data is retrieved (known as a *drill-out* operation) from the data warehouse on demand.

Wide-open Connectivity

The name of the game is getting at your data. With Oracle Express OLAP, it does not matter where your data resides. Punch it, crunch it, and get the data out the door. The first, as well as the most basic, reason is that the tools are built using Oracle standard mechanisms that provide turnkey SQL access to all ODBC data sources. *ODBC* stands for open database connectivity and enables the connection between many tools (e.g., MS Visual Basic) and SQL databases. *Turnkey access* refers to the ability to use the Express tools and be able to communicate with a vendor's data source with little or no intervention. In the case of Oracle, Express is married to the database, which allows for the tightest possible integration of an analytical tool to the data repository. Not all the data may reside in an Oracle database; Express allows wide-open connectivity. It is critical that your data warehouse be able to get at operational system data and other external data sources quickly and easily. With access to SQL data sources using ODBC, you can see that getting at the data is not going to be an obstacle. What we have found in our travels is that using Oracle Express is as simple as installing the software. We reiterate throughout this book that time to market is critical. With Oracle Express you spend your time enabling the users to get at their data rather than installing complex software that requires gobs of time to implement and configure.

The interchange of data between an Express multidimensional database and data stored within relational databases is termed SQL Reach-Through. Some key SQL commands are shown in an Express program in the next listing:

```
argument num_emp text
sql connect EVAN identified by SALTER
sql connect NORMAN identified by NADROJIAN
sql connect BESDESMITH identified by NANCY
sql connect SAUER identified by CHRIS
sql connect DEFWAYNO identified by FRANCIS
sql declare get_employee cursor for select count(*) from employee
sql open get_employee
sql fetch get_employee into :num_emp
report num_emp
```

The SQL command passes instructions written in SQL to the ODBC driver from Express, allowing free interchange of data between multidimensional and relational structures. Defining an Express program or formula (we will define the Express database entity formula later in this chapter) is generally the approach used to fetch data on an as-needed basis.

Standard Operating Environments

Not all operating systems are created equal. Not all computer shops are running UNIX. Many times you have to purchase hardware just to enable the software you want to run. Oracle Express software, like the Oracle8 Server, runs on many hardware platforms. There is no need to acquire an additional machine—you are able to run the Express Server on the same machine your existing Oracle8 implementation operates on. You do not have to use your existing hardware, but it is important that at least the option exists if you so choose. The Oracle Express Server runs on:

- Windows NT 3.5x and 4.0
- UNIX offerings such as
    - Solaris2/SunOS5
    - Sequent DYNIX/ptx
    - Digital UNIX
    - NCR UNIX SVR4 MP-RAS
    - HP-UX
    - IBM AIX
    - SunOS4
    - Pyramid/Siemens Nixdorf
    - Data General Aviion
- Open VMS from Digital
- MVS/TSO from IBM

NOTE
Not all versions of OES run on all versions of the operating systems in the previous list.

One-stop Shopping

How many times have you heard this from a software company's support organization—"Sorry, that's not our problem, please call vendor X." With Oracle Express, you have one-stop shopping. OES offers a single, integrated software architecture. It is tightly integrated with existing relational systems and can be used as a cache for relational data or as a data storage mechanism of its own. Remember the MOLAP and ROLAP discussion we had in Chapter 16? With Oracle Express, you have the choice of storing your data in a multidimensional database, a relational database, or a combination of the two.

Oracle Express empowers your users with tools that allow them to do their day-to-day analysis without having a propeller head (i.e., a very technical person) sitting at their side. With the Express toolset, users can define their own functions; they are not limited to what Oracle Express provides or what programmers have put together on their behalf. This provides maximum flexibility by not conscripting users to the set of functions built into the tool. As users explore their data with Oracle Express, they have the ability to slice and dice, and drill-down lower and lower until they get the answers they need.

NOTE
There is a point where the drill-down operation stops due to the level of detail stored in the warehouse.

For example, if your data warehouse stores every item on a purchase order over the past ten years, you will be able to drill-down to that level of detail. On the other hand, if your warehouse stores summaries of past purchase orders, you are only allowed to dig to that summary level. This leads into two issues that pop up time and time again when designing and implementing a data warehouse:

■ How much detail needs to be in the warehouse?

■ How far back should that detail data be stored (i.e., the number of years kept in the warehouse)?

The users no longer rely on computer professionals to interpret and implement their requests. On their own, they carry on standard discovery exercises that include looking for top and bottom performers, comparing current period performance against a previous period, and drilling down from highly summarized data to more detail.

Integration with the Data Warehouse

The interchange of data with a data warehouse can be achieved quite a bit easier using the Relational Access Manager (RAM) module, provided with Express. The RAM module specifically provides a bridge, or dynamic link between a relational data that is specifically constructed in a star schema, the same as discussed in Chapters 5 and 7 (a data warehouse), and Express objects. To facilitate this link, RAM uses a standard set of tables it stores in the target relational database.

The GUI front end to the Relational Access Manager is the Relational Access Administrator (RAA). It bundles all that is necessary to connect Express with relational data. The RAA module charts the data and information in relational tables to corresponding Express entities. It then has a build process that creates the multidimensional structures within the Express database with hooks for retrieving data from a data warehouse during run time.

Oracle Express Server (OES)

The basic requirement for OES is 20MB of disk space (or 20,971,520 bytes); with the default demo database, this can climb as high as 60MB. The installation is a standard Windows-based routine we have all come to know and love. When the process completes, there will be an "Oracle Express Server" program group with Express Service Manager, Express Configuration Manager, and a handful of documentation and release note icons.

NOTE
We have used a very simple, conservative Windows NT 4.0 server configuration when quoting disk space and memory requirements.

Overview

OES was designed to meet the demanding OLAP requirements of enterprise-wide, state-of-the-art, and future computing environments. There are three components to the OLAP application architecture provided by OES:

   1. The data sources   A combination of relational databases, legacy information systems, and data warehouse repositories. These information stores can cross vendor platforms and contain a hodge-podge of SQL-based databases accessible through the ODBC connectivity mechanisms.

2. **The Express Server**   The icing on the cake, so to speak, where the communication and processing is facilitated to allow clients to access the desired data, slice and dice it as they see fit, and spit out results that support decision-making processes.

3. **The client software**   Other Express components such as OEO or OEA; a Microsoft Excel Add-In, as well as interfaces for Microsoft Visual Basic, a Microsoft Windows Dynamic Link Library, OLE, and C or C++. OLE (object linking and embedding) is an industry standard mechanism that allows Windows client software to share objects.

Once information systems professionals have isolated the end-user requirements and issues that drive the desire to create an OLAP solution, they can stage the desired data in the OES. *Staging* involves creating a temporary storage area on the server. Often, derived summary data is stored permanently on the Express Server, and the detail data that produced the summaries is read directly from the warehouse during OLAP sessions.

Communication Infrastructure

The heart of Express is an advanced calculation engine and a shared, multidimensional data cache. Entry points to OES include the following:

■ **Client/server**   The familiar architecture where a desktop computer (client) interacts with a large centralized data source (server), with a communication-enabling network transport.

■ **Peer to peer**   Communication between two Express databases on the same or different machines; even though we use an OES example, peer to peer is a term used throughout the industry.

■ **Express Web Agent**   A facility that permits dynamic generation of Web pages directly from Express as users slice and dice their data.

Client/server communications for either Windows or UNIX is available for the Express Server via a library of C functions. This library of functions is known as *SNAPI* (structured *n*-dimensional application program interface) and acts like Oracle's Net8. Net8 is one of the pieces in the network that enables communication between clients and the Oracle8 Server. There are two flavors of SNAPI:

■ Local SNAPI for Personal Express (PC-based version of Express database).

■ Remote SNAPI for the Express Server—apart from the connect functions the versions are identical.

The Express Communications Architecture (*XCA*) facilitates Express server to server communications (or server to Personal Express). This communication architecture is used mainly in Express applications that have distributed databases.

The Express Web Agent is an interface that allows Express OLAP functionality through a Web browser. We are now going to have a look at the Express data model and some ways to conceptualize OES, and how it differs from the more relational database background many of us come from.

Express Data Model

Relational thinkers beware! In contrast to the techniques for designing OLTP systems, which rely on tables and relationships, the Express data model is multidimensional, using *variables*, *dimensions* and *hierarchies*. Multidimensional models are typically about numeric data, such as values and counts and are used to solve problem statements like, "What is my sales by product over time, by geographic location?"

A multidimensional model is designed to support the reporting and analytical needs, and can best be described by contrasting it with the relational model in the following ways:

■ A multidimensional model's information is structured in slices of time instead of detailed transactions.

■ OLTP systems can provide details such as those used in audit trails—multidimensional models are better for looking at the overall picture.

■ Relationships are definitive or explicit in the relational model while implicit in the multidimensional model.

The primary elements of the Express data model are dimensions, variables, formulas, and relations. Each of these is introduced in the pages following.

Dimensions

Dimensions keep creeping into our discussions; we have defined and discussed them in a number of places. Within Express, a combination of dimensions organize and index the data stored in a variable or calculated by a formula, uniquely identifying each occurrence within the database. *Dimensions* are typically hierarchical (a hierarchy is a relation, which we will talk about later in this section). Applied in a financial application, a time dimension may be grouped by fiscal year, quarters, months, and days. Dimensions can have numerous hierarchies, which, if we take again our time dimension, could also be based on calendar year.

Variables

A variable is described as an array, which holds data values. Some people, mainly those who have worked extensively with spreadsheets (typically, those finance users who live and breathe MS Excel or Lotus) refer to variable as a "cell." Another term that would probably be more familiar is a "fact" associated with a star schema. The variable is typically a number that may be representing units sold or cost of goods sold. Variables are not limited to storing numeric values. Descriptive variables store textual data such as descriptive labels for products.

Formulas

Formulas are derived data items that are calculated dynamically, a convenient way of saving and using complex or frequently used expressions. The resulting value is never stored—just its definition. Express calculates the values of the formula whenever it is invoked. Profit margin is an example of a formula. Formulas can reference variables as well as other formulas.

Relations

Relations link the values of one dimension with the values of another and capture one of the two most common types of relationships:

■ One to one—the fact that a person can have one and only one surname.

■ One to many—the fact that a person can have one or more phone numbers.

Relations are most commonly used to capture hierarchies, a top-down, one-to-many relationship. Express can use these relations to perform aggregate functions dynamically or narrow the scope of an operation.

Figure 17-2 shows examples of a dimension with a relation and variables.

After discussing the main components of the Express data model (caught your interest yet?), it now makes sense to move on and have a look at working with data on the OES; afterwards, we will look at the Express Administrator interface.

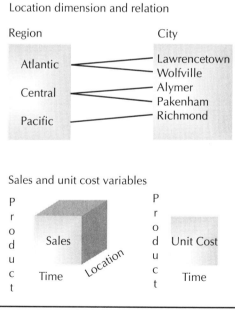

FIGURE 17-2. *Common Express items*

Working with Data on the Oracle Express Server

To become familiar with multidimensional data and the Oracle Express Server, we will use the Express Analyzer to have a look at a briefing. A *briefing* looks like an everyday report. What's different about a briefing is that the information stored within is directly linked to the data, dimensions, measures, tables, and relationships. What this means is that a briefing can actually come alive merely by a click of the mouse on an object such as a graph. Views of information displayed in a briefing change as the user changes the data selection. After double-clicking the Express Analyzer icon in the Express Client group, you will be connected to the Express Server.

NOTE
If your Express Server administrator has implemented some security features using Oracle Express' permissions system, you will need to supply login information before being hooked up to Express Server.

Figure 17-3 shows a page from the sample briefing. Before discussing selection of dimensions, let's look at some important areas on this page. The briefing page reports on regional sales broken down by time period (with eight values), channel (with three values), product division (with four values), and geographical areas (with five values). Note how there is a drop-down pick list beside time period and channel and not the other dimensions. Express has the other dimensions broken down on the display. Product is broken down into its four values (total product, audio division, video division, accessory division) plotted on the graph with different-sized rectangles. As well, the five possible geographical areas (world, Americas, Australia, Europe, and Asia) are accounted for in the display. The user can slice and dice the regional sales data using any combination of time period and channel.

The cube icon in the upper left-hand corner of the dimension bar in Figure 17-3 is called the *selector button* and brings up the Selector dialog box, where the user selects the dimension values to display. The dialog box,

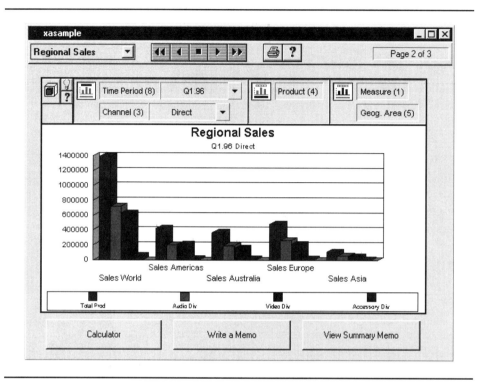

FIGURE 17-3. *Sample briefing page*

shown in Figure 17-4, includes geographical area, division of product, time period, and distribution channel dimensions.

Suppose you want to change the content of the data being displayed in the graph. You simply click on the List button on the button bar along the top of the Selector dialog box to bring up a screen from where you choose what to display. Express uses the standard "+" and "-" sign convention in lists to indicate where drill-down can be performed. Figure 17-5 shows the List dialog box where the geographical areas are broken out.

Note how "World" has been broken down into continents, and how Europe has been expanded into its drill-down components. Drill-down is possible until there is no plus sign indicator beside a list member. Had we clicked on the plus sign beside Europe, we would open up the country dimension for France. With the drill-down indicator turned on (i.e., the plus sign), France could be expanded into the city dimension, allowing one to specify cities like Paris, Bordeaux, and Dijon.

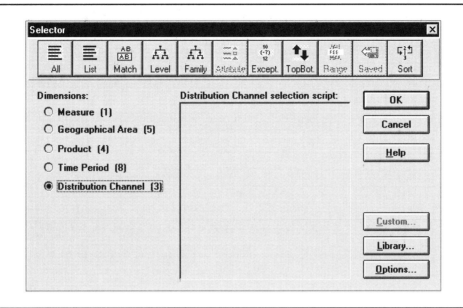

FIGURE 17-4. *Selector dialog box*

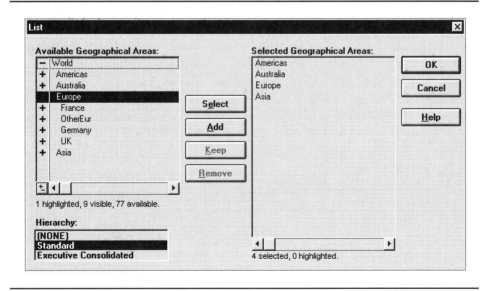

FIGURE 17-5. *Geographical areas drill-down*

OEA builds, then redisplays a graph based on what has been selected on the Selector and List dialog boxes. It's worth having a look at the Hierarchy area of the list box shown in Figure 17-5. There are three selections in this area—NONE, Standard, and Executive Consolidated. The breakdown of the geographical areas changes when each value in this pick list is highlighted. The Standard view breaks Asia down into Japan and China, and each country into a few of its biggest cities (e.g., Tokyo, Japan and Beijing, China). The Executive view drill-down stops with country; there is no city-based drill-down.

It's all fine and dandy to speak about working with data in OES—let's look around the OEA and become familiar with its look and feel.

A Tour of Oracle Express Analyzer (OEA)

When using OEA, you will spend most of your time with the elements contained in its main window. Let's discuss these elements, what they are called, and how they assist you while using the product.

NOTE
The number preceding each element refers to the areas numbered in Figure 17-6.

1—Menu Bar

This is the familiar menu found at the top of many windows. Many options in each pull-down menu are standard (e.g., Save As or Exit from the File menu); others are OEA-specific, such as the Briefing Browser, Database Browser, and Object Inspector display option dialogs under the Windows option.

TIP
The size and amount of text displayed in the icons on the Express window can be adjusted by selecting Window on the menu bar, followed by the Toolbars option on the subsequent pull-down menu.

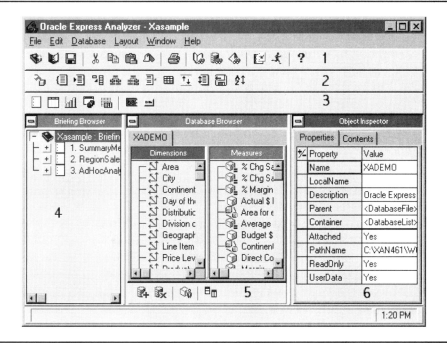

FIGURE 17-6. *Express Analyzer main window*

2—Selector Toolbar

This provides quick access to the Selector dialog box shown in Figure 17-4. The Selector tool is on the far left of this toolbar. Let's look at the various buttons on this toolbar (moving from left to right); using these buttons provides rapid access to the types of slicing and dicing the analyst does with the multidimensional data.

- *All* button invokes the Select All dialog box to choose all the values in the selected dimension or all the dimension values in the current hierarchy.

- *List* button brings up the List dialog box, where you are presented with a list of dimension values.

- *Match* displays the Select by Matching Characters dialog box, where you can specify characters to look for in dimension values.

- *Level* button brings up the Select by Level dialog box when the selected dimension has an associated hierarchy. There may be a hierarchy defined for the region dimension that breaks the dimension down by state and city.

- *Family* button brings up the Select by Family dialog box, where you choose values based on a group of related dimension values.

- *Attribute* button brings up the Select by Attribute dialog box, where you choose dimension values that share a particular characteristic.

- *Exception* button opens up the Select by Exception dialog box to select dimension values based on the data values in a particular measure or on the way those data values compare with data values in a second measure. Exceptions are usually based on numeric comparisons such as where sales have exceeded a dollar amount specified by the analyst.

- *Top/Bottom* button invokes the Select Top/Bottom dialog box, where you select dimension values based on the top or bottom range of data values in a particular measure.

- *Range* button invokes the Select by Range dialog box, where you define start and end time markers within which dimensions values should be included.

- *Saved Selection* button displays the Saved Selection dialog box, where you choose a previously saved dimension selection.

- *Sort* button displays the Sort Selection dialog box, where you specify how to sort dimension values. Sorting can be done many ways, including alphabetic, ascending or descending, and based on each value's order in the active hierarchy.

3—Toolbox

This contains icons that are selected to create Express Analyzer objects such as pages, tables, graphs, banners, and buttons. These objects become part of briefings, and some end up being used to present results to the user.

Developers are familiar with this interface as a shortcut to creating objects, headings, pictures, and screen prompts for their programs.

4—Briefing Browser

The Briefing Browser displays an outline for each open briefing as well as a briefing that is in the midst of being created. As shown in Figure 17-7, the detailed expansion uses the plus and minus sign indicators to indicate where drill-down can be performed.

Since there are three pages to this briefing, the screen shown in Figure 17-7 has three page indicators entitled "SummaryMemo," "RegionSales1," and "AdHocAnalysis1." Express Analyzer uses the same icon to classify each element as it does on its corresponding element in the main window shown in Figure 17-6. The right mouse button opens up a series of menus whose choices depend on the type of element selected. Double-clicking the left

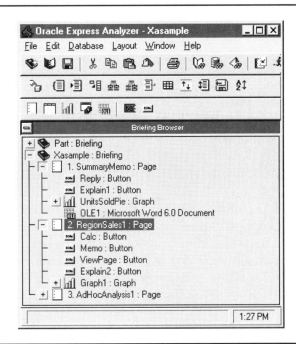

FIGURE 17-7. *Briefing Browser object detail*

mouse button on a briefing brings up the Briefing Editor; double-clicking the left mouse button on a page (or any element in a page) brings up the entire page in Edit mode with that object selected. Double-clicking on the content of an object (i.e., the title of a graph) does nothing.

Let's drill-down and look at some characteristics of the Calc button and then the Time Period selection on the Regional Sales page of this briefing. Double-clicking on the Calc button brings up an Editing Regional Sales worksheet. Clicking the right mouse button over the Calculator button on that worksheet invokes a pop-up menu from where you can define characteristics of the button including color characteristics, font and font size, border, fill color, and name. The first five options in that pop-up menu are "Duplicate," "Edit," "Inspect," "Delete," and "Set QuickAction." Clicking the right mouse button over the Time Period brings up a different pop-up menu with options "Inspect," "Select data," and "Aggregate." We'll first have a look at what happens when selecting Inspect from both elements' pop-up menu, then look at QuickAction for Calc, and Select data and Aggregate for Time Period.

INSPECT   The Object Inspector invoked by selecting Inspect is shown in Figure 17-8; this inspector is discussed in its own section later on, called "6—Object Inspector." For properties with settings such as Yes or No, double-clicking the left mouse button toggles the setting. For other properties, you can type the new setting directly into the property sheet. Some properties have an ellipsis (...) next to the property name. When you double-click on the property name, a dialog box appears. For properties with settings that you can choose from a list, a pull-down list appears when you click on the value in the Property column.

QUICKACTION   Figure 17-9 shows the QuickAction selection box for the Calc button. *QuickActions* are predefined functions used to customize the behavior of an object without the need to write or rewrite any code. The content of the Arguments section of this window depends on what Action is currently selected. The Arguments section changes to a page reference entry area when "Goto Page" is highlighted in the Actions area.

SELECT DATA-TIME PERIOD   This menu option brings up the Selector dialog box, as shown previously in Figure 17-4. When deciding what data to select for an object, you will begin to fully appreciate the

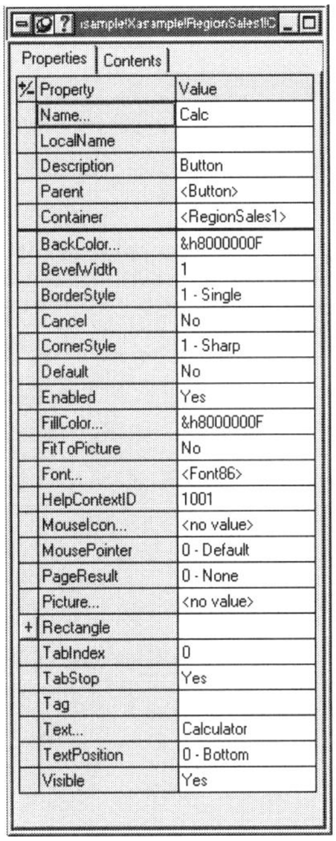

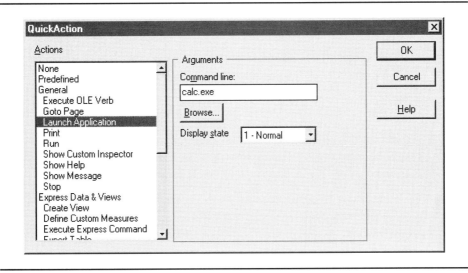

FIGURE 17-8.   *Object Inspector*

FIGURE 17-9.   *QuickAction selection of Calculator button*

options and choice that can be programmed into OEA. You will become readily familiar with selecting attributes, defining exceptions, and specifying ranges.

AGGREGATE-TIME PERIOD   This is where you specify the aggregation type such as total, average, smallest, or largest, as well as the aggregation dimension such as month, year, or quarter. By clicking on the Change Selection button, you can specify an alternate hierarchy and level to use for forming the aggregation. Express pays special attention to problems that can come up with embedded totals when doing aggregations. *Embedded totals* are predefined levels of aggregation built into a hierarchical dimension. Suppose you choose a hierarchy that contains Q1 (for the first quarter of the fiscal year) data as well as numbers from June to August that fall into Q1. An aggregation that chooses Q1 as well as these three months will produce distorted results; the aggregate total will actually be twice what Q1 is supposed to be. In this case, you should use the Change Selection dialog box to ensure you are aggregating values at the correct level in a hierarchy.

5—Database Browser

The Database Browser is used to view attached databases, and the dimensions and measures they contain. Figure 17-10 shows the database browser for the XADEMO database, with the dimensions on the left and the measures on the right.

Four buttons sit at the bottom of the screen when using the database browser:

- *Attach a Database* is a quick way to make a different Express database available to the current session, and brings up an Attach Database dialog box.

- *Detach the Active Database* closes the active database; you must close the active project or briefing before detaching a database that is in use.

- *Create Custom Measures* invokes the Custom Measures dialog box, where users can fine-tune their analysis to suit their individual requirements. Any custom measures the users create are stored

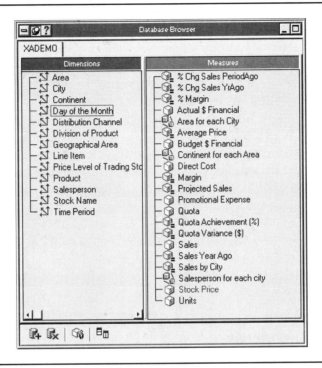

FIGURE 17-10.   *Database Browser for XADEMO database*

locally in a system project file. As the user attaches to a database when starting up an Analyzer session, the custom measures in the project file are created in that database for the life of the session.

- *Change Splitter Orientation* cascades the two browser panes horizontally or vertically—this is a toggle button.

NOTE
When a session ends, any custom measures that may have been created in the attached database are deleted.

The Database Browser has one tab for each attached database. Each tab has two panes. The left pane lists the dimensions in the attached database and the right pane displays measures within that database. As you move around the dimensions pane, the color of the measures changes to indicate which are available for each dimension. A right mouse button on any dimension brings up a pop-up menu with the Inspect option. Selecting that option invokes the dimension's property sheet.

A right mouse button while positioned on a measure displays a pop-up menu with the options "Inspect," "Table," and "Graph." Inspect on this menu also invokes the selected measure's property sheet. Choosing Table or Graph brings up a new page for the active briefing. Express builds the appropriate object into the new page and then displays the page. When you close the window showing the new page, you are asked whether you want to add the new page to the briefing.

TIP
You can set an option in Express Analyzer to automatically add each new page to the current briefing.

6—Object Inspector

The Object Inspector is used to view and set properties for an object, as well as to examine its contents. There are two tabs on the Object Inspector:

- *Properties* tab is where objects are viewed and property settings are massaged.

- *Contents* tab lists objects or components that are part of the object you are inspecting.

Once familiar with placing the Object Inspector on the Express desktop beside the Briefing or Database Browser, you will find it the only way to go. As you move around the Database or Briefing Browser, the contents of the Object Browser pane change to show the properties and contents of the selected object. Notice how the Object Inspector displays the properties for the XASAMPLE briefing as the sole briefing object is selected in Figure 17-11.

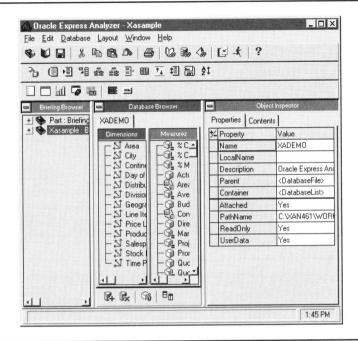

FIGURE 17-11. *Properties for XASAMPLE briefing*

TIP
*When working with the Object Browser,
context-sensitive help can be invoked by
pressing F1 on the keyboard with a property
name selected.*

For example, suppose you are looking at the Property tab in the Object Inspector for the XASAMPLE briefing, and you want to inspect the Parent property of the briefing. Before looking at the value for Parent, you could assure yourself you know what a Parent means in the Express context. You would select the text in the Value column of the property folder and press F1 to view the screen shown in Figure 17-12.

TIP
We recommend you use this property sheet context-sensitive help feature as you familiarize yourself with the jargon used by Oracle Express Analyzer.

Let's have a look at what is going on behind the scenes with the Express Administrator, the component used to configure databases for use with Express Client tools.

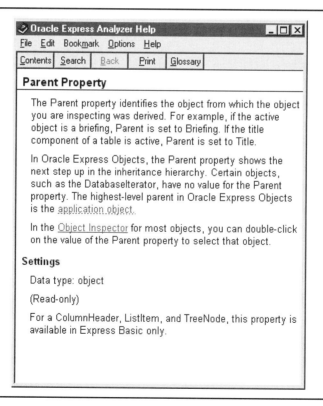

FIGURE 17-12. *Parent Property Help screen*

The Oracle Express Administrator (OEA)

The Express Administrator is distributed on the Express line of products CD. This is the tool that you use to administer the Express product; it helps you create new databases, define dimensions, and do many other tasks you need to perform prior to turning an OLAP application over to the user community. To install Express Administrator, run Setup.exe on your CD-ROM. When the installation completes, you will find an Administrator icon in the Express Client program group. Let's briefly look at some tasks that can be accomplished setting up a new database using the Express Administrator.

Creating a New Database

After double-clicking on the Administrator icon, a blank Administrator worksheet will appear. To create a new database, you select New Database from the File pull-down menu on the Express Administrator main menu bar. Alternatively, you can click on the leftmost icon on the main menu bar to bring up the dialog box shown here:

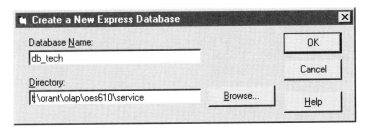

We entered DB_TECH as the new database name, then clicked on OK. The Administrator then presents you with a Database Browser window specific to the DB_TECH database being created. There will be the default tree of objects displayed underneath the DB_TECH header. To define an object using one of the seven types, right-mouse click anywhere on the Database Browser worksheet, then choose Define from the pop-up menu that appears. You can also use the menu bar, with options such as Dictionary, Define, Dimension, and Formula.

NOTE
The same pop-up menu appears regardless of where you right-mouse click.

Let's define a dimension, a variable, and then a formula derived from the variable. Right-mouse click on the worksheet, select Define, then Dimension from the pop-up menu. You must enter a Name for the dimension, and select a datatype from the picklist in the General folder. When done, click on the Define button, as shown in Figure 17-13.

After creating the dimension, click on Close to return to the Database Browser worksheet. The Administrator will display the new dimension under the Dimension branch of the database object tree. Now let's create a variable called Sales to hold information about Product. Right-mouse click in the Database Browser, Define a Variable, enter the name **sales**, and give it a datatype of Decimal. Express supports several datatypes, including integer and text. Sales will be dimensioned by Product, and normally would be dimensioned by other business tracking categories such as Region and

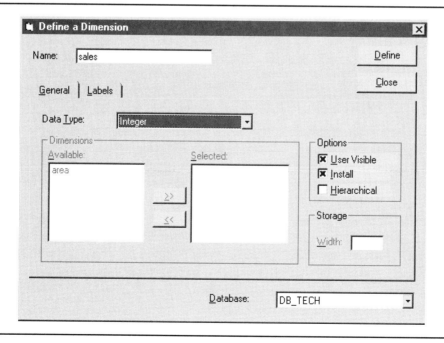

FIGURE 17-13. *Define a Dimension dialog box*

Time. Double-click on "Product" to dimension Sales by Product. Close the dialog box to return to the Database Browser.

Let's finish off this brief introduction to the Administrator by creating a formula. First, right-mouse click on the worksheet, choose Define, then Formula from the pop-up menu that appears. In the Define Formula dialog box, enter a name and select a data type from the picklist. Express presents you with a list of available dimensions and allows you to transfer dimensions back and forth to the select dimensions upon which the formula will be built. We have selected the Product dimension, then entered the formula "sales/12" to instruct Express how to arrive at the value for the formula we have named "monthlysales_avg." This will divide the Sales measure values by 12, creating a measure that is derived from existing Sales data. Figure 17-14 shows this dialog box with our data entry; the exercise is completed by clicking on Define.

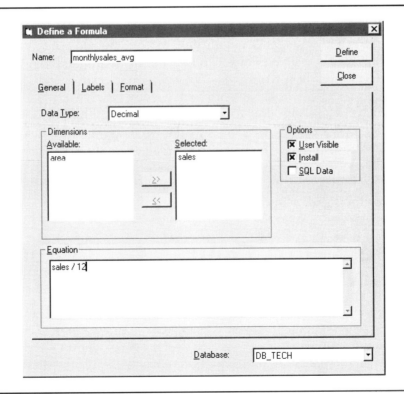

FIGURE 17-14.   *Define a Formula dialog box*

Working with an Existing Database

This activity is similar to the creation activity, except the database exists and must be attached to the current session. An Express database is attached by clicking on the Attach Database icon (second from the left on the main menu bar) or selecting Attach Database from the File option on the main menu bar.

NOTE
You can have more than one database attached at a time. Be careful when defining objects using the Express Administrator that they are created in the correct database. Until you become a seasoned user of the OEA, we recommend working with one database at a time.

To detach a database when required, use the Detach Database icon (third from the left) or select Detach Database from the File option on the main menu bar. This section helps you get your head around the power and look and feel of the OEA. Most of the activities are accomplished with mouse clicks and some text data entry.

Let's back up a bit and do a checkpoint for the administrators reading this chapter. Many DBAs (in a perfect world, we would be able to say "all DBAs") have gone through the exercise of creating a database to sit under relational technology such as Oracle8. As we look at setting up and working with OES, we are now going to spend a few minutes looking at the process of defining the OES database.

Express DBA Course 101 (Younger Sibling of the DBA)

In this section is a brief outline of some of the things that should be considered when defining an Express database. Before we look at these considerations in the definition of an Express database, we should first look at how we would be designing the multidimensional model it will represent.

Designing the multidimensional model is a top-down process with three major steps:

- First, decide what business process the database is to be capturing, such as sales processing.

- Next, identify the values or variables, such as sales amounts or unit costs. This information is almost always numeric.

- Last, identify the lowest level of detail in which the values are to be analyzed. These elements will be the dimensions with possible hierarchies.

NOTE
Contrary to popular belief, and the advice given by some experts, we feel it is mandatory to engage the services of high-end technical data-aware personnel when rolling out an OES-based solution.

The DWA (data warehouse administrator), ex DBA, is an integral piece on the OES team. The Express databases, just like the Oracle8 databases, should be protected in a way similar to their relational counterparts. Prying eyes and fingers can do more damage than good. Keep the curious out. Only allow those who know what to do and when across the moat into the multidimensional castle. This familiar warning was also called the Blair principle in two of our previous works. Now let us look at what we should look out for when defining an Express database.

The Database

As with a relational database, the Express database is where the schema is developed. Once you create a database, Express objects can be defined. The names of these objects must satisfy the following:

- The length of the object name cannot exceed 16 characters.

- The first character must be a letter or an underscore.

- Letters, numbers, periods, and underscores are allowed.

Express will give you an error if you violate any of its naming restrictions. Also, Express can have multiple databases attached simultaneously. One of the main purposes of attaching multiple databases is to separate application code from data. This allows sharing of source code to different sources of data (other Express databases) and is especially helpful if the code takes up several megabytes. Express processes multiple attached databases in a top-down fashion. With this in mind, uniqueness of names of objects is important if planning on attaching multiple databases. Take the following into account when using multiple databases:

- If duplicate object names exist among multiple attached databases, the name of the first object encountered in the attachment order of the databases is used.

NOTE
This can be a Trojan horse—suppose you attach a database named with a variable of SALES and it supercedes another one named SALES. You may end up working with the "wrong" SALES variable for hours without realizing it!

- When defining database objects, they are created in the current database.

- Database objects can only be modified in the current database.

- A dimension in one database cannot dimension variables in another database.

Now it's time to marry some theory with practice—especially the definition of dimensions, hierarchies, variables, and formulas.

Defining Dimensions

Dimensions are the backbone of the Express database. Dimensions must be created before any variables using those dimensions can be created. Efficiency can be gained by sharing dimensions among variables, whenever possible. Once you have decided on the optimal order of the dimensions (discussed in the section "Defining Variables"), use the same order for all variables that might be accessed at the same time.

Defining Hierarchies (A Relation)

A *hierarchy* is a relation created by associating dimension values in a parent-child relationship. This is the major relation defined within Express. The Express Administrator has a feature that at the time of definition can specify if that dimension will be hierarchical. A dimension can have one or more hierarchies, which identify the values that contribute to subtotals and totals in the data.

Defining Variables

When defining a variable, the order in which the dimensions are listed is extremely important because it affects both processing time and disk storage. Variables should be defined with dimensions ordered to match the order in which users are likely to view data (or order of varying). The first dimension identifying a variable should be the fastest varying, the second the next fastest varying, and so on until the last dimension identifying the variable is the slowest varying.

A variable can be dimensioned by up to 32 dimensions. However, a variable defined with more than eight or ten dimensions should not be a regular occurrence! This makes for a very unmanageable and literally difficult to understand variable. Data can then be added manually through OEA into the variable. Data can also be imported using the data loader programs or the Express Administrator's import function, which we will review later in this section.

NOTE
The Express Administrator can not view a variable that is defined with more than six dimensions; OEO can.

Use of Formulas

It is recommended that formulas be used whenever possible. The benefits of using formulas is that they are always up to date and there is no need to store them; the data are assembled as the formulas are calculated at run time.

NOTE
There is a drawback, however. The data must be calculated each time the formula is invoked. This is slower than accessing stored data.

After doing the high-level physical definition of the database, as we have discussed in the last few sections, we think about bringing data into OES. Let's spend a minute on importing data into and exporting data from OES.

Import/Export

Once a database is created and dimensions and variables are defined, the structure is available to read data into the database from a file. There are three types of files you can import data from:

■ **ASCII** Text data, either delimited by a special character or positioned in a fixed-length field. These two input types are shown here:

```
-- Fixed length where each information item reserves the same
-- number of characters regardless of the length of the data in
-- the field
Roberto         Prendin         Gloucester          ON
Rose            Stevanovic      Lees                ON
Speedo          Guilfoyle       Glebe               MI
-- Delimited data where a special character defines the end of
-- one field and the beginning of the next.
Roberto%Prendin%Gloucester%ON
Rose%Stevanovic%Lees%ON
Speedo%Guilfoyle%Glebe%MI
```

■ **Relational Database (SQL)** An ODBC connection that can be saved in a file containing the information on the relational structure extracted directly from a repository built using relational technology such as Oracle, Sybase, Informix, or CA/Ingres.

■ **Express Interchange Format (EIF)** An approach to extracting data from OES along with the definition of that data required to rebuild the information in another Express database. This is similar to the functionality and features delivered with good old export and import against the Oracle8 Server. These two tools are discussed in Chapter 8 as players that enable the ability to move data into the warehouse already resident in an Oracle database.

Before importing data from any source, the structure of the data in the source file must be known. The data structure determines the dimensions, variables, relations, and other Express objects needed to store the data properly in the Express database.

NOTE
In this context, import and export are not the same programs used by many DBAs.

To import data from a SQL data source, a connection to the relational database must exist. The SQL file creates a data loader program. The alternative to importing data is connection to SQL databases directly using Express Relational Access Manager. The last type can easily be imported because the file is from an Express database. Express exports its data and database structure from a source database to an EIF file format only. Thus the structure of the Express database importing the data does not have to be known using this option, as it did for the other sources. This is because when importing the data, the definitions are imported as well. It is important to note that the object names within the import file should not exist in the target database.

The diplomas are ready—you have successfully passed this introductory course (remember, your first student loan payment is due soon). Let's get our hands dirty looking at OEO, where the developer can build OLAP applications with which the end user will interact.

Oracle Express Objects (OEO)

Install OEO by running the Setup.exe program on your CD.

NOTE
This setup program we speak of can be found using the Start Menu|Find|Files or Folders in the Windows taskbar.

You may get asked a number of questions about the location of the Personal Express software and Express Analyzer. In most cases, you will simply click OK to carry on based on the directory names suggested by the install program. When you are done, you will have an "Oracle Express Objects" icon in the Express Client program group.

Overview

OEO is an object-oriented application development tool for creation of graphical OLAP client/server applications. Using OEO, developers build applications for the end user comprising standard display objects such as tables and graphs. With OEO, you have the capability to incorporate OLAP functionality into your current development environment. The briefings produced by OEO are open-ended. End users can control what data is displayed and format the output to their liking. This blends well with forecasting and formulation of material for sales promotions.

NOTE
We believe the open-ended architecture of OEO makes it the ideal candidate for OLAP development and rapid deployment.

With OEO, as an OLAP solution is delivered to end users, there are enough doors left open that the users can "play with the data" to their hearts' content. OEO gives you the ability to extend the OLAP development environment. For example, a checkbox is a common function all users in Windows applications are used to working with. This product enables the OLAP world to meet the non-OLAP world and vice versa. This means that your end user has the access to the same functions and capabilities as a seasoned developer. They both can incorporate OLAP objects into their development environment and simple briefings.

OEO lets the developer organize data and presentation mechanisms into a briefing in the same way as we discussed with Express Analyzer. Another attribute of OEA is that it is the player for any application developed in OEO. Express makes extensive use of data-aware objects. *Data-aware* objects allow the users to choose what measures they wish to view, and how these measures will be presented via the suite of sophisticated OEO elements. The programming language the developer uses with OEO is compatible with Microsoft's Visual Basic (or *VB*). Visual Basic is an accepted standard in the Windows development environment; so many application development people know Visual Basic, and thus the transition to application development with OEO is painless. Much of the power of OEO can be summed up using three words so native to the object-oriented application developer's vernacular:

- **Encapsulation**   The details of the implementation of an object are hidden from external objects. Objects perform services for one another, without the calling object knowing anything about what goes on inside other objects. Using encapsulation, objects do their thing after receiving stimuli from an external source; often, the same triggering mechanism used for more than one object causes different objects to behave differently.

- **Inheritance**   The ability to establish a new class of object, taking on the attributes and methods of the old class. After a new class of objects inherits the characteristics and behavior of the old class, attributes can still be added or taken away where necessary. This allows you to reuse much of your code in similar functions instead of the old way—copy old code and make changes.

- **Polymorphism**   Involves the ability of objects to behave differently depending on the circumstances under which they are invoked. Think of the OK button on two Windows dialog boxes. When acknowledging a message from Windows, clicking on OK simply causes the information window to close; when entering a file name the first time you save a document in a word processor, clicking on OK causes the data to be written to disk and the window to disappear. Same object, different behavior.

Object-oriented development environments support these three techniques and drive the approach programmers take to developing systems.

We stress time to market and end-user productivity when looking at OEO. Data-aware objects save valuable developer time and accelerate delivery of applications. Users become self-sufficient when empowered to create their own new ways of looking at their data by availing themselves of the power of these objects.

OEO possesses prepackaged modules for OLAP processing, and lives and breathes the multidimensional database structures so fundamental to a bona fide OLAP solution. Advanced analytical features such as forecasting, statistics, modeling, and financial functions are all part of OEA and OEO. They are there today—not promised "for a future release." Let's have a look around OEO.

A Tour of Express Objects (OEO)

As with OEA, you will spend most of your time in OEO working with the elements in its main window. The OEO main window is shown in Figure 17-15.

NOTE
The number preceding each element refers to the areas numbered in Figure 17-15.

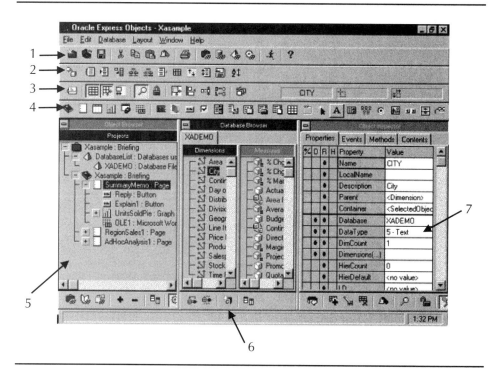

FIGURE 17-15. *OEO main window*

1—Main Window Toolbar

This area provides quick and easy access to the most frequently used features in OEO. Besides the standard Windows menu options, such as New, Open, Save, Cut, Copy, Paste, and Undo, there are a few OEO-specific buttons to access the Object Browser, Database Browser, Object Inspector, and the Basic Editor. This toolbar, as well as other toolboxes, can be moved anywhere on the screen by clicking an area unoccupied by icons, positioning it where desired, then releasing the mouse button.

2—Selector Toolbar

This toolbar provides quick access to the Selector dialog box and Selector tools as discussed in the same named section in the Express Analyzer section of this chapter. We find the consistency in interface between the developer-centric OEO product and the end-user-centric Express Analyzer to be a very strong feature in the whole Express suite of tools.

3—Layout Toolbar

This area provides easy access to the Object Editor and display properties that can be set from the layout menu. Some buttons on this toolbar help keep your workspace from becoming too cluttered. This always happens when working in a strong Windows-based application development environment. There are some nifty shortcuts that cascade or tile multiple windows, size two or more selected windows to the same dimensions, or help organize the spacing between a number of objects on the same page.

4—Toolbox

This area of the main window holds icons that help the developer create objects in OEO, such as pages and graphs. When OEO opens, this toolbox is a vertical floating window below the main window. By default, the toolbox starts out with four groups of buttons. You can also resize the toolbox, and this is where you can click on a button in the first group (the six icons in area 4 to the left of the leftmost vertical separator in the toolbox) and drag to create a new briefing object, page object, table object, graph object, Express output object, or OLE object. Regardless of what group's button you click, when you drop the selected object, OEO opens up a worksheet (page) to define and associate other objects with the one just created.

5—Object Browser

The Object Browser, when first brought up, lists all open projects in the familiar outline format. There are two other panes to the Object Browser, as shown in Figure 17-16.

The three panes in the Object Browser provide a view of the active objects from a project, briefing, or inheritance perspective. The Object Browser tends to get cluttered with a hodgepodge of windows all over the desktop. OEO provides a number of organizing buttons on the bottom of the

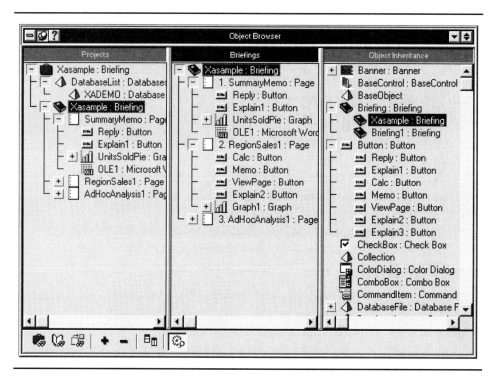

FIGURE 17-16. *Object Browser*

Object Browser to quickly collapse or expand the selected outline, organize the panes vertically or horizontally, or quickly bring one of the panes back into focus if it is no longer displayed.

6—Database Browser

Use the Database Browser to view attached databases and their dimensions and measures. This Browser in OEO is used exactly the same way as it is with the Express Analyzer component discussed earlier in the chapter. If you have attached more than one database, the Database Browser displays a tab on a separate folder for each.

TIP

The browsers can either float on the desktop, be constrained by the main window pane, or a combination of the two; as well, the toolbox can also appear as a menu bar.

7—Object Inspector

The Object Inspector is used to view and set properties, events, and methods for a selected object and to examine the object's contents. There are four tabs in this Inspector:

- The *Properties* tab allows you to view and set properties for the selected object. When new objects are added to a project or briefing, it takes on a set of default attributes; you will more than likely visit this folder at once to set its properties.

TIP

We recommend getting into the habit of visiting the properties of all new objects as they are created. Don't rely on your memory and say to yourself, "I'll do a complete pass of all the objects at the end and set their properties then."

■ The *Events* tab allows you to specify how to handle events as they happen during execution of the application. We found this tab and the functionality buried beneath quite intriguing. It is very complete, and it is a definite aid when developing applications and ensuring you touch all your bases. Figure 17-17 shows a sample Add Event dialog box with a picklist of events in the "After," "Before," "Do," and "Request" family of events.

■ The *Methods* tab allows you to view methods defined for the selected objects and specify when they are called. A *method* is a predefined action that can be called from an event handler for an object. When you double-click on a value displayed in the Method column of this tab, the Express Basic Editor pops up where you enter, edit, compile, and debug your code.

■ The *Contents* tab allows you to view the contents of the currently selected object. Suppose the currently selected object is a page. If that page contains a number of buttons and other controls, they will appear when the Contents tab is selected.

Time to move on. The material we have covered so far in this chapter should serve as a quick introduction to the Oracle Express solution. We

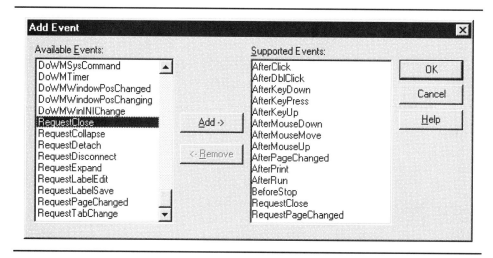

FIGURE 17-17. *Add Event dialog box*

hope you were paying close attention—there will be a test Tuesday afternoon. To round out this chapter, we are going to have a look at two custom analyzers, OFA and OSA, with hooks directly into the Oracle Cooperative Applications for the former. The Relational Access Manager (RAM), as you will see, is the icing on the cake; it enables the conduit of information between the data warehouse and the OLAP cube. Without RAM, information sharing can be done but is not anywhere close to as robust.

Oracle Financial Analyzer (OFA)

OFA is an integrated solution able to ingest information from spreadsheets, legacy systems, and Oracle General Ledger (GL), part of the Oracle Cooperative Applications toolset. There is a sophisticated administrative interface that ensures users only get to see what they need to perform their day-to-day activities without compromising security. This enforces one of the fundamental bottom lines of OLAP-based access to warehouse information—ensure users are not permitted to view in the warehouse what they cannot in the operational system data sources. Organizations can tailor OFA to react to their corporate structure using their own terminology, such as cost center, responsibility center, branch, region, or whatever. OFA requires Version 3.x or higher, with a minimum of 12MB of memory, in the Windows environment. UNIX platforms supported include HP-UX, Sun OS/4, IBM AIX, and Sun Solaris 2. Integration with GL and other general ledger solutions gives the biggest bang for the OFA dollar. Let's have a brief look at this feature.

Integration with Oracle GL

OFA brings to life the claim that companies can utilize their GL data seamlessly in an OLAP environment. They can slice and dice their information from day one, enlivening the many hooks from OFA directly into the GL relational structures. As the GL technology evolves, so will OFA without the need for adopters to redo administration in OFA to reflect the changes to GL. The data captured in GL easily maps to OFA hierarchies, dimensions, variables, and other multidimensional technology entry points. Periodic refreshing of the cube ensures that data integrity between the relational and OLAP environments is preserved at all times.

For us, the biggest single reason that will encourage organizations to adopt OFA as their analysis tool is the tight coupling with the Oracle relational database solution. OFA allows data to be locked so updates to financial data cannot be done while others are performing analytical exercises. OFA can analyze sections of the chart of accounts on their own, using existing calendar and currency information.

Key Features and Capabilities

Oracle believes OFA can play a key role in your information analysis solutions due to the following features:

- Ad hoc query, including the ability to analyze current and historical information doing variance and performance analyses. OFA can work directly with data stored in MS Excel.

- Financial modeling with over 100 analytical functions, and hooks to perform time-series analysis. OFA can ingest general ledger and nongeneral-ledger data simultaneously as input to forecasting, planning, and simulation exercises.

- Standard industry reporting and graphical output including line, bar, and area formats with a familiar drag-and-drop facility to reformat views of the cube data.

OFA empowers users to do their own analysis without the traditional wait for others to gather, program, and deploy reports on their behalf. Oracle Applications in the finance arena claims that, "Financial analysis requires information not only for executives, but also for a broader set of people who want to make better decisions on a daily basis. With Oracle Financial Analyzer, all authorized people in your organization can find the data they need, drill-down as necessary, and see the results in seconds— without waiting for MIS or even corporate accounting involvement. The analysis can be as sophisticated as you want because our online analytical processing (OLAP) tools support full multidimensional analysis—far surpassing conventional reporting tools" (source: *www.oracle.com/ products/applications/html/finance.html*). We could not agree more! Let's move on and have a brief look at Oracle Sales Analyzer.

Oracle Sales Analyzer (OSA)

OSA blends a sophisticated analytic interface with inherent intelligence about marketing and sales data. The result is a flexible analytical tool easily customized to suit your specific needs regardless of the slant of your sales organization. Empowering the user community with the tools to analyze sales and marketing data is the heart of the OSA solution. OSA can access practically any data source seamlessly, removing the need for the ongoing involvement of a company's information systems (IS) department.

Knowledge gleaned from corporate sales information using OSA can easily be distributed on the Web or using other mechanisms. Its tight integration with OES delivers advanced multidimensional query and analysis capabilities. Coupled with a library of predefined calculation types, Oracle sees OSA as a one-stop-shopping solution for sales information analysis. These calculation types can be extended and saved by the user to ingest the multidimensional data in OES and present it in a way familiar to the end user. Templates in the OSA product deliver exception and ranking reports to the user with little or no extra programming. A *template* is a preprogrammed solution with built-in functionality that accelerates the creation of sophisticated output. Think of a template as a fast path to the production of a common set of reports.

OSA provides flexibility accessing corporate data from any or all of the following sources:

- Oracle-based operational systems
- Non-Oracle-based operational systems
- Enterprise data warehouse
- Sales and marketing data mart

Using the Relational Access Manager (as discussed in the next section), OSA can read data directly from a relational data warehouse or data mart—viewing aggregate-level data in OES and more detailed information at the same time stored in strictly relational technology. OSA is integrated with the Oracle Data Mart Suite—Sales and Marketing Edition as well as the Oracle Applications Data Warehouse solution. Let's now look at the

Relational Access Manager, in effect the glue that holds many of the OLAP products together in an integrated solution.

Relational Access Manager (RAM)

The Oracle Express Relational Access Manager allows Express to access data stored in a relational database—normally a data warehouse, but any system implemented with relational technology. It should be noted that RAM has some design-related requirements for use with a data warehouse—the schema can be a star, as discussed in Chapters 5 and 7, or can be a superset of the star such as a snowflake. The *snowflake* involves leaving some of the lookup or dimension tables normalized. Secondary dimensions' relationships are to other dimensions rather than the fact table due to their still being normalized. Figure 17-18 shows a snowflake schema; notice how SECTOR_DIM is related to REGION_DIM that hangs off TERRITORY_DIM. If the model were strictly star rather than snowflake, the information (i.e., SECTOR_NAME from SECTOR_DIM and REGION_NAME from REGION_DIM) in the sector and region dimensions would be captured in the TERRITORY_DIM dimension table.

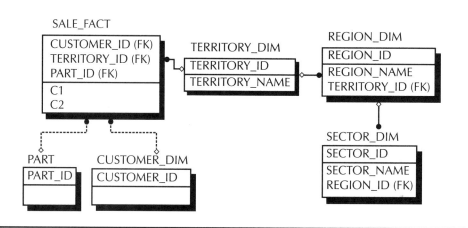

FIGURE 17-18. *Snowflake schema*

Figure 17-19 shows the welcome screen displayed after RAM is invoked.
    Though data warehouses are designed primarily for getting data out to
the users, it is the Express OLAP tools that provide users with the analytical
capabilities they crave. This helps in their quest for enlightenment regarding
all aspects of their company's performance and, hopefully, profits. Through
RAM, data can be manipulated and displayed from a data warehouse into a
multidimensional structure without the need for storage within the Express
database itself. This multidimensional format allows for easy data selection
by the users without requiring them to be familiar with the actual relational
structure within the data warehouse. There are three components to
the RAM:

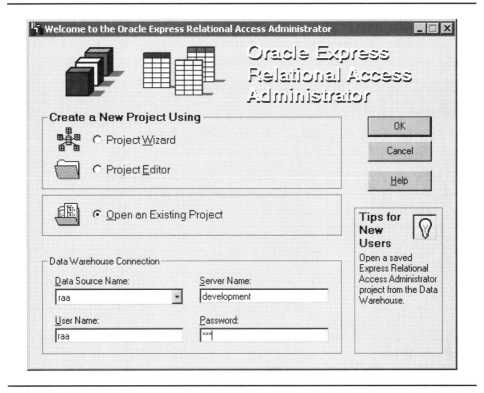

FIGURE 17-19.   *RAM startup screen*

- **Relational access administrator**   A GUI enabling the user to define an Express multidimensional model and how it accesses data from a relational database.

- **Build module**   A module using a file that contains information on building a new Express database or updating an existing one.

- **Run time module**   A run time module that contains utilities that retrieve data from a relational database at run time.

These components are key in the operation of RAM comprising three phases: definition, build-update, and online. Let's look at these three phases.

- **Definition**   This first phase of operation uses the Relational Access Administrator module. The Express data model along with its associated mappings to a data warehouse is defined along with various characteristics of the Express database. These definitions are constructed in what is known as a project and are stored within the data warehouse.

NOTE
RAM must have database tables created within the data warehouse for it to store its projects.

- **Build-update**   The build module uses the project defined within the definition phase to build the Express database. In building the Express database it must

  - Read the project from the data warehouse

  - Create the Express database and the multidimensional model

  - Populate the Express database with the data mapped from the data warehouse

- **Online**   After the build-update is complete, requests can be made for data from the data warehouse that has not been extracted (built within the build-update phase) on an as-needed basis using the run time module. This information is temporarily stored in the Express database and is lost when the user has finished its session.

Figure 17-20 shows an open project in RAM where variable units within the PSIS warehouse are mapped to the multidimensional variables within the OES model.

Oracle Web Agent (OWA)

Tada! Here a Web, there a Web, everywhere a Web Web. It seems you can't even go to the corner store without hearing those three letters—W E B. The Express Web Agent is the piece that allows you to create Express applications that can be run on any Web browser, made up primarily of the following components:

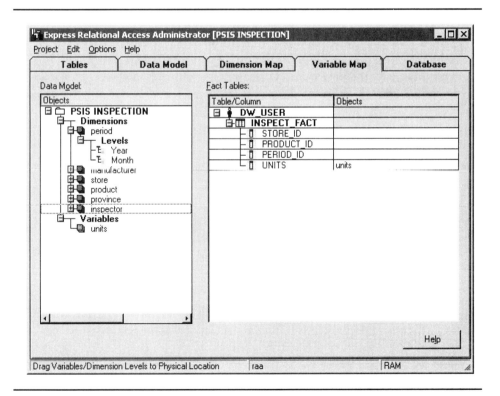

FIGURE 17-20.   *Mapping warehouse to multidimensional variables*

- **Web listener**   This part receives and processes requests from a browser to view documents or execute programs.

- **Web listener interface**   This enables communication between the browser and the Web server.

- **Web agent modules for Express Server**   This supports communication between Express Server and the Web listener.

- **The developer's toolkit**   This is used to generate HTML tags and produce Internet Web pages. *HTML* stands for Hypertext Markup Language, a development environment responsible for the production of many Web pages you see on the Internet.

Oracle promotes the thin client—the majority of the processing is done on the server with not much more than presentation mechanisms on the client. The four components we just listed are server based, with nothing other than a Web browser on the client (remember all those 8088s we mothballed in the mid to late 80s—that's 1980 to be Y2K compliant).

Even though you can use any Web listener with the Web Agent, Oracle recommends you use their Web server. The Express Web Agent CD delivers two types of interfaces—the Oracle Web Request Broker cartridge and the common gateway interface (CGI) program. Other than many differences inherent in the two approaches, the former is resident in memory after the first request is initiated whereas the latter terminates when the request is complete.

NOTE
Oracle may ship CDs with more than these two listener interfaces in the future as the products develop.

The CGI program requires no configuration on Windows NT, as it is configured automatically during the Express Web Agent installation procedure. CGI configuration will have to be performed after a UNIX installation, changes to the ServerObjectID, or the desire to Web-enable new Oracle instances. This ServerObjectID is part of the binding string typically used to identify a service running on the host. For example, on a Windows NT machine, access to Oracle8 is made possible by a service called OracleServiceORCL. Let's now move on and have a look at how an Express Web application works.

The Workings of an Express Web Application

The Express Web Agent user's guide suggests that there are eight stages to the execution of an Express Web application. The next few items describe the events that will take place as the user interacts with the Web document with the Express Web Agent buried under the covers.

1. Using Netscape Communicator, Internet Explorer, or any other popular Web browser, a user opens up an HTML document and clicks on a hyperlink to Express Server.

2. The browser sends a message to the Web listener in the form of a URL (uniform resource locator). For example, the URL *home.istar.ca/~masint/* will send you to the home page of an Oracle database systems provider in Canada's capital (that's Ottawa for those who want to know).

3. Based on the text (i.e., the URL), instructions are sent via CGI or Web request broker to OES. OES attaches the appropriate database, then assembles the data required to satisfy the user's request.

4. The data is passed back to the browser with predetermined hyperlinks embedded in the text where appropriate. If so desired, the data in the view passed back to the user is manipulated by clicking a hyperlink.

5. If user is done, or the machine is not yet locked up, our browser session is terminated. If user has clicked hyperlink, go to step 2.

Lets review—just like using the right exit on the interstate, this is not rocket science. As developers, database administrators, and data warehouse implementers, we are all well versed at connecting to an Oracle database (step 2), asking a program after login (step 3), and viewing the data passed back based on our request (step 4). It's simply a little bit a different way of doing the same old thing with a few perhaps unfamiliar components.

The possibilities are endless. The next listing shows a very simple HTML document with a call to the Express Web Agent embedded in the text highlighted in bold. Following that, Figure 17-21 shows the resultant browser output.

```
<html>
<head>
<title>Our Company's Web Site</title>
</head>
<body>
<h1>Spexwest Systems Inc.</h1>
<h1>All your Express Server requirements</h1>
<h1>One stop shopping at your fingertips!</h1>
<h1>Reasonable Rate$$ -- Let's Express Ourselves for YOU</h1>
<p> The time of day .... neat eh!
<p>
<a href="/ows-bin/oowa.exe/ExpSrv610/dbxwdevkit
        /xwd_init?sales/xwd_apppg.create/simple_html">
What an interesting web site .. if you only knew!
</a>
</body>
</html>
```

Three words come to mind when we start thinking of publishing to the Web—way too cool! Speaking of cool—let's take the next express out of here. In the next chapter, we are going to have a look at an interesting phenomenon with data warehouses. Suppose you collected every possible piece of information you could ever think of for the purposes of analysis exercises. Suppose you could then ask your data to tell you things you never knew before. Suppose you could predict the future. Next time you are at the local convenience store, when at the checkout counter, pick up a handful of black licorice pipes. Are they parked there (i.e., so close to the cash register where customers inevitably have some time on their hands) for a reason? Big time! Not too many people can resist spending the few extra pennies (once the candy is there anyway). Ever wonder why the local BMW dealer moved the parts counter from the other side of service to right beside the high-end automobile showroom? Big time! Those expensive wheel covers on the 67Z sure would look nice on my coupe and, since the parts counter is right there, might as well get a few for myself. Knowledge discovery in databases—gleaning of information from your data that identifies trends and patterns—is also called "data mining," the subject of the next chapter.

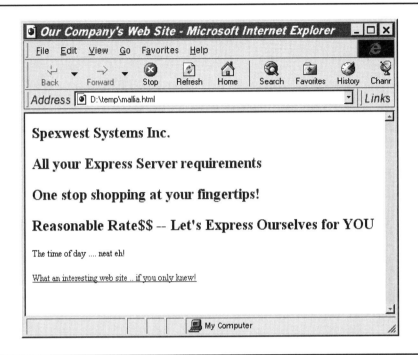

FIGURE 17-21. *HTML source code with Express hyperlink*

By the way, data mining has shown that parking irresistible treats close to the checkout counter leads to increased candy sales; close proximity of the parts counter has been shown to accelerate customer impulse buying of big ticket items for their babies (yes, a synonym for the car!). Carry on McDuff.

CHAPTER

18

Data Mining

his chapter is dedicated to data mining, a component of the data warehousing solution. Data mining is also called knowledge discovery in databases (KDD). There are many solutions out there from many vendors to assist the data mining process. Companies spend large amounts of time and money in collecting data; the data mining process helps discover what is going on with the data and the exercise of turning data into business information.

Partners are a large component of Oracle's data warehouse solution. The Warehouse Technology Initiative (WTI) brings Oracle and many third-party data warehouse vendors together in an attempt to provide more robust global data warehouse solutions. Without the WTI partners, Oracle's data warehouse solution would be missing components. Rather than reinvent the wheel, Oracle has decided the missing links will be filled by skilled third-party vendors. This decision opens up a suite of sophisticated products from non-Oracle companies, allowing Oracle to concentrate on a robust data-warehouse-centric database product—the Oracle8 Server. This is a wise decision. Oracle concentrates on what it does best and allows dedicated professionals from other organizations to do what they do best. Oracle has deliberately refined the familiar phrase, "Jack of all trades, master of none," to "Jack of a few trades, master of what they do best." This is a wise business decision.

What Is Data Mining?

Data mining is a discovery process that allows users to understand the substance of, and the relationships between, their data. Data mining uncovers patterns and trends in the contents of this information. The concept is nothing new. Perhaps what has catapulted it to the forefront in some organizations is the benefits of the exercise on a short- and long-term basis. Table 18-1 shows an interesting piece we found on the Internet regarding steps in this evolution (source: www.santafe.edu/%7Ekurt/text/dmwhite/dmwhite.shtml, © Pilot Software Inc.).

Advances in the speed of the desktop computer coupled with robust software solutions have allowed companies to sift through data at speeds unheard of a few years back. With the development of faster CPUs and storage devices, the sky is the limit. Companies need not be restrained by the overwhelming amount of data they have captured since their electronic

Evolutionary Step	Business Question	Enabling Technologies	Product Providers	Characteristics
Data collection (1960s)	"What was my total revenue in the last five years?"	Computers, tapes, disks	IBM, CDC	Retrospective, static data delivery
Data access (1980s)	"What were unit sales in New England last March?"	Relational databases (RDBMS), Structured Query Language (SQL), ODBC	Oracle, Sybase, Informix, IBM, Microsoft	Retrospective, dynamic data delivery at record levels
Data warehousing and decision support (1990s)	"What were unit sales in New England last March? Drill down to Boston."	Online analytic processing (OLAP), multi-dimensional databases, data warehouses	Pilot, Comshare, Arbor, Cognos, Micro-strategy	Retrospective, dynamic data delivery at multiple levels
Data mining (emerging today)	"What's likely to happen to Boston unit sales next month? Why?"	Advanced algorithms, multiprocessor computers, massive databases	Pilot, Lockheed, IBM, SGI, numerous startups (nascent industry)	Prospective, proactive information delivery

TABLE 18-1.   *Evolution of Data Mining*

business solutions sprang to life. As early as 1996, the META Group reported that 19 percent of respondents to a survey they conducted were working on data warehouse projects in excess of 50 gigabytes; the same survey results expected that number to climb to 59 percent before the end of that calendar year alone.

Essentially, data mining provides methods and means for efficient representation and storage of large volumes of information, the extraction and transmission of that material to a disparate user community, and the means to analyze, interpret, and display that information in a useful manner. Let's move on and have a look at relationship and pattern discovery through data mining.

Discovery

It's remarkable how relationships between data sometimes must be discovered. They are not readily evident without inspection, and they must be brought to the surface. This is an everyday occurrence evident in all areas of our lives. In the province of Ontario, for example, the last six digits of a person's driver's license are the year, month, and day of birth. Without this understanding, the three data elements shown in Figure 18-1 seem unrelated.

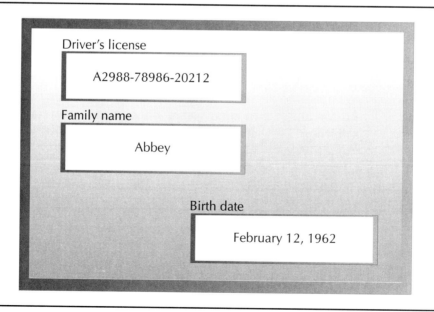

FIGURE 18-1. *Three seemingly unrelated data elements*

A data mining exercise could discover the relationship highlighted in Figure 18-2.

Discovery deliberately goes out with no predetermined idea of what the search will find. There is no intervention in the process by the end user; the data mining discovery process wades through the source data looking for similarities and occurrences of data, which allow grouping and pattern identification. In the electronic data warehouse environment, this process must be able to do its thing in a relatively short time period. Rapid delivery of results is crucial to the adoption of a data mining product.

So much data is captured in some operational systems that the contents of seemingly unimportant data elements can easily become lost in the big picture. Suppose the customer address tracking component of a system insisted the ZIP code be entered when new customer information is recorded. This is deliberate. Until the information embedded in this code becomes useful to the analyst, the ZIP code hides itself in a network of other customer-related data, such as contact name, credit limit, and payment method. Every time an invoice is generated, the ZIP code tags along and

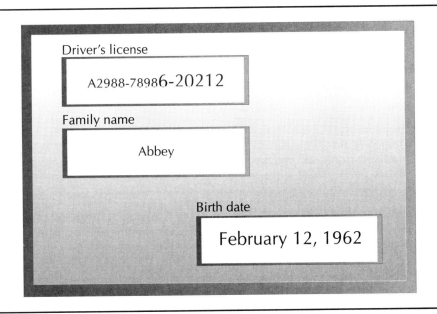

FIGURE 18-2. *Three elements after mining their dependencies*

appears on the header of the bill, as well as on the address on the envelope. The complete address record for each customer can yield invaluable geographical information of where customers are located. Knowing streets, cities, and building numbers is useful, but the ZIP code allows the pinpointing of segments of large areas within heavily populated urban areas. In this way, the substance of data becomes important, and data element values can provide enormous payoff when absorbed by a data mining initiative.

Relationships

Mining corporate data can throw light on a wide assortment of previously unknown relationships. How many times do you look at two or more sets of data that, on the surface at least, seem to have little resemblance to one another? Discovery of relationships can best be illustrated by looking at an everyday occurrence, such as our buying habits at the corner store.

Suppose it's early evening and you have just gone to the corner store to pick up a loaf of bread and some milk. As you grab the bread, a brightly colored bag of corn chips catches your eye. Hey, why not? At the dairy section, while you choose the milk, your wandering eyes see the red foil wrapping on a box of bite-sized cheese morsels. Guess what? These products have been deliberately placed in close proximity to one another. This chain of stores has gone about a data mining effort to study previously unknown relationships between purchases by Jack and Jill consumer. Discovering relationships is key to successful marketing. In our retail store, the parallel movement of products has been uncovered by looking for relationships between customer purchasing habits. Ever wonder why the red licorice box is placed beside the cash register? Investigation determined a direct relationship could be inferred between the amount of money spent (or wasted?) on junk food at the cash register and nonjunk food products purchased by the same customer.

In operational or data warehouse systems, the data architect and design personnel have meticulously defined entities and relationships. In this context, an *entity* is a set of information containing facts about a related set of data. The discovery process in a data mining exercise sheds light on relationships hidden deep down in many layers of corporate data.

Patterns

The benefits of pattern discovery to a business add real value to a data mining exercise. No one can accurately predict that person X is going to perform activity Y in close proximity with activity Z. Using data mining techniques and systematic analysis on warehouse data, however, this prediction can be backed up by the detection of patterns in behavior.

A temporal component exists in pattern discovery. Parallel behavior over a two-week period can uncover a pattern that could become the reason for the implementation of a new marketing endeavor. On the other hand, detection of this behavior over a longer six-month period adds more credibility to the suggestion that a pattern has been detected. Patterns are closely related to habit; in other words, the likelihood of an activity being performed in close proximity to another activity is discovered in the midst of identifying a pattern.

You probably remember the saying; "It's like trying to compare apples and oranges." If this comparison identifies a pattern in behavior, the comparison may be valid, and it should be the basis for a discovery exercise in your warehouse data.

Data mining allows companies to see their information in ways unheard of previously. As you know, some operational systems, in the midst of satisfying daily business requirements, create vast amounts of data. The data is complex, and the relationships between elements are not easily found by the naked eye. Along comes special data mining software and pouf! It's not exactly that easy, but without software from a handful of Oracle's data warehouse partners, the data mining process seems insurmountable. The true nature of data mining is shown in Figure 18-3. Using data mining as a tool, data becomes information.

Data is made up of a series of characters which, on their own, mean nothing. Grouped together to form data elements, they start to take on meaning. When subject to a data mining effort, these same data elements can yield a wealth of information.

Businesses have only a fixed amount of dollars and time to spend on knowledge discovery initiatives. When companies look at the short- and long-term benefits of data mining, all those dollars and all the time invested will pay off many times in the long run. DataMind Corp., a major player in

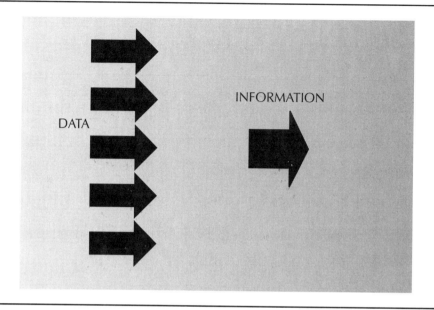

FIGURE 18-3. *Data mining in a nutshell*

the industry, identifies three segments in the data mining marketplace
(source: www.datamindcorp.com/dmabout.html):

- Assisted data mining products generally require expensive, massively
  parallel computers and significant assistance from a vendor to "glue"
  together various pieces of technology. This has been a traditional
  approach for data mining where the vendor is contracted to perform
  lengthy, on-site analysis of corporate data to try and find deeply
  buried information. This often results in 6–9 months worth of work
  to come up with one or two "chunks of gold." Engagements usually
  cost upwards of $300,000.

- The desktop data mining market includes vendors whose products
  are oriented to a PC environment with the ability to perform mining
  functions on an extract of data, typically the result of a SQL query.
  Vendors in this space offer a "slice" of data mining functionality,
  often bolted on with query and report writing facilities. In this way,
  users can experiment with data mining on small result sets to get a

feeling for how data mining might play a role in their overall analysis techniques. These products are typically priced in the $495–$2,000 range.

■ Applied data mining is a new category of software filling a gap between easy-to-use desktop interfaces and high-end data mining complexity by focusing on specific business problems. Based on popular client/server and Web/server architectures found today in nearly all Information Technology organizations, applied data mining solutions focus on making customers self-sufficient— performing their own regular data mining activities so as to gain benefits every day, across the organization. Products to perform applied data mining hunts are priced between $50,000 and $250,000.

Benefits of Data Mining

The primary benefit of data mining is the ability to turn *feelings* into *facts*. When meeting with coworkers, how many times do you say, "I just have a gut feeling that product X is more attractive to consumer group Y than the rest of our customer base." This feeling can become a fact when it's armed with the ability to sift through corporate data, looking for patterns of behavior and habits of customers. The fundamental benefit of data mining is twofold.

Data mining can be used to support or refute feelings people have about how business is going. It can be used to add credibility to these feelings and warrant dedication of more resources and time to the most productive areas of a company's operations.

This benefit deals with situations where a company starts the data mining process with an idea of what they are looking for. This is called *targeted* data mining. Data mining can discover unexpected patterns in behavior, patterns that were not under consideration when the mining exercise commenced. This is called *out-of-the-blue* data mining.

Let's look at a number of tangible benefits the data mining process can bring to companies, and how nicely these benefits fit into two kinds of data mining exercises.

Fraud Detection

All too often businesses are so caught up in their daily operations that they have no time or personnel to dedicate to uncovering out of the ordinary business occurrences that require intervention. These events include fraud, employee theft, and illegal redirection of company goods and services toward the employees trusted with their management. Many companies use sophisticated surveillance equipment to ensure their workers are doing their jobs and nothing but their jobs. Examine the following types of fraud, whose evidence could be easily uncovered by a system of data mining:

- A group of clerks in a retail building supplies chain is systematically short-shipping orders and hiding the discrepancy between the requisition for goods and the freight bill going out with the delivery. This could be uncovered by analyzing the makeup of bona fide orders, and what is found to be a premature depletion of corresponding stock.

- A retail clothing giant notices an unusual number of credit vouchers going out on one shift every Saturday morning in their sportswear and athletic shoes departments. By analyzing the volume and amounts of credit voucher transactions, management would be able to detect times when volume is repeatedly higher than the norm.

- After auditing payroll at a factory, a company notices an excessive amount of overtime over a six-week period for a handful of employees. Through a data mining effort, they uncover a deliberate altering of time sheets after management signature has been obtained.

- Using data mining, a banking institution could analyze historical data and develop an understanding of "normal" business operations—debits, credits, transfers, etc. When a frequency is tacked onto each activity as well as size of transactions, source, and recipient information, the institution can go about the same analysis against current transactions. If behavior out of the norm is detected, they engage the services of internal, and perhaps external, auditors to resolve the problem.

Fraud detection is seen primarily as out-of-the-blue data mining. Fraud detection is usually an exploratory exercise: a data miner will dive headfirst into a data repository and sift through vast amounts of data with little or no predisposition as to what will be found.

Return on Investment

A significant segment of the companies looking at, or already adopting, data warehouse technology spend millions of dollars on new business initiatives. The research and development costs are astronomical. An oil company can spend upwards of $35 million (U.S.) on an oil rig. Data mining historical data from within the company and any government or other external data available to the firm could help answer the big ticket question: "Will the effort pay off?"

Everyone has struggled with time. So little seems to exist, and so much needs to be accomplished. Most workdays are supposed to last seven to nine hours. Time management has become crucial in this day and age. In a business environment, where a finite number of hours exist in a day, wading through data to discover areas that will yield the best results is a benefit of data mining. This is your return on investment. Business decision makers always try to dedicate the most time and resources to initiatives with the best return. Looking for the best way to proceed, given a finite amount of dollars and people available, is a form of targeted data mining.

Scalability of the Electronic Solution

The major players in the data mining arena provide solutions that are robust and scalable. A *robust* data mining solution is one that performs well and can display results in an acceptable time period. The length of that acceptable time period depends on factors such as the user's past experiences and expectations. A common occurrence may be for one person to prepare a set of parameters and variables for a data mining exercise, press the ENTER key, and go off to a meeting. Two hours later, the computer screen sits full of the mining results, patiently waiting for the user's return. On the other hand, another user may sit impatiently in front of the screen, fingers drumming on the table top, waiting for what seems a light-year for results (in this situation, three to five minutes can seem an eternity). Successful mining software providers' products can ingest anything from small amounts of data all the way up to voluminous amounts. The ability to work with a wide range of input datasets is part of this phenomenon called *scalability*. Another component of scalability is the ability to deploy a data mining solution on a stand-alone personal computer, on a small group of computers tied together by a local area network, or on an enterprise-wide set of corporate computers. The transition from single to multiple users must be both transparent and seamless to the users and easy to deploy for the professionals responsible for a company-wide or workgroup-wide data mining effort.

Data Mining Assists the Decision-Making Process

As companies flatten their layers of management, they look for ways to empower employees to collect the information required to make the decisions that affect the lifeblood of their businesses. Traditional discovery methods are cumbersome. Even though the data sits somewhere in an information repository, it is hard to find. Data mining can fast-track the discovery process and allow for targeted marketing initiatives at identified segments of the population.

Decision making should be driven by knowledge of past performance, consumer behavior, and discovery of patterns and trends. Suppose a communications carrier discovered a new service offering boosted Q1 sales. The marketing effort concentrated on customers whose spending habits were between $50 and $125 per month. Through data mining, the company discovered the majority of purchases of this service were from two-income families. How did they discover this? Armed with some data mining software, they analyzed the number of phone numbers listed for their customers and found the following pattern: accounts with three different numbers listed represented over three-quarters of the new service purchases. Guess where their next targeted marketing effort concentrated?

The concept of data mining can be applied to many real-life situations with no relation to information technology. Next time you're watching a major league baseball game and the announcer tells you this batter has struck out against a left-handed pitcher with the bases empty only three of the last 102 times, think of data mining. This is the facet of data mining that looks for trends; it is the same phenomenon that stirs baseball statisticians to keep what appears to be useless information. Predicting the future is power!

A finite amount of time exists to decide what business initiatives to do next. Data mining assists the decision-making effort because it can wade through corporate data warehouse information with the click of a mouse button. As the management layer is reduced, middle- or lower-management personnel are encouraged to make inventive decisions about how much time should be spent on marketing initiatives. Data mining vast amounts of corporate data places the information required to make decisions at these people's fingertips. What once was a missing link in the data mining arena—that is, computer Windows-based solutions that fully automate the process—has been filled by the vendors highlighted in this book, coupled with an ever growing number of others.

Data mining helps transform vast amounts of data into information. Isolated occurrences of data elements are of little or no use. When those elements are mined, relationships extracted, and patterns discovered, they become useful information. This information can be likened to the iron ore pulled from more traditional mines: the data is the raw material and the information is the commodity of business.

Data Mining Techniques

Remember when computers first became popular? They seemed like magic. The more you got into the ins and outs of how a computer performed operations and looked at some programming languages, the more you understood and discovered there was no magic. Data mining uses a number of techniques to discover patterns and uncover trends in data warehouse data. By looking briefly at three of these techniques, you will begin to see that data mining, as well, is not magic.

Neural Network

Neural network-based mining is especially suited to identify patterns or forecasting trends based on previously identified behavior. A *trend* identifies a movement in habit based on past behavior. The stock market is a perfect place for the identification of trends. When NASDAQ commodity ORCL's price over the last six months is analyzed, you may be able to predict a trend in share price over the next number of weeks. Prediction immediately springs to mind when discussing neural net mining activities—the act of delivering intelligent recommendations based on the information buried in corporate data.

The roots of this type of processing are based on what was been learned from work done on the human body's central nervous system. Knowledge can be learned from a set of widely disparate, complex, or imprecise data. There are three layers to the network: the bottom layer receives inputs, the hidden (middle) layer performs the work, and the output layer presents the analyst with outputs. In a marketing organization, the inputs could be historical information pertaining to the spending habits of clients in close proximity to the time the company undertook significant new marketing initiatives. The hidden, or middle, layer processes incoming information and passes results, in the form of patterns and trends, to the output layer. The input layer, the hidden layer, and the output layer are made up of nodes. These *nodes* are another term for processing elements, which are likened to the neurons in the brain; hence, the terminology *neural network*.

When this network is trained on the information in the input layer, it takes on an eerie human-like component as it becomes expert at ingesting seemingly unrelated elements of data and spitting out results to the output layer. The number of nodes, though unknown in the hidden layer, decreases as the results rise to the surface and are spewed out by the output layer. Figure 18-4 shows the structure of a neural network and how each node in every layer is interconnected to each node in the adjacent layer.

Suppose the network shown in Figure 18-4 weighed factors affecting the risk of loaning money to a segment of the general public. At the input layer, each node would contain information related to a single factor about the borrower, such as the following:

- Age

- Checking account bank balance

- Annual income

- Credit rating

- Years at current job

- Marital status

- Monthly balance carried on charge card

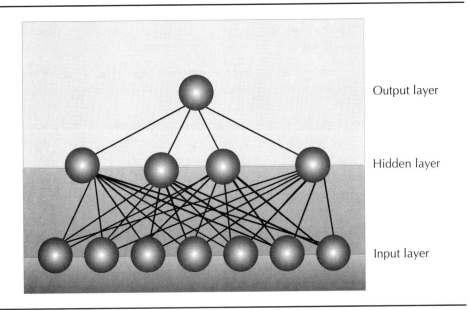

FIGURE 18-4. *Neural network structure*

Association Discovery

This technique involves studying sets of data and attempting to show associations between the occurrences of attributes within that data. Association discovery attempts to uncover similar occurrences of data values within records and produces output that can be expressed as a rule: "Eighty-six percent of the patients seen by Clinic A for hernia repairs also required intervention for a stomach-related ailment within the next six months."

A confidence factor is uncovered when mining using association discovery or association rules. The *confidence factor* is expressed as a percentage and is a measurement of the power of a prediction. Examine the following two statements:

- An 80 percent chance exists that consumers will purchase a coffee table when they acquire a new sofa and at least one other piece of living room seating.

- A 65 percent chance exists that when consumers buy a new house, they will also purchase a dishwasher.

Even outside the data mining arena, you could state that you are more confident the first purchasing habit would repeat itself than the second. By extending this type of statement, and by being able to back it up with knowledge gleaned from your data warehouse or operational system data, imagine the power this knowledge could impart to your business decision making.

When expressing data mining association rules, we speak of left-hand side (LHS) components and right-hand side (RHS) components of the association rule. When determining a confidence factor, look for the percentage that the event (in this example, purchase of a coffee table) on the RHS will occur at the same time as the two events on the LHS (in this example, the purchase of a sofa and at least one other piece of living room seating). The LHS can be one or more events, whereas the RHS tends to be a single event. Once data is mined and associations are detected, examined, and weighed, companies can decide what marketing decisions would make good business sense.

Look at one high-return item and one medium-return item at a fictitious automobile dealership called GYT Motors, which sells recreational vehicles and medium-size cars. Using association rules, it would be wise for GYT to create an environment where potential purchasers may go for a recreational vehicle. By mining client purchasing information, GYT may determine an association exists between

    air conditioning & camping supplier promotion ----> RV sales

with a confidence factor of 63 percent. So that sales are not lost to customers who definitely are not interested in a recreational vehicle, GYT has covered that base by uncovering the association

```
same price wagon ----> medium-sized car sales
```

The association discovery can uncover relationships between what appear to be completely unrelated circumstances. These circumstances can have dramatic effects on how a company does business. Odd as it may seem, the associations discovered when mining data can approach the absurd! Perhaps GYT Motors may decide to move its parts department to a location between the showroom and the service department. They have discovered a high probability exists that people who need to walk past the parts counter when they have their vehicles serviced will stop and spend money on "that part they have been meaning to pick up, but never seem to have the opportunity." A popular soft ice cream vendor near where we live built a drive-through last winter. Coincidence? We think not.

Classification

Classification involves grouping data together based on a set of similarities predefined by the analyst before the exercise begins. This technique examines data already classified and grouped together based on application of a membership rule. This membership rule may have a time component, for example, a calendar year, a fiscal year, a month of the year; a geographic component, for example, east or west of the Mississippi River; or a quantitative component, for example, clients with annual expenditures above or below a predetermined amount.

One of the more common applications of this technique is in the area of customer retention. Customer groups are classified and examined as almost separate entities, at which point one can decide how to retain the different groups of customers. This technique conjures up the familiar expression "whatever the traffic will bear." Victoria's Secret discovered clientele in New York City were willing to purchase apparel regardless of the price. Why, then, would they discount this commodity to attract a loyal return customer? In line with that expression, the traffic will bear a price of $XX, so no need exists to price the good at $.8XX.

Clustering

Clustering involves clumping similar sets of data together from a larger and more massive dataset. Unlike the classification technique, the clustering technique discovers the groupings as it works with the input data.

Similarities are identified that lead to the segmentation of large datasets made up of members that resemble each other. Once the clusters and their members are identified, generalizations, patterns, and trends can be uncovered based on the characteristics of the members of each cluster.

Think back to your feeling the last time some edict delivered by a politician made you angry. You might have said to yourself: "Wouldn't it be nice if little insignificant me could change that edict?" Well, "little insignificant you" clustered with 10,000 other "little insignificant people" with similar opinions could bring about that change. A clustering technique could be used to assemble a set of opinions, to study the properties of those opinions, and to derive a handful of clusters that represent large numbers of voters. The bottom line of this technique is the discovery that what appeared to be entirely unrelated data values and attribute values within a given set of records actually contain information with a clear set of similarities. You run across clustered results in everyday life. Figure 18-5 illustrates how previously unrelated data shows overlap after going through the application of a data mining clustering technique.

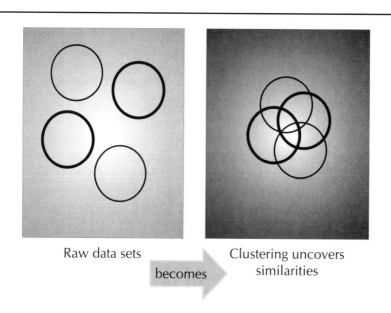

Raw data sets

becomes

Clustering uncovers similarities

FIGURE 18-5. *Clustering uncovers similarities*

The statement "75 percent of all pickup truck owners will always buy pickups" might have been derived using some form of clustering. Most likely, the answers from all the respondents was not a simple YES or NO, but other answers which, when clustered together, indicated an overall satisfaction with pickup trucks three times out of four; hence, the figure 75 percent.

Sequential Discovery

Sequential discovery attempts to find patterns between events that occur in a progression over a period of time. To make the process meaningful in the supplier/purchaser framework—for example, retail sales—the time component of the data being analyzed is decided on beforehand. Once this decision is made, the data miner has a handle on the volume of data to be inspected and the process begins.

This mining technique can be used to search for commodity purchasing patterns that repeat themselves. If a trend or repetitive pattern is found in the nature of purchases, the data mining effort concentrates on looking for more occurrences of the same habits. Data mining analyzes sets of records about purchases, looking for frequently occurring patterns over the selected time period. Suppose you uncover a specific set of purchases that precedes the purchase of a dishwasher. This information can be used to direct a marketing plan at a set of existing clients whose purchases conform to this pattern.

Data Mining Solution Checklist

What are clients looking for in a data mining solution, and how can the choice affect the integration of knowledge discovery into an existing set of decision-making resources? Some items on the checklist are mandatory; others are desirable.

Direct Access to Oracle (SQL) Database

The total warehouse solution provided by Oracle is the best of breed. Significant attention should be paid to the data repository where data warehouse data is stored, and this is where Oracle is the obvious choice.

Desirable—a data mining solution should be able to provide quick, easy, and rapid access to data held in an SQL database.

Visual Analysis Capabilities

"A picture is worth a thousand words"—this is never more applicable than in a situation where you are mining data. The sheer volume of the data being analyzed coupled with the wide range of results being presented require visual output capabilities.

Mandatory—a data mining solution must produce output in a graphical, visual manner.

Coupled with this ability, because so much output is presented in columnar and matrix report format, a mining tool must support common drag-and-drop features where objects in the output can be moved to another axis on a graph. A *columnar* report is the familiar rows and columns output shown in Table 18-2. It displays descriptive information—in this case, critical quantity and manufacturer code—about a single entity.

NOTE
The data in the next two tables does not represent factual information and is "cooked" for the sake of illustrating matrix reports.

When the intersection points define a relationship between the column and row measurements, the report is a *matrix* report as shown in Table 18-3.

The number 0.72 in the boldface cell in Table 18-3 means a 0.72 percent chance exists that drivers between the ages of 20 and 24 will have a fender bender in the next year (notice how the *1-year* value is selected in the time frame column) if they drive between 31 and 60 miles per day.

Part Number	Critical Quantity	Manufacturer Code
ABN-2322	15	TH8892A
ABH-2918	10	HJ87662
ABM-0922	225	UJ8831L

TABLE 18-2. *Part Characteristics*

Time Frame	Miles	Age 16–19	Age 20–24	Age 25–30
1 year	5–30	1.21	0.87	0.33
2 years	31–60	1.26	**0.72**	0.35
3 years	61–99	1.34	0.70	0.31

TABLE 18-3.   *Age of Driver Vs. Miles Driven per Day Over a One-year Time Frame*

A data mining product must allow the user to click on the *3-years* cell in the matrix report output and to have the output immediately transformed to a state representing the three-year time frame results. This transformation is shown in Table 18-4.

Ability to Ingest Large Volumes of Data

Because the volume of data fed to a data mining tool can be so large, the tool must process loads of data in short time periods. Some tools have a Microsoft Excel interface, which allows users to work with their data in a familiar environment when the amount of incoming data is small. When mining the multigigabyte data warehouse, a robust mining tool can deliver results in real time.

Mandatory—given the common size of the data warehouse repository, the data mining tool must be able to ingest extremely large volumes of data.

Time Frame	Miles	Age 16–19	Age 20–24	Age 25–30
1 year	5–30	1.97	0.92	0.31
2 years	31–60	1.32	**0.76**	0.37
3 years	61–99	1.22	0.88	0.39

TABLE 18-4.   *Age of Driver Vs. Miles Driven per Day Over a Three-year Time Frame*

Sensitivity to the Quality of Data

When mining large datasets looking for patterns and trends, data mining software must be sensitive to the quality of the input data. When one or more attributes in that data is the source of a mining effort, you must ensure missing or incomplete data have not skewed the output and affected the outcome of the analysis. Data mining software must not only be able to compensate for that data, but it must also be able to report on the amount of bad data ingested to assist the analyst in deciding the validity of the results.

The Future of Data Mining

The foundation of data mining is nothing new—the desire to conduct business based on the past behavior of customers. With the advent of larger and more powerful computers, data mining technology is primed to take off over the next few years. Not long ago, electronic data mining solutions were few. A glut of technology exists on the market now, and it's still growing.

The biggest reason data mining has a bright future is the computing power of today's high-end machines. One of the industry's hottest phrases is *parallel processing*. This type of processing is so well suited to data mining, it can easily be derailed by hardware not robust enough to ingest and analyze multiple gigabytes of data. It seems you cannot turn around without stumbling on yet another bigger and better parallel computing solution.

As a new breed of frontline employees contribute to the business decision-making process, arming them with data mining technology makes so much sense. These individuals live and breathe the business operations, experience firsthand contact with consumers of the company's products and services and, therefore, are players in selection of future business endeavors and initiatives. They may not actually make the final decision, but they are responsible for giving recommendations based on their frontline knowledge of the business. Ever-increasingly sophisticated electronic data mining solutions enable these players to make recommendations to upper management.

The foundation of data mining has been around for some time. Machine learning and artificial intelligence are two disciplines dedicated to training machines to learn from past experiences and, based on that training, make predictions about the future. Naturally, many have based their Ph.D. theses on machine learning, and a wealth of books, journals, and technical conferences exist worldwide dealing with the subject of data mining.

In Chapter 19, we are going to have a look at data warehousing and the Web. With the advent of the thin client, and the widespread adoption of browser-based solutions, desire to publish OLAP and other query results to the Web is spreading like a grass fire out of control.

CHAPTER
19

Data Warehouse and the World Wide Web

ake up and open your eyes—the Information Highway is upon us. Information is the key to knowledge; knowledge is the key to maintaining your organization's competitive edge. Companies that lose their competitive edge wither and die. The Internet is the world's first virtual library, with nearly unlimited information available to those who know how to unlock the secrets held within. The Internet also represents the most efficient distribution mechanism for goods and services in the history of civilization. Every time a new way to distribute goods and services evolves, a substantial business opportunity is created. In the early days, it was the Sears Corporation's "Wish Book." It was the first firm to dominate mail order as a way to distribute goods and services. Another good example of an early adopter is the Tupperware Corporation; they distributed goods and services through a home network. They realized early on that the housewife was an untapped resource. The point is that any time a way to distribute goods and services evolves, early adopters are able to exploit a major business opportunity. Minimally, the Internet represents a very efficient way to offer goods and services—perhaps the most efficient method ever. Think of how we can now instantly get software product updates over the Web. A company we use to develop 35mm film now offers an Internet option. We are able to download the digitized images of our pictures as soon as they are ready. By using this option, we get the best of both worlds—we can use a high-end camera and still have a digitized image; we can also get the pictures quicker. As the consumer, I am given a choice.

As we all know, a free market is able to offer its consumers far better goods and services at much better prices than the alternative. This is due to the effect competition has on the marketplace. The Internet represents the purest form of competition we have ever had in the history of the world. It is now having an impact on the free world that is as profound as the industrial revolution. How businesses transact business is being retooled as we speak today. Our children are growing up in an age where how they obtain products and services is being redefined. The paradigm is changing.

They are growing up in an age where the information of the ages is available to all, quickly and easily. The traditional barriers to knowledge acquisition are being eroded away as we speak. The problem in the future will be the filtering of information, so you do not become information overloaded. With such drastic changes taking place, it's no wonder the evolution of your data warehouse is being altered. A data warehouse is about information and getting at it. These new Internet-enabling technologies are changing the way users harvest the information contained within the warehouse. The Internet is making it easier to obtain the information, maintain the information, and deploy the information to your stakeholders no matter where they reside.

In this chapter, we discuss

- What the World Wide Web is

- What an intranet is

- Why it is more cost effective to build and deploy applications over the Internet

- What some of the current trends taking place are

- How fast it is all happening

- What the business value of creating an intranet is

We will make the business case for you—that the warehouse of today and in the future will be Web-enabled. Now that we have grabbed your interest, read on.

What Is the Internet

To better understand the Internet, let's take a look at its roots. The Internet came about by research sponsored by the United States government. It is interesting to note that the relational database also came about due to research by the United States government. There was a need to sort through large amounts of information quickly. Oracle Corporation's early customers were mostly U.S. government-sponsored projects. The goal with the Internet was to build a network that would provide the military with communications even in the event of a nuclear war. Isn't it funny that many people are worried that the Internet might come crashing down someday when, by design, that would be near impossible. To take it down would mean you would have to disable every Internet server. By design, the Internet would automatically reroute the requests around failed servers. The Internet is designed to just keep chugging along.

The Internet by design is also the first truly open network standard. Since the military was made up of many different computers running many different operating systems, they needed a network standard that would tie them all together. Today, the Internet is all about open standards:

- Any computer

- Any network

- Any software

- Accessed by any server, worldwide

The bottom line—you get a very fault-tolerant network that is able to talk to virtually any computer, across any network, running virtually any software.

What Is the World Wide Web

The World Wide Web is really the Internet with graphics. In 1993, Marc Andreessen created Mosaic, the first graphical user interface for the Internet. The creation of Mosaic brought graphics to the Internet. This made it easy to use, and what's more, Mosaic was available free of charge for any user to download. (We find it ironic that the trend is still to offer a browser free of charge for the download.)

This now meant anyone could navigate the Internet—yes, even you. It had taken the Internet from the once sacred realm of only the highly technical person (another name for a propeller head) to John and Susan Q. Public. We have come a long way since the creation of Mosaic in 1993. We now have many universal browsers to choose from. The two most widely used browsers are Netscape Navigator and Microsoft Internet Explorer. These browsers make it easy for the Internet to deal with all types of data, ranging from sound to video and text.

To navigate the Web, you must have a starting point. Think of a home page as the starting point. Just as Dorothy in *Wizard of Oz* had the yellow brick road, you have the home page. The home page is your key for locating information (we like to think of information as the Emerald City), which then employs HTTP (Hypertext Transfer Protocol). HTTP links you up to the information that your browser provides you with in the form of graphics, text, live audio, live video, and even live 3-D. With hypertext, your browser will be able locate and receive music and voice from the Web pages you view. Yes, you can even see and play movies from your browser. Through the use of a VRML (virtual reality modeling language) viewer, you will be able to view pages in 3-D.

Hypertext will link you to this information, no matter where it resides on the Web. So, with HTTP and a universal browser, it would be possible to have a picture of Dorothy in the *Wizard of Oz*. When you used the mouse on the computer and clicked on the image of Dorothy, the hypertext link (that's what a graphical user interface is all about, using the mouse to navigate) would take you to another location on the Web. This is another location where additional information on the *Wizard of Oz* is available. This information could be anywhere in the world; it all happens transparently to the user with a simple mouse click.

With this enhanced graphical capability, anyone can easily navigate the Internet, and millions do. Susan Q. Public has embraced the Internet in a major way. With its massive embrace by John and Susan Public, you now have a very viable commercial platform to do business. This is a very important point—with the deployment of browsers like Internet Explorer from Microsoft, the Internet has become a viable commercial platform to do business on. This ability to do business on the Web is fueling a growth unlike anything the marketplace has ever seen before. In fact, no matter what trends you choose to examine, they all show you loud and clear that we are embracing the Internet at a very fast pace. It is the business tool of today, with the architecture to survive tomorrow.

How Fast Is the World Embracing the Internet

When we think of a real fast trend that is overtaking the world, we think of the PC revolution. When we examine the facts a little closer, we learn that in the year 1997, approximately 27,000,000 PCs were sold. This is a far cry from the 250,000 that were first sold approximately 15 years ago. Yet when we think about this, this is an incredibly fast-growing trend. When we compared these numbers to the growth of the Internet, an Internet year equals three PC years. Yes, you read it right: an Internet year equals three PC years. What has taken the personal computer 15 years to accomplish, the Internet will accomplish in less than five years.

When one looks at Internet domain name registrations, the growth rate is phenomenal! These are *URL* designations of a Web site. Simply put, a URL is an Internet address or a uniform resource locator (a yellow brick road for finding something). An example of a URL is "http://www.dbtinc.com". Think of this as your road map to any given Internet site.

A survey we found produced by the InterNIC organization showed that in the year 1993, when the Mosaic browser was first available for download, there were 5,946 registrations for domain names. This represented a substantial increase from the previous year when there were only 2,845—in fact, well over double-digit growth from the previous year. In the year 1997, it was estimated there would be 1,500,000 registrations. Ninety percent of these registrations were for commercial use. You can tell a commercial Web site since it will always end in ".com". For example, the Web site for Database Technologies Inc. is "http://www.dbtinc.com". Table 19-1 is a quick guide to the meaning of the various Web site designations.

The Internet explosion is happening so fast, there are already discussions about adding more designations. Just as many parts of the world outgrow their postal codes or phone area codes, don't be surprised if we quickly outgrow our Internet designations. Look at how quickly an email address has become almost as popular as a phone number.

Designation	Purpose
.com	Commercial use
.edu	Education
.org	Organization
.net	Network
.gov	Government

TABLE 19-1. *Definitions of Internet Designations*

The trend that really caught our attention was a recent rating that showed TV viewership was down due to Internet usage. According to the survey, close to 60 percent of the people who participated are watching less TV. Over 85 percent of the people are using the Internet more. Over 40 percent admitted that they are watching less TV due to the fact they are using the Internet more.

Do we think that the Internet will ever replace television? No, we don't believe it will. Think about it—we still have radio and we still have newspapers. What is clear to us is that the Internet is a very powerful communication tool. It is a very efficient way to reach the masses. Just as television offered advantages over radio and radio offered advantages over newspapers, the Internet offers significant advantages over its predecessor. For example, would you rather watch a Stanley Cup hockey game on TV or listen to it on the radio. We would rather have the rich medium of TV. But each medium has its advantages and disadvantages.

We think this point was best illustrated by the recent death of Princess Diana. It was a very tragic accident. People all over the world turned to the TV to help them with this loss. The Internet was just not equipped as a medium for dealing with this tragic accident. Clearly, TV was a much better medium for dealing with emotions. After the funeral, people turned to the Internet. It was a much better medium for discussion groups and distributing the facts. Through discussion groups, people were able to better deal with the loss. It is an excellent and very efficient tool for disseminating information. This ability to effectively disseminate information is one of the major reasons it is an ideal match for your data warehouse. Later in this chapter, we will discuss the advantages of building and deploying a warehouse using Internet-enabling technologies. For now, let's take a closer look at what an intranet is.

What Is an Intranet

An *intranet* site is where one or more applications reside, accessed using one of the universal browsers like Netscape Navigator or Microsoft Internet Explorer. Since it is an intranet site, the applications reside within the firewall and are accessed using technologies like TCP/IP, HTML, or Java. The primary purpose of intranet sites is to service internal customers.

An *Internet* site is similar to the intranet site, except the applications reside outside the firewall. They are accessed using the same technologies as the intranet site. The primary purpose of Internet sites is to service external customers. An average Internet site typically contains marketing information.

When you look at these two definitions, you realize there is not much difference. So, let's simplify the definition. An intranet is a small-scale version inside your organization of your Internet site. An intranet is all about communication within your business.

Up till now, if a business wanted to communicate with its employees, it would turn to traditional means, which included everything from mail to phone and email. Yet in most companies, if you surveyed the employees, the number one problem would be communication. No wonder we are trying to solve our communication problems with very old solutions. An intranet has proven itself an excellent way to disseminate information within an organization in much the same way the Internet has proven itself an excellent way to disseminate information outside your organization.

The Evolution of Intranet(s)

Originally, an intranet site was just a billboard of company information. For example, if someone had a human resource question, it was much easier to get on the intranet and search for the needed information. Corporations found it was easier to keep the intranet up to date than the monstrous task of keeping each employee up to date. Like a brochure or billboard, what you see is what you have. The same issues applied to sales and marketing literature on the intranet. In today's world, companies cannot wait for the literature to come back from the printers—it is always needed yesterday. Using the old methods, no matter how hard you tried, someone got missed. Face it—companies need access to information yesterday. So, intranet applications were used to supply up-do-date information on products.

Everyone knows how to use a universal browser, but try to teach your employees how to use a traditional client/server application—good luck. The fact is, with the Internet, once you publish the information, everyone knows how to access it. So information published on the company intranet was ending up in everything from client presentations to training modules. Intranets are helping corporations be more competitive and better informed. Once established, the next step was to allow strategic customers and suppliers into the intranet. Why not provide a key supplier the information they need to work with you smarter? Why not let a customer access the information you have about them and, if they choose, update it? Why not let an employee fill out a 401k change form or a T4 short online? Table 19-2 compares the types of information classically found on a company's intranet (for internal use alone) vs. the Internet (for both internal and external use).

One of our customers does automobile fleet management for their clients. They track and approve purchases made with the fleet cards they issue. In the old days, if their clients wanted to issue a new fleet card for their new employee, they would call up an operator and place the order. If clients wanted a report of their activity, they would call up and request the report. Within a few days, it would arrive in the mail. Today, their clients have the option of getting reports via an intranet application. They can literally slice and dice the data online. They also have the option of ordering additional fleet cards online. The intranet application is helping them to be more competitive and at the same time more responsive to their customers.

Another great example of an intranet at work is the Federal Express intranet site. In order to use it, you must be a customer, so by definition this is not an Internet site. It contains nonpublic information. If you want to track your package, you are empowered to do so yourself. You can get at the information when you want—this is a much better alternative for both Federal Express and the customer. For Federal Express, they get transactional efficiency. It is cheaper and faster to have the customer working the intranet site than to pay an operator to deal with the phone calls. For the customer, it means no waiting in phone queue lines, and getting the service when they want it.

	Internet	Intranet
Information type:	Marketing, financial, investor	Proprietary, all forms of company information
Audience:	Prospects, John Q. Public	Employees, strategic partners
Purpose:	Informative, only outgoing, billboard in nature	Collaborative, two-way, interactive

TABLE 19-2.   *Comparison of Internet to Intranet*

These types of applications are being built in a fraction of the time and cost that it would take for a traditional client/server approach. They are allowing companies to communicate, collaborate, and transact online with their employees, customers, and key strategic partners. The marketplace is adopting Internet-enabling technologies at a feverish pace. Now let's see what some of the costs of an intranet might be.

A Closer Look at an Intranet

Many times in our careers, we have heard about these wonderful technologies that would be ideal if we had a million dollars to burn and many months of effort to waste. If we were in the shoes of an individual trying to determine whether to Web-enable a data warehouse, we would ask the questions, "How much does an intranet cost?" and "What are the gotchas?" Well, the startup costs are typically very low. You probably have most of the components of the intranet in-house already. What you will get in the long run are the hidden costs.

We think the CIO of a very large cruise line put it best: "I built a Web site and now I need a team of people to maintain it." When we looked at this particular Web site, he was right—he did need a team of people to maintain it. He had the largest static "billboard" site we had ever seen. They had not harnessed the power of Internet-enabling technologies at all. They had not linked the Web site up to a database, so every time there was a price change, they needed to rebuild the Web site. If it had been married to the database, every price change in the database would have automatically been reflected in the Web site by the built-in database links. The point is, watch out for the hidden costs. Technology is like any other tool—a great help when used for the right job. Use the billboard approach for the static data, and use a database link for the dynamic data.

The Intranet and Security

Don't believe everything you read in the newspapers or hear on TV. You can make an intranet very secure. As with any security, you have to decide how much you want and how much you are willing to spend to get it, then reconcile the two. For example, on many PCs, it is possible today to buy software that will encrypt all the data so that no unauthorized eyes could ever look at every document. Yet, we have never known of any firm to use it widely outside of a secure U.S. government installation. The reason for this is quite simple. The costs far outweigh the benefits associated with it. This same thinking process applies to your intranet site. You can have as much or as little security as you want. Just be willing to pay the price.

Open Society (Collaboration) Vs. a Closed Society

The other issue with security is the type of working environment you want for your team—an open society where lots of information is available for all to see or a closed society where each team member is given information on a need-to-know basis. For example, in a closed environment, the sales force might only know about their own customers and other customers within their sales region. So when making a call on General Electric, their knowledge of that account is limited to that sales region's experience.

In an open environment, they would have access to all other regions' sales information. This means that when a salesperson in Alaska calls on General Electric, he or she would be able to collaborate with other salespeople in the firm to see what they know about General Electric. Perhaps someone in the Boston office has been working with General Electric for awhile and might be able to offer insights. The negative side to this is that when a person leaves the firm, he or she will have valuable information about the company's activities that span beyond their normal reach. This also applies to the strategic vendors you let into the intranet. Yes, they will have information about your firm that will help them to be a smarter ally; at the same time, they will have information that, placed in the wrong hands, could hurt you. It has been our experience that the benefits of allowing the free flow of information to your strategic vendors and employees far outweigh the occasional leakage of information over time. Just be smart about it. If it's confidential company information, then label it as such. It will reinforce the need to be prudent with its use. Also, choose your allies well.

Advantages of an Intranet

Let's now take a closer look at the advantages of deploying new applications using Internet-enabling technologies. For all the reasons that it makes sense to build new applications with Internet technologies, it makes sense to build your warehouse with this technology and deploy it over an intranet.

Single Point of Entry

How much time has been wasted in information technology organizations over the years trying to teach people how to use different applications that have been created? Each application has a different look and feel. Each application has a different keystroke sequence to invoke it. Each application has a different command sequence to use it. Each machine has a different operating system with a different set of commands associated with it. With the universal browser, you have one entrance point into your systems. Once you have learned how to use the browser, you have mastered the knowledge needed to use all applications. You don't need to be retrained with each new application that is developed. With an intranet application, you have access to all the information, applications, and data from one window.

The closest thing we have ever had to this historically is the Apple Macintosh. If you used one Macintosh program, you were well on your way to understanding them all. With the universal browser and an intranet, you have one window into all the systems. No longer do you have to launch five different applications to answer one question. You have one-stop shopping.

Single Source for Information

It is easier to keep an intranet updated with information and have everyone go there for information than to take on the horrendous task of informing everyone. For example, if you put all the marketing information online on an intranet site, it would be much easier to keep it accurate and up to date than to go through the traditional process. Let's face it, snail mail (a term of affection for the U.S. Postal Service), company-wide meetings, newsletters, voice mail, and so forth just don't work.

By having everyone share a common knowledge base (in this example, the marketing intranet site), you are ensuring a strong, cohesive voice. Everyone sees the same message, everyone is drinking from the same well. It's in everyone's best interest to make sure the message is accurate and the well is safe. Over time, team members add their base of knowledge to the total base, making it better for themselves and everyone else in the process. What you get is a growing base of knowledge that helps everyone be more successful. By its very nature, the intranet is a collaborative technology. Over time, the application will become more and more interactive and collaborative.

Transactional Efficiency—A Great Partnering Tool

The intranet is both a partnering tool and a customer tool. By allowing your strategic partners access to your intranet, you streamline their ability to do business with you. You are empowering them with the tool they need to get the information they need from your organization. For example, as a business alliance member with Oracle Corporation, we can search their intranet site for competitive bulletins, white papers, and sales presentations. This type of information is critical to helping my firm close business. When we close business, it means increased product and service business for Oracle. Many consulting firms are joined at the hip with Oracle, whether Oracle and the consulting firms like it or not. Every time they close a deal, they are pulling Oracle products and services with it. In the old days, we would make this request of the local office and hoped for the best. The workload of the salesperson at the time would determine how quickly they turned our request around. By allowing me access to the intranet site, we get/they get transactional efficiency. It is easier for Oracle Corporation to respond to our needs, making it easier for us and other companies to do business with them. It also gives me transactional efficiency. We get the answer quicker, making us more responsive to my customers. The bottom line—this makes intranet sites a great partnering tool.

Transactional Efficiency—A Great Customer Tool

Allowing customers access to your intranet site gives both you and them transactional efficiency. The best example of this at work is the Federal Express intranet site. When I want to track a package, we can now go online and check the status of my order. This is empowering customers with a tool to get the information they need from Federal Express quickly and easily. This gives the customers what they want, when they want it. FedEx is making it easy for the customer to do business with them. Both sides get transaction efficiency out of this. For FedEx, they are now able to meet the customers' needs in a much more cost-effective manner. This makes FedEx much more competitive, which makes the customer much happier.

Lower Training Costs

We have discussed this in many different ways already. Once people learn how to use a browser, they then have the skillset they need to transact business over the Internet without any additional training. The training costs associated with deploying an intranet application are substantially lower.

Lower Maintenance and Deployment Costs

An intranet is based on open standards. It is cheaper to deploy an intranet application than a traditional client/server application. The network costs are substantiality reduced. The cost of the browser is next to nothing, since almost everyone is giving away the software. The cost to update the browser is practically nonexistent. In the old days, if one wanted to deploy a nationwide application, it meant sending out teams just to install the software. Today, the users can update the software without any systems personnel interaction. The browser will run on any hardware. Deploying a new application does not mean upgrading the hardware.

The icing on the cake is that it's all based on open standards. The Internet represents the purest form of competition we have ever had. You will have lots of alternative choices on every component of the application. This will bring down costs. Open standards mean lower acquisition costs and lower deployment costs, along with lower maintenance costs.

Yes, a Square Peg Fits in a Round Hole

Yes, the universal browsers will run on any machine. No matter what the hardware, software, or operating system, anyone can access the Intranet site. You will be able to connect and communicate among all your disparate platforms. As we said, a square peg now fits in a round hole.

Full Range of Multimedia

An intranet application allows you the full range of multimedia. You can have sounds, graphics, videos, etc. This brings application design to a new high point. When conveying information, you have a much greater toolkit of options to choose from.

Infrastructure

Much of what you need for your intranet site you already have. This is a real advantage, since you are able to leverage investments the corporation has already made. You also do not need to build, train, and manage new project teams anymore.

Communication

If you surveyed most employees of a corporation, they would say the number one problem today within the corporation is communication. They feel like they are getting the mushroom treatment. Unlike a mushroom, employees do not thrive in the dark. Well, an intranet site will foster and enhance communication. Your employees will feel better, your customers will feel better, and your strategic partners will feel better. You will find your organization collaborating more and coordinating much better.

Creativity and Innovation

It seems that by the very nature of business, we tend to stifle creativity and innovation. When we want creative thinking, we typically put our bright bulbs in the boardroom and say "go at it." We also always seem to ask the same people over and over. Do you do your best thinking in a boardroom? We know we don't. An intranet site usually helps companies get back their creative and innovative spirit.

Disadvantages of an Intranet

Let's take a closer look at some of the known disadvantages. There are always two sides to each argument, and it would be best to discuss some points on the other side of the coin.

Do I Need Consultants

Yes, you do. This technology is still on the bleeding edge. The skillset for this talent is in such high demand that the highest concentration of the talent is currently with consulting companies. It has been our experience that it is better to bring consultants in than to risk the time loss and mistakes if you do not. A great of example of this is firewall technology. It is changing at a very rapid pace. Most organizations, unless they are very large, will find it cheaper to outsource this firewall component. Can you risk the consequences of a mistake? Does your firm really need a team of graphic artists? Our experience has shown us that the most successful intranet projects are completed by a team of consultants working with employees.

What About My Competitors

They have it, too. They are building and deploying intranet sites. They are trying to use this technology against you. It is a race, and the early adopters usually will own the playing fields. They will also be able to see what you are up to on any information you post that is not secured. It will be easier for them to learn about you, since more information about your business is in the hands of more people than ever before.

Full Range of Multimedia

Just because you can use it, doesn't mean you should. I have seen intranet sites that are so multimedia intensive they just don't work. Everything in this world should be done with moderation. If you are not careful, you will have a Web site that is a great showcase for what technology can do, but without purpose—like an architect building a great monument to himself or herself, but you creating something that can't be lived in.

Security

It is much easier for critical business to get outside the corporation. This is because critical information is now in the hands of more people than ever before. You must pay much closer attention to how you treat proprietary information.

Too Much Data, I Can't Take It

With an intranet site, you are now empowering people. Some people take to power while others allow power to overtake them. If you are not careful, people will become information overloaded.

Intranet Summary

Internet-enabling technology is here to stay. Businesses cannot afford to be like ostriches and bury their heads in the sand. It won't go away. To ignore these trends just gives your competitors another edge against you. Internet technology is cheaper to deploy, faster to deploy, easier to use, and cheaper to maintain. Any application you are building today should be looking at how they can be placed on the intranet.

A data warehouse is all about information and getting people access to it. Every major data warehouse vendor has an intranet strategy. If they don't have an intranet strategy, get a new vendor because they are in trouble and won't be in business much longer. This is the way of the world. It is changing at a very fast pace. Each vendor is leapfrogging the others at every turn. What is clear is that deploying the warehouse using Internet technologies makes good sense. The goal of this chapter was to provide you with a very solid grasp of the Internet and provide you with the facts on why you should consider an intranet-enabled warehouse for you organization.

We feel that any warehouse product that does not have a strategy for dealing with the Internet is making a mistake. We also feel the future of warehousing is with Internet-enabling technologies. We feel that the combination of the warehouse and the intranet will change your organization for the better. It will help transition your organization into a learning organization. A business will only have a sustainable competitive advantage when it becomes an organization that can learn and adapt. That's what a warehouse is all about, empowering people with the knowledge and tools they need to solve their problems. From this, the business will learn to adapt.

An organization must establish a common knowledge base. This must be a collaborative knowledge base. It must establish two-way communication into and out of the warehouse from each business unit, each strategic partner, and its customers. In this way, over time, the knowledge base feeds itself and those stakeholders around it. This knowledge base will become so vast that tools will have to be established to assist in the filtering process. Business cannot afford to let go of any scrap of information about itself that may someday hold the key to being more competitive. The combination of an intranet and the warehouse is the key to helping a business thrive and survive.

We are just about ready to close this Oracle8 data warehousing saga. You have been very patient and well behaved, waiting for the material we deal with in the closing chapter. Chapter 20 looks at tuning the Oracle8 data warehouse—*tuning*, the act of taking your ideas and translating them into technological solutions, then ensuring the solution keeps your user community happy. Impossible, you say? We think not!

CHAPTER
20

Tuning the Warehouse

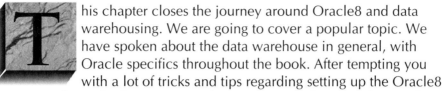

his chapter closes the journey around Oracle8 and data warehousing. We are going to cover a popular topic. We have spoken about the data warehouse in general, with Oracle specifics throughout the book. After tempting you with a lot of tricks and tips regarding setting up the Oracle8 VLDB (very large database), we need to cover general tuning ideas and some specifics that we have gleaned from our experience working with large information repositories. Let's get started looking at the shared pool where Oracle keeps ready-to-execute SQL statements.

NOTE
Follow the tips we make after most sections in this chapter to get the biggest bang for your tuning dollar (or peso, lira, pound, shekel, yen, shilling, etc.).

The Shared Pool

Regardless of how you access your warehouse, the shared pool is the heart of SQL statement processing. In this section we are going to look at processing the four most common types of SQL statements—**select**, **insert**, **update**, and **delete**. At all times, but especially critical during the load phase, a SQL statement is executed only after one of the following conditions has been met:

- It must be a perfect match against a SQL statement resident in the pool whose status is valid.

- If a matching statement is not in the pool, the statement is preprocessed and loaded into the shared pool, and marked as valid.

It is wise to ensure there is enough space in the shared pool to accommodate the most frequently used SQL statements so this preprocessing phase can be avoided. The Oracle documentation set suggests there are eight steps in processing **select** statements and five in the three other types, upon which we are going to concentrate. Let's briefly look at the steps in processing SQL statements; this discussion will help show why shared pool sizing is so important to assist the warehouse tuning exercise.

Select Statement Processing

Once a SQL statement is received by Oracle for processing, the first step is to allocate a segment of memory to enable further processing. This memory is called a *cursor*. Once that has been established, we move on to the parse phase; the statement is picked apart into its components. The following list details a few operations performed during this phase:

- The syntax is checked to ensure the words passed to Oracle form a bona fide SQL statement with a combination of reserved words and object names. *Reserved words* are used by Oracle (e.g., **select**, **order**, or **group**), mean something to Oracle, and can therefore not be used for table names.

- The table and column definitions in the data dictionary are inspected to ensure they are valid.

- Object privileges in the data dictionary are surveyed to ensure the user owns or has access to the tables referenced in the statement.

- The statement is compared against statements resident in the shared pool, looking for a match. If one is found, that statement is used in place of the one just received.

- The optimal execution plan is determined.

- The statement is loaded into the shared pool.

NOTE
The size of the shared pool affects the number of SQL statements that can be held. This adds impetus to allocating as much memory as possible for this pool.

This is the most time-consuming phase of SQL statement processing. In an ideal world, Oracle would be able to hold the most popular SQL statements and they could be executed continually on behalf of those received continually as your users interact with the warehouse.

NOTE
A significant portion of the time required to place a statement in the shared pool can be avoided if Oracle can reuse a statement already in the pool.

The nature of the results for the query is determined. Oracle figures out the characteristics of the data that qualifies for the result set. Values are assigned to the variables referenced in the statement. In high school algebra, we used to call these "unknowns;" think of the logic involved in solving the following equation—the value of "x" must be known before the process can make a decision.

```
if x < 12 then
    do this
else
    do that
end if
```

Non-select Statement Processing

There are no query results to be presented when the SQL statement involves an **insert**, **update**, or **delete** operation. As a result, there is no need to describe results, define output, or fetch the rows of a query. Most statements that start with one of these three SQL operators do not contain any other SQL statements unless they contain a subquery. A *subquery* is a query within another SQL construct such as that shown in the next listing. The **delete** statement shown is actually two statements in one. The result set from the subquery is assembled in memory, then the comparison against HIRE_DATE in PERSON is performed to see what rows should be deleted.

```
delete person
  where hire_date <=
        (select max(end_date)
           from per_stat
          where occ_code is not null);
```

After this overview of SQL statement processing, let's move on to looking at the three initialization parameter file entries that affect shared pool sizing and processing.

Three SHARED_POOL Parameters

There are three parameters in the initialization parameter file related to the shared pool:

1. SHARED_POOL_SIZE   Controls the amount of memory allocated to this SQL cache. It is indicated using an integer alone or an integer followed by **K** or **M**. The former instructs Oracle to multiply the number before by 1,000,000 and the latter by 1,000.

2. SHARED_POOL_RESERVED_SIZE   Instructs Oracle to set aside the specified number of bytes as a reserved area. Coupled with the next parameter in this list, this setting helps satisfy large requests for space in the pool and keep fragmentation to a minimum.

3. SHARED_POOL_RESERVED_MIN_ALLOC   Instructs Oracle to consider satisfying requests above this amount in the reserved rather than the unreserved area of the shared pool.

We call the space derived by subtracting the reserved size setting from the total size of the pool the *unreserved area* of the shared pool. Regardless of the reserved size and the setting over which requests become candidates for this reserved area, Oracle tries to first allocate space in the unreserved area of the pool. To illustrate the way these three parameters interact, inspect the data in Table 20-1.

Deciding Values for These Parameters

The load phase requires a shared pool size conducive to large requests for space in the pool. The two largest space requests are those for large PL/SQL program compilations, **create index** statements, and **alter table add constraint** statements with the **using index** syntax used to create primary keys. There are so many indexes created during the load phase that we recommend sizing for these three parameters according to the following tip.

TIP
During the load phase, we recommend setting the reserved size to ½ the total size of the shared pool, and the minimum allocation entry the same as the reserved size.

shared_pool_size	20MB
shared_pool_reserved_size	5MB
shared_pool_reserved_min_alloc	2MB

| | Largest Chunk Free Space in | | |
Request	Unreserved	Reserved	Results
3000000	8000000	2500000	Placed in unreserved area since the request can be satisfied without looking in the reserved area
3500000	2000000	4000000	Not enough space is free in the unreserved area; placed in the reserved area since it is larger than minimum allocation and enough space can be found in the reserved area
1500000	1000000	3000000	Oracle error since not enough space can be found in the unreserved area and the request does not qualify for the reserved area (i.e., smaller than minimum to be considered for reserved)

TABLE 20-1. *Shared Pool Parameter Settings and Space Requests in Shared Pool*

Day-to-day access to the warehouse is a different story. The requests for space in the pool are almost exclusively for **select** statements, and we see very few (if any) large requests for shared pool space. The following tip sums up our suggestion for sizing during the daily access phase.

TIP
During the daily access phase, we recommend setting the reserved size to 20 percent of the total size of the shared pool, and the minimum allocation entry to ½ of that set for reserved.

Table 20-2 illustrates the application of those tips for a few different-sized pools in the load and daily access phases.

The total amount of space allocated on your warehouse machine for the shared pool should be expressed or figured out as a percentage of the total amount of memory at your disposal. Let's make a recommendation for this setting, then move on to the next issue in tuning the warehouse.

Phase	Pool Size	Reserved Size	Minimum Allocation
Daily access	100MB	20MB	10MB
	300MB	60MB	30MB
	30MB	6MB	3MB
Load	100MB	50MB	50MB
	300MB	150MB	150MB
	20MB	10MB	10MB

TABLE 20-2. *Parameter Relationships During Warehouse Phases*

TIP
Start sizing the shared pool by using 30 – 40 percent of the memory available on the machine. The shared pool and the database block buffer cache (whose controlling parameter is discussed in the "Important Parameter Description" section later in this chapter) are the two parameters that have the most effect on the amount of memory Oracle8 tries to acquire when the warehouse is started.

Miscellaneous Features

This section will lump together a number of miscellaneous features in Oracle8 that assist tuning the warehouse. There is definitely no shortage of books, articles, newsgroups, conferences, and technical publications that cater to the tuning requirements of large information repositories running with the Oracle8 Server. Let's get started.

Read-only Tablespaces

By default, information in the Oracle database, collected logically and physically into an assortment of tablespaces, can be created, updated, and deleted through the familiar SQL statements **insert**, **update**, and **delete**. Tablespaces are, by default, in read/write mode. Oracle offers an alternative called *read-only tablespaces* whose data is static and cannot be changed until the tablespace is taken out of this mode. Read-only tablespaces offer the following two main advantages in the data warehouse environment:

1. They eliminate the need to perform ongoing backup of large, static portions of the warehouse. Read-only tablespaces are backed up once, and those backups can be used as part of a recovery process any time in the future after the backup has been written.

2. They require no resources such as locks and latches that Oracle maintains on information as it is worked with by the users of the database. *Locks* protect the integrity of the data in the database that prevent destructive interaction between transactions accessing the same resource. *Latches* are mechanisms defined by Oracle to protect

data structures in the shared memory allocated to Oracle. There is an adage that nicely sums up the differences (and similarities) between locks and latches—locks are to data as latches are to memory.

Precious time used to perform unnecessary backups of tablespaces in read-only mode can be used to back up dynamic information. Since these tablespaces require no resource management as mentioned in the second point, Oracle only need worry about the data resident in read/write tablespaces. The following SQL statements are used to take tablespaces in and out of read-only mode:

```
alter tablespace XXXX read only;
alter tablespace XXXX read write;
```

During warehouse refresh, all the target tablespaces must be in read/write mode. If you attempt to put data into any tables that reside in a read-only tablespace, you will get the following error. The solution is to take the tablespace out of read-only mode and rerun the code that generated the error.

```
insert into finance …
            *
ERROR at line 1:
ORA-00372: file 210 cannot be modified at this time
ORA-01110: data file 210: 'T:\ORANT\DATABASE\FINANCE.DBF'
```

We would suggest using the following two code segments if you have any read-only tablespaces in your warehouse. The first lists the tablespaces in read-only mode, the second, if you decide to use it, places all tablespaces back in read/write mode.

```
/* ---------------------------------------------------------- */
/*   Oracle8 Data Warehousing      Oracle Press 1998          */
/*                                                            */
/*   rolota.sql        Read-only look and take.               */
/*                                                            */
/*   Corey, Abbey, Abramson, Taub                             */
/* ---------------------------------------------------------- */
spool rolook
select tablespace_name
  from sys.dba_tablespaces
```

```
 where status = 'READ ONLY';
spool off
--
-- Only run the output from this part if you want ALL your
-- tablespaces taken out of read-only mode.
--
set echo off feed off pages 0 ver off trimsp on
spool takoutro.sql
select 'alter tablespace '||tablespace_name||' read write;'
  from sys.dba_tablespaces
 where status = 'READ ONLY';
spool off
set echo on feed on
--
-- Uncomment (i.e., remove the double dash) the next line if you
-- want to run output from previous SQL statement.
--
-- start takoutro
```

The only other problem we have experienced with read-only tablespaces is trying to put a tablespace in this mode and receiving the error "ORA-01640: cannot make tablespace read only with active transactions." The secret here is to get the session that may be in the midst of working on a transaction against data in the desired tablespace to save or abandon its work. Then, simply reissue the **alter tablespace** command. All that we have discussed here can be accomplished using the Storage Manager in Oracle Enterprise Manager (*OEM*), as shown in Figure 20-1.

TIP
Consider using read-only tablespaces for your static date. In partitioned tables, when separate partitions are in their own tablespaces, pieces of the table can be in read-only mode while other partitions are in read/write mode.

Temporary Tablespaces

We have talked in a number of places about temporary workspace used primarily by Oracle to build intermediary tables to satisfy queries and for

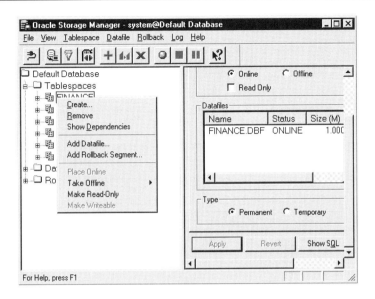

FIGURE 20-1. *Altering status using Storage Manager*

sorting activities. We recommended in Chapter 7 to point all users at a dedicated temporary tablespace. Let's take that recommendation one step further, along the lines of the following:

- You should consider having more than one temporary tablespace. Suppose the data is being loaded into multiple schemas at the same time, owned by FINANCE and PERSONNEL. By having each using its own temporary workspace area, the clashing of their requests for the same resource will be minimized. The SQL statement to accomplish this resembles the following:

```
SQL> alter user finance temporary tablespace finance_tmp;
User altered.
SQL> alter user personnel temporary tablespace personnel_tmp;
User altered.
```

- You should mark temporary tablespaces as type "temporary." This is done using the checkbox in the Type area of the screen shown in

Figure 20-1 by clicking Temporary, or the following statement in SQL*Plus:

```
alter tablespace finance_tmp temporary;
```

The only caveat about this command is when you inadvertently try to make a tablespace temporary that contains data. You will get the error "ORA-01662: tablespace 'ABCD' is non-empty and cannot be made temporary," where ABCD is the name of the tablespace in question. You return a tablespace to the mode allowing it to hold objects by issuing the command:

```
alter tablespace finance permanent;
```

When a tablespace is marked as type temporary, you allow for improved sort activity—it can reduce overhead, allow concurrent sort operations to better coexist with one another, and avoid space management activity in the tablespace during sorting. You might find some interesting information regarding active sort activity looking in the V_$SORT_SEGMENT data dictionary view belonging to SYS.

TIP
Flag all your temporary tablespaces as type "temporary" to improve sorting activity in the warehouse as a whole.

Parallel Aware Optimizer

In Chapter 7 we discussed parallelism and the cost-based optimizer (CBO). CBO has intelligent features built in that are sensitive to parallelism. Looking at parallel execution options and availability is fundamental to the choice of the most optimal execution plan chosen by the CBO. Access path choices take into consideration the number of processors (CPUs) and the number of drives upon which the data retrieved for the query resides.

The initialization parameter file entry OPTIMIZER_PERCENT_PARALLEL instructs the optimizer about how much weight to give to parallelism as access paths are determined for queries. The parameter can be set from 0 to 100. Low settings favor index scans and high settings favor table scans.

TIP
Only consider setting this parameter if you are
using the parallel query feature discussed in this
chapter as well as in Chapter 7. If you are using
parallel query, you may start by setting this
parameter to 50 and seeing how happy you
and your users are with performance.

Read-ahead Mechanisms

Queries involving large amounts of data can get bogged down for a number
of reasons:

- Insufficient memory to accommodate sort operations

- Amounts of I/O required to access the volume of data

- Fragmentation of the data in the objects being read

- Inability of software to partition work and to allow activities to run
  concurrently with one another

Oracle addresses this final bottleneck in the list by ensuring that queries
against large tables are optimized by using read-ahead mechanisms. This
permits a set of data to be read from disk as a previous set of data is being
processed. This feature exploits parallel query technology and supports
overlap between processing and I/O operations.

Direct Option with Export

Export is Oracle's utility used to extract data from the database and place
it in a compressed binary file. This compressed file is only readable by
Oracle's import utility. Many readers are familiar with export. DSS architects
work closely with database administrators, who incorporate export into the
suite of mechanisms used to move data from operational Oracle systems
into DSS. Invoking export with the following command line can speed the
extraction process by as much as 100 percent:

```
exp80 userid=darch/pword tables=(fin,inv,geo,trn) direct=true
```

Conventional path export uses the SQL **select** statement to extract data from tables. Data is read from disk into a buffer cache, and rows are written to the export file. Direct path export extracts data much faster than a conventional path export by reading data directly, bypassing the SQL **select** statement layer command processing, and saves on data copies whenever possible.

Hash Join Processing

To satisfy queries in the data warehouse as well as in operational systems, relational database management systems use a join operation. A *join* involves bringing data together from two or more tables to assemble a common result set for a query. The following listing shows what a join operation entails. The tables being joined are in **boldface**; the columns in those tables equated to each other are in *italics*:

```
select person.hire_year, department.dname,directorate.dir_name,
       person.full_name
  from person,department,directorate
 where person.dept_id = department.dept_id
   and department.dir_id = directorate.dir_id;
```

When tables are joined, the database management system needs to construct a number of dynamic temporary tables to manage the volume of data. Sort activity is time-consuming. With optimal management of the memory structures that support the Oracle database, many of the sort operations can be done in memory. Look at Figure 20-2 to see where sorting is done and how some of the work may need to be done on disk, as well as in memory.

Figure 20-2 shows 2MB of memory available for sorting (2,097,152 bytes). The work required to answer the query generates 4MB (4,194,304 bytes) of data that need sorting. Oracle will use both disk and memory to sort because sorts to disk are much slower than those done in memory. Hash joins bypass the sort phase of query execution by using an in-memory hash table built on the fly as the query is processed. Sort operations consume massive amounts of computer resources and, in a perfect world, sort would be eliminated or its resource requirements diminished. With hash join processing, sorts are minimized (completely in many cases), which is the next best thing to complete elimination.

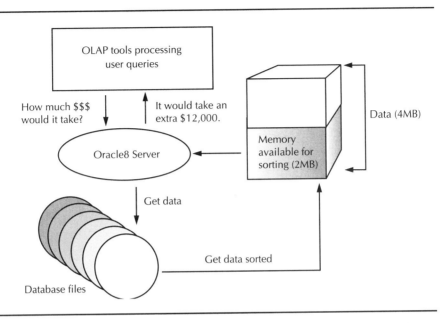

FIGURE 20-2. *Data to sort is more than available memory can accommodate*

Hash join processing can dramatically aid processing complex queries, which involve large amounts of data. Processing these queries when indexes are not used is extremely labor and resource intensive. This happens often in a DSS environment where a significant number of the queries are ad hoc. The data architect can painstakingly index the warehouse, only to find queries that suppress existing indexes are being passed to the database. *Index suppression*, whether deliberate or inadvertent, means indexes on the tables mentioned in the query cannot be used for accessing the data.

Enabling Hash Joins

To use hash join functionality, there are three new parameters to set in the data warehouse initialization parameter file (commonly referred to as "init.ora"):

I. HASH_JOIN_ENABLED   When set to "TRUE" allows the optimizer to consider a hash join when it deems appropriate.

2. HASH_AREA_SIZE   Measured in bytes; the default is twice the value in the parameter file for SORT_AREA_SIZE—values of 655,360 are not unheard of and would set aside 640 kilobytes of memory for this special processing mechanism.

3. HASH_MULTIBLOCK_IO_COUNT   Higher values are good for I/O efficiency up to a point, above which the expected positive effect may slow things down.

To find the current values of these entries, try the following:

1. Enter Server Manager with the command **svrmgr30**.

2. Enter the command **connect internal** and the secure password (usually **oracle**).

3. Enter the command **show parameters hash** and receive output similar to the following listing:

```
NAME                                TYPE     VALUE
----------------------------------- -------  -------
hash_area_size                      integer  0
hash_join_enabled                   boolean  TRUE
hash_multiblock_io_count            integer  8
sequence_cache_hash_buckets         integer  10
```

TIP
The value for HASH_AREA_SIZE in the previous listing is 0, even though it is two times the value for SORT_AREA_SIZE.

Example
Suppose TABLE_A and TABLE_B are being joined with the hash join approach. If TABLE_A will fit into memory, Oracle loads TABLE_A and then builds a hash table using its column values. This hash table can be used for in-memory lookups. A *lookup* refers to the activity of searching through a list of values to find a match. TABLE_B is scanned on disk; then its rows are selectively compared against the hash table copy of TABLE_A, looking for matches.

When TABLE_A is larger than the amount of memory available for hash join processing, Oracle will do the following:

1. Split TABLE_A and TABLE_B dynamically into more manageable partitions, using an internal hash function.

2. Load the smaller of the two partitions into memory and build the hash table for that partition, as mentioned in the previous example.

3. Scan the rows in the other table partition, looking for matches.

When hash join is enabled, the cost-based optimizer uses this approach, after looking at the size of the tables involved in a join operation, the amount of available memory, and the indexes in place on the joined tables.

TIP
Hash join processing, in some cases, means indexes are not needed. When the hash table is built in memory, it alone can achieve benefits similar to, if not many times greater than, indexes.

Governors

Ad hoc query and analysis is one backbone of processing intrinsic to the data warehouse decision support arena. Administrators go out of their way to ensure resources are managed efficiently, but must look at ways to control user requests. Many query and analysis tools have governors, and there is a way to implement resource limits via the Oracle8 Server. A *governor* limits the resources that can be used by processes that access the data resident in the Oracle repository. These limits can be time based (e.g., total allowable connect time) or counter based (e.g., the maximum number of read and write requests) and mapped to groups of users. Governors are nothing new; remember the last time you saw an 18 wheeler (some call it a tractor trailer or semi) with a sign on the side that said "Maximum 90kmh". A governor keeps the speed from going over 90kmh. Let's look at the governors available with Oracle8, also called *profiles*.

A profile is a group of settings that control resource consumption on the Oracle8 database. When you install the Oracle Server, there is a **default** profile created and all users who can connect to the database use this profile automatically.

Creating a Profile

This activity, usually carried out by the DBA, starts with the familiar statement **create profile** followed by the profile name. Let's look at the keywords and parameters usually included and set with this SQL statement. Table 20-3 shows the most common items usually set as a profile is created.

Resource	Meaning	Unit
sessions_per_user	Controls the number of concurrent sessions that can be running using the same account	Integer
cpu_per_session	Limits the CPU time per session, where a session is defined as the time between which a user connects to the database and either disconnects or reconnects as another user	Hundreds of a second
cpu_per_call	Limits the total processing time for an individual SQL statement passed to the database	Hundreds of a second
idle_time	Limits the length of inactivity during a user session, after which the session is terminated	Minutes
logical_reads_per_call	Limits the number of blocks read from memory or disk for the processing of an individual SQL statement	Integer
logical_reads_per_session	Limits the number of blocks read from memory or disk for the life of a user session	Integer

TABLE 20-3. *Limits Usually Set*

Let's look at setting up a profile through the SQL*Worksheet from OEM. After connecting to the database (usually, though not always, as **internal/oracle**), enter the SQL command, as shown in Figure 20-3, and receive "Statement processed" from Oracle.

Assigning Profiles

In situations where you need to control the amount of resources consumed by your user community, profiles are worth investigating. To enliven the limits set in the **create profile** command, you must do the following:

- Collect the names of users or roles that need to be restricted using the profile(s) just created.

- Assign the desired profile to users or roles with the **alter user profile XXXX;** where **XXXX** is the profile name. We discussed roles in Chapter 12 as a method of lumping users together in a group. Roles can be the object of the **alter user** command that gives profiles to users.

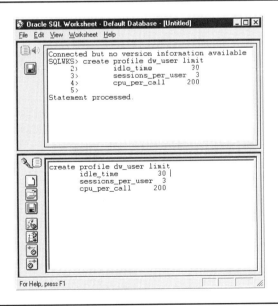

FIGURE 20-3. *Creating a profile in SQL*Worksheet*

■ Put the entry RESOURCE_LIMIT = TRUE in the instance initialization parameter file and restart the database.

The following type of error message is displayed when users exceed a limit specified in their profile. This one is related to IDLE_TIME; the error text when other limits are exceeded is different, but regardless of the limit exceeded, users will receive the "ORA-01012: not logged on" message if they try to do anything without reconnecting.

```
ORA-02396: exceeded maximum idle time, please connect again
```

Changing Profiles and Resetting Users

The whole concept of implementing profiles can be a political hot potato. Seasoned administrators report that after going through a fact-finding exercise with the heads of the user community, they just cannot gain enough of a consensus to go ahead and implement resource limits via profiles. Often after their implementation, you need to change a limit for a profile; this is done using the following code as an example:

```
alter profile dw_user limit idle_time 60;
```

If you need to set a user or role back to the standard set of resource limits given to the default profile created when Oracle8 was installed, issue the following command:

```
alter role dw_user profile default;
```

All the work we have discussed in this section can be accessed from OEM and the Security Manager as shown in Figure 20-4.

Information about defined profiles is stored in the DBA_PROFILES data dictionary view shown in the next listing:

```
SQL> desc dba_profiles
 Name                            Null?    Type
 ------------------------------- -------- ----
 PROFILE                         NOT NULL VARCHAR2(30)
 RESOURCE_NAME                   NOT NULL VARCHAR2(32)
 RESOURCE_TYPE                            VARCHAR2(8)
 LIMIT                                    VARCHAR2(40)
```

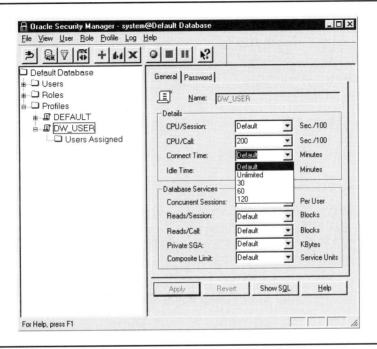

FIGURE 20-4. *Working with profiles in OEM*

The Initialization Parameter File

This section will look at this parameter file, discuss the types of entries, and walk through those that will get you the best tuning results in the data warehouse. Some entries can have a remarkable effect on the performance of Oracle in the data warehouse arena. Two distinct activities or operational phases exist in a data warehouse, and many entries in this parameter file differ from one phase to the other:

1. The load phase, where data is migrated from other systems, transformed in some cases, and placed in the Oracle repository.

2. The daily phase, where the warehouse is static and the users are hitting the data with query tools and OLAP tool(s) of choice.

NOTE
When any changes are made to entries in the initialization parameter file, the database needs to be shut down and restarted for the new values to take effect.

Types of Entries

Entries in the initialization parameter file fall into one of three categories:

1. Those that impose database-wide limits. The amount of space allocated for sorting is determined by SORT_AREA_SIZE, which falls into this type of entry. Suppose the number 4194304 is specified; 4MB of memory is automatically allocated for sorting when a user session initiates sort activity.

2. Those that specify names and locations of files. By default, Oracle8 places its assortment of trace and log files in locations that, in our opinion, do not make the most sense from a logical perspective. The entry USER_DUMP_DEST that defines where Oracle will write user process trace files, for example, may specify a network drive dedicated to application trace files, and the entry may specify T:\ORACLE\TRACE\USER rather than letting the value default to D:\ORANT\RDBMS80\TRACE.

3. Those that set upper limits on characteristics of the sessions working with the Oracle database or the number of processes that can access the database simultaneously. Oracle allocates a chunk of memory called a *cursor* to process SQL statements. The entry OPEN_CURSORS places an upper limit on the number of cursors that an individual user session may have open at one time.

Important Parameter Description

For each parameter covered, we will zero in on its meaning and then recommend a value. Unless specified, the value for each parameter should be set the same for both phases. More details on these and more parameters are available in *Oracle8 Server Administrator's Guide*, as well as many other

books, including *Oracle8 Tuning* (Oracle Press/Osborne/McGraw-Hill, 1998, by Corey, Abbey, Dechichio, Abramson).

BITMAP_MERGE_AREA_SIZE

This entry determines the amount of memory to be allocated to merge bitmaps retrieved from a range scan of bitmap indexes. Bitmap indexes were discussed in Chapter 10, where we made recommendations about when they should be used. The default is 1MB and, if you use bitmap indexes extensively on large tables (in excess of 100,000 rows), it should be doubled or tripled.

COMPATIBLE

This parameter controls what features can be enlivened when a database is in use. Significant changes incorporated in subsequent releases of the Oracle software require setting this entry accordingly. The caveat about this parameter lies in the inability to use current release functionality if the value is set to a previous release. The default for this parameter is 8.0.0, and most administrators never change its value. We mention it here in case you ever get compatibility error messages when working with a new release of Oracle8.

CREATE_BITMAP_AREA_SIZE

This parameter controls the amount of memory allocated for bitmap index creation. In Chapter 10 we discussed *cardinality* as a measurement of the number of distinct values in a column with respect to the number of rows in its table. Very low cardinality in a column makes it a candidate for a bitmap index. The default for this parameter is 8MB, which is sufficient in most situations. Since the creation of bitmap indexes is planned during warehouse rebuild, you may raise this parameter to 12MB or even 16MB to speed up creation.

DB_BLOCK_BUFFERS

This figure controls the size of your data cache. The *data cache* is where all your data passes through before being displayed to the user as results to an OLAP query. The data cache is measured in Oracle data blocks. A *data* block is a chunk of space in the database with sizes ranging from 2 kilobytes (2,048 bytes) up to 16 kilobytes (16,384 bytes). Allocate as much to this data cache as the computer can handle. For example, 256-megabyte and 512-megabyte machines are common these days. A block size of 4Kb is becoming the most common. The size of the data cache is the product of the value for this parameter and the database block size. Thus, a DB_BLOCK_BUFFERS entry of 10,000 with a 4Kb block size gives you a data cache size of 40,960,000 bytes or 40MB. Choosing the optimal value for DB_BLOCK_BUFFERS is a two-step process:

1. Set this parameter somewhere between 25 and 30 percent of your total computer memory. This is the same for the load and daily phases of warehouse operation. Table 20-4 shows some sample parameter values based on this recommendation, with available memory and data cache size measured in megabytes.

2. Let the user community access the data warehouse for a while and run the following SQL*Plus program after at least one full day of use. If the database that holds the data mart or warehouse is open and in use for longer than a day at a time, run this program once a day and inspect the output. The program must be run from the SYS Oracle account; zero as a value in the STATE column of X$BH indicates a buffer in the data cache does not hold any data.

Memory	Parameter	Data Cache
64	5000	19.53
128	10000	39.06
256	20000	78.12
512	40000	156.24

TABLE 20-4.   DB_BLOCK_BUFFERS Values to Size of Data Cache

```
/* ---------------------------------------------------------- */
/*  Oracle8 Data Warehousing      Oracle Press 1998            */
/*                                                             */
/*  db_block.sql        Look at database buffer usage.         */
/*                                                             */
/*  Corey, Abbey, Abramson, Taub                               */
/* ---------------------------------------------------------- */
set pages 0
select 'DB_BLOCK_BUFFERS is '||value
  from v$parameter
 where name = 'db_block_buffers';
select decode(state,0,'FREE','Other'),count(*)
  from x$bh
 group by decode(state,0,'FREE','Other');
```

Output from this script will be similar to one of the following two listings:

```
-- Sample 1: Of the 8000 blocks in the data cache, all are in use.
-- Note there is nothing returned for FREE.
DB_BLOCK_BUFFERS is 8000
Other                8000
-- Sample 2: Of the 8000 blocks in the data cache, 600 are not in
-- use.
DB_BLOCK_BUFFERS is 8000
FREE                 600
Other                7400
```

The values returned for FREE by this query are important. Setting of the DB_BLOCK_BUFFERS parameter can be assisted by applying the following logic:

```
maximum setting = available memory / 2 / database block size
optimal = FALSE
if FREE is consistently 0 then
   increase DB_BLOCK_BUFFERS by 10%
   loop until optimal = TRUE
     if new value for DB_BLOCK_BUFFERS >= maximum setting then
        optimal = TRUE
     elsif FREE is consistently 0 then
        increase DB_BLOCK_BUFFERS by 10%
     end if
   end loop
end if
```

The goal of this exercise is to make the FREE value 0 and the OTHER value the same as the value for DB_BLOCK_BUFFERS, coupled with as large a value as will consume no more than 50 percent of your available computer memory. We used 30 percent as a starting point, but the final total you want is 50 percent.

DB_FILE_MULTIBLOCK_READ_COUNT

The value for this parameter controls the number of Oracle blocks read during one I/O operation during a sequential scan. If I/O is a concern in your database, setting the value of this entry high is a good idea. I/O is one of the primary activities in a data warehouse environment.

TIP

Set the value for this parameter to 16 or 32. A maximum value may be allowed, which depends on your computer's operating system and version number.

DB_FILES

This parameter controls the number of database files that may be open by Oracle concurrently. In a data warehouse environment with partitioning and separation of the fact and dimension tables into separate database files, the default for this parameter is too low.

NOTE

Set the value for this parameter to an artificially high value, around 1,024.

DBLINK_ENCRYPT_LOGIN

This parameter controls whether or not passwords sent from a client to a server to verify a connection are encrypted. If it is set to TRUE on the server and the ORA_ENCRYPT_LOGIN environment variable is set to TRUE on the client, passwords are encrypted using a modified Data Encryption Standard algorithm.

TIP

*As an extra layer of security, set this parameter
value to TRUE.*

DBWR_IO_SLAVES

The "dbwr" acronym refers to the system support database writer process.
By default, Oracle spawns a single database writer process; it is the only
process that performs write operations to the warehouse. It services user
requests. When this parameter is set, the database writer will use additional
processes to perform these write operations, all under control of the master
writer process. Keep in mind that the additional processes should be
counted when you look at setting the PROCESSES parameter a little later
in this chapter.

TIP

*Set this parameter equal to the number of disk
drives upon which the warehouse data resides.*

OPEN_CURSORS

A *cursor* is a segment of memory allocated to process all SQL statements.
The default value for this parameter is too low.

TIP

*The value of this parameter should be 400–600
for the daily phase and something equal to this
number or less for the load phase.*

PROCESSES

This entry controls the maximum number of concurrent processes that can
connect to, or participate in, the management of the Oracle8 Server. The
default value in most environments is 50, which is too low.

TIP

*Set the value for this parameter to between 128
and 256 to start. If you find the value is too
low, it may need to be revisited.*

RESOURCE_LIMIT

Setting up profiles for the users of your data warehouse allows you to restrict the processor, or CPU, time that can be consumed by a user during a single session, as well as a number of other session-related resources. After a profile is created and resource governors specified, the limits are only enforced when this parameter is set properly.

TIP

This parameter should be set to TRUE.

ROLLBACK_SEGMENTS

During the daily phase of the data warehouse, few or no transactions are happening and the size and number of rollback segments should be small. During large data loads, the number and size of rollback segments must be increased.

TIP

In the daily phase, acquire two or three private rollback segments, each sized at about 20 megabytes and each with ten equally sized extents. In the load phase, acquire six to eight private rollback segments, each sized at about 100 megabytes, and each with 20 equally sized extents.

SORT_AREA_SIZE

This parameter controls the amount of memory that is dedicated to each request for sort operations. It is a value in bytes and the default of 64Kb (or 65,536 bytes) is not enough for either phase of warehouse operations.

TIP

This parameter should be set to somewhere between 1,048,576 and 2,097,152 (or 1 to 2 megabytes) for the load phase and twice that for the daily phase.

STAR_TRANSFORMATION_ENABLED

Transformation is a process that the optimizer goes through that changes the wording of SQL statements to allow for more efficient processing without altering the results. In its simplest form, the following listing shows how a query may be transformed:

```
select surname,given,tot_sal
   from person,salary
 where person.pin = salary.pin
   and person.pin = 100981;
-- Is transformed to the following so the PIN columns in both
-- tables can be compared against a constant for faster access.
select surname,given,tot_sal
   from person,salary
 where salary.pin = 100981
   and person.pin = 100981;
```

Setting this parameter to TRUE instructs the optimizer to weigh the advantages of transforming star queries when selecting an access path for a query against a star schema. The star transformation is a cost-based transformation and, in a nutshell, does the following:

■ Generates and remembers the best plan it can produce without the transformation

■ Sees if the query is a candidate for the star query transformation

■ If the query qualifies, generates a plan with the star transformation

■ Based on a comparison of the cost estimates between the best plans for the two versions of the query, decides which plan to use—the transformed or untransformed

The optimizer with Oracle8 is star query aware, looking for opportunities to enable special processing routines when it finds the following characteristics in tables passed for query processing:

I. A join between one very large table and two or more small tables. The terminology "very large" and "small" are difficult to translate into absolute numbers; they are used in comparing the sizes of the tables involved in the join compared to one another.

2. The large table (also called the *fact* table) has a multicolumn primary key.

3. Each column in that primary key is part of a foreign key constraint pointing at one of the smaller tables (also called *dimension* tables).

TIP

Set this parameter to TRUE for both phases of data warehouse activity. During the load phase, more than likely there are no star schemas in the intermediary processing schemas so this parameter will be ignored anyway.

Some of the parameters we have discussed in this section list different values for the load and daily phases of data warehouse operations. We now spend some time on how to use multiple initialization parameter files with your Oracle8-based data warehouse.

Starting Oracle with Different Initialization Parameter Files

We have spoken about the initialization parameter file in this chapter and some other places in this book. Since the environment within which Oracle operates depends so much on the setting of the parameters we discussed in the previous section, starting with different values may be a fact of life for your warehouse.

Line Mode Server Manager

This is the workhorse of the DBA interfaces to the Oracle8 Server, run in a DOS Window. Specifying the name of an initialization parameter file as the database is started is done using the following steps:

1. Enter the command **svrmgr30** to start Server Manager and find yourself positioned at the SVRMGR> prompt.

2. Enter the command **connect internal** and enter the password when requested.

3. Enter the command **startup pfile={directory name followed by init file name}** and Oracle responds with the size and makeup of the components of the SGA, followed by messages about how the database is mounted, then opened. This is shown in the next listing in bold.

```
SVRMGR> startup pfile=g:\phase\load\initdwh.ora
ORACLE instance started.
Total System Global Area      12071016 bytes
Fixed Size                       46136 bytes
Variable Size                 11090992 bytes
Database Buffers                409600 bytes
Redo Buffers                    524288 bytes
Database mounted.
Database opened.
```

NOTE

The information between the brackets in step 3 depends on the hardware upon which the Oracle database is running.

The directory name followed by the name of the initialization parameter file is placed following the **pfile** keyword on the **startup** command. If the server supporting your warehouse is either Windows NT or UNIX based, log onto the server using the account that is the owner of the Oracle software when running line mode Server Manager.

NOTE

There is a GUI version of Server Manager that was distributed for Windows and X-terminals. It is not certified to run against Oracle8 and its distribution was discontinued with Version 7.3 on most platforms.

OEM Instance Manager

Startup using different parameter files is accomplished from the OEM Instance Manager. After invoking the Instance Manager and clicking on Initialization Parameters, you will see the first of two settings folders as shown in Figures 20-5 and 20-6—Basic Tuning and Instance Specific.

Values for the displayed parameters are set by placing the cursor on the line to change and entering a new value. The Apply and Save buttons become active once you have started making changes to parameter values. When you are done working with the entries you wish to change, click on Save to store the values in a different configuration file.

When the database is closed, the Status folder shows a red traffic light. To start the warehouse with different parameter configuration files, you select Database Open from the four choices in this folder displayed beside

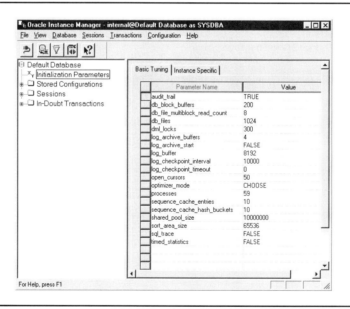

FIGURE 20-5. *Basic Tuning folder*

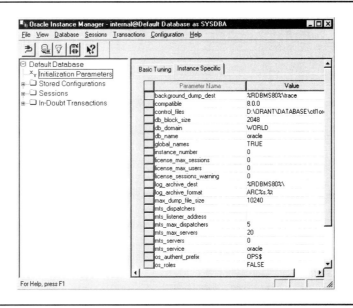

FIGURE 20-6. *Instance Specific folder*

the traffic light. Oracle brings up a dialog box from which you can select your desired configuration, as shown in Figure 20-7.

Notice there are two choices—OEM Stored Configuration and Local Parameter File. Since we chose Save from the Status folder, ours are saved in the OEM tables. You can export the OEM configurations to a local file, then propagate that file to other clients if you decide you are happy with the performance of your warehouse using a particular set of parameter values. This is done by highlighting Stored Configurations, then clicking the right mouse button to bring up the drop-down menu shown in Figure 20-8.

Add this to your bag of tricks supporting the data warehouse on Oracle8. So many times we need to tweak the Oracle environment to accomplish task A, wishing we had at our disposal a set of parameters to optimize the running of task B. The material discussed in the last few sections shows you how to do it from the client using OEM, and from the client or the server using Server Manager.

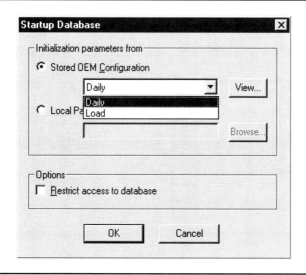

FIGURE 20-7. *Choosing a configuration*

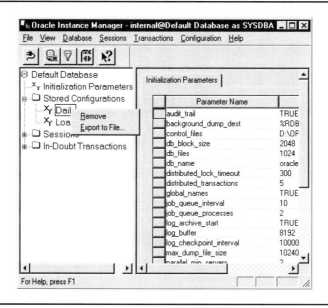

FIGURE 20-8. *Saving OEM Config to local file*

The discussions and recommendations made in this chapter highlight the most important issues when using Oracle8 to support your data warehouse activities. No shortage of technical information exists about Oracle and how to leverage its power best to deliver a data warehouse solution to an eager user community. As well, this chapter terminates the saga called Oracle8 data warehousing. We hope this book provides you with a practical guide to building a successful data warehouse. When we looked at many of the data warehouse books on the market, they seemed to concentrate on the theoretical side of the technology. The reality is that many data warehouse projects fail due to poor project management. Many also fail because the right team was never pulled together. Some initiatives never get off the ground because they did not use the right set of tools. We hope our approach, that is, all facets of the project—from technology to people—provides you with the guidance you need to be successful. Remember Jeremy in *Yellow Submarine*: "So little time, so much to know," and SO MANY places to get that knowledge!

INDEX

O

Q

R

Get Your **FREE** Subscription to Oracle Magazine

Stay informed and increase your productivity with every issue of *Oracle Magazine*. Inside each FREE, bimonthly issue, you'll get:

- Up-to-date information on the Oracle RDBMS and software tools
- Third-party software and hardware products
- Technical articles on Oracle platforms and operating environments
- Software tuning tips
- Oracle client application stories

Three easy ways to subscribe:

1 MAIL: Cut out this page, complete the questionnaire on the back, and mail to: *Oracle Magazine*, 500 Oracle Parkway, Box 659952, Redwood Shores, CA 94065.

2 FAX: Cut out this page, complete the questionnaire on the back, and and fax the questionnaire to **+ 415.633.2424.**

3 WEB: Visit our Web site at **www.oramag.com.** You'll find a subscription form there, plus much more!

If there are other Oracle users at your location who would like to receive their own copy of *Oracle Magazine*, please photocopy the form on the back, and pass it along.

☐ **YES! Please send me a FREE subscription to <u>Oracle Magazine</u>.** ☐ **NO, I am not interested at this time.**

If you wish to receive your free bimonthly subscription to *Oracle Magazine,* you must fill out the entire form, sign it, and date it (incomplete forms cannot be processed or acknowledged). You can also subscribe at our Web Site at **http://www.oramag.com/html/subform.html** or fax your application to *Oracle Magazine* at **+415.633.2424.**

SIGNATURE (REQUIRED) ✓ _____ **DATE** _____

NAME _____ TITLE _____

COMPANY _____

STREET/P.O. BOX _____

CITY/STATE/ZIP _____

COUNTRY _____ TELEPHONE _____

You must answer all eight of the questions below.

1 What is the primary business activity of your firm at this location?
(circle only one)
01. Agriculture, Mining, Natural Resources
02. Communications Services, Utilities
03. Computer Consulting, Training
04. Computer, Data Processing Service
05. Computer Hardware, Software, Systems
06. Education—Primary, Secondary, College, University
07. Engineering, Architecture, Construction
08. Financial, Banking, Real Estate, Insurance
09. Government—Federal/Military
10. Government—Federal/Nonmilitary
11. Government—Local, State, Other
12. Health Services, Health Institutions
13. Manufacturing—Aerospace, Defense
14. Manufacturing—Noncomputer Products, Goods
15. Public Utilities (Electric, Gas, Sanitation)
16. Pure and Applied Research & Development
17. Retailing, Wholesaling, Distribution
18. Systems Integrator, VAR, VAD, OEM
19. Transportation
20. Other Business and Services ____

2 Which of the following best describes your job function? *(circle only one)*
CORPORATE MANAGEMENT/STAFF
01. Executive Management (President, Chair, CEO, CFO, Owner, Partner, Principal, Managing Director)
02. Finance/Administrative Management (VP/Director/Manager/Controller of Finance, Purchasing, Administration)
03. Other Finance/Administration Staff
04. Sales/Marketing Management (VP/Director/Manager of Sales/Marketing)
05. Other Sales/Marketing Staff ____
TECHNICAL MANAGEMENT/STAFF
06. Computer/Communications Systems Development/ Programming Management
07. Computer/Communications Systems Development/ Programming Staff
08. Computer Systems/Operations Management (CIO/VP/Director/ Manager MIS, Operations, etc.)
09. Consulting
10 DBA/Systems Administrator
11. Education/Training
12. Engineering/R&D/Science Management
13. Engineering/R&D/Science Staff
14. Technical Support Director/Manager
15. Other Technical Management/Staff
_____

3 What is your current primary operating system environment?
(circle all that apply)
01. AIX
02. HP-UX
03. Macintosh OS
04. MPE-ix
05. MS-DOS
06. MVS
07. NetWare
08. OpenVMS
09. OS/2
10. OS/400
11. SCO
12. Solaris/Sun OS
13. SVR4
14. Ultrix
15. UnixWare
16. Other UNIX
17. VAX VMS
18. VM
19. Windows
20. Windows NT
21. Other ____

4 What is your current primary hardware environment? *(circle all that apply)*
01. Macintosh
02. Mainframe
03. Massively Parallel Processing
04. Minicomputer
05. PC (IBM-Compatible)
06. Supercomputer
07. Symmetric Multiprocessing
08. Workstation
09. Other ____

5 In your job, do you use or plan to purchase any of the following products or services
(check all that apply)

SOFTWARE	Use	Plan to buy
01. Accounting/Finance	☐	☐
02. Business Graphics	☐	☐
03. CAD/CAE/CAM	☐	☐
04. CASE	☐	☐
05. CIM	☐	☐
06. Communications/ Networking	☐	☐
07. Database Management	☐	☐
08. Education	☐	☐
09. File Management	☐	☐
10. GIS	☐	☐
11. Image Processing	☐	☐
12. Laboratory Control	☐	☐
13. Materials Resource Planning (MRP, MRP II)	☐	☐
14. Multimedia Authoring Tools	☐	☐
15. Office Automation	☐	☐
16. Order Entry/ Inventory Control	☐	☐
17. Programming/Systems Development	☐	☐
18. Project Management	☐	☐
19. Scientific and Engineering	☐	☐
20. Spreadsheets/ Financial Planning	☐	☐
21. Systems Management Products	☐	☐
22. Workflow	☐	☐
HARDWARE		
23. Macintosh	☐	☐
24. Mainframe	☐	☐
25. Massively Parallel Processing	☐	☐
26. Minicomputer	☐	☐
27. PC (IBM-Compatible)	☐	☐
28. Supercomputer	☐	☐
29. Symmetric Multiprocessing	☐	☐
30. Workstation	☐	☐
PERIPHERALS		
31. Bridges/Routers/ Hubs/Gateways	☐	☐
32. CD-ROM Drives	☐	☐
33. Disk Drives/Subsystems	☐	☐
34. Tape Drives/Subsystems	☐	☐
35. Video Boards/Other Multimedia Peripherals	☐	☐
NETWORK/COMMUNICATIONS		
36. Communications Controllers	☐	☐
37. Local Area Networks	☐	☐
38. Modems	☐	☐
39. Wide Area Networks	☐	☐
SERVICES		
40. Computer-Based Training	☐	☐
41. Education/Training	☐	☐
42. Maintenance	☐	☐
43. Online DatabaseServices	☐	☐
44. Support	☐	☐
45. **None of the above**	☐	☐

6 What Oracle products are in use at your site? *(circle all that apply)*
SERVERS
01. Oracle7
02. Oracle Media Server
03. Oracle7 Workgroup Server
04. Personal Oracle7
05. Oracle Rdb
TOOLS
06. Designer/2000 (CASE)
07. Developer/2000 (CDE, Forms, Reports, Graphics)
08. Oracle Media Objects
09. Oracle Power Objects
APPLICATIONS
10. Oracle Financials
11. Oracle Human Resources
12. Oracle Manufacturing
13. Other ____
14. **None of the above**

7 What other database products are in use at your site? *(circle all that apply)*
01. CA-Ingres
02. DB2
03. DB2/2
04. DB2/6000
05. dbase
06. Gupta
07. IMS
08. Informix
09. Microsoft Access
10. Microsoft SQL Server
11. Progress
12. Sybase System 10
13. Sybase System 11
14. Sybase SQL Server
15. VSAM
16. Other ____
17. SAP
18. Peoplesoft
19. BAAN
20. **None of the above**

8 During the next 12 months, how much do you anticipate your organization will spend on computer hardware, software, peripherals, and services for your location? *(circle only one)*
01. Less than $10,000
02. $10,000 to $49,999
03. $50,000 to $99,999
04. $100,000 to $499,999
05. $500,000 to $999,999
06. $1,000,000 and over

OMG